The Forked Juniper

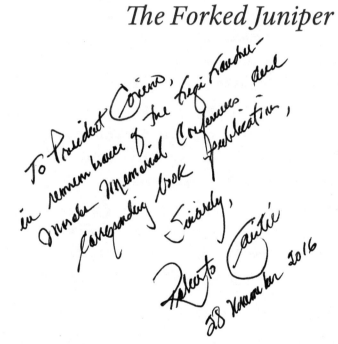

To President Córeno,
in remembrance of the Tripi Gaucher
Ornrobe Memorial Conference and
corresponding book publication,

Sincerely,
Roberto Cantú
28 November 2016

CHICANA & CHICANO VISIONS OF THE AMÉRICAS

The Forked Juniper

CRITICAL PERSPECTIVES ON RUDOLFO ANAYA

Edited by Roberto Cantú

UNIVERSITY OF OKLAHOMA PRESS : NORMAN

Library of Congress Cataloging-in-Publication Data

Names: Cantú, Roberto, editor.
Title: The forked juniper : critical perspectives on Rudolfo Anaya / edited
   by Roberto Cantú.
Other titles: Critical perspectives on Rudolfo Anaya
Description: First edition. | Norman, Oklahoma : University of Oklahoma
   Press, 2016. | Series: Chicana and Chicano visions of the Américas series ; 17
Identifiers: LCCN 2016013240 | ISBN 978-0-8061-5485-5 (hardback) |
   ISBN 978-0-8061-5486-2 (paperback)
Subjects: LCSH: Anaya, Rudolfo A.—Criticism and interpretation. | Mexican
   Americans in literature. | New Mexico—In literature. | BISAC: LITERARY
   CRITICISM / American / Hispanic American.
Classification: LCC PS3551.N27 Z67 2016 | DDC 813/.54—dc23
LC record available at https://lccn.loc.gov/2016013240

The Forked Juniper: Critical Perspectives on Rudolfo Anaya is Volume 17 in the
Chicana & Chicano Visions of the Américas series.

The paper in this book meets the guidelines for permanence and durability of
the Committee on Production Guidelines for Book Longevity of the Council on
Library Resources, Inc. ∞

1 2 3 4 5 6 7 8 9 10

To
Rudy and Patricia

Now, take the owl, go west into the hills until you find a forked juniper tree, there bury the owl. Go quickly—

—Rudolfo Anaya, *Bless Me, Ultima*

Contents

Acknowledgments

I would like to thank the contributors to this book for their groundbreaking essays and collegial cooperation throughout the editorial process. I also thank David Ellis for his amiable agreement to do the interview. The fourteen authors—most of them personal friends and colleagues for more years than we dare to count—expressed a communal enthusiasm and ready willingness to contribute to a book that would be a critical and generational homage to a writer whose work has beguiled and bewitched us for more than forty years. We have all been Tony or Ultima since 1972, the year *Bless Me, Ultima* was released. My special appreciation to the anonymous reviewers whose commentaries added to the scholarly precision and high standards of the published essays. My heartfelt thanks to Kathleen A. Kelly, acquisitions editor at the University of Oklahoma Press, for her professional guidance in the publication of *The Forked Juniper*; to Bethany R. Mowry, editorial assistant, for her timely and graceful assistance; to Emily J. Schuster, manuscript editor, for her energetic and enthusiastic direction throughout the editing process; to Melanie Mallon, copyeditor, for her meticulous assistance in the editing of the book; and to Robert Con Davis-Undiano for bringing us to the University of Oklahoma Press with his characteristic generous and welcoming spirit. Lastly, but closest to me, I thank my wife, Elvira, and our three children—Victoria Guadalupe, Isabel, and Roberto—for their love and the spiritual ties that unite us for all eternity, like Anaya's readers to Ultima's owl.

—Roberto Cantú

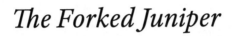

The Forked Juniper

Introduction

Roberto Cantú

América, cifra de nuestros comunes desvelos
—Alfonso Reyes, *Ultima Tule* (1942)

The Forked Juniper: Critical Perspectives on Rudolfo Anaya consists of thirteen chapters and one interview written exclusively for this volume by prominent literary critics from Germany, Mexico, and the United States.[1] The book is partitioned into four interdependent quadrants that, like the Zia solar symbol or New Mexico's state flag, find dialectical unity—thus plural, critical, and creative—in their inner composition. The first section, titled "Rudolfo Anaya and Narratives of the U.S. Southwest," opens with a chapter by Ramón A. Gutiérrez, who transports his readers back to colonial New Mexico so that we may imagine, reenact, and go through what he calls the spells, hexes, and magic of those days. Inspired by Rudolfo Anaya's *Bless Me, Ultima*, Gutiérrez recalls his early life as a *manito*, or native, of New Mexico, growing up like Antonio Márez Luna, afraid of La Llorona and of witches while walking along the Río Grande at night. Gutiérrez writes a detailed cultural history of eighteenth-century New Mexico, carefully tracing the surge of trials of so-called witches accused of having the power to bewitch, bodily seduce, or spiritually seize local men and women of Spanish ancestry. Drawing from personal research in Mexico's Archivo General de la Nación and painstaking examination of records dating back to the Inquisition, including recent scholarship of New Mexican folklore, Gutiérrez explains the historical and cultural background of Anaya's inaugural novel, clarifying the cultural conditions that allowed witches and *curanderas* (folk healers), such as Ultima, to be accused of witchcraft.

3

The chapter by Heiner Bus points to a southwestern branch of American literary history associated with the "Land of Enchantment" founded on the nostalgia for a pre-industrial United States and on the repressed contradictions and paradoxes that defined U.S. modernity and the idealized view of its national expansion in the nineteenth century. Bus studies the work of American writers from the late nineteenth century to the twentieth for whom the Southwest functioned as the last frontier and a desperate refuge from the pitfalls of modernity and the machine age. Bus establishes a contrast between writers known for their negative views on Native and Mexican cultures in New Mexico (e.g., John G. Bourke) and those who saw the Southwest as a romantic utopia, such as Charles F. Lummis and a group of writers who fell under his influence, among them Mary Austin.[2] Heiner Bus localizes his critique on two of Austin's books, *The Flock* (1906) and *The Land of Journeys' Ending* (1924), the first set in California, and the second, in New Mexico. Bus examines how Anaya's novels—such as *Bless Me, Ultima* and his Sonny Baca narrative cycle, from *Zia Summer* (1995) to *Jemez Spring* (2005)—respond critically to the contrasting traditional American views on Native and Mexican cultures, thus transcending both the negative and the "Land of Enchantment" representations by Bourke, Lummis, and Austin. Active and imaginatively critical on several trenches, Bus also overturns much of Chicano literary criticism centered on *Bless Me, Ultima*, contesting the tendency to judge the novel's ideological core as one of nostalgia, and proposing instead that Anaya, through *Bless Me, Ultima*'s main character, Antonio Márez Luna, "provides the reader with a fictional model of culture in action that celebrates not a nostalgic backward glance but the freedom of choice to combine the best from the past and the present."

José E. Limón's chapter is a comprehensive and interdisciplinary analysis that searches for points of contact between Mexican American prose fiction and social conditions in the United States from the 1970s to the present. Taking Anaya's *Bless Me, Ultima* as a generational narrative that differs from recent Mexican American literature, Limón opens his chapter with an analysis of Anaya's novel in the context of the time when it was written—the late 1960s, during the age of rock 'n' roll, as well as the anti-Vietnam and radical youth movements of the era—and in light of other Chicano novels, by Tomás Rivera and Rolando Hinojosa, written in the early 1970s. Limón studies the optimism, iconoclasm, and sense of direction of the protagonists in narratives by Anaya, Rivera, and Hinojosa according to their attitudinal divergences from relatively recent prose fiction by Mexican American writers Oscar Casares (*Brownsville*, 2003), Manuel Luis Martínez (*Drift*, 2003), and Manuel Muñoz (*The Faith Healer of Olive Avenue: Stories*, 2007), whose narratives are examples of the generational despair and disillusionment of young Mexican American males. Limón's careful analysis is grounded in recent theoretical and social studies that attempt to clarify the condition of U.S. working-class minorities, particularly of Mexican American males, during times of recession, continued discrimination, and downsizing in the United States.

In María Herrera-Sobek's study of Anaya's *Jalamanta: A Message from the Desert* (1996), she contends that it can be read both as a novel and as a significant illustration of Anaya's sense of spirituality and well-known concern for the environment, therefore of humanity's connectedness to nature and the universe. Herrera-Sobek claims that Anaya's *Jalamanta* transcends ethnic and national categories, reaching an international readership through the language of fable, parable, and myth. With the application of interpretive models taken from *The Hero with a Thousand Faces* (1973), by Joseph Campbell, and from *Les rites de passage* (1909), by Arnold van Gennep, Herrera-Sobek interprets *Jalamanta* as the narrative of a hero's exile in triadic form—his separation from the community, his initiation, and his return. The far-reaching analysis includes Greek, Hindu, and Mesoamerican myths, as well as philosophical and political traditions referenced or implicitly contained in *Jalamanta*, a work by Anaya that has not been carefully studied before. Herrera-Sobek's important contribution establishes a critical breakthrough in Anaya studies.

The book's first section closes with Robert Con Davis-Undiano's chapter, in which he illuminates the idea of Aztlán—the mythical origin of the Aztecs and, according to *El Plan Espiritual de Aztlán* (1969), the origin of Chicanos by rights of lineage—tracing the concept from its articulated expression of ancestral ethnic foundation in Oscar Zeta Acosta's *The Revolt of the Cockroach People* (1973), to the more recent *spiritual* reconceptualization of the notion of Aztlán in Rudolfo Anaya's novels, particularly in *Shaman Winter* (1999). Davis-Undiano examines Chicano literary expression of the intervening thirty years, finding different and contrasting concepts of "homeland" (not of birth but as the *re-creation of a lost place*, thus as a cultural construction); land itself (not for profit and commercial reasons, but for the sustainable local stewardship of the homeland); and identity (not one of a claimed ancestry back to the mists of time, but Anaya's "New World" concept with its notion of a spiritual Aztlán and its north/south orientation, which connects the Américas and peoples from all parts of the world—Europeans, Africans, Asians, and Native Americans). The guiding thread of this chapter runs through the Chicano Movement and the Chicano Cultural Renaissance, therefore from Alurista and Oscar Zeta Acosta to Rudolfo Anaya, Reies López Tijerina, Luis Valdez, and recent Chicano literary criticism. In a tight and comprehensive chapter, Davis-Undiano reminds us that the multicultural dream of becoming a composite "American" (being everyone and no one in particular) must be resisted in favor of another dream proposed by Anaya in his Sonny Baca novels, namely that people must claim a personal legacy from their past to live as fully as possible in the present moment. As an example of a truly engaged ethical criticism, Davis-Undiano asserts that "other cultural perspectives can be known through the lens of one's own heritage, but one must first take possession of that heritage based in history and ties to a place."

Monika Kaup's chapter opens the book's second part, "Anaya's Poetics of the Novel," by situating *Bless Me, Ultima* in the hemispheric aesthetic context of the baroque, understood no longer as an art category associated with a European era, but as a global appropriation of a Western eighteenth-century aesthetic by artists born in former European colonies, from Mexico and Brazil to Asian countries—in other words, peoples and sites formerly linked by trade and cultural exchange through the Spanish and Portuguese empires. Drawing on influential theoretical works on the baroque in Spain and in Latin America by Eugenio d'Ors (Spain), Irlemar Chiampi (Brazil), and Alejo Carpentier (Cuba), Kaup explores the cultural and historical relations between *Bless Me, Ultima* and baroque architecture, art, and literature in Mexico and in the U.S. Southwest. Kaup's chapter sets a new standard in Anaya studies as well as in Chicano literary criticism through the global and interdisciplinary range of her analysis.

Francisco A. Lomelí conjoins in his chapter a partial autobiography; a historical account of the emergence of Chicano literary theory and criticism and its mature branching in different directions; and, in passing, a summary of his recently published book of essays. Lomelí brings to memory the general dismissal or outright rejection in academic circles of Chicano and other ethnic literatures during the 1970s, as well as their eventual and rightful entry into the literary canon. He describes the early Chicano literary field as one in which those with different viewpoints and ideological positions engaged in polemical exchanges. Lomelí underscores the lack of early consensus among Chicano and Chicana literary critics about how to classify Chicano literature: by theme, by ethnicity, by the author's politics? As a post-1965 literary possibility? Lomelí recognizes Luis Leal as the literary critic who taught him the importance of periodization in cultural studies, along with a literary imagination that incorporates, as a form of liberation, identifiable roots in the early history of what is now the U.S. Southwest. In Lomelí's words, such archival work transformed his view of Chicano and Chicana literature, allowing him to "leap from limbo to center stage in order to reclaim a rightful place in modernity by bringing into question our long-standing invisibility and second-class status." He adds that Anaya's writings express "the oldest myths and legends in the United States," thus providing a mirror "by which the Chican@ community sees itself and wonders about its place in time and space."

Enrique Lamadrid offers an all-inclusive and insightful examination of Anaya's work—his novels, plays, short stories, and essays—interpreted as "performances" in the sense proposed by Victor Turner: namely, as a "ritual drama" or stage "where performance becomes a process of transformation for both the group and the individual." Anaya's writings—affirms Lamadrid—tell stories of origin, cultural conflict, a search for meaning and identity, all configured as ritual dramas that connect the audience/reader to the land, to history, and to a larger world through myths originating in Mesoamerica, Egypt, India, or Greece. Anaya's inclusion of myth in his writings, argues Lamadrid, is not part of a "fantasy heritage," but is an "ancient system of signification, which mediates cultural contradictions, ecological change, and historical conflict." Yet, Anaya's work is not all solemn and unsmiling: Lamadrid points to the "pícaro" dimension in Anaya's writings, in which irony, satire, and parody function as a self-immunization against any pretentiousness, in the manner of a Chicano Mark Twain. Anaya confronts serious questions in our modern world, such as drugs, violence to people, and the degradation of ecosystems and of human dignity. According to Lamadrid, this interplay of performances, including *vatos* (homeboys) and *vates* (prophets), constitutes the core of Anaya's cultural authority in the literary ritual dramas of New Mexico and the world.

Mario Acevedo is a prolific and rising Chicano gothic writer whose mastery of political satire and humorous tales of a Chicano vampire named Félix Gómez have produced a multivolume series. In his chapter Acevedo recalls his youth in Las Cruces, the land of his birth in southern New Mexico, where he was raised as a Baptist and thus with no felt connection to his fellow Catholic *nuevomexicanos*, whom he viewed as quaint, superstitious, and with traditions and history that, like old buildings, should be demolished and discarded. This attitude changed when in name of "urban renewal," most of downtown Las Cruces was bulldozed and "torn down to make way for the new and to fatten the wallets of a chosen few." Dreaming of being a novelist, he eventually looked to Rudolfo Anaya and his use of the gothic in *Bless Me, Ultima* and in the Sonny Baca novels, such as *Shaman Winter* (1999), and began to embrace the old traditions and the New Mexico gothic. With his characteristic humor and irony, Acevedo discusses his background as a writer and the aspects of his art that disclose the depth of his readings, the personal commitment to his writing, and the work ethic that have cemented Acevedo as one of our most successful writers from New Mexico in the genre of gothic fiction.

Rosaura Sánchez, one of the foremost literary theorists and critics in Chicano literature, opens the third part of this book, titled "History, Ancient Genealogies, and Globalization," with a landmark study of the figuration of time and space in Anaya's Sonny Baca detective narrative quartet. A popular genre, detective novels have achieved a salient presence among contemporary Mexican writers (e.g., Paco Ignacio Taibo

II), as well as in Chicano and Chicana literature in which, according to Sánchez, Anaya's novels best display the intersection of multiple realities, including evil and crime in their political and social forms, as well as in their metaphysical manifestations. The representations of social reality next to a dimension beyond the real, and the presence of the historical juxtaposed to the ahistorical discourses in Anaya's writing, are read by Sánchez as the dissonant intersections of postmodern and premodern temporalities, with the spiritual plot featuring triumph over the material reality of evil. Sánchez's proposed theoretical and interpretive analysis results in an all-embracing reading of the Sonny Baca narrative quartet, with *Shaman Winter* considered to be Anaya's "creative best, blending elements of speculative fiction with elements of the marvelous." Sánchez claims that this novel "is Anaya's most historically grounded account of New Mexico's past, which serves as the basis for exploring dreams" and, by implicit association, the history of the Américas. Sánchez holds that given the cyclical sense of time in Anaya's work, it follows that the reenactment of dreams will be continuous in a narrative that turns on a "perpetual present," with a parallel reality in cyberdream or cyberspace, where a global and universal consciousness turns into a possibility of world awareness for Anaya's readers.

Horst Tonn develops his analysis from the logical connection that Anaya makes in "The New World Man" (1989), an essay in which Anaya confirms his sense of place in New Mexico bound to a simultaneous felt relationship to the pre-Columbian traditions of the hemisphere and to his avowed sense of being a "citizen of the world." To better conceive of Anaya's sense of regional and world relations and to fully understand what the "global" signifies in Anaya's writings, Tonn ventures into questions regarding "cosmopolitanism" in current theoretical discourses. Quoting Tom Lutz on the topic of American regionalism, Tonn advances the notion that cultural differences are not grounds for different identities but are the constitutive elements of a larger literary identity in which ethnicity, region, history, and class are not foundational but relational. In his analysis of Anaya's writings, specifically the travel narrative *A Chicano in China* (1985), Tonn proposes that "the ways in which these texts explore the ongoing calibrations of one's relationships to nation, region, local

spaces, and so forth," leads to reflections on Jacques Derrida's argument
for refugee rights, and on Ulrich Beck's "realistic cosmopolitanism," as
these arguments relate to issues of "otherness" and international boundaries in our increasingly globalized world.

John M. D. Pohl's chapter is a prominent example of recent scholarly
findings in Mesoamerican cultural history, stemming from his ongoing
archaeological research in areas of long-range trade routes, dynastic alliance systems, the acquisition of exotic status items (such as turquoise),
and shifting political relations in what is now Mexico and the U.S. Southwest. Pohl points to a long-forgotten economic system that linked more
than fifteen language groups from Oaxaca, Jalisco, Nayarit, Zacatecas,
Chihuahua, New Mexico, and Arizona during the late postclassic period
(A.D. 950–1521), a system that included Eastern Nahuas, Mixtecs, and
Zapotecs. The "politics of history," according to Pohl, has resulted in
constructed and restricted identities for Mexicans (with the Aztecs as
the symbol of national identity), while in the United States, "the hunting tribes and the pueblo-dwelling peoples, together with the colonizing
Spanish and indigenous peoples from Mexico, [are viewed] as a vestigial
population largely detached from their natural surroundings." According
to Pohl, new research has unveiled the coexistence and alliances between
the Anasazi of Chaco Canyon (A.D. 950) and the Toltec capital of Tula
based on a macroeconomy that spanned across the Southwest and northern Mexico, resulting in the influence of the Anasazi on its southern allies
in the intensification of their social stratification, generated by the dynastic lineages involved in an aggressively expanding trade system. This
dominant political and economic system was challenged and temporarily
displaced by the emergent Aztec empire in the fifteenth century. Pohl's
findings and research in the field show that the disaffected Native nations
allied themselves with Hernán Cortés in the destruction of Tenochtitlan,
the Aztec capital, with Tlaxcaltecas at the helm of the exploratory and
colonizing advances of Spaniards to the north, particularly to present-day
New Mexico. "By the middle of the sixteenth century"—Pohl argues—
"Tlaxcalteca caciques together with other Eastern Nahua, Mixtec, and
Zapotec cacicazgos across the plain of Puebla and Oaxaca were sponsoring pioneer expeditions of settlers into northern Mexico and the American

Southwest." Eventually this led to Tlaxcalteca unity with the Pueblo peoples against Spaniards in the revolts of the sixteenth and seventeenth centuries. Two important points emerge from Pohl's chapter. First, when Chicano writers such as Rudolfo Anaya express a close cultural affinity to Mesoamerican civilization, this is no "cultural fantasy": the concrete historical and cultural relations are now being confirmed by recent research, headed by Mesoamerican scholars who are questioning obsolete views of the U.S. Southwest. Second, the Chicano idea of Aztlán, in its variant as a Mexica-centered myth, shall eventually undergo revision.

In the closing chapter, Spencer R. Herrera claims that humanity's "genetic code" includes mythmaking, storytelling, and community building, an ancient human heritage that endows life with meaning. But myth retelling, as in Anaya, does not involve repetition of an inherited myth: it must be recreated, reenacted, and reinvented, as Anaya does in his children's books, of which Herrera studies four—*Roadrunner's Dance* (2000), *The First Tortilla* (2007), *How Hollyhocks Came to New Mexico* (2012), and *How Chile Came to New Mexico* (2014). Commenting on world myths, Herrera sees in their variety and differences the beauty of mythmaking. To fortify his argument, he alludes to Nigerian novelist Chimamanda Ngozi Adichie, who writes and speaks about "the danger of the single story"; Spencer asserts that access to diverse stories and narratives has the potential to be life changing. In *How Chile Came to New Mexico*, for instance, Anaya rewrites the myth of the introduction of chile seeds to the Pueblo people through trade with Mexico. The story involves a journey by Young Eagle, who travels through Chihuahua on his way to the valley of the Aztecs, while holding the turquoise necklace of his young beloved, Sage, for protection. On his return, he presents the seeds to Sage's father as a symbol of betrothal, and Sage's father accepts the offer. According to Herrera, "Anaya affirms that we can trace the origin of chile seeds we use in our modern diet back to the seeds Young Eagle brought to New Mexico." Anaya's reinventions of myths ironically contain seeds of historical truth: this myth retold by Anaya contains the story of a trade system that involved elite trade items (such as turquoise) and tales of dynastic marriages and alliances, in keeping with John Pohl's archaeological findings and scientific deductions. Herrera's analysis of Anaya's four children's books, with references to Mesoamerican and Judeo-Christian myths, is a fitting conclusion to the chapters included in this book.

In my interview with David Ellis, he recounts how he wrote, produced, and directed his recently released film *Rudolfo Anaya: The Magic of Words*, which took him about nine years to complete. David shares interesting anecdotes about the making of this film, his conversations with Anaya over the duration of this project, and his overall experiences with the persons who made this film possible—Rudolfo and Patricia Anaya, and the people of New Mexico.

As these chapters illustrate, Rudolfo Anaya (b. 1937) belongs to the first generation of Chicano writers who pioneered and charted one of the most vigorous and theoretically grounded ethnic literatures in the United States.[3] He emerged as a Chicano writer unlike any other in the early 1970s, with his novel *Bless Me, Ultima* (recipient of the 1972 Quinto Sol Award), and worked his way toward creative years of narrative experimentation and the steady development of his literary art in other novels, short fiction, essays, drama, and children's stories.[4] Firmly embedded in the cultural history of his native New Mexico, Anaya's writings are known for their animated landscape descriptions and the traces of autobiography that recreate, from a nuevomexicano point of view, a more inclusive canvas of the American Southwest. His novels often turn into settings for discord and violent encounters between forces of good and evil—from the regional to the international—and for the aggressive national expansionism that spread westwards in the nineteenth century under the banner of modernity.[5] Placed in this setting, Anaya's modernity is *antimodern*, similar to a long-established tradition in American letters from Thoreau's "plain living and high thinking" to the new regionalism of the 1930s, but with a different and much older idea of origins, reaching back to Spanish and Pueblo histories and their narratives of conflict and nation building, which Anaya deftly critiques, subsumes, and retells in *Bless Me, Ultima* and later novels.[6]

In an autobiographical essay included in *Focus on Criticism*, Anaya looks deep into and beyond New Mexico to plot the recovery of world cultures and civilizations that modern-day Chicanos are heirs to:

> For those who had lived close to the oral tradition of the people, the literary inheritance was clear. From Spain, from the

Mediterranean world of Catholics, Jews, and Arabs, from the borrowing of medieval Europe, from the dozens of waves which swept over the peninsula of Spain to evolve the characters of those groups, into the Mexico of the Americas with Cortez, to be enhanced with the serious magic of the pre-Columbian Indians, north into the heart of Mexico, north up along the Rio Grande, a rich world view came to sustain the people. In the *cuentos*, in the oral tradition, the view of the world was kept alive, and it was fed to us with *atole* and *tortillas*, filling us with the wonder of creation. ... But the inheritors of this fantastic world view and heritage were most often at the bottom of the socio-economic system. . . . My interest with Mexican thought continues to grow. I will not rest until the people of Mexican heritage know the great cultures and civilizations they are heirs to from that country to the south.[7]

Conjuring oceanic images that turn into vivid holograms of past rivalries and conquests, and of the rise and fall of civilizations, Anaya's language seeks its articulation in the ebb and flow of maritime metaphors ("from the dozens of waves which swept over the peninsula of Spain," "to the Mexico of the Americas"), in a back-and-forth rhythm of phrases and allusions to the Mediterranean and the Gulf of Mexico, coupled as the Columbian pathway of encounters, trade, war, and the amalgamation of more complex cultures ("north up along the Rio Grande"). The result is the eventual hybridization and confederation of peoples ("Catholics, Jews, and Arabs" and American Indians), as in Virgil's *Aeneid*—Rome's famed epic—where Trojans confront native Italian tribes; quarrel, fight, and mix their bloods—and in due course become Romans.[8] Anaya tacitly directs our attention to the term "Latino," but uplifts the word to a higher level: not as an ethnic or racial category, but as the sign of a historical and cultural legacy of Chicanos and peoples of Latin America who are the rightful heirs to this "fantastic world view and heritage." This passage provides a glimpse of Anaya's own quest as a writer, to reclaim by rights of ancestry a heritage of great cultures and civilizations that have shaped the history of that country to the south, the two *originating* sources of the Chicano heritage: the Mesoamerican—from the Mayas and Aztecs to the Pueblos ("north up along the Rio Grande")—and the Mediterranean, with its Catholics, Jews, and Arabs. The mythical core in Anaya's view of Chicano culture and literature is Aztlán, understood as the historical archetype of the southward journey of ancient Chichimeca peoples who descend, from remote times to the present, toward central México to combine, transform, and claim the metropolitan civilization as a fundamental source of nuevomexicano cultural history.

Like most Mexican Americans born in the Southwest, Anaya grew up exposed to distorted notions of his regional birthright and customs, portrayed as "primitive, agrarian, and otherwise former ways of life."[9] Recent scholarship has revealed how wrong this generalized notion has been. In Donna Pierce's study on Asian trade goods in colonial New Mexico during the centuries-long Manila Galleon trade, she contends that "archaeological and documentary evidence indicates that New Mexico participated in the international trade market and the globalization of culture from the earliest days of settlement."[10] Pierce points to archaeological evidence of female dresses made of multicolored silk, household goods such as Chinese porcelain, ivory beads and fans, camphor chests, Japanese kimonos, and East Indian chintz (*indianilla de colores fina*).[11] New Mexico traded its hides, woolen goods, and piñon nuts, "indicating that [New Mexico] actively participated in the global trade of the period by both exporting and importing goods."[12] New Mexico, once part of Spain's global empire, became a cultural island after Mexico's wars of independence and a southwestern territory after the 1846–1848 U.S.-Mexico war.

To go back in time and to return with a reclaimed heritage—this back-and-forward movement is exemplified in the prefatory note to Gaspar Pérez de Villagrá's *Historia de la Nueva México, 1610*. The series editors—Genaro Padilla and Erlinda Gonzales-Berry—emphasize an important point: "*Nuevomexicano* literature has been virtually ignored in mainstream literary histories of the United States and the Southwest."[13] It is significant that 1992, the year of this edition, marked the Quincentennial of the Discovery of America, commemorated on the basis of an epic poem that recounts—in the manner of Virgil's *Aeneid* ("the bible of the renaissance epic")—the embattled confrontations and the subsequent merging and intermarriages between Spaniards and Pueblos from New Mexico.[14]

Mexican poet and essayist Alfonso Reyes studied Gaspar Pérez de Villagrá (Puebla, New Spain, 1555–1620), focusing not on the latter's military history but on his membership in the first generation of poets born in colonial México. Reyes claimed that Pérez de Villagrá was known for a poetic sensibility inspired and shaped by Mediterranean models as well as by classical Náhuatl poetry, which expresses a feeling and view of the world learned from songs by Texcocan poet Nezahualcóyotl and other Náhuatl masters. According to Reyes, Villagrá had access to Náhuatl poetry in translations into Spanish by Fernando de Alva Ixtlilxóchitl (1577–1648), a historian whose maternal ancestors were the lords of Tenochtitlan and Texcoco.[15] Religious colleges established by Franciscans, Dominicans, and Jesuits in New Spain began to train the children of the Native nobility according to a comprehensive curriculum, including classical languages such as Latin and Greek. The Native people's intelligence and powerful retention were noticed also in commoners, such as Antonio Valeriano (Azcapotzalco, 1531–1605), who surprised and surpassed his teachers in the mastery of Latin. This cultural mission in the New World, unfurled by various religious orders in New Spain as a humanist foundation dating back to Greco-Roman antiquity, would produce, in Reyes's words, México's golden age in poets, such as Sor Juana Inés de la Cruz (1648–1695); Juan José Eguiara y Eguren (Mexico City, 1696–1763), who wrote the first colonial history of New Spain, *Bibliotheca Mexicana*, in Latin; Diego José Abad (Jiquilpan, Michoacán, 1727–1779), translator of Virgil into Spanish; Francisco Javier Alegre (Veracruz, 1729–1788), translator of Homer's *Iliad* from ancient Greek to Latin; and, among others, the Jesuit scholar who was the culmination of this Mexican Renaissance: Francisco Javier Clavigero (Veracruz, 1731–1787), one of the salient scholars on Mesoamerica, fluent in classical Náhuatl, Mixtec, and Otomí, and in European languages such as Latin, Greek, French and Italian.[16] Memory traces of this tradition were fed to nuevomexicanos with atole and tortillas, filling them with the wonder of creation.

Most of this classical heritage was forgotten after México's post-Independence civil wars, the foreign invasions, and the 1846–1848 U.S.-México War. The result was México's embrace of liberalism and nationalism, two modern tendencies contemptuous of a nation's "colonial" era and of its cultural affiliation with metropolitan and foreign centers. Carlos Fuentes remembers, in his autobiographical book *Myself with Others*, that during his youth he had a Marxist teacher who maintained that it was un-Mexican to read Franz Kafka; a fellow writer assured him that reading Marcel Proust was a way to "Proustitute" oneself. Fuentes adds: "To be a writer in Mexico in the fifties, you had to be with Alfonso Reyes and with Octavio Paz in the assertion that Mexico was not an isolated, virginal province but very much part of the human race and its cultural tradition; we were all, for good and evil, contemporary with all men and women."[17]

Thinking through questions of "appearances" and "apparitions," and of their association with writing and reading, Octavio Armand opens a book and invites us to read what is simultaneously a rainbow, the sun, and a column of fire: thus, under not enough light, or in the blinding glare. How to read a page under such conditions? Armand casts a few rays of light on an "other" reading possibility:

> Dije que ya todos podemos leer el Apocalipsis de San Juan en edición de bolsillo. No dije, ni tenía que decir, que en esa edición el Apocalipsis será leído, y solo puede ser leído, como literatura. Popularidad devastadora: las profecías resultan legibles únicamente como literatura. Relato de ciencia ficción, novela gótica, poema surrealista: lo único que el Apocalipsis no puede ser es una escritura sagrada. Como tal—como algo que signifique o pretenda significar exactamente lo que quiere decir—la Revelación de San Juan resulta ilegible. La edición de bolsillo excluye a un lector: el creyente.

> [I said that all of us can now read St. John's Revelation in paperback. I did not say, nor did I have to say, that in such edition Revelation shall be read, and can only be read, as literature. A devastating popularity: prophecies are legible only as literature. A narrative of science fiction, a Gothic novel, or surrealist poem: what Revelation can not be is a sacred text. As such, and as something that pretends to mean or signify exactly what it wants to avow—the Revelation of Saint John—is beyond legibility. The paperback edition excludes one reader: the believer.][18]

The opening paragraph in *Bless Me, Ultima* contains the blinding glare and intensity of expression in Antonio's remembrance of things past, told in tongues as he reenacts his first encounter with Ultima and the revolution she brought to his senses—tactile, visual, and no less significant, his sense of origins and history ("Let me begin at the beginning. I do not mean the beginning that was in my dreams and the stories" [1]).[19] The recollection of this momentous meeting with Ultima manifests itself as a Proustian temporal experience in which the past is relived as the present, and the future is one with the instant ("Time stood still, and it shared with me all that had been, and all that was to come" [1]), a point in time's convergence that reveals the purpose and fulfillment of Ultima's advent: "I have come to spend the last days of my life here, Antonio" (11).[20] These first reading impressions disclose two important narrative features: one, Ultima's revelations of Antonio's true destiny (that is, to be instrumental in her own death—the novel's plot—and therefore the instrument of Ultima's *sacrifice* in order to reintegrate the communal body); second, the reader's comprehension of a larger view of "American" history through *Bless Me, Ultima*, past and present. Antonio's remembrance of a youthful experience of temporal fusion and mystical transport virtually expands one's reading of *Bless Me, Ultima* beyond the mere storyline, particularly in readers who know about the history of the Spanish conquest, the conversion of the Native population, the apparition of the Virgin of Guadalupe to Juan Diego in the Tepeyac hill, and the religious traditions that flowed north along the Río Grande.[21]

Early readings of *Bless Me, Ultima* mostly followed a form of subjectivity in conformity with the era and questions of ethnic identity; thus, Antonio Márez Luna's self-interrogation ("will I be a Márez or a Luna?") is interpreted as a dialectic with its own Chicano resolution: Antonio as a mestizo with Indian and Spanish ancestry. Antonio's fundamental question of existence, however, is transposed early in the novel from the question of cultural identity to one associated with a *fated function*, in which his future would be determined not by his father's or mother's lineage but by Ultima's intervention in the family quarrels after his birth, resulting in her claim to be the sole possessor of the key to his fate (*"only I will know his destiny"* [6, italics in the original]). At this level of interpretation, one can begin to read—in the sense of to interpret and comprehend—*Bless Me, Ultima* in the light of its Marian iconography (the apparition of the Virgin of Guadalupe to Juan Diego; Ultima's "apparition" to [Juan] Antonio) and the configurations of the new sacred (the golden carp) as opposed to the dogma of the traditional Catholic Church:

> Ultima came to stay with us the summer I was almost seven. When she came the beauty of the llano unfolded before my eyes, and the gurgling waters of the river sang to the hum of the turning earth. The magical time of childhood stood still, and the pulse of the living earth pressed its mystery into my living blood. She took my hand, and the silent, magic powers she possessed made beauty from the raw, sun-baked llano, the green river valley, and the blue bowl which was the white sun's home. My bare feet felt the throbbing earth and my body trembled with excitement. Time stood still, and it shared with me all that had been, and all that was to come. (1)

Antonio's remembrance of past experiences and impressions is narrated in a raw, sensory language that offers interpretive paths along the lines of a coming of age story or a tale of ethnic identity.[22] Yet it can be read, on the contrary, as a textual microcosm of the novel itself, in the sense of containing essential plot elements and narrative space where different fields of knowledge and a people's cultural unconscious converge—as in the prelude "Descent into Hell" in Thomas Mann's *Joseph und Seine Brüder* (Joseph and his brothers, 1933–1943), or in Carlos Fuentes's "Aztec" soliloquy in *La región más transparente* (Where the air is clear, 1958). Only then can Anaya's art of the novel manifest its quest for a broad literary range, structural subtlety, and a polyphony of cultural discourses. Guided by such reading possibilities, the reenactment of Antonio's memories of a conflict-ridden ancestry illuminates the purpose of Ultima's arrival, the regional and global implications of her acts of magic, and the cultural foundation that gives meaning to her actions. Set within the symmetry of regional and global violence, the conflicts between the peoples of the llano (the Márezes) and the river valley (the Lunas) find their international correspondence with World War II: namely, the atomic bomb tests in

Alamogordo (July 16, 1945) and clear allusions to them in the pages of *Bless Me, Ultima*. In a world-historical setting expressed through apocalyptic imagery—to be read as *revelation* in the sense of perception, and as an *event*, hence as the "end of the world"—Ultima enters the narrative in a forked manner, as the apparition to a Juan Diego (Juan is Antonio's middle name), with the function of healing the region known for its history "full of blood, murder, and tragedy" (19), first of Spaniards or Mexicans against American Indians, followed by that of Anglo-Americans against Mexicans.

Rhetorically inscribed in *Bless Me, Ultima* in such an apocalyptic sequence, the historical conflicts of the region—and particularly in the town of Guadalupe—constitute a synchronic gathering of Johannine communities representing different times and places, from Ancient Rome (St. John on the island of Patmos), to the Spanish conquest (the apparition of the Virgin of Guadalupe to Juan Diego at México's Tepeyac hill in 1531), to Ultima's "apparition" in 1944 to (Juan) Antonio in Guadalupe, a town located near a hill and surrounded by water, thus an archetypal figuration of Patmos. From this particular viewpoint, *Bless Me, Ultima*, like Carlos Fuentes's *Terra Nostra* (1975), reads like a long reflection on world empires—celestial and of this world—and therefore as a narrative with interpretive choices made possible by the rhetorical functions of animated surfaces, apparitions, oneiric experiences, and vision trances of "new worlds" found in islands, peninsulas, and entire continents, from Europe, Africa, and Asia to the shores of the New World.

Anaya's inaugural novel led the way to a regionalism in Chicano literature that could only be theorized and understood in the 1990s within the sphere of its international implications. Therefore, this understanding is *in retrospect* and as part of a process of literary differentiation that originated in the U.S. Southwest, thereafter branching out toward the four cardinal directions, which symbolically give meaning to a world that finds unity through the temporal swing between moments of harmony and the ever-recurring threats of chaos and wars of aggression.[23] To memorialize, to rethink a manifold ancestry, and to evoke the rivalries as well as the unification of peoples who discover a higher destiny for humanity—these are the guiding themes in Anaya's writings about New Mexico's cultural history.[24]

NOTES

1. Some of the included chapters were especially commissioned for this book; however, most of the volume's chapters are selected and expanded versions of papers read by leading Anaya scholars at the Conference on Rudolfo Anaya: Tradition, Modernity, and the Literatures of the U.S. Southwest, held at California State University, Los Angeles, on May 2–3, 2014. For more information about this conference and the program, visit http://rudyanayaatcalstatela. blogspot.com.

2. Lummis saw his work as part of the New School of American History, with A. F. Bandelier as its leading figure. Lummis's "break" with an official school of American History marks a stand in favor of a critical change in established perspectives on the American frontier and on Native Americans, Mexicans, and, implicitly, on African Americans. In his preface to *The Spanish Pioneers* (1893), Lummis makes the following important observation: "In this country of free and brave men, race-prejudice, the most ignorant of all human ignorances, must die out. We must respect manhood more than nationality, and admire it for its own sake wherever found,—and it is found everywhere. The deeds that hold the world up are not of any one blood" (11). Lummis adds a positive view on Spain and her achievements in the Americas: "Had there been no Spain four hundred years ago, there would be no United States today. It is a most fascinating story to every genuine American,—for every one worthy of the name admires heroism and loves fairplay everywhere, and is first of all interested in the truth about his own country" (91). Published in 1893, *The Spanish Pioneers* marks an evident commemoration of the 1492 Columbian "discovery" of America and a hymn on behalf of Spanish conquistadors and their descendants; ironically, the book precedes by five years the decisive war between the United States and Spain and the transformation of the former into an emerging global power.

3. In César A. González-T.'s book of essays titled *Rudolfo A. Anaya: Focus on Criticism* , he lists several conferences on Chicano literature hosted by various European campuses, such as the Johannes Gutenberg University Mainz, Germany, in July 1984, and at the Germersheim campus, July 1990; the University of Paris, March 1986; and the University of Barcelona, June 1988 (xv). In less than two decades, Chicano literature had reached an international readership. To date, Anaya has a growing number of readers in the Américas and, through translations into many world languages, in other parts of the world, such as France, Germany, México, Russia, and Turkey.

4. For a fuller discussion of Anaya's biography and of his novels published between 1972 and 1999, including their critical reception, see my article "Rudolfo A. Anaya." For a study of Anaya's autobiography as the thematic core of his New Mexico trilogy—composed of *Bless Me, Ultima* (1972), *Heart of Aztlán* (1976), and *Tortuga* (1979)—see my article "Surname."

5. See Slotkin, "Recovering the Mission."

6. For Henry David Thoreau's phrase and the new regionalism in American letters, see Ellis, *Beyond Borders*, 13, 129.

7. Anaya, "An Autobiography," 386–87.

8. After Jupiter's command that Juno end her hostility toward Aeneas, she replies: And now I yield, and quit this loathsome war. / I have one solemn request of you. . . . When soon / (Let it be) they make peace with happy weddings, / And form alliances with laws and treaties, / Do not command the native Latins / To change their ancient name, nor become / Trojans and be called Teucrians, nor to change / In language or in dress. Let Latium be, / Let Alban kings rule through the ages, / And let the Roman stock be strong / In Italian manhood. (Virgil, *Aeneid*, 12.988–99) Jupiter consents (12.1005–12).

9. Ellis, *Beyond Borders*, 129.

10. Pierce, "At the Ends of the Earth," 155.

11. Ibid., 174.

12. Ibid., 180.

13. Padilla and Gonzales-Berry, Prefatory note to *Historia*, xv.

14. Ibid., xxii.

15. See Reyes, *Letras de la Nueva España*, 297.

16. Ibid., 301, 375.

17. Fuentes, *Myself with Others*, 23.

18. See Armand, "Una lectura de la luz," 430–31, my translation. For a study of Octavio Armand's poetry and essays, see Gotera, *Octavio Armand contra sí mismo*.

19. Text references are to page numbers form the 1972 edition of *Bless Me, Ultima*.

20. The trinitarian dimension in Ultima's funeral requests underscores the unorthodoxy of her approach to religious and cultural customs: she asks Antonio (1) to burn her medicines and herbs—associated with her magic and power to heal—somewhere near the river, and (2) to bury her owl in the hills—the spiritual setting for apparitions and miracles—under a forked juniper tree. Antonio, as if to emphasize Ultima's freedom from cultural conventions, concludes his narrative with an unexpected disclosure: (3) Ultima is really buried at the end of his storytelling, therefore an act of remembrance, implying that she is again "awakened" to life each time he retells the story of her actions and willful engagements with the world's evil—intolerance, fratricidal conflicts, and by symbolic association, world wars. The mythical cluster defined by fire, sacred trees, and rituals of burial and resurrection also appear in James George Frazer's underlying argument in *The Golden Bough*, through his study of trees in sacred groves (King of the Wood), the priesthood of Diana, the making of fire through the friction of wood, and divine lightning and thunder. Frazer alludes to the golden bough's early source being Virgil's *Aeneid*, where the reader can confirm the Sibyl of Cumae's "chant in eerie riddles," warning Aeneas that in order to enter and come out of Avernus, he must first find the golden bough

"Hidden in a darkling tree . . . held sacred, / To the goddess below" (Virgil, *Aeneid*, 10.175–77). Frazer, however, goes further afield in his reflections on this mythical cluster, locating universal equivalents in nations that have lived in the U.S. Southwest for thousands of years, such as the Senal and Maidu of California, and in other nations who dwell in British Columbia. These North American peoples chanted myths about the world originally being a vast ball of fire, with its blazing element retained in trees, liberated each time two sticks of wood are rubbed together. Frazer explains that trees that are forked or double in portion due to lightning are major features of an American Indian metaphysical system, and quotes directly from his sources: "[L]ightning is nothing but the Great Man himself descending swiftly out of heaven and *rending the trees* with his flaming arms" (Frazer, *Golden Bough*, 568, my emphasis). In *Bless Me, Ultima*, the reader descends back to humanity's myths of fire, of conflict and death, and rises "awakened" to life again. An in-depth reading of *Bless Me, Ultima* would allow us to trace the Franciscan substitution of the oak with the juniper tree in relation to New Mexico's penitente tradition; the Franciscan theological sense of history and its millenarian implications in the cult of the Virgin of Guadalupe; and their devoted readings of Virgil's *Aeneid* and of St. John's Revelation. As an opening path to such a reading, consult Phelan, *Millennial Kingdom*.

21. For a fuller development of this analysis and a critical discussion of different interpretations of *Bless Me, Ultima* during the 1970s and 1980s, see my article "Apocalypse," 59–63.

22. See the selection of articles on *Bless Me, Ultima* published between 1973 and 2007 and collected in Trudeau, *Contemporary Literary Criticism*, 1–118.

23. For a brief exposition of the regional and theoretical differentiation within Chicano literature after 1990, see my foreword to *Latino Los Angeles*.

24. Mexican poet Estela Alicia López Lomas, born in Guadalajara (México) but raised in Tijuana—thus facing daily the "reality" of México's border with the United States—translates the otherness of America into the palpable and understandable through the writings of Lewis Carroll and Ezra Pound, in which crossing the border can be a sudden fall into a rabbit hole that leads to other forms of madness and delirium, or where "translation" of distant languages and cultures opens possibilities for the fertile and critical understanding of the civilization one lives under. See her award-winning books of poetry, *Alicia en la cárcel de las maravillas* and *El último monolito de la noche*.

BIBLIOGRAPHY

Anaya, Rudolfo A. "An Autobiography." In *Rudolfo A. Anaya: Focus on Criticism*, edited by César A. González-T., 359–88. La Jolla, CA: Lalo Press, 1990.

———. *Bless Me, Ultima*. Berkeley, CA: Quinto Sol, 1972.

Armand, Octavio. "Una lectura de la luz." In *Contra la página: ensayos reunidos, 1980–2013*, edited by Miguel Aguilar Carrillo, 420–34. Santiago de Querétaro: Calygramma, 2015.

Cantú, Roberto. "Apocalypse as an Ideological Construct: The Storyteller's Art in *Bless Me, Ultima*." In vol. 362 of *Contemporary Literary Criticism*, edited by Lawrence J. Trudeau, 51–69. New York: Gale Group, 2014.

———. Foreword to *Latino Los Angeles in Film and Fiction: The Cultural Production of Social Anxiety*, by Ignacio López-Calvo, xi–xvii. Tucson: University of Arizona Press, 2011.

———. "Rudolfo A. Anaya." In *Dictionary of Literary Biography*, vol. 278, 7th series, *American Novelists Since World War II*, edited by James R. Giles and Wanda H. Giles, 11–20. New York: Gale Group, 2003.

———. "The Surname, the Corpus, and the Body in Rudolfo A. Anaya's Narrative Trilogy." In *Rudolfo A. Anaya: Focus on Criticism*, edited by César A. González-T., 274–317. La Jolla, CA: Lalo Press, 1990.

Ellis, Reuben J., ed. *Beyond Borders: The Selected Essays of Mary Austin*. Carbondale: Southern Illinois University Press, 1996.

Frazer, James George. *The Golden Bough: A Study in Magic and Religion*. Abridged. New York: Digireads, 2011.

Fuentes, Carlos. *La región más transparente*. Edición conmemorativa. México: Alfaguara, 2008.

———. *Myself with Others*. New York: Farrar, Straus, and Giroux, 1988.

González-T., César A., ed. *Rudolfo A. Anaya: Focus on Criticism*. La Jolla, CA: Lalo Press, 1990.

Gotera, Johan. *Octavio Armand contra sí mismo*. Madrid: Efory Atocha, 2012.

López Lomas, Estela Alicia. *Alicia en la cárcel de las maravillas*. Quintana Roo: Nave de papel, 1995.

———. *El fuego tras el espejo*. México: Instituto Municipal de Arte y Cultura, 2002.

———. *El último monolito de la noche*. México: Consejo Nacional para la Cultura y las Artes, 2004.

Mann, Thomas. *Joseph and His Brothers*. Translated by John E. Woods. New York: Everyman's Library, 2005.

Padilla, Genaro, and Erlinda Gonzales-Berry. Prefatory note to *Historia de la Nueva México, 1610*, by Gaspar Pérez de Villagrá. Edited and translated by Miguel Encinias, Alfred Rodríguez, and Joseph Sánchez. Albuquerque: University of New Mexico Press, 1992.

Pérez de Villagrá, Gaspar. *Historia de la Nueva México, 1610*. Edited and translated by Miguel Encinias, Alfred Rodríguez, and Joseph Sánchez. Albuquerque: University of New Mexico Press, 1992.

Phelan, John L. *The Millennial Kingdom of the Franciscans in the New World*. 2nd rev. ed. Los Angeles: University of California Press, 1970.

Pierce, Donna. "At the Ends of the Earth': Asian Trade Goods in Colonial New Mexico, 1598–1821." In *At the Crossroads: The Arts of Spanish America and Early Global Trade, 1492–1850*, edited by Donna Pierce and Ronald Otsuka, 155–82. Denver, CO: Denver Art Museum, 2012.

Reyes, Alfonso. *Letras de la Nueva España*. 1948. Reprinted in *Obras completas*, vol. 12, 281–390. México: Fondo de Cultura Económica, 1960.

———. *Ultima Tule*. 1942. Reprinted in *Obras completas*, vol. 11, 9–153. México: Fondo de Cultura Económica, 1960.

Slotkin, Richard. "Recovering the Mission: Mexico Westerns, 1965–1968." In *Gunfighter Nation: The Myth of the Frontier in Twentieth-Century America*, 560–577. New York: Atheneum, 1992.

Trudeau, Lawrence J., ed. *Contemporary Literary Criticism*. Vol. 362. New York: Gale Group, 2014.

Virgil. *Aeneid*. Translated by Stanley Lombardo. Indianapolis, IN: Hackett, 2005.

PART 1

Rudolfo Anaya and Narratives of the U.S. Southwest

1

The Spell of New Mexico

THE WITCHES AND SORCERERS
OF COLONIAL NEW MEXICO

Ramón A. Gutiérrez

This chapter owes its inspiration to Rudolfo Anaya's novel *Bless Me, Ultima*. Back in 1972, when the novel appeared, I was a young man of twenty-one. As a *manito*, a native New Mexican, reared along the banks of the Río Grande on the south side of Albuquerque, I grew up with stories of El Cucuy, of La Llorona, of the ghosts and spirits that regularly traveled along the río at night looking for souls, and of the *brujas* and *curanderas* who brought both evil and good into the world. As a young boy, growing up, much like Antonio Márez Luna, I knew several women in the neighborhood who approached Ultima, la Grande, for their knowledge of curing with native plants and herbs. Women who knew how to lift the hexes that witches cast, curing everything from *mal de ojo* (evil eye) to *empacho* (indigestion). Let me transport you to another time and place, to colonial New Mexico, to the spells, hexes, and charms of those days.

It was an April night in 1734, recalled María Manuela de Armijo. It must have been eight o'clock, or thereabouts. Outside on the streets of Santa Fe, New Mexico, all was abolutely still. Inside María's house, the day's end had brought a peaceful hush. The evening embers in the hearth had begun to crackle and pop. Already Cayetano Moya, María's husband, had retired. And all the children had been blessed and safely tucked in. María bolted shut the windows and door to her house. She blessed herself with the sign of the cross, said her evening prayers, and climbed into bed for a night's rest.

But there would be very little rest for María that night. Moments before she fell asleep, a witch entered the house. Bellowing like a raging bull, barking like a dog, with yips and yaps and harrowing cries, the witch, whom María recognized as the *coyota* Nicolasa Romero, kept shouting out in an ugly cry: "Puta! Puta! Gran Puta!" (You whore! You whore! You big whore!) María tried to scream out in terror, but the cords in her throat were silent. No one heard her desperate cries. "Praised be the Blessed Sacrament," she prayed. "Glory be Saint Anthony," she mumbled helplessly as the witch fondled María's body, caressed her breasts, and did with her as she pleased. And though María's husband, Cayetano, was in bed beside her, he saw and heard absolutely nothing. Then, just as suddenly as Nicolasa Romero appeared, she disappeared into the night.[1]

In the 1700s church authorities in New Mexico launched several investigations into accusations that certain women were practicing *brujería* (witchcraft) and *hechicería* (sorcery), as well as making people ill by giving them *mal de ojo*.[2] Witnesses described the making of love potions and charms wives used to win back the affections of their husbands, the brews that were being cooked to win back lovers, and the hexes that spurned mistresses were placing on the private parts of their former partners. Unlike the witch crazes of Europe and New England, which were often sparked by famine, disease, and factionalism, in New Mexico a fear of witches and sorcery was rather constant in the 1700s. Nothing particularly unusual seemed to provoke the accusations and investigations, or at least nothing that was reported in the historical documents of the time. New Mexico then was in a constant state of war against nomadic Indian enemies, who attacked with impunity. These indigenous enemies were being constantly captured, baptized, and placed into Christian homes as slaves, and so their numbers residing in Spanish households were rapidly rising in the eighteenth century. Captured Apaches and Comanches lived in close quarters with their masters, the women often laboring as housekeepers, wet nurses, and cooks with unfettered access to food, which was often described as the most effective means to bewitch or hex an unsuspecting victim.

Pueblo Indian women were also being sexually assaulted, wooed, and seduced by Spanish men. From such activities illegitimate children were being born who were immediately exiled from Pueblo Indian towns. These infants, often left abandoned at the nearest church and registered in the baptismal books simply as *"hijo de la iglesia, padres no conocidos"* (child of the church, parents unknown) were incorporated into Spanish households as servants, or *criados*. Such strays and slaves, known collectively as *genízaros*, were stigmatized by their ancestry, deemed dishonored by their work, the victims of considerable public stigma and suspicion. It was out of this fear of the Indian enemy living within that the Spanish colonists of New Mexico accused a number of Indian and mestiza women of witchcraft and sorcery. These women were accused of all sort of heinous acts, particularly of plying love magic and of being in cahoots with the devil to make Spanish men impotent. Imagine the two worst things that could happen in a society at war with the Apaches and Comanches: falling in love with the enemy, thus weakening the society's protective resolve, and having impotent Spanish soldiers (*machos capados amariconados*) who were defenseless against their Indian enemies.

The witchcraft accusations and the investigations they triggered in eighteenth-century New Mexico tell us a great deal about the cultural preoccupations of this society. The racial exclusivity of the area's so-called Spaniards was being eroded by the process of mestizaje. Spanish men, both single and married, were cohabiting with Indians, which was quickly increasing numbers of illegitimate mestizos, numbers only compounded by the proliferation of abandoned strays. If the racial distinctions that allowed Spaniards to lord over Indians were to continue unchallenged, marriage and social mixing had to be tightly regulated. Witchcraft and sorcery denunciations and the investigations they precipitated were precisely the tool Spanish New Mexicans and imperial authorities used to police local racial boundaries. In a moment, we will see specifically how and why all of this happened, but for now, bear in mind that the major accusation against Indian women denounced as witches was that when they engaged in the sexual act, they were always on top. They had control over Spanish men, so totally dominating them that they could ensnare their affections and regulate their erections. Such sexual inversions of the established gender order were extremely subversive, or so opined the Spanish colonial authorities. How could an Indian woman dominate a man? How could a woman have more power than a man? In short, how could Indian women be on top?

Obviously, only by being in cahoots with the devil could such things transpire. In the learned writings of celibate priests, these witches were bad mothers. They were sexually provocative, sinful, and aggressive Eves, who did not accept prescribed gender roles. They were powerful, aggressive, and usurped male prerogatives of authority, or so claimed their accusers. They were by definition shameless women, who had supernatural powers because they slept with the devil. The evil of the night was their domain; under the cover of darkness, they performed their nefarious deeds. The witch, Nicolasa Romero of Santa Fe, was seen riding around on a broomstick one night in 1734. The broomstick, a sign of a woman's domesticity by day, became a giant phallic symbol, the essence of masculinity, when placed between her thighs at night. On December 24, 1745, the very night commemorating Christ's birth, Michaela de Contreras was said to have transformed herself into a big black cat. In this form she attacked a man named Antonio de Orianda, forcing him to fornicate with her and to defile the sanctity of his matrimonial vow.[3] Santa Fe's residents complained of seeing the Indian witch Juana de la Cruz flying about inside an egg, spying on all the men she controlled with her evil potions.

Witches were attackers and deceivers using what was impure and demonic to pollute the pure and holy. They subverted the social order sanctioned by religion. María Domínguez of Santa Fe was prosecuted in 1734 because of the trances she could induce in men with her peyote potions. While under the spell of María's enchanting drinks, men could see the past and the future before their very eyes. And even more demonic still, with her peyote potions, María could gain the affections of any man she desired.[4]

In 1719 Josepha de la Encarnación of El Paso, a woman accused of witchcraft, told María Vélez that if she wanted to know if her husband loved another woman, all she had to do was "toss a caterpillar's cocoon into a fire; if it swelled, he loved another woman." But if "a woman dreamt of raging bulls, this was a sign that she would be pursued by men who loved her."[5]

Witches were known to shatter the limitations of time and space. Beatriz de los Angeles magically transported herself from Santa Cruz de la Cañada, in northern New Mexico, to Senecú, a town just north of El Paso, or a distance of some two hundred miles. Beatriz's only purpose for this travel was to torment María Granillo, on whom she had placed a hex. Though Fray Gerónimo Pedraza tried to exorcize María's demons, he did not have much success.[6] On two occasions during 1731, Michaela de Contreras was seen by several witnesses in two different towns on the same day; these towns were separated by hundreds of miles.[7] And even though the door and all the windows to María Manuela de Armijo's Santa Fe house were securely bolted, as you will recall, Nicolasa Romero entered without constraint.

Witches possessed powers they had obtained from the devil and displayed behaviors that were inappropriate to their gender. Subverting the gender hierarchy enshrined in the honor code and moral order sanctioned by the Catholic Church was precisely the reason that authorities pursued New Mexican Indian and mestiza women as witches and sorceresses. Let us examine a few of more cases to illustrate these points.

In 1745, Beatrice de la Cabrera was investigated by the Inquisition because of the accusation leveled against her by María Rosa Telles Jirón of El Paso. María Rosa told the Inquisition's representative that one day while out in a maize field with Beatrice de la Cabrera, a man named Juan José Romero arrived on horseback. After a brief chat he began to argue bitterly with Beatrice. While still exchanging heated and foul-sounding words, Juan mounted his horse and galloped away, not heeding Beatrice's command that he return at once. "So he does not want to come back," Beatrice said to María Rosa. "Wait a minute and watch how he will return." As she said this, Beatrice reached into her sash and rubbed something; then, something just short of miraculous occurred. In an instance, Juan returned. Later, after Juan and Beatrice had spoken, Juan left again, but this time in a friendly and romantic mood. Quite stunned by what she had seen, María Rosa asked Beatrice how she had performed something so incredible. Beatrice pulled from her sash a white cloth pouch that contained a small wheat cake into which a special weed had been baked. If a woman baked this cake, explained Beatrice, "a man would not abandon his woman, but rather would love her until she tires of him." With this weed, Beatrice could control any man she desired.[8]

In another case, from 1731, Felipe de Ayudo of Socorro denounced Michaela de Contreras as a witch because she had place a hex on him, which had left him sexually impotent. "Michaela left me like a woman," Felipe protested, "putting a spell on my [private] part so that I cannot cohabit with other women." Asked by Fray Andrés Varo, the local representative of the Inquisition, how he knew that Michaela was the source of his affliction, Felipe explained, "When I am with other women I cannot, and only with the said Michaela can I." Felipe claimed that he finally broke the spell by beating Michaela up, "giving her a round of kicks with my spurs, and even though I caused great scandal, from that moment I felt great relief and have been able to function again."[9] Other townspeople complained about Michaela's sinister powers as well. She had hexed the wife of Nicolás Sierra, leaving her so sick that "she was passing her brains through her nose."[10]

Even priests were not immune from the devil's handmaidens. In 1743 the Franciscan friar stationed at the Indian pueblo of Isleta was hexed by Gertudes Sánchez of Santa Fe. Gertudes was accused of sorcery and of having entered "a pact with the devil," for after she secretly placed a weed in the food of Fray Pedro Montaño, the priest began "to love Gertudes very much."[11]

María Padilla accused Magdalena Sánchez of Santa Cruz de la Cañada of plying the sinister craft. Magdalena told her in 1748, "if you want a man to desire you, or if you do not want to lose the one that already loves you, take a few kernels of corn and chew them. Next fetch a pinacate [a big black bug that looks like a cockroach]. Rub it together with the corn in your hands. Call the man you want, or the one you do not wish to lose. And while pretending to be affectionate, let some of the corn kernels fall on his head." This, Magdalena assured María, was a sure way to gain the affections of a man, particularly if one's age and physical attributes had failed to attract him.[12]

Examining these and many other New Mexican cases of witchcraft and sorcery as a whole, certain patterns emerge. Mostly Indian and mestiza women were accused of having such malevolent supernatural powers. In no instance was a man accused. The victims were usually Spanish males, though a few females were also afflicted. Michaela de Contreras, for example, was accused of hexing women and men alike.

Who were the accusers? In only one case did a Spanish male step forward to denounce an Indian or mestiza as a witch, when Felipe Ayudo complained to the Inquisition that Michaela de Contreras had made him sexually impotent with other women. Reading the extensive documentation on this case, we learn that Felipe had had a long-standing adulterous relationship with Michaela. His affliction and the beating he gave her to free himself from her hex occurred only after he had tired of their adulterous affair. He thus justified the great scandal of publicly beating a woman who was not his wife by arguing that Michaela and the devil had made him act this way. He had not been in control but was Michaela's pawn.[13]

In the majority of witchcraft and sorcery cases, the denouncers were either the wives or close female relatives of the bewitched men, troubled that the affections of their men had been stolen through some malevolent means. These women sought to understand why their husbands had cooled to their affections, grown distant and remote, and taken mistresses. Wives could imagine no other explanation than the work of Indian witches and sorcerers.

The 1708 witchcraft denunciation that doña Leonor Domínguez of Santa Fe leveled against three Indian women from San Juan Pueblo, two of whom had disabilities, illustrates this point very well. On May 7, 1708, doña Leonor wrote to New Mexican governor don José Chacón Medina Salazar y Villa, seeking his intercession.

> I Doña Leonor Domínguez, native resident of this Province, wife of Miguel Martín, appears before your lordship . . . being extremely ill with various troubles and maladies which seem to be caused by witchcraft, having been visited by persons practiced and intelligent in medicine. Wherefore, I cite them, and having just suspicions of certain [persons] . . . I know that there have been many examples in this Province of persons of my sex who have been possessed by witchcraft with devilish art, as is well known and perceptible in Augustina Romero, Ana María, the wife of Luiz López, and María Luján, my sister-in-law, and other persons. . . . And having just suspicions of certain persons notorious for this crime . . . I ask

that you may be pleased to [order?] one of your agents [to come] to
the house and habitation where I am staying to . . . take my legal
declaration and solemn oath of what passed between me and the
three Indian women of the Pueblo of San Juan, whom I suspect [of
witchcraft] promising to declare the occasion, cause and reasons
for my suspicion, and in order that likewise it may be seen from the
condition in which I find myself, which is also a matter of public
knowledge and notoriety. . . . I swear, by the Lord God and the
Holy Cross, that it is not from malice but from exhaustion that I
solicit relief, and I implore and need the royal aid through you.[14]

On May 13, 1708, New Mexico's governor dispatched Juan García de
la Riva, Santa Fe's constable, along with a notary, to take doña Leonor's
formal deposition at the house of her brother-in-law, Tomás Girón. The
constable found doña Leonor in bed, quite ill and clearly suffering. When
García de la Riva asked her under oath why she wanted to denounce the
three Indian women, she explained:

On Holy Thursday last in the church of the town of Santa Cruz,
while praying, beside me sat an Indian woman of San Juan called
Catherina Luján, and further off was [Catarina Rosa], who is the
wife of [Diego] Zhiconqueto, the Indian painter. I heard this Catherina Luján say to the wife of the said Indian [painter]: "Is this the
wife of Miguel Martín?" "Yes, it is" [she responded]. . . . I then heard
the wife of the Indian painter and one of her daughters [named
Angelina Pumazho] say to the said Catherina Luján: "Now." And
the latter said: "Not yet." Full of terror, I left that place where I was
kneeling, and fell on my knees closer to the altar. This time the
[painter's] wife said to Catherina: "It would be better now." And
while still on her knees the said wife of the Indian [painter] came
close to me and put her hand on [my] back beside [my] heart. Then,
as she did so, [my] entire body began to itch, and I [manuscript torn]
have not lifted my head since then . . . whence I am persuaded that
the [Indian women are why I suffer].[15]

Doña Leonor went on to certify that she was twenty years old and had
failed to sign her declaration because she did not know how to write.

On May 15, 1708, after reading doña Leonor's declaration, the governor had all three Indian women arrested, transported to Santa Fe, and imprisoned in leg irons until they could be interrogated about doña Leonor's illness. In the week that followed, their depositons were taken. All three women denied even being in church on Holy Thursday; they had been there on Palm Sunday. They denied having spoken to doña Leonor and vigorously protested ever touching her or even coming close to her. According to Pueblo Indian lore, witches seize the power of their victims by stealing their hearts, which is precisely what doña Leonor claimed Catalina Rosa had done when she had placed her hand on doña Leonor's back near her heart. When questioned about doña Leonor's stolen heart, the Indian women said they knew nothing.

The governor, puzzled by the contradictory depositions he read, and hoping to sort out the facts, ordered a new deposition taken with doña Leonor by a much more aggressive interrogator, Gaspar Gutiérrez de los Rios, New Mexico's war captain. On May 22, 1708, Gutiérrez questioned doña Leonor, who again told the same story. But now when asked why she suspected the Indian women as witches, she explained:

> My suspicion of the said Catalina [Rosa] . . . is because when coming from the farm, in [the] company with my husband, Miguel Martín, [en route] to the village of San Juan to get a little lime, I asked him to leave me at the house of Catherina Luján. Instead my husband deceived me and took me to the house of Catalina Rosa, and because of this, I quarreled with my husband. Catalina Rosa offered us some roasted meat and beans. My husband told me to eat. But I replied that I was fasting. Catalina said to me, "What? Today? Sunday? You are fasting?" At that moment, a neighbor named Martín Fernández said to me: "Eat what they give you, it won't hurt you because this Indian woman is your husband's mistress."[16]

Doña Leonor further declared that one day while chatting with Alfonso Rael, her husband's cousin, she had learned from him that her husband had two Indian mistresses in Taos Pueblo and another one in San Juan Pueblo. On reading this second, more extensive cross-examination of doña Leonor, the governor concluded that the charges against the Indian women were "false, futile, and despicable," born of pure malice and jealousy. She had accused the Indian women falsely because she knew that two of them had stolen her husband's love. Indeed, claiming that they stole her heart, the symbol of love in Western thought, is not insignificant.

The accusations against New Mexican witches and sorcerers can be read at several different levels. On the surface, they were first of all statements about the problematic nature of marriage as an institution. Given that parents arranged most marriages for the sole purpose of forging economic and social alliances, with little concern for the wishes and desires of the actual partners, it was to be expected that adultery became one way of escaping from an indissoluble sacramental state. When wives discovered that their husbands had mistresses or were clandestinely cavorting with a concubine, some of them, out of desperation resorted to the black arts, to Indian and mestiza women who knew how to control men with love magic.

The Pueblos believed that corn kernels contained a person's breath and spirit and that witches attacked individuals by stealing their hearts and their breath. Thus when Juana Sánchez sought the assistance of a San Juan Indian woman "so that her husband would not maltreat her, and so that he would end his illicit friendship with his mistress and would love her [Juana]," the woman gave her "two kernels of blue corn with inverted hearts" and various weeds. Juana was told to chew the corn and weeds into a paste that she was to rub on her husband's heart. This way she would win back his heart and his love.[17] Beatrice de Pedrasa received similar advice so that she too "could win back her husband's heart . . . and so that he would love her and treat her well."[18] Some women made concoctions with their husband's urine. Others fashioned dolls in the likeness of their spouse and stuck pins in them. Whatever the means, the desired end was identical: to win back the love of the man they had taken in matrimony.[19]

God-fearing men could not admit their frustration with marriage and their adulterous activities, which according to church teachings was a sin. Admission of this to the authorities could result in harsh punishment. By blaming one's behavior on supernatural forces of evil, on the devil and his handmaidens, the witches, the defect was placed in a realm beyond human control. Clerics certainly believed in the reality of the devil. Numerous times during the colonial period, friars stated that the snakes Pueblo Indians venerated were the devil, who had enslaved the Indians in their most notorious sin, that of lust.[20] So when men blamed their affairs on being hexed, they were presenting religious authorities with an explanation that seemed perfectly valid. Because clerics and theologians believed that God might punish his servants through the activity of witches and sorcerers, investigations had the effect of giving notice to the community that adultery and fornication were intolerable illicit activities.

Even though no one was ever severely punished for this sin in colonial New Mexico, the mere threat of prosecution, and the knowledge that if guilt were established, one could be tortured and burned at the stake, made people tremble, blame others for their own behavior, and conjure up witches as responsible for what they themselves had willfully done.[21]

What does the symbolism of sexual inversion in these accusations tell us? Why are Spanish men and women so fearful of Indian women, whom they claim are rendering their men impotent, thereby inverting the natural model of domination by which men control women? I suspect that we can begin to answer these questions demographically. When the Spanish returned to New Mexico to reconquer the kingdom in 1693, having been routed from the area during the 1680 Pueblo Revolt, they returned to their old ways of life, resettling in a pattern of broadly dispersed farms. Almost immediately this dispersion made them easy targets for nomadic Indian raiders, who by 1700 had been armed by the French and English, become expert equestrian warriors, and developed particular ferocity. The Spanish farms, with their well-stocked granaries and their immense flocks of cattle, sheep, and hogs, were easy prey. The Pueblo Indians, in their walled towns and terraced compounds, designed precisely to ward off enemies, were able to defend themselves more easily. From 1693 to roughly the 1780s, New Mexico's Spanish farms were constantly under attack. Such depredations forced Spanish farmers eventually to construct walled towns.

Warfare became a way of life for the Spanish settlers, who were constantly staging raiding parties to seize slaves and to avenge the loss of life and livestock. The Apaches, the Utes, the Navajos, and the Comanches always engaged in rather exact retaliation.

The central cultural anxiety during New Mexico's eighteenth century centered on how, precisely, the largely Indian slave, servant, orphan, and stray population living in Spanish towns would participate in the body politic. Living side by side with their masters, the females often shared the master's bed, and if not his, certainly those of his brothers, sons, or other male kin. New Mexico's sex ratio during the 1700s shows that in most Spanish settlements, Indian and mixed-blood women far outnumbered Spanish men, there being approximately eighty men for every one hundred women.[22] The majority of Indians who entered Spanish households as slaves were women and children. Nomadic Indian warriors were deemed too disruptive to settled life and thus were either killed in battle or sold to work in the silver mines of northern México, the henequén plantations of the Yucatán Peninsula, or the sugar fields of Cuba. Many more Spanish men than women died defending the area against nomadic attack. Thus, in New Mexico, there were many more single and widowed females than there were sexually active men.

What happens when there are too many women? According to demographers Marcia Guttentag and Paul Secord, women are valued merely as sex objects. High rates of illegitimacy occur. Men, but not women, have a high rate of remarriage and take a fair amount of sexual license. In such societies, note Guttentag and Secord, women "feel powerless, resentful, rejected and angry . . . [and often] intensify efforts to change the balance of power between the sexes."[23]

The sex ratio imbalance that New Mexico experienced between 1760 and 1820 reverberated through the body politic and manifested itself in pronounced racial anxieties about the promiscuous mixing of the races. Declarations of racial standing began to appear in legal documents that previously had not mentioned them. Before 1760, most official records listed only a person's religion and whether they were *vecinos*, or propertied citizens. After 1760, everyone was additionally classified by race and color—at precisely the moment when racially mixed marriages rose precipitously. Census data from 1760 to 1820 show a rising incidence of widow-headed households, high rates of illegitimacy, and a blurring of racial boundaries among mixed-bloods at marriage.[24]

Anthropologists tell us that witchcraft accusations are often a way of clarifying a society's social boundaries. When the boundaries of a group's privileges are perceived to be under attack, witchcraft accusations are effective counterattacks. Viewing race mixing and the sexual liberties rampant in eighteenth-century New Mexico as the attack, the question becomes: Whose privileges were being threatened? Obviously, it was the local Spanish nobility whose honor and racial status in society were at stake. Their social primacy was fundamentally tied to the sexual purity of their women and the sexual avoidance of Indian slaves, ex-slaves, and mixed-blood women. The birth of illegitimate mixed-blood children in large numbers threatened the boundary separating Indians and Spaniards. If mestizaje was left unchecked, over time it would surely create contentiousness over personal identities, social belonging, communal loyalty, and the rights that citizenship guaranteed in terms of land and water.

The symbolic anthropologist Mary Douglas, in her book *Purity and Danger*, notes that groups are often perceived to have particular functions in relationship to the totality of the social body. When social boundaries blur, the anxiety is often expressed as pollution fears, with the actual body parts invoked, serving as privileged symbols for those fears.[25] In patrilineal societies, women's reproductive bodies are routes of entry into social groups. Thus, when New Mexico's nobility expressed concern over the deterioration of their socio-racial status and privileges, they did so in the language of pollution, as a concern for the integrity of their bloodlines and for the protection of their women. The aristocratic privileges that Spanish conquistadores had bequeathed to their children in the early 1600s had come to be seen by the 1700s as an innate quality of their blood. Since maternity is undeniable while paternity was not, the Spanish nobility tried to protect their social status by guarding the sexual purity of their females and by frowning on marriage and sexual mixing with Indians and members of the lower races. To ensure that the latter did not occur, from 1760 clear into the 1820s, New Mexico's nobility begged the church to allow them to marry close relatives, marriages that the church defined as incestuous, arguing that if they were not allowed to do so, they would have to marry racial inferiors, metaphysically taint their pure aristocratic blood, and slowly lead to the destruction of the integrity of the state and of its hierarchical order.[26] The church agreed.

The concerns New Mexico's *españoles* voiced over race mixture and the necessity of closing ranks to protect their corporate identity in a period of rapid social change had a paradoxical aspect to them. They were the active agents of what was transpiring. Both they and the clergy complained about the sexual comportment of acculturated Indian women and mestizas, yet they openly cavorted with them in scandalous ways, claiming that the devil, Indian witches, and the charms of sorcerers made them do it. They claimed that Indian and mestiza women, not Spanish men, lived in concubinage, practiced polygamy, fornicated with abandon, and celebrated rituals of debauchery and sexual perversion. These accusations reveal a deep distrust and fear of these women, perceived as wells of lust, passion, and heathen friskiness.

Lest my point here be misunderstood, let me state emphatically that what we know about Indian women, particularly those accused of witchcraft, comes to us through the eyes of Spanish colonial priests and secular officials. These are often perverse stereotypes. They are racist caricatures, which tell us more about Spanish fears and anxieties than they tell us about Indians. The thoughts, attitudes, and behaviors of Pueblo, Apache and Comanche women, of course, would be very different. But as largely illiterate and dominated groups, they left few, if any, records that preserve the integrity and complexity of their thoughts.

The sex role inversions recorded in witchcraft accusations against Indian and mestiza women accused of practicing love magic were born of demographic fears, sparked by a growing number of Indian and mixed-blood women in Spanish towns, and exacerbated by the growth of a mestizo population through Spanish-Indian marriages and cohabitation, as well as by the diffusion of Indian values and ideas about sexuality into Hispano society.

In all of these witchcraft investigations, the "natural" model of domination provided by the male subordination of females became a metaphor for the conflict over socio-political power and the racial ordering of this hierarchical society. Sexual inversion and women with control over men

were extremely dangerous, warned the seventeenth-century Spanish
theologian Tomás Sánchez:

> *[M]ulier supra virum,* or the woman on top of the man in sexual
> intercourse is contrary to the order of nature. It is natural for man
> to act and for woman to be passive; and if the man is beneath, he
> becomes submissive by the very fact of his position, and the woman
> being above is active; and who cannot see how much nature herself
> abhors this mutation? Because in scholastic history it is said that
> the cause of the flood was that women, carried away by madness,
> used men improperly, the latter being beneath and the former
> above. . . . Women did change the natural use into that which is
> against nature.[27]

The Indian witches of eighteenth-century New Mexico were accused
of turning the world topsy-turvy, of controlling male genitalia, of transforming *machos* into passive effeminates, and—through their reproductive capacities—of threatening the very exploitative racial order on
which colonial society stood. In many ways these accusations were but
the last gasp of a racial order. Extensive biological mixing in New Mexico
among Spaniards, Pueblo Indians, and genízaros by 1800 had created a
truly mestizo society, one in which the population had profoundly mixed
and melded. These groups were working beside one another on the same
land, cultivating the same crops and livestock by the same techniques,
nominally worshiping the same god, and daily sharing food, affection,
and love.

Let me conclude by making explicit the implicit in this chapter. I
have focused only on the witchcraft accusations against the Indian and
genízara women of eighteenth-century New Mexico. The church considered these Indians *gente sin razón,* or mere children lacking reason and
therefore unable to understand the error of their ways. When found guilty
of such crimes, they were usually scolded, given mild penances, and urged
to curb their ways. Spanish men and women were deemed *gente de razón,*
who knew better than to seek charms, have hexes cast, and enter into
pacts with the devil to win love. When they were found guilty, the full
force of the law fell on their backs.

NOTES

1. *Inquisición* 1734, legajo 858, expediente 1, folio 508, Archivo General de la Nación (Mexico City), hereafter cited as AGN.

2. Kamen, *Spanish Inquisition*; Fintz Altabé, *Spanish and Portuguese Jewry*; Greenleaf, *Mexican Inquisition*. The 1528 executions are noted in Greenleaf, 26.

3. *Inquisición* 1745, legajo 892, expediente 1, folio 258, AGN.

4. *Inquisición* 1745, legajo 849, expediente 1, folio 601, AGN.

5. *Inquisición* 1719, legajo 553, expediente 47, folios 242–45, AGN.

6. Scholes, "First Decade," 222.

7. *Inquisición* 1731, legajo 892, expediente 1, folio 256, AGN.

8. *Inquisición* 1745, legajo 913, expediente 8, folios 150–54, AGN.

9. *Inquisición* 1731, legajo 892, expediente 1, folio 256, AGN.

10. Ibid., folios 250–70.

11. *Inquisición* 1743, legajo 914, expediente 13, folio 35, AGN.

12. *Inquisición* 1748, legajo 901, expediente 1, folio 235, AGN.

13. *Inquisición* 1731, legajo 892, expediente 1, folios 250–70, AGN.

14. A complete transcript of this case can be found in Twitchell, *Spanish Archives*, 2:142–63. Letter quoted on 142–43.

15. Ibid., 144.

16. Ibid., 157.

17. *Inquisición* 1631, legajo 372, expediente 16, folios 1–5, AGN.

18. *Inquisición* 1632, legajo 372, expediente 16, folios 19–20, AGN.

19. Declaration of María de la Vega Martínez, *Inquisición* 1632, legajo 372, expediente 1, folio 14, AGN; Declaration of María de Albisu, *Inquisición* 1661, legajo 593, expediente 1, folio 95, AGN. See also Parsons, "Witchcraft," 204–10.

20. Hammond and Rey, *Rediscovery of New Mexico*, 100–101; Hammond and Rey, *Don Juan de Oñate*, 637.

21. Scholes, "First Decade," 195–241.

22. Taken from the census enumerations listed in the following: *Spanish Archives of New Mexico*, 1790, reel 12, frame 428; 1794, reel 13, frame 560; 1820, reel 20, frames 498–99, New Mexico State Records Center and Archives, Santa Fe.

23. Guttentag and Secord, *Too Many Women?*, 20–21.

24. Gutiérrez, *When Jesus Came*, especially pages 271–336.

25. Douglas, *Purity and Danger*.

26. Gutiérrez, *When Jesus Came*.

27. Sánchez, *De sancto matrimonii sacramento*, 37–38.

BIBLIOGRAPHY

Douglas, Mary. *Purity and Danger: An Analysis of Concepts of Pollution and Taboo*. London: Penguin, 1970.

Fintz Altabé, David. *Spanish and Portuguese Jewry: Before and After 1492*. Brooklyn, NY: Sepher-Hermon Press, 1993.

Greenleaf, Richard E. *The Mexican Inquisition of the Sixteenth Century*. Albuquerque: University of New Mexico Press, 1969.

Gutiérrez, Ramón A. *When Jesus Came, the Corn Mothers Went Away: Marriage, Sexuality, and Power in New Mexico, 1500–1846*. Stanford, CA: Stanford University Press, 1991.

Guttentag, Marcia, and Paul Secord. *Too Many Women? The Sex Ratio Question*. Beverly Hills, CA: Sage, 1983.

Hammond, George P., and Agapito Rey, eds. and trans. *Don Juan de Oñate: Colonizer of New Mexico, 1595–1628*. Albuquerque: University of New Mexico Press, 1953.

———. *The Rediscovery of New Mexico, 1580–1594: The Explorations of Chamuscado, Espejo, Castaño de Sosa, Morlete, and Leyna de Bonilla and Humaña*. Albuquerque: University of New Mexico Press, 1966.

Kamen, Henry. *The Spanish Inquisition*. New York: New American Library, 1965.

Parsons, Elsie Clew. "Witchcraft Among the Pueblos: Indian or Spanish?" In *Witchcraft and Sorcery*, edited by Max Marwick, 204–10. New York: Penguin, 1990.

Sánchez, Tomás. *De sancto matrimonii sacramento*. Antwerp: n.p., 1607.

Scholes, Frances V. "The First Decade of the Inquisition in New Mexico." *New Mexico Historical Review* 10 (1935): 222.

Simmons, Marc. *Witchcraft in the Southwest: Spanish and Indian Supernaturalism on the Rio Grande*. Flagstaff, AZ: Northland Press, 1974.

Twitchell, Ralph Emerson. *The Spanish Archives of New Mexico*. 2 vols. Cedar Rapids, IA: Torch Press, 1914.

2

Disenchanting the
"Land of Enchantment"?

SENSE OF PLACE IN MARY AUSTIN
AND RUDOLFO ANAYA

Heiner Bus

In "Introduction: Beyond the Land of Enchantment," which opens the collection of scholarly essays titled *Nuevomexicano Cultural Legacy: Forms, Agencies, and Discourse*, Francisco A. Lomelí, Victor A. Sorell, and Genaro M. Padilla define the subject of the volume in contrast to outsider views of New Mexico:

> [I]ts spiritual qualities have been simplified and commodified by outsiders who have mythified its "enchanting" qualities, at the same time ignoring its paradoxes and contradictions. . . . The essays in this book make visible the presence of these stories, stories that reference New Mexico's mixed origins and testify to its capacity to accommodate outside influences without losing its native character.

These investigations into the past and present of New Mexico led them, in part, to "the region's distinct matrix for storytelling: its geography, best emblematized through its *llanos*, and its demographic *mestizaje* (mixture)."[1]

The mythification of the "Land of Enchantment" and of the entire Southwest, or the ignorance of its paradoxes and contradictions, is certainly closely connected with the mood of some sections of American society at the end of the nineteenth century, disenchanted by the pitfalls of modernism and the machine age, longing for a regeneration through physical and intellectual activity, thus establishing the nostalgic image of a preindustrial superior American identity. The Southwest replaced the frontiers of the westward movement as the scenery of Anglo-American invigoration, offering a last refuge from the irritations of the modern age, especially for "a whole class of financiers, philanthropists, journalists, writers and artists."[2] The new playground of the nation as defined by these newcomers competed with an ideology calling the Southwest "the American Congo," because as John G. Bourke set down in a magazine article in 1894, "[T]hrough the centre of this unknown region . . . courses the Rio Grande, which can be more correctly compared to the Congo than to the Nile the moment that the degraded, turbulent, ignorant, and superstitious character of its population comes under examination."[3] It was Charles F. Lummis (1859–1928), the most enthusiastic popularizer and mastermind of the new image, who for Robert E. Fleming was "a wonderfully perceptive and skillful recorder of the Southwestern scene, a freethinker who evaluated stereotypes of the Indians and Mexican Americans and replaced them with true-to-life portraits, a crusader who forced his readers to re-examine their beliefs about these minorities, their country, and themselves."[4]

In "Charles Fletcher Lummis and the Orientalization of New Mexico" (2002), Ramón A. Gutiérrez vehemently contradicts this utterly positive assessment: "If New Mexico could be conceived as an oriental place, as an Egypt locked in a time warp in the past, New Mexicans could be romantically depicted as specimens of degenerate races destined to col-lection in museums and extinction on the earth."[5] The question is whether Lummis's influence was so prevalent that he could substantially shape the publications of a fairly diverse group of journalists and writers engaged in promoting the image of the Southwest at the end of the nineteenth cen-tury and in the first three decades of the twentieth.[6] Out of this group, the critic Fleming classified Mary Hunter Austin (1868–1934) as one of Lum-mis's dependents.[7] My analysis of two of her books set in the Southwest, published in 1906 and 1924, explores the sense of place evoked by the choice of perspective and narrator; by the interaction between the past, present, and future; the characterization of the Southwest as a unique place in transition; and the interrelation between man and the landscape.

I then examine the same elements in two novels, of 1972 and 1995, by the insider Rudolfo Anaya. In my conclusion I compare the works of these writers, separated by roughly half a century, and single out major convergences and divergences.

Mary Austin began her career as a writer in California's Owens Valley about eight years after she had moved there. After publishing poems and stories in children's magazines and in the *Overland Monthly*, she succeeded in gaining access to the prestigious *Atlantic Monthly* with "A Shepherd of the Sierras" (1900) and "The Last Antelope" (1903). With her first book-length study, *The Land of Little Rain*, she entered the hall of fame for nature writers in 1903.[8] In her next books, she populated her new conquered territory with people typical of this place, those who lived close to nature, namely the Indians and the sheepherders. They became the protagonists of *The Basket Woman* (1904), *Isidro* (1905), and *The Flock* (1906). In *Mary Austin and the American West*, Susan Goodman and Carl Dawson characterize her books as contributions "to a growing literature of California that drew attention to the 'exotic' (meaning Indians, Mexicans, and early Spanish colonists), yet there had never been anything quite like it."[9]

The first chapter of *The Flock* establishes a frame for the story by relating the history of sheepherding in Alta California, in a landscape that has preserved its basic features for more than two centuries. Thus Austin creates continuity between the Spanish beginnings and her own life "in the clutch of great Tedium" (13), relieved by the coming of the flock, the subject of the following chapters.[10] Whenever she deals with the Spanish pioneers, she stresses the extraordinary challenges posed by the environment only to be met by heroic human efforts.

A first-person narrator enters the stage at the conclusion of the historical section: "What I have to do here is to set down without prejudice, but not without sympathy, as much as I have been able to understand of the whole matter" (11). She continues on this note in her direct address, in a sort of self-introduction—"I suppose of all the people who are concerned with the making of a true book, the one who puts it to the pen has the least to do with it" (11)—and calls the collective of the local people the true authors.[11] Consequently, the narrator plays a subordinate part, though she immediately afterward characterizes herself as an expert on the annual rhythms of nature, including the movements of the wandering shepherds and their stories.[12] Thus she can close her "Preface which is not on any account to be omitted" with a programmatic statement on the meaning of her theme for herself, for the "Friendly Folk in Inyo," and her potential readers: "In this land of such indolent lapping of the nights and days that neither the clock nor the calendar has any pertinence to time, I call on the eye of my mind, as it were, for relief, looking out across the moon-colored sands" (13).[13] So readers are asked to commit to a narrator with great expertise gained through the experience that structured her personal life. She presents herself as a humble recorder when she authenticates her story through the collective memory of Inyo's storytellers.

From their reminiscences, this narrator reconstructs the history of sheepherding in Inyo County with a focus on the second half of the nineteenth century. What she adds to this record are the "epic" descriptions of the landscape changing with the seasons. There she remains a somewhat withdrawn figure, though the still ongoing repetition of these cycles provides her with an authority she cannot claim for herself in the story, on the movements of the flocks, which at the time of writing her book had become a matter of the recent past.

The ten subsequent chapters are devoted to the long trail of the flocks and their hired herders, as they move at the end of spring on the still-open range, from their southerly winter quarters to the northerly summer pastures in the Sierras. Now and then readers are reminded of the presence of the narrator through rhetorical interjections and direct addresses, creating a sort of dialogue with them, inviting readers to participate in an argument without substantially and permanently reducing the distance to her material.[14] Only very seldom does she let herself get carried away to emotional statements, such as when she confesses her irritation about the loss of romance by the introduction of technical improvements in the sheep business.[15] In general, her few personal statements remain in the indeterminate, never endangering the status of the objective observer and recorder. This changes when she retells the history of Ranchos Tejón in chapter 12, and when she preaches her gospel of the wilderness and its effects on man in chapter 13.[16]

Parts of that gospel are foreshadowed in the chapters on the long trail, though it moves through a fairly docile wilderness. But even such an unspectacular landscape produces heroes: the sheepherders lead a heroic life in the "Great Outdoors" by their "devotion . . . to the necessities of the flock" (98) and the mastering of precarious situations.[17] They are nomadic individuals exposed to "full . . . elemental experiences" (61), persons with a fine sense of beauty and the goodness of the earth, people "who come from sojourning in that country as if the sheer nakedness of the land had somehow driven the soul back on its elemental impulses. You can imagine that one type of man exposed to it would become a mystic and another incredibly brutalized" (97).[18] Obviously, the good shepherds (101) of *The Flock* have made their choices. And they are further ennobled when the flock approaches the wall of the Sierras: "[T]he Indians named them '*Too-rápe*,' the Ball players. They line up as braves for the ancient play, immortally young, shining nakedly above, girt with pines, their strong cliffs leaning to the noble poises of the game. It is evident . . . that God and a poor shepherd may admire the same things" (80). Here, readers are persuaded to include the narrator in this exclusive club. Likewise they are invited to share her delight and gladness while watching the sheepherders at leisure and pursuing their profession in a landscape appealing to the senses of beauty and harmony (106, 130–31).

As mentioned, the narrator does not ignore the fact that the sheepherder's wholesome way of life was becoming a matter of the past.[19] Quite early in the book, the agents of change and doom are identified: "cowboys, homesteaders, provincials with little imagination and no social experiences" (64). Even more destructive are the conservation and national parks movement, the establishment of national reserves, the reorganization of water and land management, the introduction of taxes and licenses, all of them causing "bitterness and violence" (169), though on the other hand, the narrator admits that the sheep also cause considerable damage to the land and could become a plague.[20]

As the disappearance of the sheep industry seems inevitable, readers are confronted with the price to be paid in chapter 12, which returns to the splendors of life on the open range, focusing on Ranchos Tejón in Inyo County, a place especially dear to the narrator roughly between 1850 and

1875. Consequently, she includes more references authenticating and personalizing her story. "Ranchos Tejón" opens with a precise statement of purpose: "[T]he most likeable features of the old California sheep ranches are departing. That is why I am at the pains of setting down here a little of what went on at the Ranchos Tejón before the clang of machinery overlays its leisurely picturesqueness" (215).[21]

The story becomes a eulogy on "the best of mission times" (231), the owners of the ranch, and the benevolent treatment of their multiethnic employees. This patriarchal idyll could develop because "the original owner" of the place in the 1850s "must have had extraordinarily the faculty of dealing with primitive people" (219).[22] That owner, whom the narrator had actually met, was Edward Beale, superintendent of Indian affairs.[23] Beale, who had bought the farm and "was the first to discover, or to give evidence of it, that it is wiser for Indians to become the best sort of Indians rather than poor imitation whites" (219), was the perfect descendant of the local founding fathers.[24] Austin characterizes one of the Indian workers on the ranch as someone "who saveys the tempers and dispositions of men, who knows the Tejón better than its own master, the man whose hand should have been at the writing of this book" (224).

Direct references to the previous eleven chapters are quite seldom. Again and again, nostalgia becomes the determining mood, as in "It was against this backdrop of wild beauty, mixed romance, and unaffected savagery" (234), or when she mentions her camel bell: "Hanging above my desk, swinging, it sets in motion all the echoes of Romance" (227). The "high, clean color of romance" (239) enters the tales about the long drive. It all comes together in the final paragraph of this chapter, where she more or less identifies herself with scenes typical of the shepherd's life:

> If you ask me at a distance from its mirage-haunted borders, I
> should be obliged to depreciate . . . but once inside the territory
> of the badger, I basely desert from this high position, frankly glad
> of so wide a reach of hills where mists of grey tradition deepen to
> romance, where no axe is laid wantonly to the root of any tree, and
> no wild thing gives up its life except in penalty for depredation.
> Most glad I am of the blue lakes of uncropped lupines, of the wild
> tangle of the odorous vines, of the unshorn water-shed; glad of

certain clear spaces where, when the moon is full and a light wind ruffles all the leaves, soft-stepping deer troop through the thickets of the trees. (249–50)

In the final chapter, "The Shade of the Arrows," the narrator is preoccupied with her gospel of the interdependence between human life and the wilderness: "There is no predicating what the life of the wild does to a man until you know what arrows he interposes between himself and his influences" (255).[25] After this fairly general introduction, she returns to the particular business and region, focusing on the shepherd as the representative of a productive and wholesome life in nature. Without being able to talk about it, the shepherd's "unhoused nights" (262) generate his sense for the beauty of the land "beyond the question of its service . . . because he exhibits its natural reactions" (258), which include the acceptance of disaster; of "the natural and ineradicable difference of kind" (266); of human isolation, which she defines as "a social divorcement without sensible dislocation" (261); and an appreciation of the large processes "going on independently of the convenience and the powers of man" (264). To arrive at and maintain this state of mind, one definitely needs what she calls the "arrows" protecting from the "assault it [the wild] makes on the spirit" (266). And she concludes with a personal statement: "Knowing all that the land does to humans, one could go fearsomely except that the chiefest of its operations is to rob one finally of all fear—and besides, I have always had arrows enough" (266).

Mary Austin's *The Flock* introduces a narrator deeply impressed by the seasons and moods of a specific landscape. From the immediate past, she takes her representative man, the shepherd whose job asks him to live in harmony with nature. The nostalgic perspective on this profession, pursued in an ideal human and natural environment, clearly signals that all this has come to an end. Yet some of the landscape features invite the readers to explore their responses to what is still wild. This foreshadows a basic theme of her 1924 book, *The Land of Journeys' Ending*, in which she moves into the heart of the Southwest, a move she justifies in her autobiography, *Earth Horizon* (1932), as follows: "What I felt in New Mexico was the possibility of the reinstatement of the hand-craft culture and of the folk drama," and "I liked the feel of roots, of ordered growth and progression, continuity, all of which I found in the Southwest."[26]

The Land of Journeys' Ending (1924) opens on a note of caution—"This being a book of prophecy, a certain appreciation of the ritualistic approach is assumed for the reader" (vii)—which is extended into an appeal to Austin's colleagues: "Anybody can write about a country, but nobody can write truth who does not take into account the sounds and swings of its native nomenclature" (viii).[27] Her subject calls for an appreciation of American Indian and Spanish names, "since there are aspects of every country impossible satisfactorily to describe except in rhythms that have a derivative relation to the impression the land makes on its inhabitants" (viii). Thus, she foreshadows some of her themes and her procedure, namely "prophesying the progressive acculturation of the land's people" (viii). Of course, this is also "a book of topography" (viii) and guidebook for the reader or reluctant tourist, because "if you read my book conscientiously, you will have nothing to fear" (ix). Her final remark in the preface concerns the perspective of her "attempt to describe the country by the effect it produces on the author" (ix).

Unlike in *The Flock*, the table of contents does not indicate a systematic thematic or chronological order, though her first chapter, "Journey's Beginning," gives another historical introduction to "all country east of the Grand Cañon, west and north of the Jornada del Muerto. . . . Go far enough on any of its trails, and you begin to see how the world was made" (3). She advises the traveler to read the history of the place "from the faces of the men who first made it habitable . . . seeing ever so short a way into the method of the land's making, men became reconciled to its nature" (4). About "the Amerindian savage and the unlettered American pioneer," she says that they "married the land because they loved it, and afterward made it bear" (5), whereas others solely exploited it.

From the beginning, the first-person narrator reveals herself as Mary Austin, who takes readers with her on her excursions into the geography, history, and cultures of New Mexico and, as in the final chapter of *The Flock*, confronts them with a prophecy.[28] This prophecy comes as no surprise because the fifteen essays contain many hints at what she has called a "land ethic" derived from the intensive interaction between man and the land, which is defined as

all those things common to a given region, such as have been
lightly or deeply touched upon in this book; the flow of prevailing
winds, the succession of vegetal cover, the legend of ancient life;
and the scene, above everything the magnificently shaped and
colored scene. . . . [T]hese are the things most quickly and surely
passed from generation to generation. (438)[29]

For the American Southwest, this means an awareness of "an aboriginal
top-soil culture, rich in the florescence of assimilation, to which was added
the overflow from the golden century of Spain, melting and mixing with
the native strain to the point of producing a distinctive if not final pattern
before it received its second contribution from the American East" (439).
Thus, she excludes some of the more recent American "gifts." In the next
paragraph, however, she declares: "It is, in fact, hardly three quarters of
a century since the flag of American federation was raised in the plaza
of Santa Fé. And already the land bites sharply into the deep self of the
people who live upon it" (440), though they still need a period of "realiza-
tion and general adoption of native symbols for experiences intimate and
peculiar to the land. The profoundest implications of human experience
are never stated rationally, never with explicitness, but indirectly in what
we agree to call art forms, rhythms, festivals, designs, melodies, objective
symbolic substitutions" (440). She is so convinced of the success of this
process that she even "predicts the rise there, within appreciable time,
of the *next* great and fructifying world culture" (442) on the basis of her
idealistic evaluation of the cultures and her firm belief in the forces of
natural selection:

Three strains of comparative purity lie here in absorbing contact,
the Indian, the Spanish, and the so-called Nordic-American,
for by distance, by terror of vastness and raw surfaces, the more
timorous, least adaptive elements of our population are strained
out. Of these three the Spanish serves chiefly to mollify tempera-
mentally the aboriginal strain, so that in New Mexico and Arizona
we approach nearest, in the New World . . . the energetic blond
engrafture on a dark, earth-nurtured race, in a land whose beauty
takes the breath like pain. (442–43)[30]

The deadline Austin sets for the fulfilment of her prophecy is "within the time of your children's children" (443). Though she claims that the aboriginal and Spanish cultures are still visible in architecture, vital customs, and significant landmarks, they are only echoes of their former golden ages. She confirms her optimism with a very personal statement:

> Even so, I suspect, the quality that the conquistadores wrote into the land, as they passed by here, will outlast the brisk conventionalized patterns stamped over it since 1848. If I did not believe this, I should not so wish that I could make my home here. . . . I can think of no place more suited to my purpose. But if not to live, then, perhaps, equally to my purpose to be buried here. (230–31)

At this point, it is quite significant that she ignores the influx of Mexican labor since 1900 as a revitalizing element comparable to the heroic multiethnic sheepherders and the laborers of *The Flock*. But for her, these people cannot claim a journey's ending in the Southwest.

Austin's prophetic authority is based on her studies of the lore of the land, her understanding of its cultures, and her intimate geographical knowledge, acquired on her excursions with archaeologist Adolphe F. Bandelier, botanist Daniel T. McDougal, and painter Gerald Cassidy. She claims that she is actually writing her book "on the lower slopes of Sangre de Cristo" (72) and introduces herself as an expert in American Indian rhythms and being drawn to Native life, which "is the absence of those strains and resistances that stiffen us against the wind forever blowing from some quarter of the universe across our souls" (73).[31] Visiting the cliff dwellings, she feels "the enchantment of mystery" (81), which combines with her strong powers of imagination and her expertise in various fields to enable her to conjure up scenes of daily life in "The Days of Our Ancients" or "The Cities That Died," especially that of the Pueblos, "the only existing human society that ever found, and kept for an appreciable period, the secret of spiritual organisation" (238).[32] "By a swift reach of spirit" she is capable of "making [herself] one with them [the Penitentes]" (358).[33] Her respect and "the deeply rooted ill breeding of the American public . . . constrains me . . . to set down here far less than I know of what goes on in the moradas and in the hearts of the Penitentes" (353–54).

Her occasional restraint blatantly contrasts with Austin's poignant criticism of the newly arrived Americans who "despised the Spanish-speaking even more than they did the Indian" (197), "the souvenir-hunting propensities of the American tourist" (159; see also 352–53), the architecture and educational programs of the Indian Bureau (91, 197), international boundaries (198), and modern times in general: "Over all the inestimable treasure of their culture lie our ignorance and self-conceit as a gray dust. Yet still, in that dust, blossom and smell sweet, concepts for the lack of which our age goes staggering into chaos" (244–45).[34] Such an enthusiastic, occasionally sentimental (but in many passages thoughtful) mediator and propagator of the continuity of significant life and cultures in a spectacular landscape in the past, present, and future invites readers and prospective tourists with equal gifts of perception and willingness to distance themselves from the negative trends of the present in order to share her love of "the land's undying quality" (231) and her optimism about its future.[35] For Austin the Southwest, "still a place in which the miraculous may happen" (337), figures as an open-air museum, with the promise of the reinstitution of a peaceful society of mutual respect and learning from one another, a model in which the binary opposition of constant change and continuity has been suspended.

Discussing some of the migration routes of the "Hohokum" (Hohokam), Austin reaches "the fabled valley of Aztlán" (101) and quotes historical records as evidence that some of the Indian tribes "came out of seven caves, and 'these caves are in a country which we all know to be toward the north.' . . . There are two provinces in this country, one called Aztlán . . . from which the last of the Nahuatl tribes set out" (102). Later in her book, she prophesies the reemergence of hitherto submerged cultures: "I expect to see it rise here, on this ground, within a generation or two in forms of music and dramatic and pictorial art of a quality which takes its savour from the land" (340). Accepting her observation that "there is much that is better told in fiction" and "may just as well be told in any way that makes a good story" (195), and linking this with her prophecy, we could easily interpret the rise and flourishing of Chicano literature in the Southwest as a partial fulfillment of her predictions. All the more as, for instance, some of the concepts of Chicano authors about the interaction between man and landscape correspond with hers.

Introducing the anthology *Writing the Southwest,* Rudolfo Anaya defines the spirit of a place as "a set of historical, cultural, and language traditions," including the myths of the place because "those primal images are our connection to human history, hieroglyphs of the spirit which help us transcend our daily life and feel connected to a purpose in the universe."[36] They are retained as collective memory, not only in the stories of violence and evil, but also in those of order and harmony. Though Anaya is aware of the onslaught of "rugged individualism" on the communal spirit in the larger framework of the Westernization and its "obsession with development," he believes in the healing powers of "the stories of origin, the gods, the proper ceremonies and rituals, the relationship of the people to the spirit world." Thus, the writer in the Southwest is obliged to listen to the "voices of the ancestors, the hum of the earth itself," which become "a catching of dreams, the catching of stories" that will "transport the reader into the very core of the mythic and poetic world of the story."[37] This belief becomes even more evident when he sets the Southwest into the larger context of the confrontation and reconciliation of different cultures. In a conversation with David Johnson and David Apodaca, Anaya defined the Southwest, or rather Aztlán, the Chicano homeland, as the meeting place of an East-West axis that is "fundamentally a Freudian axis, and a way of explaining everything that we do as human beings through sexual impulse as opposed to a North-South axis that is always looking for a reconciliation. . . . It sees a polarity but it also sees a unity which the East-West axis doesn't provide." In consequence, "all of Chicano culture, or a great deal of it, is talking about the reconciliation of self within the community, within the communal self, which is exactly what Jung says."[38]

The design of *Bless Me, Ultima* (1972) as a first-person narrative makes all constituents of the novel's sense of place part and parcel of Antonio's memories, recalling his formative years with the curandera Ultima at the conclusion of his childhood and adolescence, which coincides with the death of Ultima. Choice of perspective and chronology make the reader witness his gradual liberation from the anxieties and dependencies of a child through observation, experience, and his growing powers of critical assessment. Consequently, the memories of Anaya's protagonist possess an existential quality. Even the location of the Márez home in the small

New Mexican town of Guadalupe, across the river on "the rocky wild hill" at "the beginning of the llano, [where] from here it stretched away as far as the eye could see" (26), is deeply meaningful as a compromise between his father's and his mother's places of origin and their respective modes of subsistence competing for influence on Antonio's destiny.[39] From several overheard arguments between his parents, he learns about the Márez "men of the sun" (29), "freethinkers" (31), claiming the heritage of "an exuberant, restless people, wandering across the ocean of the plain" (6), enjoying the freedoms of vaquero culture, as opposed to his mother's descent from the Lunas "men of the moon" (29), devout Catholics, farmers "tied to the earth" (6) of the river valley. Unlike Austin, Anaya presents New Mexican Spanish culture not as uniform but as diversified according to the varieties of land use. Though Antonio forever cherishes close family ties, those distinctions soon impede unrestrained loyalties. These remain reserved for the guide through his individuation, Ultima, who once admonishes him in one of his dreams: "You have been seeing only parts . . . and not looking beyond into the great cycle that binds us all" (126), thus reconciling the llano with the river valley culture. Much earlier, when Ultima came into the Márez household, Antonio's sensual perceptions had already indicated such syncretism:

> I saw for the first time the wild beauty of our hills and the magic of the green river. . . . I felt the song of the mockingbirds, and the drone of the grasshoppers mingle with the pulse of the earth. The four directions of the llano met in me, white sun shone on my soul. The granules of sand at my feet and the sun and the sky above me seemed to dissolve into one strange, complete being. (12–13)[40]

Antonio's dreams repeat significant events, either intensifying anxieties or offering strategies for conquering them. In *The Land of Journeys' Ending*, Mary Austin also hints at the importance of dreams in Indian cultures because "a deeper level of experience is uncovered," but elsewhere her dreams are triggered by a momentary feeling of harmony with nature and turn into the sort of drowsiness Washington Irving's narrator falls into when entering Sleepy Hollow.[41] Her dreams resemble those of Antonio's father, composed of many nostalgic backward glances into the life of the vaqueros (57–58, 131) and romantic notions of a better future in California. When he eventually submits to reality, he is also able to agree with his son's own rational choices for his destiny (261). Antonio's search for identity is structured by dreams and nightmares as well as by Ultima's seasonal excursions to the llano to collect healing herbs and roots, the cycles of planting and harvesting of the Luna family at Puerto de los Luna, and the schedules of church and school.[42]

Antonio remembers listening to cuentos and legends quite frequently (14, 52, 128, 130–31, 145). As a child he more or less automatically accepted their wisdom, but his accumulating store of new insights provokes questions and asks for adaptations to his developing individual system of values, without totally negating the blessings of the collective experience.[43] The myth of the golden carp, for instance, strengthens his belief in an understanding and forgiving Virgen de Guadalupe and merely supplants that of a punishing God, a belief forced on him by the priest.[44] This "pagan god" (119), which "the grown-ups can't see" (120), presumably "a god of beauty, a god of here and now ... made the world peaceful" (252): "Seeing him made questions and worries evaporate, and I remained transfixed, caught and caressed by the essential elements of sky and earth and water. The sun warmed us with its life-giving power, and up in the sky a white moon smiled on us" (252). In collaboration with Ultima's teachings and Antonio's actual encounters with reality, the myth of the golden carp even suspends binary oppositions, such as Márez versus Luna heritage, thus liberating and empowering Antonio.[45] Now he can strive to become "a true man of learning" (188) "because in the end understanding simply means having a sympathy for people" (263), as his father finally argues.

Anaya's choice of theme and perspective provides the reader with a fictional model of culture in action that celebrates not a nostalgic backward glance but the freedom of choice to combine the best from the past and the present. Constant initiations into new realities and their interpretation by Ultima and Antonio's parents, as well as the vital stories, legends, and myths, supply him with tools to face the future courageously, independently, and optimistically. His father in the end confirms Ultima's gospel of the reconciliation of alleged opposites when he postulates: "A wise man listens to the voices of the earth, Antonio" (202). His own conversion was caused by recent radical changes in land use—for example, "The rich rancheros sucked the earth dry with their deep wells, and so the heavy snows had to come to replenish the water . . . so now the wind picks up the barren soil and throws it in their faces" (201–202)—and the aftermath of the war and probably of nuclear testing in New Mexico (200–201). Antonio accepts these explanations because for him, they appear to be more rational than the priest's, especially when Ultima and his father cooperate and offer him a complete vision of past, present, and future:

> "There is power here, a power that can fill a man with satisfaction," my father said.
>
> "And there is faith here," Ultima added, "a faith in the reason for nature being, evolving, growing—" And there is also the dark, mystical past, I thought, the past of the people who lived here and left their traces in the magic that crops out today. (242)

Part of this system of values is recognizing change, as Ultima tells Antonio: "You are growing, and growth is change. Accept the change, make it a part of your strength" (259). When he leaves for a summer with the Lunas in El Puerto, his father observes:

> "Ay, every generation, every man is a part of his past. He cannot escape it, but he may reform the old materials, make something new—"
>
> "Take the llano and the river valley, the moon and the sea, God and the golden carp—and make something new," I said to myself. That is what Ultima meant by building strength from life. (261)

These insights leave room for decisions based on individual experience, the collective wisdom of the older generations, and trust in the "magical strength that resides in the human heart" (263).

In *Zia Summer* (1995), the first of Anaya's four mystery novels, Sonny Baca solves a murder case and prevents the fatal conclusion of an antinuclear protest by a group of radical environmentalists.[46] The omniscient narrator focuses on the actions and reflections of his main protagonist; however, some of the more general statements, especially in the final evaluation of events, appear to be conclusions of both Sonny and the narrator.

The plot of the novel is carefully embedded in the seasonal moods of nature, as in the case of an unusually long dry spell of a New Mexico summer that ends with a life-giving rain during the final showdown.[47] In chapter 1 Sonny awakens to the sound of a chain saw, which is supposed to cut down the seemingly dead cottonwood in his neighbor's front yard. The cottonwood "had been witness to the last hundred years of history in the village of Los Ranchitos in the North Valley of Albuquerque. Its spreading branches had shaded don Eliseo's family for many generations" (4).[48] The tree will miraculously survive this assault and sprout new leaves after the defeat of evil: "Tonight the earth will not be burned by the deadly heat of radiation . . . the slaked earth of summer would green again" (357).

Within this larger framework of the imperilment and renewal of life, readers are introduced to Sonny Baca as a person very much aware of his family history, as his "great-grandfather, El Bisabuelo, was Elfego Baca, the most famous lawman New Mexico ever produced" (3).[49] Sonny quite willingly acknowledges this heritage together with the regional wisdom handed on to him by his advisers in the fight against evil: his old neighbor, don Eliseo; his girlfriend, Rita; and the curandera Lorenza, who will offer a traditional cleansing ceremony as closure.

Sonny is drawn into the case first through family ties and later by the extraordinary strategies of the criminals exploiting southwestern symbols and myths. So after a while, the perpetrators face a private investigator who understands their moves, chases them down, and thus saves the community and the land from further damage. Like Antonio in *Bless Me, Ultima*, Sonny finds guides empowering him with the magic and mystery of the place. So, before the action speeds up toward the final showdown, the reader finds an abundance of passages focusing on the lore of the land, which means the city of Albuquerque and the mountain areas nearby, a unique region where "a grand mestizo mixture took place. The Nile of the desert Southwest. All bloods ran as one in the coyotes of New Mexico" (6).

Like Antonio in the classic 1972 novel, Sonny is searching for an identity that will stabilize and harmonize his life. He has gone through a chaotic period and has found some sense of direction through the acceptance of his family heritage, which has to be revitalized in an environment that presents itself, on the surface, as a stage for imminent change that would violate traditional values. Sonny will discover that knowledge of these values will not only help him solve the case but also provide him with an identity with which to face the future confidently.

On his numerous trips through the cityscape and the rural environment, Sonny sees New Mexico as a unique place in its mixture of splendor and destruction, in nature and society, producing the sense of an ending as well as the hope for renewal.[50] Besides the perversion of the life-sustaining Zia symbol and the abuse of environmentalist idealism, Sonny observes violations of land rights and land use, the urban spread either making Hispanic farms and villages disappear completely or turning them into ghost towns (141–42).[51] Ambitious and pretentious developers and politicians endanger the delicate balance between land use and water availability by trying to create a "Camelot of the desert" (183), or a Disneyland in Albuquerque. In various neighborhoods, Sonny encounters homeless people (296), mounting violence statistics (181), and a growing "rift between the cultural groups" (182): "The city was an intricately patterned blanket, each color representing different heritages, traditions, languages, folkways, and each struggling to remain distinct, full of pride, history, honor, and family roots. They were clannish, protective, often prejudiced and bigoted.... At the center they were all struggling for identity" (211–12). From the group of newcomers, he singles out as main targets of his criticism "the gringo antro-poligies" (75), superficial "summer tourists" (213), and rich people in their newly built adobe homes looking for permanence where there is none, or those fulfilling their dreams in "the land of enchantment" (367) as collectors of art.[52] For Sonny "change was inevitable" (182), though it is always a mixed bag, as he learns from don Eliseo: "This place where we live is special. It is a sacred place. That's why our vecinos from the pueblos have lived here for so long. That's why people come here. But what attracts the angels attracts the diablo" (362). In one of his nightmares, Sonny reflects on his own alienation from the spirit of the place:

> His parents had given him a history, a sense of the traditions of the valley, the stories of the Bisabuelo and the heritage of the antepasados, the ancestors. . . . Getting a degree at the university meant entering a different world, and living in the vast change that swept over the land meant losing touch. Now he was returning. (378–79)

So what creates permanence in fast-changing Albuquerque? Tamara, one of the conspirators, once teases Sonny: "Oh, you are so innocent. So caught up in your cultural ways" (228). It is his old neighbor don Eliseo who formulates strategies of coping with the evils of the present without escaping into the nostalgic dream of restoring a simple past. Eliseo is a firm believer in the healing powers of Los Señores y las Señoras de la Luz daily conquering the darkness of the night at sunrise, "When the light enters our soul and gives us clarity" (203). And the old man shares the energies he receives with Sonny, giving him the strength to solve the case: "[T]here was clarity: His mind was clear, at rest, absorbing light, communing with something primal in the universe, connecting to the first moment of light in the darkness of the cosmos" (205). In the end, don Eliseo's constant support and Rita's love, her healing powers and skills as an interpreter of his dreams and nightmares, make him a transmitter of the wisdom of the elders, because "only those who believed in the soul could help put Humpty-Dumpty together again" (362).[53] Sonny certainly feels in harmony with the spirit of the place and is prepared to face the present and future in an ever-changing and renewing Southwest. It is quite significant that in this situation, the old cottonwood is revived, confirming Sonny's and don Eliseo's belief that "everything had a spirit. Tree, corn, stone, rain, clay. Everything was alive" (74).

At first glance, a comparison of Austin's with Anaya's evocations of a sense of place in the Southwest does not seem fair, because they were conceived and published in totally different sociopolitical and cultural contexts, more than fifty years apart; however, Austin's prophecies for the future of this region somewhat close the gap. Consciously or subconsciously, both writers had to consider the popular tastes of their times, for example, the notions of what attracts the interest and curiosity of their readers. Austin's chosen territory had been occupied by Helen Hunt Jackson's immensely popular novel *Ramona* (1884): "Recording the Hispanic-Mexican-Indian civilization before white settlement, *Ramona* played a major role in romanticizing southern California history."[54] Austin found a loophole for herself by documenting a segment of California's sheep business, thus saving it from oblivion, in a region she knew very well, and later by publishing a "promotional book" on New Mexico.

In her hybrid books, the constitution of a sense of place is a much more diffuse affair than in Anaya's novels because of the choice of perspective. While in Austin's books, the narrator's voice is nearly identical to the author's, Anaya's first-person perspective for *Bless Me, Ultima* and the omniscient-author perspective are nearly identical with that of his main protagonist in *Zia Summer*. Austin's sense of place is built up cumulatively, with its most obvious manifestations in the final chapters. In the preceding chapters, her explorations of the land and its people are presented by an ambitious and committed observer, with occasional backstage insight and comprehensive knowledge gained through wide reading, extensive field trips, and consultation with eyewitnesses and experts. From this detached and privileged, sometimes even egocentric, position, she is lecturing her readers. Registering the irritations and losses of the present in contrast to the glories of the past, she tends to escape into romantic and nostalgic moods, adding a moral touch to her stories, combined with an optimistic look into the future based on the values of the past cyclically bonding with seemingly new values, which are fundamentally indistinguishable from the old ones.

In Anaya's novels, the main protagonists are portrayed as insiders per se, because the establishment of a sense of place is the central means of securing an individual identity. Anaya's work is embedded in a permanent dialectic trial-and-error process with the spontaneous challenges of reality and the strategies provided by the various guides. As in Austin, access to the spirit of the place is granted through understanding and clarity, the recognition of cultural traditions combined with courageous acceptance of the changes and provocations of modern times. In a way this arrangement draws readers into the story by asking them to follow Antonio's or Sonny's gradual progress through contradictions and blind alleys toward understanding and eventual clarity. Thus, a potential escape into nostalgia and jeremiads about modern times is refused to both protagonists and readers. Consequently, a central element of the sense of place is the interaction between past, present, and the future. Both writers celebrate the continuity of the past in the present but also have doubts about the vigor and duration of this process when confronted with the strong counterforces of modernity. Whereas Anaya's protagonists are prepared to bravely face the present and the future, Austin trusts in the continuation of the cycles of collective reconciliation of old and new people and their cultures.

Austin once in a while blurs her positive and harmonious picture of the Southwest and its cultural and racial "heroic triad" with quite irritating interjections; for instance, when she refers to "swarthy people" and their "primitive mind" on Ranchos Tejón, or pronounces her admiration for the conquerors and the pioneers: "Here they brought the habits of freedom, their feuds, yes, and the seeds of the potentialities that make leaders of men."[55] Still, both authors plead for a syncretic southwestern culture, although despite Austin's proclamations for a mélange of equal elements and her radical rejection of the second and third generations of Anglo immigrants "possessing what we were still unpossessed by," Austin tends to think in terms of future Anglo dominance.[56] Anaya is more reluctant to make such general pronouncements; even his individual characters are drawn as empowered but only at the beginning of a stable life. Though his novels do not explicitly focus on the Native contribution to the spirit of the place, his main characters readily accept the wisdom of "our vecinos."[57] On the level of style, Spanish place names considerably support a sense of the uniqueness of the scenery. Austin specifically praises their precise denotation of landscape features and above all their sounds and rhythms.[58] In *Bless Me, Ultima*, the Spanish language serves as a marker for particular places and as a minor plot element.[59]

In *Mary Austin and the American West*, Susan Goodman and Carl Dawson comment on the public interest in Native cultures in Austin's times: "At the turn of the twentieth century, the American public's fascination with 'primitive' peoples, especially American Indians, had grown inversely to their annihilation."[60] Equally paradoxical was the acquisition of the Southwest as "a sane and secure place amid the world of change."[61] Peter Wild's view of the Southwest in that historical period comments on these contradictions: "[T]he land was fairly settled, with the establishment of railroads, ranches, mines, and the beginnings of today's sprawling desert cities. It was then that the fairly comfortable residents and visitors grew misty-eyed, romanticizing a desert wilderness, just past."[62] In *The Flock* Austin documented some of those changes. Nevertheless the place made her reflect about "some figment of the Original Impulse [that] begins to fumble through the teachable strong fingers toward creation."[63] And throughout *The Land of Journeys' Ending*, she expresses her longing for simplicity, authenticity, handcraft cultures, and a life reduced to bare essentials, similar to how Anne H. Zwinger summarizes part of Thoreau's ethic: "Survival puts a different edge on things."[64] Anaya's protagonists share such sentiments in *Bless Me, Ultima* in connection with the golden carp, perceived as "something simple and pure" (252), and with Sonny's reflections on the simplicity of the past, but they are soon exposed as dreams or minor components of a more comprehensive system of values.

Sonny's insight that "Landscape dictates character" (222) addresses one of the central elements of the sense of place in the works of Austin and Anaya: What does the land do to man and vice versa? On this theme, the two authors are in almost complete agreement. Basically, some of the features of the fragile and quite often fractious land prevail and give people an idea of the superhuman powers shaping the land, summoning them to adapt their lives to the land's dictates but also providing them with glimpses of beauty and magic. Still, man's invasions result in manifold changes, even inflicting serious wounds on nature. In "The Southwestern Writings of Mary Austin," in *West of the Border*, Noreen Groover Lape concludes, "Drawing on conservationist notions, Austin fashions an aesthetic theory of 'geographic determinism,' which holds that because humans are intimately connected to the land, the land determines cultural expression and personal identity."[65] Austin personalized this statement, for her genuine regional writing "has come up through the land, shaped by the author's own adjustment to it."[66] Anaya apparently is not so sure about this. Sonny, who observes the destructive effects of ambitious politicians and businessmen recklessly exploiting the land and its resources, needs the support of his guides to understand the wisdom of the traditions and myths that emanate from harmonious interaction between the land and the people who offer explanations and remedies. In the end Anaya's protagonists accept impermanence as a normal condition much more expressly than Austin does. Yet both writers subscribe to the notion that literature represents reflections on essential themes that are supposed to activate their readers, the central one being the interrelationship between character and place, which Eudora Welty briefly summarized as follows: "Sense of place gives equilibrium; extended, it is sense of direction too."[67] And in "The Writer's Landscape," Anaya points out: "When the writer has incorporated his sense of place into his art and the entire sense of the land-scape—characters, emotion, experience, detail and story—permeates his craft, the reader will respond, and that response is the beginning of a new epiphany."[68]

Anaya stands for the necessary change of perspective that privileges the people with a longer record of their journeys' endings in the South-west, claiming their homelands, place-specific identities, and their own sense of place in their books. With all the limitations of the context in which Austin was writing, she, as another "prophet of the New West," anticipated some central aspects of Anaya's vision and paved the way for a new, authentic, and partially disenchanted literary acquisition of *"Cuentos de la Tierra Encantada"* by a generation of women writers, including Fabi-ola Cabeza de Baca, Leslie M. Silko, Gloria Anzaldúa, and Ana Castillo.[69]

NOTES

1. Lomelí, Sorell, and Padilla, "Introduction," 1, 2.
2. See, for example, Irving, *A Tour on the Prairies*: "We send our youth abroad to grow luxurious and effeminate in Europe; it appears to me, that a previous tour on the prairies would be more likely to produce that manliness, simplicity, and self-dependence, most in unison with our political institutions" (55). See also Slotkin, *Regeneration through Violence* and *Fatal Environment*. Quotation from Gutiérrez, "Charles Fletcher Lummis," 12. Note that the use of "Oriental" geo-graphical names (for example, in Anaya's *Zia Summer*, 6), or the fact that the U.S. Army employed a Camel Corps in the Southwest between 1850 and 1860 (see Austin's camel bell in *The Flock*, 227) does not automatically indicate Orientalism.
3. Bourke, "American Congo," 594.
4. Fleming, *Charles F. Lummis*, 50.
5. Gutiérrez, "Charles Fletcher Lummis," 13.
6. See, for example, Rudnick, "Re-Naming the Land."
7. See Fleming, *Charles F. Lummis*, 41: "Although she was later to suggest that Lummis's ego outstripped his talents, there can be no doubt that Lummis was Mrs. Austin's mentor for a time."
8. See her treatment, for example, in Wild, *Desert Literature*, 37–41.

9. Goodman and Dawson, *Mary Austin*, 57. *The Flock* is described as an "idiosyn-cratic tour de force, Austin blends early Western history with contemporary issues sketching the evolution of sheepherding in the West and offering a plan for better use of the land" (270).

10. All page citations in the text are from the 1973 reprint of the original edition of Austin's *The Flock*.

11. Note that *The Flock* is "Dedicated to the Friendly Folk in Inyo and the People of the Book."

12. "Very little, not even the virtue of being uniformly grateful to the little gods who have constrained me to be of the audience, can be put to the writer's credit. All of the book that is mine is the temper of mind which makes it impossible that there should be any play not worth the candle" (Austin, *Flock*, 11).

13. See Lummis, *Land of Poco Tiempo*.

14. Rhetorical interjections, for example: " I have said" (Austin, *Flock*, 89), "The Flocks, I say" (87), or "as I have set them forth" (170–71). Direct addresses, for example: "You should have heard" (ibid., 121), "a chapter to be omitted by the reader who has not loved a dog" (133), "I shall put the case to you" (169), or "To convince you of" (208). In some of Austin's books, especially in her autobi-ography *Earth Horizon* (1932), her acute sense for perspective made her refer to herself "as 'Mary'; 'I-Mary' (her creative self) and 'Mary-by-herself' (her despondent and insubstantial self)." See Goodman and Dawson, *Mary Austin*, 253–54.Whenever she does reveal her emotional involvement, it foreshadows her changed attitude toward her materials in the final two chapters, for exam-ple, when she comments on the "flock minded" (Austin, *Flock*, 116).

15. Ibid.; "but as for me, the dust of the shuffling hoofs is in my eyes" (57).

16. Only twice before the two final chapters does she reveal the congruence between narrator and author: once when one of her informers calls her "Madame-who-writes-the-book" (ibid., 151), and later when she refers to "no longer ago than the time when this book began to shape in my mind" (212).

17. Authority is part and parcel of this sense of responsibility: "It is also conceivable that in the clear silences of the untroubled wild the flock-mind takes its impulse directly from the will of the herder" (ibid., 117–18). For precarious situations, see, for example, 185: "Singular, even terrifying, as evincing the insuperable isolation of man, is the unawareness of the wild kindred toward the shepherd's interests, his claims, his relation to the flock."

18. In chapter 5, the narrator refers to mankind's "progress from nomadism to com-monwealth" (72) and the strife with the ranchers who limit the free movement on the open range (74). This is the archetypical conflict between "the farmer and the cowman," only to be solved in Rodgers and Hammerstein's *Oklahoma* (1943). The appreciation for beauty and earth, for example, is described as "the sense of the earth being good to lie down upon" (73). In chapter 6 she argues, "The voice of that country is an open whisper" (93), which the shepherd is capable and willing to listen to because "every life has its own zest for those who are bred to it. No more delighted sense of competency and power goes to the

man who from his wire web controls the movement of money and wheat, than to the shepherd" (92). She quotes many examples for this competence on pages 92–94 and page 105: "There is a sort of fascination in the naïve and unrelated whittlings and paintings that proceed from men who have a musing way of life, as if when the mind is a little from itself some figment of the Original Impulse begins to fumble through the teachable strong fingers toward creation."

19. See 109–10: "This is why there have never been any notable changes in the management of the flocks since the first herder girt himself with a wallet of sheepskin and went out of his cave dwelling to the pastures." Also 121: "It is yet to be shown how long man halted in the period of stone dwellings and the sheep with him; but if it be presented that we have brought some traces of that life forward with us, might not also the sheep?"

20. See 193, when she complains that pastures are set aside "in order that silly tourists might wonder at the meadow full of bloom," and 194, commenting on the establishment of Yosemite National Park, "The sheep-men were not alone in esteeming the segregation of the Park for the use of a few beauty-loving folk, against its natural use as a pasture, rather a silly performance." These remarks clearly contradict John Muir's philosophy! See also 208–12, and the complete chapter 11, "The Sheep and the Reserves," 191–212.

21. A register well known in American literature. See, for example, Washington Irving's "The Creole Village: A Sketch from a Steamboat" (1837) or the first section of Jean Toomer's *Cane* (1923).

22. See Austin, *Flock*, 221: "But between Sebastian [an Indian employee] and Beale grew up such esteem from man to man that lasted their lives out in benefits and devotion" (221).

23. See 229: "General Beale himself showed me."

24. When speaking about Beale and the Indians, she employs the term "swarthy," which she already used for Beale's multiethnic laborers: he "began to prove the land and draw to him in devotion its swarthy people" (220). Later in the book, she refers to their "primitive mind" (233).

25. Before proceeding, she insists on the Indian's life with the land as a model without going into further detail: "And when it comes to formulating the sense of man's relations to all outdoors, depend upon it the Indians have been before you" (255).

26. Austin, *Earth Horizon*, 336, 349.

27. All page citations in the text are from the 2007 facsimile edition of Austin's 1924 *Land of Journeys' Ending*.

28. See, for example, her reference to herself on 219–20: "as I have already described them in 'The Land of Little Rain.'" On 226 she refers to Ranchos Tejón and its owner, Edward Beale, from *The Flock*.

29. See also 437: "He is the land, the lift of its mountain lines, the reach of its valleys; his is the rhythm of its seasonal processions, the involution and variation of its vegetal patterns . . . he takes it in and gives it forth again in directions and occasions least suspected by himself, as a manner, as music, as a prevailing tone of thought, as the line of his roof-tree, the pattern of his personal adornment."

30. In David W. Teague's *Southwest in American Literature and Art*, he comments on the racist undertones of such a passage: "Austin seems to have avoided the chauvinism of her time to a great extent, although some of her references to race nevertheless grate a bit on the modern ear. . . . To her credit, Austin articulated her racial theories with a fair amount of grace" (102).

31. The observant and informed reader knows that in 1923, she published *The American Rhythm*, in which she pretended to be able to guess the place of origin of any American Indian verse by its rhythm. On page 164 of *Land of Journeys' Ending*, she notes, "and you will perhaps allow that I know something of Indian rhythms."

32. See also Bandelier conjuring up *The Delight Makers* in his novel of 1890.

33. For authentic information on the Hermanos Penitentes, see Gutiérrez, "Crucifixion, Slavery, and Death," 253–71.

34. To make these points, Austin points the lives of the ancients "to correct impressions of cave-dwelling man, to discover the shy, home-loving, beauty-worshipping animal man was. Never in the cliff period so harried and hate-ridden as in this civilized age of ours" (187). See also her critiques on modern times in "Not all the fine and moving things in American history were done in English" (193), and "our English-speaking life that is mortifying and confusing" (316).

35. See, for example, "and the song rising through the clear water, . . . Ay, *Peña Hueca*, forget me never more! . . . as I think some passionate plaintive note of the Spanish occupation must continue to rise long through our strident modernism" (199).

36. Anaya, "Foreword," x, xii.

37. Ibid. xv, xiii.

38. Johnson and Apodaca, "Myth and the Writer," 84.

39. All page citations in the text are from the 1994 edition of *Bless Me, Ultima*.

40. See also "She taught me to listen to the mystery of the groaning earth and to feel complete in the fulfilment of its time . . . I had been afraid of the awful *presence* of the river, which was the soul of the river, but through her I learned that my spirit shared in the spirit of all things" (16), and "I was a very important part of the teeming life of the llano and the river" (43–44).

41. Austin, *Land of Journeys' Ending*, 260. When Austin settled down in New York in 1910, she moved into Irving's house on Riverside Drive.

42. In chapter 3, "A thin mist rose from the river . . . hid the church tower and the schoolhouse top" (34). Later Antonio defines Ultima's influence on his education: "[I]n her company I found a greater deal of solace and peace. This was more than I had been able to find at church or with the kids at school" (236).

43. See, for example, pages 4–5 on family values.

44. In one of his dreams, la Virgen de Guadalupe "smiled at the goodness of the owl" (14).

45. This reconciliation is foreshadowed in Antonio's dream after the first appearance of the golden carp. See 125–26.

46. Anaya's mysteries share a number of features with Tony Hillerman's (1925–2008) eighteen Navajo tribal police mysteries. For example, the important

contributions of a deep knowledge of local Native culture to the solution of the cases.

47. Note also the seasonal titles of Anaya's four mystery novels. A fairly similar dry spell structures the plot of Elmer Skelton's *The Time It Never Rained* (1973). See also Skelton's treatment of Mexican labor in this novel.

48. All page citations in the text are from the original edition of Anaya, *Zia Summer*.

49. For the historical Elfego Baca (1865–1945), see Bryan, *Incredible Elfego Baca*, and "Tribute to Elfego Baca—Hon. Bill Richardson (Extension of Remarks—May 10, 1995)," 104 Cong. Rec. E987 (May 10, 1995), http://Thomas.loc.gov/cgi-bin/query/z?r104:E10MY5-53.

50. Even the final victory celebration is marred by grim facts: "In the meantime radioactive waste continued to pile up. . . . One of the Indian tribes already petitioned the state for a license to set up a nuclear storage facility on their land. The storage of radioactive waste had become big business" (357–59).

51. This is also the fate of the sheep business in New Mexico, similar to the situation in California as depicted in *The Flock*.

52. This could be read as a hint at people like Mary Austin: "The old southwest was dead or dying, taken over by Californicators living in Santa Fe style and staying in touch through fax machines. The once reclusive Villa de la Santa Fé had been 'discovered' in the eighties" (222). See also a similar passage on 108.

53. Like Antonio in *Bless Me, Ultima*, Sonny has developed the skills of a future "leader of the people," as predicted by his parents. See my comparative study, "Individual Versus Collective Identity." See also a similar treatment of the theme combined with nostalgia and melancholy in John Steinbeck's "The Leader of the People," in *The Red Pony* (1937).

54. Whitaker, *Helen Hunt Jackson*, 45. Austin refers to *Ramona* in *The Flock* (223) and in *Earth Horizon* (230). Recent studies have revised earlier fairly ambiguous reviews of the novel in connection with the republication of María Amparo Ruiz de Burton's *The Squatter and the Don* (1885). See Goldman, "I Think Our Romance Is Spoiled," 65–84.

55. Horgan, *Heroic Triad*; Austin, *Flock*, 220, 223.

56. See Robert Frost, "The Gift Outright," written before 1936, reprinted in *The Oxford Book of American Poetry*, ed. David Lehman (New York: Oxford University Press, 2006), 236.

57. The myth of the golden carp was transmitted to Cico and Antonio by Jasón's Indian. In *Heart of Aztlán*, Crispín, the old blind Indian seer, plays a prominent role in the story. See my study "Presence of the Native American." See also Anaya's statement on the Pueblo (or Popé's) Rebellion of 1680 in his introduction to *Ceremony of Brotherhood*: "In that year of 1680 the land and the survival of a native culture were at stake, and those who would oppress sought to use these elements to turn people against one another. But in spite of the tyrants, a group of people emerged who had the wisdom to create a new harmony from both world views" (2).

58. See Austin, *Land of Journeys' Ending*, viii.

59. Unlike Antonio and his parents, his sister welcomes Ultima into the family in English (12). See also 80—"There was magic in the letters, and I had been eager to learn the secret"—and 188.
60. Goodman and Dawson, *Mary Austin*, 66. Lummis's *Land of Poco Tiempo*, along with sensitive descriptions of American Indian culture, also includes "On the Trail of the Renegades" (written in 1886), a rather one-sided reportage on the bloody trail left behind by "Geronimo and his co-renegades" in southern Arizona.
61. Martin, introduction to *Writers of the Purple Sage*, xiii.
62. Wild, *Desert Literature*, 6.
63. Austin, *Flock*, 105.
64. Zwinger, introduction to *Mary Austin and John Muir*, xvii. When advertising the Southwest and its preindustrial past, as Austin did, such nostalgic passages must be tolerated as a useful component. Fortunately enough, Austin's vision fundamentally diverges from the images of Willa Cather's Archbishop Lamy, who sees the people of Acoma as "rock turtles on their rock. Something reptilian he felt here, something that had endured by immobility, a kind of life out of reach, like crustaceans in their armour" (*Death Comes*, 103).
65. Lape, *West of the Border*, 140.
66. Austin, "Regionalism in American Fiction," 134.
67. Welty, "Place in Fiction," 792
68. Anaya, "Writer's Landscape," 102.
69. Hoyer, "Prophets of the New West"; Allen, "*Cuentos de la Tierra Encantada*."

BIBLIOGRAPHY

Allen, Paula Gunn. "*Cuentos de la Tierra Encantada:* Magic and Realism in the Southwestern Borderlands." In *Many Wests: Place, Culture, and Regional Identity*, edited by D. M. Wrobel and M. C. Steiner, 342–65. Lawrence: University of Kansas Press, 1997.
Anaya, Rudolfo A. *Bless Me, Ultima*. New York: Warner Books, 1994.
———. "Foreword: The Spirit of the Place." In *Writing the Southwest*, edited by David K. Dunaway, ix–xvi. New York: Penguin/Plume, 1995.
———. Introduction to *Ceremony of Brotherhood*, edited by R. A. Anaya and S. J. Ortiz, 2–3. Albuquerque, NM: Academia, 1981.
———. "The Writer's Landscape: Epiphany in Landscape." *Latin American Literary Review* 5, no. 10 (Spring–Summer 1977): 98–102.
———. *Zia Summer*. New York: Warner Books, 1995.
Austin, Mary H. *Earth Horizon*. Boston, MA: Houghton Mifflin, 1932.
———. *The Flock*. Santa Fe, NM: William Gannon, 1973.
———. *The Land of Journeys' Ending: Facsimile of the Original 1924 Edition*. Santa Fe, NM: Sunstone Press, 2007.

———. "Regionalism in American Fiction." In *Beyond Borders. The Selected Essays of Mary Austin*, edited by R. J. Ellis, 130–40. Carbondale: Southern Illinois University Press, 1996.

Bandelier, Adolph Francis. *The Delight Makers*. 1890. Reprint, New York: Harcourt Brace Jovanovich, 1971.

Bourke, John G. "The American Congo." *Scribner's Magazine*, May 1894, 590–610.

Bryan, Howard. *Incredible Elfego Baca: Good Man, Bad Man of the Old West*. With a Foreword by Rudolfo Anaya. Santa Fe, NM: Clear Light, 1993.

Bus, Heiner. "Individual versus Collective Identity and the Idea of Leadership in Sherwood Anderson's *Marching Men* (1917) and Rudolfo A. Anaya's *Heart of Aztlán* (1976)." In *Rudolfo A. Anaya: Focus on Criticism*, edited by C. A. González-T., 113–31. La Jolla, CA: Lalo Press, 1990.

———. "The Presence of the Native American in Chicano Literature (Anaya, Candelaria, Alurista, Elizondo, Mora)." In *International Studies in Honor of Tomás Rivera*, edited by J. Olivares, 148–62. Houston, TX: Arte Público Press, 1986.

Cather, Willa. *Death Comes for the Archbishop*. 1927. Reprint, New York: Vintage Books, 1971.

Fleming, Robert E. *Charles F. Lummis*. Boise, ID: Boise State University, 1981.

Frost, Robert. "The Gift Outright." In *The Oxford Book of American Poetry*, edited by David Lehman, 236. New York: Oxford University Press, 2006.

Goldman, Anne E. "'I Think Our Romance Is Spoiled,' or, Crossing Genres: California History in Helen Hunt Jackson's *Ramona* and María Amparo Ruiz de Burton's *The Squatter and the Don*." In *Over the Edge. Remapping the American West*, edited by V. J. Matsumoto and B. Allmendinger, 65–84. Berkeley: University of California Press, 1999.

Goodman, Susan, and Carl Dawson. *Mary Austin and the American West*. Berkeley: University of California Press, 2008.

Gutiérrez, Ramón A. "Charles Fletcher Lummis and the Orientalization of New Mexico." In *Nuevomexicano Legacy: Forms, Agencies, and Discourse*, edited by Francisco A. Lomelí, Victor A. Sorell, and Genaro M. Padilla, 11–27. Albuquerque: University of New Mexico Press, 2002.

———. "Crucifixion, Slavery, and Death: The Hermanos Penitentes of the Southwest." In *Over the Edge: Remapping the American West*, edited by V. J. Matsumoto and B. Allmendinger, 253–71. Berkeley: University of California Press, 1999.

Horgan, Paul. *The Heroic Triad: Essays in the Social Energies of Three Southwestern Cultures*. New York: Holt, Rinehart and Winston, 1970.

Hoyer, Mark T. "Prophets of the New West: Wovoka and Mary Austin." In *Dancing Ghosts. Native American and Christian Syncretism in Mary Austin*, 1–18. Reno: University of Nevada Press, 1998.

Irving, Washington. "The Creole Village: A Sketch from a Steamboat." 1837. In *The Western Journals of Washington Irving*, edited and annotated by John Francis McDermott, 171–80. Norman: University of Oklahoma Press, 1954.

————. *A Tour on the Prairies.* 1832. Reprint, Norman: University of Oklahoma Press, 1965.

Johnson, David, and David Apodaca. "Myth and the Writer: A Conversation with Rudolfo Anaya." *New America* 3, no. 3 (Spring 1979): 76–85.

Lape, Noreen Groover. *West of the Border: The Multicultural Literature of the Western American Frontiers.* Athens: Ohio University Press, 2000.

Lomelí, Francisco A., Victor A. Sorell, and Genaro M. Padilla. "Introduction: Beyond the Land of Enchantment." In *Nuevomexicano Cultural Legacy. Forms, Agencies, and Discourse,* edited by Francisco A. Lomelí, Victor A. Sorell, and Genaro M. Padilla, 1–8. Albuquerque: University of New Mexico Press, 2002.

Lummis, Charles F. *The Land of Poco Tiempo.* Reprint, Albuquerque: University of New Mexico Press, 1952.

Martin, Russell. Introduction to *Writers of the Purple Sage: An Anthology of Recent Western Writing.* Edited by Russell Martin and Marc Barasch, ix–xxx. New York: Viking Penguin, 1984.

Rudnick, Lois. "Re-Naming the Land: Anglo Expatriate Women in the Southwest." In *The Desert Is No Lady. Southwestern Landscapes in Women's Writing and Art,* edited by V. Norwood and J. Monk, 10–26. New Haven, CT: Yale University Press, 1987.

Skelton, Elmer. *The Time It Never Rained.* Garden City, NY: Doubleday, 1973.

Slotkin, Richard. *The Fatal Environment: The Myth of the Frontier in the Age of Industrialization, 1880–1890.* New York: HarperPerennial, 1994.

————. *Regeneration through Violence: The Mythology of the American Frontier.* New York: HarperPerennial, 1996.

Steinbeck, John. "The Leader of the People." In *The Red Pony,* 73–92. 1937. Reprint, New York: Bantam Pathfinder, 1963.

Teague, David W. *The Southwest in American Literature and Art: The Rise of a Desert Aesthetic.* Tucson: University of Arizona Press, 1997.

Toomer, Jean. *Cane.* 1923. Reprint, New York: Boni and Liveright, 1975.

Welty, Eudora. "Place in Fiction." In *Stories, Essays and Memoirs,* 781–96. New York: Library of America, 1998.

Whitaker, Rosemary. *Helen Hunt Jackson.* Boise, ID: Boise State University, 1987.

Wild, Peter. *Desert Literature of the Early Period.* Boise, ID: Boise State University, 2001.

Zwinger, Anne H., ed. *Mary Austin and John Muir: Writing the Western Landscape.* Boston, MA: Beacon Press, 1994.

3

Sweet Birds of Youth

COMING OF AGE FROM *BLESS ME,*
ULTIMA TO *THE FAITH HEALER*
OF OLIVE AVENUE

José E. Limón

Rudolfo Anaya's best-known work, *Bless Me, Ultima*, offers us a central protagonist, Antonio Márez Luna, as a young and developing male character, but in tandem with the old curandera Ultima.[1] In this chapter, I trace a certain disjunctive movement from Antonio and Ultima to the Mexican American male youth of today as represented in contemporary fiction. I close with a commentary addressing the social reality that may be conditioning these fictional representations. As a general context for Anaya's work, let me first open with the category of American youth at mid-twentieth century, surrounding Antonio and the publication of Anaya's book, which is most clearly articulated in the 1960s.

HAIL, HAIL, ROCK AND ROLL

Much has been said in learned and popular discussions of the sixties as a political and cultural moment; indeed, as I write, CNN is airing a special documentary series on the sixties. But we should always be wary of a constricted decade-focused analysis, recalling, in this instance at least, that the entire post–World War II period, especially the fifties, provided the germination stage and launching point for the sixties. If rock 'n' roll and the Motown sound were the music of the sixties, recall that Bill Haley, Elvis Presley, and Chuck Berry hit the national stage in the fifties. Even Motown was launched in this earlier decade, in 1959. Closer to our cultural concerns in this chapter, before we heard Carlos Santana's "Oye Como Va" at the tail end of the sixties, we first heard Ritchie Valens's "La Bamba" in 1958.

From the fifties through the sixties and beyond, rock 'n' roll has also been the music of youth—a particular kind of youth, as a previously unknown culture of teenagers and young adults was born into a historically unprecedented period of greater and more pervasive affluence. George Lipsitz, a leading cultural critic of this period's popular culture, notes that rock 'n' roll had decidedly working-class origins, and teenagers "raised in times of unprecedented consumer affluence . . . found more meaning and value in working-class culture than in the signs and symbols of their own emerging middle class." For Lipsitz, such youth "sought escape from the stifling blandness of 1950s popular music, but they also developed their own preferences as people anticipating life in an increasingly bureaucratic and conformist society."[2] But such music expressed its rebellious differences largely *musically*—that is, in new time measures, rhythms, chord progressions, instrumentations, and so on—although its sexually suggestive images were also new and nonconformist, as were its other images and diction from "below," such as "you ain't nothing but a hound dog."

Yet, rock 'n' roll offered a varied range of emotional and ideological registers for such youth, from playful mirth to dark tonalities and explorations of forbidden sexuality. In the fifties, one could, with Chuck Berry, "hail, hail rock 'n' roll." In 1964, young people could, with the Dixie Cups, optimistically imagine themselves "going to the chapel, and . . . going to get married," and yet, that same year, could also imagine the hard life of prostitution in New Orleans with the Animals' "House of the Rising Sun."[3] In 1965, they could begin to say in strident chords with Mick Jagger, "I can't get no satisfaction." Again, closer to our cultural concerns, but also illustrating this tonal division, the Mexican American band Question Mark and the Mysterians had to agree to change the sexually explicit title of their 1966 signature song from "69 Tears" to "96 Tears" before recording it, while another Mexican American band, Sam the Sham and the Pharaohs, offered the rhythmic, funny, and nonsensical "Wooly Bully," about Matty and Hatty learning to dance rock 'n' roll while he tells her about "a thing he saw" (supposedly a buffalo) with its "two big horns and a wooly jaw."

THE MOODY BLUES OF AMERICAN YOUTH

This youthful rebellious difference was also manifested in more discursive and traditional literary and filmic genres, where the rebellion was more evident but also had more pessimistic outcomes for such youth. Unlike rock 'n' roll, the ideological moods, tones, and registers of such fiction, drama, and film were not as varied and were principally defined in an aura of dark alienation. I take my title from the 1959 play *Sweet Bird of Youth*, by Tennessee Williams, in which the central protagonist, Chance Wayne, has misspent his youth and hopes to recover something from it, although it would now seem to be a sweet but elusive bird. In the American fiction of this period, yet another iconic American youth, John Yossarian, loses his youth in the violence filled skies over Europe in World War II in Joseph Heller's 1961 novel *Catch-22*. Youths in these fictions grapple with an alienated identity, with a lost innocence and an emerging adulthood seemingly stunted by the new consumerist and corporate culture, undergirded by the military-industrial complex, which worried even conservative president Dwight D. Eisenhower. Such a culture was then represented and promulgated by the "madmen" of the New York advertising world. This is the world—the phony world—in which there is always a catch-22, the culture of Lipsitz's "increasingly bureaucratic and conformist society," through which the depressed Holden Caulfield must suffer and negotiate in Salinger's 1951 *Catcher in the Rye*. But such a culture did not emanate just from corporate capitalism or novels. In the film *On the Waterfront*, corrupt labor unions leave Marlon Brando's young Terry Malloy saying, "I could have been a contender."[4] But the primary filmic representation of such youthful alienation surely must be James Dean as the teenager Jim Stark, who must rebel but, in 1955, is a rebel without a cause.[5] By the late 1960s, James Dean's rebel without a cause turns into Dustin Hoffman's Benjamin Braddock in the 1967 film *The Graduate*; Ben cannot accept a world of "plastic," even as the film ends in ambivalence and uncertainty, ironically in Berkeley.[6] For Mexican Americans, there is no better example of such alienation in fiction than José Antonio Villarreal's 1959 *Pocho* and its principal youthful protagonist, Richard Rubio from Santa Clara, California, who at the end of the novel faces an uncertain cultural future (a theme later recalled by another Richard, born in Sacramento—Richard Rodríguez—in his 1982 autobiography, *Hunger of Memory*).[7]

Yet in most of these cases, one senses a cause in the making, as most offer "nonconformity as a way of unleashing the nobility and heroism of the ordinary person."[8] In these works, such nobility and heroism are indeed articulated largely at the level of the ordinary individual; however, they are not always, or ever, clearly transformed into a collective and politically efficacious cause.

That cause would come in the later sixties, as such youth found expression and engagement in the anti–Vietnam war movement, in civil rights action, and sometimes just in taking their critical difference from the dominant culture. In short order, however, the white sector of that youth-led movement soon dissipated into even more alienation or into cultural vapidity, reflected in a changing music and dance, in which only the narcissistic self emerges as any kind of "hero," and the "collective" is articulated only on the disco dance floor and only in moments of "Saturday Night Fever."

POR MI RAZA HABLARÁ EL ESPÍRITU

It was a very different matter for youth of color, as such youth increasingly affirmed their besieged cultural and historical identity, although a few, like Richard Rodríguez, would refuse it. Unlike the alienated wreckage of the mostly white radical protest movement of the sixties, youth of color, and certainly Mexican American youth of this time, perdured in their political and cultural affirmation, as Juan Gómez-Quiñones and Irene Vásquez show us in their new book on this period.[9] The continuation of their struggle, even into our own time, was articulated largely through the creation and stabilization of Chicano studies academic programs but also through other allied endeavors, such as art collectives and publishing houses.

In this historical context, we can now better understand the emergence of three other emblematic youthful male figures in three works of Mexican American fiction written in the 1960s, which appear almost as a cluster in the years 1971, 1972, and 1973, with the Chicano publishing house Quinto Sol. Anaya's *Bless Me, Ultima* (1972) is set, of course, in New Mexico. Tomás Rivera's *Y no se lo tragó la tierra* (1971) and Rolando Hinojosa's *Estampas del Valle y Otras Obras* (1973) are both set mostly in southern Texas.

Unlike the ending of *Pocho,* the central protagonists in these three works clearly look toward a future of integration within their Mexican American community and solidarity with its progressive sociopolitical agenda of liberation from oppression. In Rivera's work, a young unnamed male protagonist experiences this oppression among his farmworker Mexican people as we trace his growing awareness not only of this oppression but also of certain contradictions within his native culture, including, of course, his climactic discovery that the earth will not devour him if he questions the Catholic faith that too often oppresses his community. Through his skeptical reasoning, he emerges at the end of the novel less as a Cartesian and more of a Nietzschean Zarathustrian heroic figure, who will willfully lead his people to knowledge and liberation as they collectively utter the incantatory "when we arrive, when we arrive."[10] Rolando Hinojosa also offers a progressive and liberated future for his people, although in a lower key. His youthful protagonist is Rafe Buenrostro, a figure enveloped in his people's culture in *el valle* of Texas, an envelopment that Hinojosa handles with great subtlety, as he also handles Rafe's growing awareness of the political and economic trials his community has experienced in a racist and exploitative Anglo Texas—an Anglo Texas, however, with willing Mexican American accomplices. At the end of the book, we find Rafe about to leave for the University of Texas at Austin, and even if this had been Rolando's only book, we would still know with great certainty that Rafe would eventually put his higher education toward service to his people in el valle. As we all know, however, Hinojosa has written much more—the whole of his Klail City Death Trip series of novels—and indeed in these later books, he does develop this progressive future for his young protagonist as Rafe matures into a young adult. After law school at the University of Texas at Austin, Rafe returns to the Río Grande Valley to work as a police officer, fighting the scourge of drugs, a late capitalist symptom that has descended on his beloved valley.[11]

In Anaya's *Bless Me, Ultima* we obtain a more transcendent and evocative sense of the young protagonist's emancipatory possibilities. Under the guidance of Ultima, young Antonio discovers the external oppressions that have been visited on his community, even as he also discovers that it is also capable of self-inflicted violence. But his greater discovery is his community's curative power through a synthesis of indigenous and Catholic beliefs, a power expressed through mythological forms but most centrally by Ultima, who at the end of the book and of her life appears to pass on her curative legacy to Antonio, for his use in the betterment of his New Mexican people—but really the betterment of all of us who share this fundamental cultural/religious synthesis. Following Roberto Cantú, I suggest that among Anaya's many contributions to Mexican American literature, the figure of Antonio as incarnated innocence and bountiful promise is central and enduring.[12] Yet the leading critic of Chicano literature, Ramón Saldívar, questions *Bless Me, Ultima* as a "pre-critical idealist venture," ultimately "dissatisfying," as it imposes on the reader "the burden of restoring the whole socially concrete subtext of nineteenth and twentieth century Southwestern history mythicized and reified on so many levels of utopian compensation." In offering such a negation of material history and such mythic compensation, Saldívar seems to say, the novel paradoxically achieves its enormous popularity with both "Mexican-American and Anglo audiences."[13] But even granted its utopianism, the novel nevertheless offers affirmation.

As Hinojosa continued to develop Rafe Buenrostro into a mature, socially engaged character, one might argue that Anaya has not abandoned his parallel project of cultural affirmation either, but continues this work by way of his later novels, particularly *Randy Lopez Goes Home* (2011). In this novel, Randy Lopez leaves his northern New Mexican village of Agua Bendita in his youth to make his way in the larger Anglo-dominated world, even writing a book called *Life Among the Gringos*. Although successful in that world, he nevertheless is missing something substantial in his life, and he finds it as a now older man only when he returns to the folklorically enchanted world of Agua Bendita. But here, no doubt, critic Saldívar would also find an escape from material history and a compensatory mythic idealism, a persistent theme not only in Anaya but in much New Mexican writing, sustaining New Mexico as a "land of enchantment."[14] Paralleling Hinojosa, a more materialist and as yet unwritten New Mexican fiction might turn, for example, to the question of substance abuse now plaguing northern New Mexico for its materials and plot and for a thesis of disenchantment.[15] To be sure, as with Hinojosa, one needs to consider Anaya's own turn to detective fiction; but even here, one senses a continuing, if now urbanized, compensatory folk idealism, as Anaya's youthful protagonist, private detective Sonny Baca, draws supportive sustenance from an array of mythic figures and an empathetic involvement with the New Mexican natural environment, itself part of the New Mexican mythos.[16]

Even if idealistically compensatory, *Bless Me, Ultima*; *Randy Lopez Goes Home*; and Anaya's other writings, along with Rivera's and Hinojosa's more materially historicized texts, were not in sync with the general pessimistic outlook in the dominant American fictional representation of the youth of that period and even of today. Rather, and reflecting the progressive and emancipatory potential of the Chicano and Chicana movement of those years, they seem to express a deep belief in the creative and liberating possibilities of youth, mainly of Chicano male youth. Yet these representations may have also been reflecting the arrival of Mexican-origin people into a post–World War II American society of greater possibility for a population that had previously not fully participated in the benefits of this society. Sociological historian David Montejano notes such an arrival for Mexican Americans in Texas, an arrival no doubt occurring elsewhere in Mexican America.[17]

By 1950 the effects of war-related industrialization in increasing the ranks of skilled and semiskilled laborers and clerical workers were evident. Skilled and professional workers accounted for nearly half the Texas Mexican workforce, while unskilled made up the other half. By 1970 the occupational distribution of 1930 had been reversed. The unskilled category of farm and service workers and laborers composed slightly less than a third (30.8 percent) of the workforce, while the skilled and professional workers made up slightly more than two-thirds (69.2 percent). This occupational division of thirds is evident in the 1980 data, but with a further weakening of the unskilled categories and a strengthening of the white-collar categories. In 1980, 35.8 percent of Texas Mexicans had white-collar occupations; 35.3 percent had skilled occupations; and the number with unskilled jobs had dropped to 29 percent.[18]

Montejano summarizes his findings: "The importance of these occupational changes for Mexican-Anglo relations cannot be overstated. The general effect of an expanding white collar and skilled strata within the Mexican-American community was the attainment of a measure of economic stability."[19] Such stability, as Montejano notes, was made centrally possible by a somewhat greater access to higher education, as evident in the early academic careers of the three Mexican American authors discussed here as well as in the Chicano generation of the sixties that sustained them. For Mexican Americans, the post–World War II period, at least up to 1980, was actually a time of measured and always tentative social gains and optimism, also reflected in the perceptible rise in the number of Mexican Americans elected to public office and their increasing representation in other public spheres, for example, as military officers, administrative personnel, and medical doctors, among other occupations. Though much yet remained to be done, what Montejano says of Texas was generally true of Mexican America and bears repeating: "[T]he general effect of an expanding white collar and skilled strata within the Mexican-American community was the attainment of a measure of economic stability." Elsewhere I have explored the emergence and significance of such a Mexican American social stratum.[20]

THE MEXICAN AMERICAN MALE MILLENNIUM MALAISE

Anaya, Rivera, and Hinojosa clearly defined male youth in culturally affirmative idioms for the second half of the twentieth century and into the twenty-first. Yet what about younger Mexican American writers and the continuing present moment and the future? While expanding opportunities continue today, at least for some Mexican Americans, the twentieth-century short fiction produced by a new generation of Mexican

American writers seems to tell such a different story in fiction that we may be looking at two very different Mexican Américas. Rivera's liberating figure, Hinojosa's successful yet socially aware Rafe, and Anaya's culturally sanctified and blessed Antonio, and even Sonny Baca, have given way to young male figures best characterized by "D" language: despair, disillusion, and desolation. Social sciences enable us to examine a new generation encumbered by a pervasive anxiety that does not permit it to build and expand on the social and cultural gains made by the preceding generation. In what follows, I briefly explore the works of three such new and still young fiction writers, while adducing some support from the social sciences.

One such young writer is the estimable Oscar Casares, from Hinojosa's and Rivera's southern Texas. His 2003 short story collection, *Brownsville*, examines the daily lives of the mostly Mexican Americans in that city, also his hometown, but with some focus on its youth. In one story, "Chango," we meet a twenty-something young man, Bony, probably a nickname for Bonifacio.[21] Bony spends his unemployed days sitting outside his parents' home, drinking beer and waving at passersby, much to the exasperation of his parents, particularly of his father, a police officer representative of the social gains in Texas that I noted earlier by way of David Montejano. More than occasionally, Bony adds secretive pot smoking to the beer consumption while driving around town in his old truck, listening to Pink Floyd tapes, dressed in his daily uniform of "chanclas, baggy blue jean shorts, and San Antonio Spurs jersey" (60).[22] When he occasionally speaks, he does so mostly in English, but an English of unclear half syllables and incomplete sentences, as is the Spanish that he speaks only occasionally. Conversations, such as they are, occur over humdrum dinners, mostly with his parents, as they eat takeout fried chicken, and Bony debates whether he prefers Churches or KFC.

The only spark that appears in Bony's twilight world is, oddly enough, a monkey head he finds one day. With little originality, he names it Chango (monkey), and it becomes his buddy, his conversational partner, and possibly the only object of his love in his world. Yet, harassed by the predictable objection from his parents to the monkey head, he ends up slipping the monkey head into one of Brownsville's resacas, or bayous:

"People were always talking at him and telling him how he should live. Sometimes he listened, but most times he didn't. He was just living. That's the best explanation he could give," as the story ends (67).

In another story, "Big Jesse, Little Jesse," a twenty-four-year-old male protagonist, Jesse, is a high school graduate separated from his wife, Corina. He works as an assistant manager at an electronics store in downtown Brownsville that caters to customers from Matamoros, across the border, where probably all the floor employees carry the title "assistant manager." Likely working on minimum wage plus commissions, he can afford only a small apartment with "zero furniture," consisting of a plastic lawn chair and a used mattress that he bought at a clearance sale. He can cook anything "with eggs: *frijoles con huevo, chorizo con huevo*, ham and eggs, bacon and eggs, potato and eggs," which he eats with plastic spoons and forks (110). His separation from Corina is due in part to their very different ideas about raising their son, little Jesse. His mother wants the little one to read books and do well in school, with the expectation of going to college, while big Jesse wants him to be a regular neighborhood kid like he was and learn his father's "famous around-the-back reverse layup" in basketball. Little Jesse is not into sports, preferring to read books, which upsets his father, but there is also the matter of little Jesse's physical disability—he was born with one foot shorter than the other—which also bothers big Jesse. Indeed, when big Jesse takes his son to a carnival, little Jesse's disability draws a taunt from another young father, whom Jesse calls Rata (rat), resulting in a fight between the two young dads in which big Jesse loses one of his shoes. The men are separated by the police, and as big Jesse is led away, he sees that a boy has picked up his shoe. He wants to ask for his shoe, but the cop is tugging at him. Jesse steps awkwardly

> every time his foot comes down. . . . People are laughing at the way he is walking, and telling him not to forget his shoe, that he'll need it when he gets out of jail. The boy with the shoe mimics the way Jesse walks, making him look more like a chimp than a man. This gets the biggest laughs so far. Jesse could step on his toes and look like anyone else walking out of a carnival. But he doesn't. He lets them keep on laughing. It's the only thing he can hear now. (113)

The lost shoe will link him with his son but will also metaphorically speak to a much larger disability in big Jesse, namely, as Julie Minich notes, his inability to imagine any other existence that is not bound by his precarious sense of "masculinity, heteronormativity, and able-bodied superiority," which can so easily collapse in the face of a Rata, a superiority always subject to Jesse's economic vulnerability in the new economy of the Lower Río Grande Valley. Minich argues "that it is crucial for the most vulnerable members of a social order to find new ways of imagining collectivities within that order."[23] Yet, she does not make it at all clear what those imaginary collectivities are, nor how they might be practically implemented to refashion Jesse's impoverished life. Absent such socially effective reimaginings, it falls to big Jesse to take some personal initiative in fashioning a better life for him and his son, and possibly a reunified relationship with Corina and little Jesse, who actually provide the only practically effective template for such a refashioning if only big Jesse would act on it. Minich is correct that the new socioeconomic forces in the Lower Río Grande Valley are indeed related "to larger hierarchies of race and class undergirding US national identity."[24] Those hierarchies, however, do not absolve big Jesse from acting but require even more so his reflective analysis and agency within the collectivity he should know and love best—his family—and through the only instrumentality really available to him: education. Yet, the story leaves us with little sense that he will do so.

Thus, we do not find much evidence in *Brownsville* that would encourage confidence in its Mexican American youth, especially its young males, a youthful failure witnessed by yet another young Brownsville writer, Domingo Martínez, in his memoir of growing up in that same place in the latter third of the twentieth century.[25] By comparison, the older Mexican Americans who populate *Brownsville* are far more representative of Montejano's earlier cited "expanding white collar and skilled strata within the Mexican-American community," which, as it happens, also gave forth from Brownsville the distinguished intellectual and artistic lineage of not only Oscar Casares, but also cultural historians and critics Carlos Eduardo Castañeda, Américo Paredes, and the Saldívar family of senior cultural critics and scholars (Ramón, José David, and Sonia).

If indeed Brownsville is a key Mexican American city in Texas, San Antonio may be even more so. A young fiction writer from that important city, Manuel Luis Martínez, in his novel called *Drift*, offers us the figure of Robert Lomos, a high school kid in San Antonio whose family has broken up. His dad, an itinerant jazz musician, has abandoned the family, and Robert's mother and little brother a have moved to Los Angeles, leaving Robert with his grandmother (Grams), a tough, hard-working, and thrifty woman. Admonishing him not to be a *burro*, she tells him: "You don't ever feel sorry for yourself. Nothing ever been easy for Mexicans. You don't got a choice, boy. The best you hope for is that God lets you see the problems coming so that you can get ready" (19).[26] And, to this end, she helps him get his first library card (21). But he begins to skip classes at his school and spends his days doping and drinking with his friends, even as Grams tries to steer him right by her example and advice. Though he hates classes, he nevertheless spends time at the school library, where he reads Kurt Vonnegut's *Slaughterhouse-Five*, Heller's *Catch-22*, and Hunter S Thompson's *Fear and Loathing in Las Vegas*. "Those three," he says, "kind of explained my life to me. These guys see the world filled with monsters and freaks, and the scary shit is that it's the monsters who run things and make life hard for the rest of us" (7). But this emerging literary-political sensibility gives way to the harsh realities of life after he leaves school altogether and must get some sort of job to sustain his new household, since Grams "cleans wealthy white women's houses and takes care of their complaints" (18). Through a girlfriend, and with not much formal education, he finds work in one of San Antonio's well-known barbacoa joints, preparing this meat and other foods and selling them over the counter.[27] Working "fifteen, sixteen hours straight," he especially hates working with *lengua* (tongue) because

> it means cutting into the big tongue and it gives me the willies. . . . [A] close second as far as the nausea factor is *sesos* [brains] but the people order it. I've seen a big meat-eatin' Mexican order a pound of it and say, "Hey, don't wrap it up just yet," and he'll pull out a corn tortilla and spread some of that gray gook on it and munch the brain taco down in three bites flat. I guess my face contorts into a look of disgust, because the guy smiles at me with brain goo on his teeth and he says, "Mmmm that's damn good!"

"But *ojos* [eyes] are the worst," Robert says, and the other, older Mexican workers initiate him into their workplace by forcing him to eat one of the eyes (33–34). Thus, Robert does not fit into mainstream culture nor in his own native Mexican American society, and so his drift continues as he migrates to Los Angeles to try to get back together with his family. He finds work as a busboy at a Sizzler's steakhouse, where the manager, Ayala, harasses him to no end: "[I]f you can't do the job, you'll be out on your *culo* fast around here." Robert thinks about his mom, who needs his money, and "instead of telling him to fuck off, I nod and say, 'yes, boss'" (13). The effort to reunite with his family ends in failure, and he returns to San Antonio, where he works in construction but faces periodic layoffs. To make matters emotionally worse, his grandmother dies. He will inherit her small house and a small life insurance policy payout, and perhaps that will be the foundation that will permit him to get at least a toehold on life, but the future is unclear at best. His new girlfriend, Amelia, asks him what he will do. "I tell her that I don't know, and I don't. I'm not sure that I can be a college boy. I'm a drop-out after all. But the real answer is that I don't trust myself not to fuck up. I don't trust myself to do the things I have to do to make it" (237). Encouraged by his recollections of hard-working Grams as well as Amelia's reassuring presence in his life, he says, "I won't be a burro, and I will be a man." But the story concludes on an open-ended note, with no clear resolution. Sitting on a sofa with his head on her lap, Amelia sings softly to him, and as she sings, "I listen, and the funny thing, *the really great thing*, is that somewhere in there I stop thinking about tomorrow and find that I've let myself slip into the embrace of this day" (244).

Most of the action in Martinez's novel takes place in San Antonio, Texas; however, the middle of the novel allows us to witness this new world of youth in Southern California as well. Our final writer, Manuel Muñoz, sets his 2007 short story collection, *The Faith Healer of Olive Avenue*, exclusively in California, but in the Central Valley in and around Fresno, a part of the state often ignored, not only in Chicano fiction, but in the popular imagination of California. Some of this work references coastal California, but by way of San Francisco, itself something of an innovation in such fiction. But betwixt and between these two California

locales, the theme of male youthful depression and disillusionment continues. The title of the very first story, "Lindo y Querido," references a
popular mariachi song about a continuing loyalty to México from those
forced to leave that country. It was popularized in the 1950s by the great
Mexican singer Jorge Negrete, a continuing symbol of Mexican hetero-
sexuality and masculinity. Yet, the story is about the unfulfilled love and
growth of two gay teenage boys who keep their gayness a secret. Muñoz
deftly takes advantage of Negrete's hetero-masculine identification with
the song through the masculine form of *lindo* y querid*o* to underscore that
we are dealing with two young gay men who thought of each other as
lindo (lovely) and *querido* (loved).[28]

In their high school youth, one is killed and the other seriously maimed
in a motorcycle accident returning from a secret place in the country,
where they have gone to make love. Isidro is seriously disabled and bed
ridden, for what little remains of his life. His mother, Connie, abandoned
by her husband, cares for him while also cleaning white people's houses
in Fresno. Once again, the disability of the body and that of a society that
has marginalized Connie and her family are brought into interpretive
conjunction to sustain Minich's larger study of this issue among Mexican Americans.[29] When Isidro finally passes, Connie discovers the boys'
love secret in letters he had received from the now also deceased Carlos.
Because she cannot read English, she does not really know what the
letters say, but she knows enough to understand the pencil-drawn little
hearts on the pages and the signature, "Love, Carlos," at the end of each
letter. She is momentarily judgmental, but recalling her husband's abandonment, she realizes what real love can be, even though the boys do not
live to fulfill it as adult young men, perhaps by eventually moving to the
friendlier nearby San Francisco.

San Francisco also figures in another Muñoz story, "Bring, Brang,
Brung." We meet a young gay man named Martín Grijalva, a native of
Fresno, who, while living in San Francisco, has a lover, Adrian. Notwithstanding Martín's reservations, Adrian persuades him that they should
have a son with a host mother. But Adrian dies from a sudden aneurysm,
and to make ends meet, Martín is forced to return, with his son, Adán, to
his native Fresno, a place where no one, including his family and other

acquaintances, approved of his sexual preferences nor that he left Fresno for the big city and its cultural, if not real, capital for him.

Grieving and not even sure that he really loves his son—it was Adrian's idea, after all—he takes a job in a small accounting office, which "wasn't the best of circumstances: the building was on the south side, the more dangerous part of the city after dark, and the office was situated in a converted warehouse. . . . [D]rafts of the hot afternoon air somehow snaked past the corrugated paneling and into his office which was nothing more than walls of sheetrock" (33).[30] He is also conflicted about the lower-middle-class lives that his family and other Mexican Americans live in Fresno, lives of daily making do as compared to his precious existence in San Francisco. The family and acquaintances are represented by Perla, his sister; Candi, a school secretary; and Roberta Beltrán, the school's principal. He remembers all these people—these women—as losers in high school, Roberta as "a really fat girl" (36).

Yet, these same people are now willing to set aside their former prejudices and support him and his son in various ways. Even though Perla cleans houses for people to make a living and is herself a single mom, she takes care of Adán after school. On another occasion, a boy steals money from his son at school. The boy is caught by Candi and Roberta, and Martín is asked to come to the school to meet the perpetrator. On the way to the school, Martín recalls the disdain he felt toward Candi when he first enrolled Adán at the school and now thinks he should have been kinder. When he arrives, Candi is "busy with the phones and a string of kids slumped in plastic chairs against the wall." He had thought perhaps now he might speak to her, "but she was too busy now, and he regretted how he might have misread her before, her initial spark of forgiveness, of new possibilities, of growing and maturing, and how he had wiped it out by not returning her grace" (40–41).

He then meets the school principal, Roberta Beltrán, who greets him warmly and attends to the matter at hand with great professionalism. She insists that the boy who stole Adán's money write a note of apology to Martín, but the note only reinforces his own continuing and conflicted prejudices about his community. He immediately notices the poor grammar and diction in the note, the "crabbed penmanship," the use of "brang" instead of "bring" and recalls the same problems in his mother and sister's writing. The issue of language use becomes a window onto the whole of this community's failure but also his for his inability to reintegrate himself into his community: "Diction, syntax, grammar, basic math, conceptual thinking. Symmetries, the logic of sympathy, the order of gratitude, empathy, concern, the rigor of understanding, the faulty equation of grief and anger. He had failed, too, somewhere along the line" (44).

In another Muñoz story called "Señor X," Chris, a young Mexican American small-time criminal and now convict, is released on furlough from the local detention center, gets a part-time job at a paper mill in Fresno, and lives in a shoddy apartment complex called Las Palmas. His apartment overlooks the small house of an older man named Treviño, who befriends him and has him over to eat and drink. One night when Treviño has had too much to drink, he falls asleep, and Chris takes forty dollars from the old man's wallet. Later in his apartment, he is awakened because Treviño has set his house on fire accidentally and died in the flames, but Chris makes no effort to join the neighbors of Las Palmas who are trying to help. After the fire, "sleep would not come" for him. At dawn, he "witnessed the sky turn pink and light purple over what used to be Treviño's house. I kept feeling the bills, and when the morning light arrived in all its clarity, I lay down on my bed and forced myself to sleep" (180).

Almost all of Muñoz's stories are in this vein, young Mexican American males unable to integrate themselves successfully and productively in the life of their native community, which itself seems marked by failure, a people in malaise at the turn of the twentieth century. But the title story most evokes such a sense of failure. That it is the title story and comes at the end of the collection seem to suggest that the author intends it as his summation of the argument he has been making throughout. "The Faith Healer of Olive Avenue" opens with, again, a young Mexican American male, twenty-one-year-old Emilio, originally from Texas and now living with his father near Fresno. His mother has divorced them and left town. Once again, the protagonist is found in a low-paying job, loading pallets of paper for shipment from a paper mill some thirty miles from Fresno. Muñoz offers a detailed description of the job, as if to fully render the most intimate sense of the humdrum and physically demanding occupation so that we may know it and its subjects fully. We are thus able to lend some understanding to the workers' habit of secretly and furtively drinking on the job as well as grabbing pot-smoking breaks whenever they can, although they can be fired for such infractions. Thus, we see Emilio, during a late-night shift, "scuttling into an adjoining grape vineyard to smoke a joint" during a fifteen-minute break period: "Despite having already had more than a few sips of whiskey, he hurried with the joint, trying to savor it a little before smothering it in the thick dust of the vineyard, not wanting to be late back to his post" (218). No doubt in something of a fog, Emilio operates a forklift with a very large load of pallets of paper to be loaded onto trucks. Something goes wrong with the forklift, and as Emilio gets off to inspect it, "the wood of the pallet creaked with a sound that reminded him of an old bridge back in Texas." He looked up at "the ill-wrapped boxes of paper collapsing, the wooden pallet splintering and suddenly shifting the entire weight of the load," also causing the forklift itself to turn over on its side, with "Emilio futilely raising his hands to the massive amount of weight" (218–19). He hears people screaming, but no sound comes from his mouth, although he can see that the cement floor of the warehouse has gone slick with blood—his blood—and can also see work boots leaving bloody tracks as the men lift the paper boxes one by one from his body.

He will survive but as a totally disabled young man, who refuses to leave the house out of a sense of shame and whose severe disability will also cost him his girlfriend, Catri, whom he had hoped to marry but who will marry someone else and have a baby. His father, now aging, has to lift him from his bed and then from the wheelchair onto the toilet, or onto the chair in the kitchen for their meals, or into the car, a wheelchair that will over time callus his hands, a father who has to empty the bedpan every morning and spoon-feed his son, a traditional father who comes to believe that his son's accident and condition was somehow caused by some bad person giving Emilio *el mal ojo* (the evil eye). One morning, as the father is sitting with his son in the bathroom, he suddenly says in Spanish, "*allá en Fresno vive una curandera.*" Emilio does not believe in such, but his father clearly does, and Emilio is so overwhelmed by his father's enormous difficulties in caring for him that all he can say is, "Let's go then" (223–24).

I opened this chapter with recognition of Rudy Anaya's enduring and evocative young character Antonio Márez Luna, but always in relation to another curandera, the mythic Ultima. The curandera on Olive Avenue in Fresno whom Emilio and his father will consult is at some considerable distance from Ultima, not just temporally but in in her decidedly non-mythic identity. As they meet her, she is "barefoot . . . her black T-shirt was too long for her but still covered her prominent belly, and her faded blue jeans bulged at her thighs. Her lips bore a frosty shade of pink, and around each wrist she wore the bracelets that all the television commercials swore had healing powers, the ones with the tiny balls at each end, not quite meeting" (228).

After a bit of back and forth about God, devils, and the evil eye, the woman goes into her house and then comes back with a Gerber baby-food jar, containing a cream whose application she then demonstrates. "His father took out his wallet and laid out bill after bill" in her hands, which she counted, then "folded the bills and reached deep into the black T-shirt to hide the bills in her bra" (229). They leave with Emilio convinced "that she would hold nothing but empty promises, visits extending as long as his father's wallet held out" (230). Yet every night his father tries, smoothing the cream onto Emilio's "thin legs, white, and nearly hairless, working the mixture over his knees all the way down to his ankles, over the ugly scars" (238). After his father is done with the treatment, Emilio lies in the dark and thinks of Catri, of his mother and father, of drugs and whiskey, of "love and not having it, of who had it and who got to keep it." Then he reached for the little jar of cream, opened it, "and smelled the lard, the oranges, the pepper. He took the little bit of crema that was left in the jar and worked it onto the calluses on each of his palms, a long moment of circling his fingers in the dark violet of early morning, and when he was done, they felt smooth and absolutely brand-new" (239).

Muñoz will not offer us an easy way out of this crisis of young manhood seemingly afflicting Mexican America, one that is articulated by the disability of the body as a consequence of low-wage labor. We can again connect the disabilities of the Mexican American human body and the body politic as Minich has done. Yet, while we can certainly give great causative power to the political economy and its inflictions on the human body, in this story, as in "Big Jesse, Little Jesse," we cannot help but sense that both authors are also critically evaluating what culture has become and the role of personal responsibility within that culture and within the political economy. In Muñoz's view, nothing seems to work anymore—schooling, occupations, sex, substance abuse—but he also explores the individual sense of responsibility in an ultimately unjust world. The "traditional" cure offered by the faith healer on Olive Avenue is now merely just another cream that at least makes calluses feel better, but in offering such a fake cure, the traditional curandera is now merely a charlatan and a cultural failure, (dark) light years away from Ultima as are the young men of today in comparison to the young men that defined the fiction of the early seventies, like Anaya's Antonio.

But is this only fiction? Is there any correspondence between these characters and any social reality? In *Citizens in the Present: Youth Civic Engagement in the Americas* (2013), social scientists Maria de los Angeles Torres, Irene Rizzini, and Norma Del Río remind us that youth in the West who become fully mature young adults historically have (1) left the parental home and established new living arrangements; (2) completed formal education; (3) formed close, stable relationships outside the family, often resulting in marriage and children; and (4) tested the labor market, finding work and possibly settling into a career, and achieving a more or less sustainable livelihood. They also note that in the current moment, "these measures are deeply affected by economic restructuring that has been brought about by globalization. . . . More youth are living at home, and even after completing their education, many are not finding viable employment and are postponing marriage and parenthood."[31] Torres, Rizzini, and Del Río also caution against an "artificial notion of a homogeneous 'youth'[, which] can hide the deep differences in which young people of various backgrounds experience being young," undoubtedly including racial and class marginality.[32]

Two other social scientists, Roberto Suro and B. Lindsey Powell, statistically document this millennial economic condition:

> The long-term effects of the recession will likely depress employment and incomes in Hispanic communities at least through the

end of 2004, and judging from historical experience that time span will be longer than for any other major population group. Even if predictions of a turnaround later this summer prove valid, pocketbook issues will vex Latinos for several years after the national economy recovers.

Second-generation Latinos—U.S.-born children of an immigrant parent—are now experiencing high job losses. In recent recessions Hispanic unemployment has fallen hardest on low-skilled immigrants. This time, young people who are the products of U.S. schools are experiencing the highest unemployment rate among Latinos. Many work in skilled occupations, including managers, technicians and professionals, and many are in the early years of household formation. Prolonged joblessness could prove a historic setback for them, their communities and the nation.[33]

That is, even in an economically marginalized condition, an "Anglo" culture of consumption seems to have done away with older and perhaps more socially stabilizing and more clearly ethnic Latino cultures. Young Latinos may be more enveloped in what David Harvey, Fredric Jameson, and others have critiqued as a culturally flattening, late capitalist postmodern condition.[34] Some years ago, I called attention to how this condition was already having adverse effects on Mexican American youths as early as the 1970s.[35]

Within and against such circumstances, these scholars nevertheless find substantial evidence of such marginalized youth engaging in civic action to better their conditions and those of their native communities, with projects more localized than those master narratives and activities of the sixties epitomized in the words of Crosby, Stills, Nash, and Young: "We can change the world / rearrange the world."[36] Yet it remains curiously and disturbingly the case that the contemporary Mexican American fiction I have discussed is wholly untouched by such civic action. Rather than high moral, political, or cultural purpose expressed in relatively linear narratives of development, we find the young men in Mexican American contemporary fiction—Bony, big Jesse, Robert,

Isidro, Chris, and Emilio—*in medias res* within a stylistically dispersed and thematic world, which Bill Buford has called "dirty realism," in writings that are

> unadorned, unfurnished, low-rent tragedies about people who watch day-time television, read cheap romances or listen to country western music. They are waitresses in roadside cafés, cashiers in supermarkets, construction workers, secretaries and unemployed cowboys. They play bingo, eat cheeseburgers, hunt deer, and stay in cheap hotels. They drink a lot and are often in trouble: for stealing a car, breaking a window, pickpocketing a wallet. They are from Kentucky, Alabama or Oregon, but mainly they could just about be from anywhere: drifters in a world cluttered with junk food and the oppressive details of modern consumerism.[37]

But I also wish to underscore what I trust is now obvious, namely that we have been examining a fictive world of young Mexican American working-class *males.* Is an answer, or at least some form of resolution, to this seeming contradiction between the realities and fictive depictions of marginalized youth to be found in gender? Perhaps. I close by returning to one of the social scientists noted earlier, María de los Angeles Torres, who studied youth activists specifically in Chicago. She says, "of the young people with whom we spoke, seven were males, and eighteen females. The fact that most were female was not surprising. In many countries, more females than males are involved in these kinds of projects. For the females, gender was an important part of how they defined themselves."[38] As a broader consideration of this gender disparity, it is of little consolation that Latino boys consistently score lower than their Latina counterparts in various measures of educational attainment.[39] Returning to the contemporary fiction I have examined, it is of the greatest interest that women often stand out as creative, intelligent, energetic, and supportive foils in these fictive worlds of male malaise and ineptitude. These include the ex-wife, Corina, in Casares's "Big Jesse, Little Jesse"; Grams, Robert Lomo's grandmother, and his girlfriend, Amelia, in Martinez's novel *Drift*; and, Connie, the strong, hard-working, and loving mother in Muñoz's "Lindo y Querido," as well as the three women in his "Bring, Brang, Brung." Only the regrettable curandera in "The Faith Healer" is an exception. (Although not within the scope of this chapter, an extended examination of Chicana fiction for this period would likely show women figures of even greater strength and affirmation, such as la loca in *So Far from God*, Estrella in *Under the Feet of Jesus*, and various women characters in *Woman Hollering Creek*, although Cisneros can be more circumspect on this matter, as shown in her character Clemencia in "Never Marry a Mexican.")[40]

In and of itself, gender difference may not be enough of an explanatory variable, but together with the postmodern condition, a particular kind of social emasculation may be at work against a significant sector of Mexican American male youth today, a male working-class culture that is now at some considerable distance from Rudy Anaya's Antonio and that era. To paraphrase Yeats, today this is no country for young men. To the credit of our young contemporary writers, they are witnessing and critiquing this new male sociocultural moment with unflinching candor and alerting us to a new crisis and our concomitant social responsibility in the twenty-first century.

NOTES

1. Anaya, *Bless Me, Ultima*.
2. Lipsitz, *Time Passages*, 120.
3. Originally a traditional English ballad transplanted to the U.S. South, "The House of the Rising Sun" became an African American folksong and could have also referred to a women's prison in New Orleans, hence the "ball and chain" reference in the lyrics. The traditional folksong version refers to "poor girl" rather than the "poor boy" in the contemporary version.
4. Kazan, *On the Waterfront*.
5. Ray, *Rebel Without a Cause*.
6. Nichols, *The Graduate*.
7. Villarreal, *Pocho*; Rodríguez, *Hunger of Memory*. Yet, *Pocho* is certainly preceded in its alienation and even more so by Américo Paredes's then-unpublished novel from the 1940s, *George Washington Gómez: A Mexico-Texan Novel*.
8. Lipsitz, *Time Passages*, 175.
9. Gómez-Quiñones and Vásquez, *Making Aztlán*.
10. Saldívar, *Chicano Narrative*, 74–90.
11. Hinojosa, *Ask a Policeman* and *Partners in Crime*.

12. Cantú, "Degradación y regeneración."

13. Saldívar, *Chicano Narrative*, 126.

14. Padilla, "Land of Enchantment."

15. Trujillo, *Land of Disenchantment*.

16. Anaya, *Zia Summer, Rio Grande Fall, Jemez Spring*, and *Shaman Winter*.

17. Montejano, *Anglos and Mexicans*, 298.

18. Ibid.

19. Ibid., 299.

20. Limón, "Transnational Triangulation."

21. The linguistic reduction of his name from the traditional Bonifacio (nice face) to the less than attractive Bony already marks his fate.

22. All page numbers cited in the text are from the original edition of Casares, *Brownsville*.

23. Minich, "Disabling La Frontera," 42, 45.

24. Ibid., 45.

25. Martínez, *Boy Kings of Texas*.

26. All page numbers cited in the text are from the original edition of Martínez, *Drift*. A burro is, of course, literally a small donkey, but people of Mexican origin often use it as a metaphor for someone who is dim witted, uneducated, or a simpleton.

27. Barbacoa, also called *barbacoa de cabeza*, refers to all the meat on the head of a cow, including the eyes, brains, and tongue, which is pit cooked over hot coals or steamed in an oven for a long time until tender. Very much a working-class food, it is consumed with tortillas and salsa throughout much of México and Mexican America, often as a festive ritual meal on weekends. See Montano, "History of Mexican Folk Foodways."

28. "Mexico Lindo y Querido" was written by Chucho Monge in 1943.

29. Minich, *Accessible Citizenships*.

30. All page numbers cited in the text are from the original edition of Muñoz, *Faith Healer*.

31. Torres, Rizzini, and Del Río, *Citizens in the Present*, 12.

32. Ibid., 5.

33. Suro and Powell, *New Lows from New Highs*, iii.

34. Harvey, *Condition of Post-Modernity*; Jameson, *Postmodernism*.

35. Limón, *Dancing with the Devil*. See especially chapter 5, "Emergent Postmodern Mexicano."

36. From the song "Chicago," written by Graham Nash (New York: Atlantic, 1971).

37. Buford, *Dirty Realism*, 4.

38. M Torres, "Chicago Youth Activists," 31.

39. "Educational Achievement," The Boys Initiative, accessed December 2, 2015, www.boysinitiative.org/facts-figures/educational-achievement.

40. Castillo, *So Far from God*; Viramontes, *Under the Feet of Jesus*; Cisneros, *Woman Hollering Creek*.

BIBLIOGRAPHY

Anaya, Rudolfo A. *Bless Me, Ultima.* Berkeley, CA: Quinto Sol, 1972.

———. *Jemez Spring.* Albuquerque: University of New Mexico Press, 2005.

———. *Shaman Winter.* Albuquerque: University of New Mexico Press, 2009.

———. *Randy Lopez Goes Home.* Norman: University of Oklahoma Press, 2011.

———. *Rio Grande Fall.* Albuquerque: University of New Mexico Press, 2008.

———. *Zia Summer.* New York: Warner Books, 1995.

Buford, Bill. *Dirty Realism: New Writing from America.* Cambridge: Granta Publications, 1983.

Cantú, Roberto. "Degradación y regeneración en *Bless Me, Ultima:* el chicano y la vida nueva." In *The Identification and Analysis of Chicano Literature,* edited by Francisco Jiménez, 374–88. New York: Bilingual Press, 1979.

Casares, Oscar. *Brownsville.* Boston, MA: Back Bay Books, 2003.

Castillo, Ana. *So Far from God.* New York: Norton, 2005.

Cisneros, Sandra. *Woman Hollering Creek, and Other Stories.* New York: Vintage, 1992.

Gómez-Quiñones, Juan, and Irene Vásquez. *Making Aztlán: Ideology and Culture of the Chicana and Chicano Movement, 1966–1977.* Albuquerque: University of New Mexico Press, 2014.

Harvey, David. *The Condition of Post-Modernity.* Cambridge: Blackwell, 1989.

Heller, Joseph. *Catch-22.* New York: Simon and Schuster, 1961.

Hinojosa, Rolando. *Ask a Policeman: A Rafe Buenrostro Mystery.* Houston, TX: Arte Público Press, 1998.

———. *Estampas del Valle y Otras Obras.* Berkeley, CA: Quinto Sol, 1973.

———. *Partners in Crime: A Rafe Buenrostro Mystery.* Houston, TX: Arte Público Press, 2011.

Jameson, Fredric. *Postmodernism, or the Cultural Logic of Late Capitalism.* Durham, NC: Duke University Press, 1992.

Kazan, Elia, dir. *On the Waterfront.* Los Angeles: Columbia Pictures, 1954. Film.

Limón, José E. *Dancing with the Devil: Society and Cultural Poetics in Mexican-American South Texas.* Madison: University of Wisconsin Press, 1994.

———. "Transnational Triangulation: Mexico, the United States, and the Emergence of a Mexican-American Middle Class." In *Mexico and Mexicans in the Making of the United States,* edited by John Tutino, 236–56. Austin: University of Texas Press, 2012.

Lipsitz, George. *Time Passages: Collective Memory and American Popular Culture.* Minneapolis: University of Minnesota Press, 1990.

Martínez, Domingo. *The Boy Kings of Texas: A Memoir.* Guilford, CT: Lyons Press, 2012.

Martínez, Manuel Luis. *Drift.* New York: Picador, 2003.

Minich, Julie Avril. *Accessible Citizenships: Disability, Nation, and the Cultural Politics of Greater Mexico.* Philadelphia, PA: Temple University Press, 2013.

————. "Disabling La Frontera: Disability, Border Subjectivity, and Masculinity in 'Big Jesse, Little Jesse' by Oscar Casares." *MELUS* 35 no. 1 (2010): 35–52.

Montano, Mario. "The History of Mexican Folk Foodways of South Texas: Street Vendors, Offal Foods, and *barbacoa de cabeza*." Ph.D. diss., University of Pennsylvania, 1992. *ProQuest* (AAI9308630).

Montejano, David. *Anglos and Mexicans in the Making of Texas, 1836-1986*. Austin: University of Texas Press, 1987.

Muñoz, Manuel. *The Faith Healer of Olive Avenue: Stories*. Chapel Hill, NC.: Algonquin Books, 2007.

Nichols, Mike, dir. *The Graduate*. Los Angeles: United Artists, 1967. Film.

Padilla, Laura. "Land of Enchantment, Land of mi Chante: Four Arguments in New Mexican Literature." Ph.D. diss., University of Texas at Austin, 2006.

Paredes, Américo. *George Washington Gómez: A Mexico-Texan Novel*. Houston, TX: Arte Público Press, 1990.

Ray, Nicholas, dir. *Rebel Without a Cause*. Los Angeles: Warner Bros, 1955. Film.

Rivera, Tomás. *Y no se lo tragó la tierra / And the earth did not part*. Berkeley, CA: Quinto Sol, 1971.

Rodríguez, Richard. *Hunger of Memory: The Education of Richard Rodríguez*. New York: Godine, 1982.

Saldívar, Ramón. *Chicano Narrative: The Dialectics of Difference*. Madison: University of Wisconsin Press, 1990.

Salinger, J. D. *Catcher in the Rye*. New York: Little, Brown, 1951.

Suro, Roberto, and B. Lindsey Powell. *New Lows from New Highs: Latino Economic Losses in the Current Recession*. Washington, DC: Pew Hispanic Center, January 24, 2002.

Torres, Maria de los Angeles. "Chicago Youth Activists: Home Matters in Their Search for Democracy." In *Citizens in the Present: Youth Civic Engagement in the Americas*, edited by Maria de los Angeles Torres, Irene Rizzini, and Norma Del Río, 145–72. Urbana: University of Illinois Press, 2013.

Torres, Maria de los Angeles, Irene Rizzini, and Norma Del Río, eds. *Citizens in the Present: Youth Civic Engagement in the Americas*. Urbana: University of Illinois Press, 2013.

Trujillo, Michael. *Land of Disenchantment: Latin/o Identities and Transformations in Northern New Mexico*. Albuquerque: University of New Mexico Press, 2009.

Villarreal, José Antonio. *Pocho*. New York: Doubleday, 1959.

Viramontes, Helena María. *Under the Feet of Jesus*. New York: Plume, 1996.

Williams, Tennessee. *Sweet Bird of Youth*. New York: New Directions, 1959.

4

The Nature of *Jalamanta*

RELIGIOUS, PHILOSOPHICAL, SPIRITUAL,
AND POLITICAL INTERCONNECTIONS IN
RUDOLFO ANAYA'S ECOLOGICAL NOVEL

María Herrera-Sobek

> We will meet on the Path of the Sun,
> Seeking internal clarity and peace.
> We meet as brothers and sisters,
> Knowing each soul reflects the other.
> —*Jalamanta*, book epigraph

Many of Rudolfo Anaya's works are characterized by a strong spirituality and a deep concern for the environment. His novels, in particular, exhibit a love and respect for nature and a spiritual connection with the universe and all its manifestations, both animate and inanimate. *Bless Me, Ultima* (1972) is a prime example of how Anaya encodes his ecological belief system into the narrative's structure, but it is not the only one. In this chapter, I posit that Anaya's *Jalamanta: A Message from the Desert* (1996) is infused with spiritual discursions on humanity's interconnections with nature and the cosmos and underscores his central philosophical position that the universe and all that is within it, whether sentient or not, are interconnected. In *Jalamanta*, the Chicano author constructs a unified philosophical, religious, spiritual, political, and ecological tract, incorporating the literary structure of the novel as a vehicle to articulate and inscribe his philosophical thoughts in these areas. By "novel," I reference two definitions of the

---

All page numbers for quotations from Rudolfo Anaya's *Jalamanta* refer to the 1996 edition.

genre: Margaret Anne Doody's, found in her book *The True Story of the Novel* (1996), and Ian Watt's definition as stated in *The Rise of the Novel* (1957). Doody's description is comprehensive in scope and critiqued for its all-encompassing grasp. She classifies a literary work as a novel if it has three basic structural components: "[I]f it is fictional, if it is in prose and if it is of a certain length" (quoted in MacKay 2011, 21). A more traditional and accepted characterization is the one offered by Ian Watt:

> The novel is a full and authentic report of human experience, and is therefore under an obligation to satisfy its reader with such details of the story as the individuality of the actors concerned, the particulars of the times and places of their action, details which are presented through a more largely referential use of language than is common in other literary forms. (quoted in MacKay 2011, 23)

Jalamanta fits both definitions of the novel offered by these critics.

Jalamanta consists of twenty-seven chapters with a simple plot: the protagonist, Amado, meaning beloved, but renamed Jalamanta while wandering in the desert, returns from exile to his faithful and loving partner, Fatimah. At the urging of local exiled community members, Jalamanta begins to expound on multiple philosophical subjects regarding what he learned and reflected on during his nomadic existence in the barren lands of the desert. His teachings are viewed as unorthodox and dangerous by the local moral authority (also cited as central authority), a militaristic and dictatorial group in power. He is eventually betrayed to the harsh ruling elites by a childhood friend and is taken prisoner to be interrogated and most likely severely punished. Each chapter in *Jalamanta* focuses on specific metaphysical issues related to the mind, body, and soul. In particular, the novel incorporates the theme of Maya's veil as a metaphor for all that prevents humans from acknowledging their true selves and that inhibits them from perceiving the "light" that will lead them to a harmonious existence, happiness, and world peace. The title, *Jalamanta*, composed of two words—*jala*, meaning "pull" as in pull off, and *manta*, or cloth—clearly depicts the function of the protagonist, who will aid his community in pulling the wool from their eyes, so to speak, and in this manner help them achieve a more enlightened life.

The *Jalamanta* narrative also adheres to the paradigmatic model of the adventure of the hero monomyth as elucidated by myth scholar Joseph Campbell in his study *The Hero with a Thousand Faces* (1973). The hero's monomyth in turn is based on the rites of passage as first postulated by Arnold van Gennep in his ground-breaking work *Les rites de passage* (1909). The basic structure of the rites of passage includes the tripartite elements of separation, initiation, and return.

The adventure of the hero monomyth as posited by Campbell include these structural components:

    I. Departure
        1. The Call to Adventure
        2. Refusal of the Call
        3. Supernatural Aid
        4. The Crossing of the First Threshold
        5. The Belly of the Whale
    II. Initiation
        1. The Road of Trials
        2. The Meeting with the Goddess
        3. Woman as the Temptress
        4. Atonement with the Father
        5. Apotheosis
        6. The Ultimate Boon
    III. Return
        1. Refusal of the Return
        2. The Magic Flight
        3. Rescue from Without
        4. The Crossing of the Returned Threshold
        5. Master of the Two Worlds
        6. Freedom to Live (Campbell 1973)

Of course, not all the elements cited above are present in the *Jalamanta* hero monomyth. Campbell warns:

Many tales isolate and greatly enlarge upon one or two of the typical elements of the full cycle (test motif, flight motif, abduction of the bride; others string a number of independent cycles into a single series as in the *Odyssey*). Differing characters or episodes can become fused, or a single element can reduplicate itself and reappear under many changes. (1973, 246)

Campbell's summary of the monomyth covers the main elements: "A hero ventures forth from the world of common day into a region of supernatural wonder: Fabulous forces are there encountered and a decisive victory is won: the hero comes back from this mysterious adventure with the power to bestow boons on his fellow man" (1973, 30).

Jalamanta begins the adventure of the hero monomyth with the return of the protagonist who bears that name. Convicted of heresy as a young man by the moral authority, the ruling powers from the Seventh City of the Fifth Sun, he was exiled to the unforgiving and deadly environment of the desert for thirty years. While wandering in that arid and desolate region, Jalamanta encountered wise elders who saved his life and soul. These prophets helped him to see the light, to become spiritually enlightened: "In the desert I became a new person, and during my initiation my guide named me Jalamanta: Jala means to pull, and mantas means veils. I am Jalamanta, he who pulls away the veils that blind the soul" (26).

The desert became a transformative space for the protagonist; a rebirth transpired in the womb of this inhospitable wasteland. After roaming for thirty years in that bleak geographical space, Jalamanta is energized from his experience and from the knowledge he has gained through his own introspection and self-reflection as well as the teachings of the local prophets. When a twinge of doubt clouds his mind, he tells himself: "Dispel the doubt. . . . You have crossed the desert and spoken to the elders of many tribes. They have shown you the Path of the Sun. Walk with clarity in your heart and speak with clarity. Everything else will give way to that truth" (25).

After Jalamanta's spiritual transformation while in exile, he returns to his community to impart the knowledge he has gained, in keeping with the hero monomyth journey. He is warmly received by the people who live outside the limits of the Seventh City. Here he begins to teach the philosophical and spiritual insights he gained during his banishment. His teachings, while welcomed by the people in the community, are viewed as subversive and revolutionary by the oppressive police state, the Seventh City of the Fifth Sun, which enforces the proper way to think and behave.

Jalamanta's subversive teachings are the platform through which Anaya articulates his different belief systems: philosophical, religious/spiritual, ecological, and political.

Jalamanta, therefore, is an important contribution to the study of Anaya's overall literary oeuvre. It aids the Anaya reader in understanding the author's past and future writings, because in this rather unusual novel are inscribed the various belief systems extant in his other more "traditional" creative writings. In the pages that follow, I examine some of the major belief systems presented in *Jalamanta* and the influences that have aided in shaping the worldviews expressed therein.

PHILOSOPHICAL BELIEF SYSTEM
Greek Philosophical Influences

Anaya's fictional narrative exhibits close connections with the early Greek philosophers. A significant portion of the novel, for example, is structured as a dialectic exchange between "prophet" and "disciples." Questions regarding the cosmos, God, and ethics are posed by different members of the community to the newly returned desert wanderer. Jalamanta proceeds to answer the questions with long discourses into the nature of the earth and the cosmos as well as of the body, mind, and soul of human beings and other entities. He shares key philosophical concepts with ancient Greek philosophers from approximately 585 B.C., such as the unitary principle. For example, Thales believed in a unitary principle of explanation for the fundamental question of "What is the source of all things?" (Allen 1991, 2). For Thales, the single primordial element, water, was "unbounded"; he further believed that this water was "alive" (2). Anaximander, from the same era, also adhered to a unitary principle of explanation, although he did not tie it to water but tied it to the "Boundless" (3). As Reginald E. Allen explains in his book *Greek Philosophy: Thales to Aristotle* (1991), Anaximander thought that "the universe is bound to a single principle . . . and that nature is one whole" (3). On the other hand, another Greek philosopher, Anaximenes, posed the concept of matter as that out of which all things are made. He further speculated that this primordial "stuff" was alive, "ensouled," and made of air (4).

A second major concept found in *Jalamanta* is that of harmony. Here again, we find parallels with the philosophy of Anaximander, who first posited that "balance or harmony is a principle of nature and the equilibrium of the world process is its product." (Allen 1991, 4). The views of the well-known philosopher Socrates are also inscribed in Anaya's philosophical work. The edict "Know thyself," found on the portals of the temple at Delphi, is a fundamental commandment in *Jalamanta*. Socrates explains in Plato's *Apology* that our goal in life "is to make one's soul as good as possible," since this will lead to human happiness, and "human happiness is based on self-knowledge" (Allen 1991, 17) Socrates, like Jalamanta, challenged Greek rules and customs via the Socratic method of teaching (17). Through this method, Socrates achieved his goal of making each person listening to his lectures arrive at his or her own conclusions regarding moral values and "truths" (18). As is well known, Socrates was put to death for his revolutionary teachings. As Allen describes it, the social fraying of the Athenian fabric gave impetus to the unraveling of Greek society and the rampant distrust of citizens pitted neighbor against neighbor (18). Allen asserts:

> Socrates's relentless examinations often called in question the rules and customs of conventional Greek morality. The very basis of his ethics challenged the morality of social habit in the name of a higher morality of spiritual aspiration. Each man must see his own good, must come to understand for himself. The goal is the autonomous moral life of the wise man, which cannot be governed by any set of rules imposed from without. But the latter part of the fifth century, particularly in Athens, was a time of social disorder, a time when men were in doubt who did not know how to doubt. For many Athenians, the old order, which they knew to be passing away, became a symbol of all that was fair in the life of Greece; criticism became heresy and change, unthinkable. And because Socrates criticized, and refused to give over, he was regarded as a sophist and put to death. The charge against him could hardly have been more ironic: He had corrupted the youth and introduced strange gods. (1991, 18)

Jalamanta is also castigated by the moral authority for his supposedly heretical beliefs. The conclusion of the novel is open ended, for the protagonist is taken in to the offices of the moral authority for questioning, and since he does not agree to recant nor to cease teaching his vision of the world, the reader is left to surmise that he will be exiled again, imprisoned, or even put to death.

Jalamanta, in a similar manner to Socrates, teaches that to know oneself we have to be free from all that prevents us from seeing the true light; the words "clarity" and "light" are important nouns in the narrative and are repeated numerous times throughout the chapters. A crucial activity necessary for achieving enlightenment and for being able to "know oneself" is to eliminate the "veils" that hide the truth from us. Jalamanta declares:

> A veil is an illusion that blinds the soul. . . . Anger, hate, bigotry, greed, excessive pleasures and gratification, and many other selfish desires take possession of the mind and body. When one gives to those desires, the care of the soul is neglected and forgotten. Those veils block the clarity of vision that we seek. I teach a way of knowledge, a way to remove the veils that blind the soul. (26)

The Nature of the Universe

In *Jalamanta's* chapter 4, "The First Creation," Anaya (via Jalamanta) delves deeply into what he perceives is the nature of the universe. For the protagonist, the sun is the embodiment of the "energy and imagination of the First Creation" (41), and he perceives the First Creation as "love that was the seed in the womb of time" (43). Equally important, the sun—or "Parent Sun," as he calls the big incandescent star—is a critical component of the cosmos, for "sunlight is a reflection of the vital energy of the universe," and this "reflection is all we know of the First Creation" (42). Furthermore, Jalamanta affirms that the First Creation is an "act of Divine Love" (43) and that the "light of the First Creation spread through the universe" (46). It is clear from reading the novel that Anaya adheres to the big bang scientific theory of the origins of the universe, mainly that the universe was created at one point in time with a big "bang," or explosion. Jalamanta also links creativity and imagination with the creation of the cosmos, as well as with love (80). For him, the nature of the Universal Spirit is tightly bound with love and with God; that is, God and the Universal Spirit are one and the same. These thoughts also coincide with some biblical teachings, which I come back to later in this chapter.

The Nature of the Soul

Anaya's conceptualization of the soul in *Jalamanta*, as an immortal entity, resonates with Pythagoras's (b. 570 B.C.) theories of the soul, that, "the soul is immortal and can experience incarnation in various forms of animal life" (Allen 1991, 6). In addition, Jalamanta's teachings coincide with those of Socrates and Plato, who regarded the soul as immortal as well as divine and rational (ibid., 19). The prophet Jalamanta declares that everything dies; that there is birth, growth, and death; and that "The body dies, but the soul lives on returning to the cosmic wind and the light that sweeps around the universe" (129). Furthermore, "Our light within is a reflection of the soul of the universe, and so it is part of the consciousness of the universe," and all of us contribute to this expanding consciousness (130).

The soul is a very important element in the *Jalamanta* narrative. Jalamanta begins at the outset, in the first chapter, "The Exile Returns," with a definition of the soul, which he considers "an entity of light within" and an "essence that seeks clarity" (3). Issues that may prevent the soul from achieving clarity are the "veils" that cast shadows on the soul and "hide the light" (3). The prophet posits a tripartite structure in a person's overall makeup: the body, the mind, and the soul, with the body being the "temple of the soul." Given the three divisions of a person's structural makeup, problems arise when the mind and the body supersede the soul's function. The mind creates different "selves" with numerous needs and desires, while the body becomes engrossed with its own needs. It is the soul that can "transcend the limitations of the mind and body. The soul yearns to be one with the Universal Light" (18). Nevertheless, the soul can also be fooled, and Jalamanta cites "anger, hate, bigotry, greed, excessive pleasures and gratification" as activities that can act as veils that prevent the soul from seeing true reality (26). Only when clarity is achieved can the soul merge with the consciousness of the universe (28). Another significant issue related to the soul is the concept of harmony. Jalamanta informs his audience that the soul needs to be free of strife and tension, which the desires of the mind and body create. We can achieve freedom from these negative energies by meditation, by walking the Path of the Sun and letting the light into our souls. Morning meditation, when the sun's rays begin to peek from the night's darkness, is especially effective in clearing the mind from the shadows of strife and disharmony. The soul yearns to be in communion with other souls, especially the soul of the universe.

Anaya dedicates chapter 9, aptly titled "The Soul," to detailed discussions regarding the nature of the soul and defining it via Jalamanta as "reflections of that imaginative birth that brought the first spark into consciousness. The stream of light in the universe is uninterrupted; it flows from the First Source outward, like a wind of light sweeping across the universe. Our souls are reflections of that consciousness, part of that cosmic wind" (80). Furthermore, Jalamanta contends that "the essence of the soul is love" (83) and later adds: "The essence within that resonates to the clarity of light is what I call the soul" (85). While the mind and the body disappear when death overtakes them, the soul remains because the composition of the soul is pure energy and cannot die. The protagonist posits that the soul is immortal. Nevertheless, the soul can become "fragmented" from the veils visited on it or from the crisis one experiences when filled with doubt. The author calls this "The Dark Night of the Soul" and expounds on this aspect in chapter 22, "The Fragmented Soul." Although the soul cannot perish, since it is pure energy and, according to the laws of thermodynamics, "energy cannot be created or destroyed," it can become fragmented. When this happens, a healer can be summoned to help the individual reconfigure (heal) his or her soul and become whole again. Jalamanta tells his listening audience how a healer works in putting back together a fragmented soul: "The healer becomes a guide, someone who knows that injury to the soul means the soul has taken flight. The healer teaches you to fly to recover your soul" (167).

The Nature of God

Jalamanta's conceptualization of the nature of the universe is closely linked to the nature of God, or what he denominates as the Universal Spirit, which I interpret to mean God. The First Creation, or the birth of the universe, is related to an act of Divine Love. This act of Divine Love emanates from God—the Universal Spirit. This light connects to our souls and to the Universal Spirit. Furthermore, by joining our souls, which are pure energy, to the Universal Spirit, we merge and become God. Jalamanta wonders if the audience is ready to hear his most startling viewpoint: "[T]he purpose of clarity was to become God. . . . [T]he person on the Path of the Sun was filling the soul with light, and that was the path of becoming God" (85). This concept of "becoming God" is reiterated: "The soul is the Holy Grail filled with love and light and that in seeking unity with the Universal Spirit the soul was becoming God" (90). In other words, when the soul is infused with light, it joins the Universal Spirit's energy and becomes one entity.

This concept of becoming God is easy to understand if we subscribe to the theory that our essence as human beings, our souls, are indestructible because they are pure energy. When we die, this energy merges with the Universal Spirit (read energy) of the universe. This conceptualization of the nature of God and the expanding universe, plus the concept of humans becoming God, is expressed in Incan religious philosophy. Carlos Mendivil Capaerth, in his book *El Imperio de los Inkas: The Story of the Inkan Empire* (2014), explains the Incan concept:

> For the Inkan philosophers, the world was divided into three dimensions: The Heavens, the Earth and the Underground World. The Heavens were called **Hanan Pacha** and there dwelled the gods and the souls of human beings who became gods through their own efforts. The **Amautas** would say that it was the common and inexorable destiny of the whole of mankind to truly become human beings and afterwards, gods. The **Kay Pacha** is the Earth where the humans live. Life was seen as a long trip; an odyssey to return or re-unite with our Origin and End; God. The **Ukhu Pacha** is the Underground world, under the earth, where the **Huari** dwell

and where the souls of humans rest after death, waiting for their next opportunity to live and thus, continue on the return trip to God. (67; boldface in the original)

The concept of humans becoming gods is an old one, shared by various religions, as can be seen in the Incan religion.

RELIGIOUS INFLUENCES
Biblical

Jalamanta is infused with religious concepts acquired from four main areas: biblical scriptures, Hinduism, Aztec cosmology, and Incan religious teachings. I comment on the Incan concepts above and focus on the other three areas in this section. The Judeo-Christian biblical teachings are evident throughout *Jalamanta*; for example, the structure of the novel is based on the figure of Jesus. Jalamanta is portrayed as a Jesus-like figure, full of wisdom and love for his fellow human beings, for the earth, and for the environment. Many of his teachings, such as love and respect for one another, respect for the animal world and for our earth, as well as concepts of immortality, are closely linked to biblical precepts and teachings.

In the Bible, there are similar teachings regarding loving one another. In I John 4:7 (King James Version), John preaches: "Beloved, let us love one another: for love is of God; and every one that loveth is born of God, and knoweth God." In I John 4:8 the preaching continues: "He that loveth not knoweth not God; for God is love." And I John 4:11 states: "Beloved, if God so loved us, we ought also to love one another." And finally in I John 4:21, the above philosophy of love is reiterated: "And this commandment have we from him, That he who loveth God love his brother also."

Jalamanta, like Jesus Christ, spends time in the desert (thirty years to be exact) meditating and gaining self-knowledge, and then returns to preach what he has learned to his community. Also, as Jesus was betrayed by Judas, Jalamanta is betrayed by Iago, his friend, to the moral authority, whom we assume will find him guilty and imprison him, exile him once again, or even execute him for the supposed crime of heresy.

Aztec Cosmology

Aztec religious expressions are found in the concepts related to the belief of previous eras on earth. The Aztecs believed they were presently living in the era of the Fifth Sun. Earlier there had existed four different eras, or Suns, on earth, which had been born, developed, and then destroyed. The Fifth Sun is invoked in several chapters of the *Jalamanta* narrative. It is particularly salient when Jalamanta presents an optimistic view for the future. He informs members of the community listening to his teachings that we are living in the era of the Fifth Sun, and that the era of the Sixth Sun, it is hoped, will be one of harmony, love for one another, and understanding. Miguel León-Portilla informs us that:

> Para el pensamiento náhuatl, el mundo había existido no una, sino varias veces consecutivas. La primera fundamentación de la tierra había tenido lugar hacia muchos milenios. Otros cuatro soles o edades habían existido antes de la época presente. Durante todo este tiempo había habido una cierta evolución en espiral en la que aparecieron formas cada vez mejores de seres humanos, de plantas y de elementos. (1986, 7n1)

> [For Náhuatl thought, the world had existed not once but several consecutive times. The original founding of the world had occurred several million years ago. There had existed four other Suns, or epochs, previous to the present one. During these consecutive periods, a certain evolution, spiral like, transpired in which the new forms of human beings appearing were superior to the previous ones; this was also true for plants and other elements of the earth.] (My translation)

León-Portilla quotes a poem, "Los soles o edades que han existido" (The suns or epochs that have existed), in which all five Sun periods are described, including their demise. The poem begins

> Se refería, se decía
> que así hubo ya antes cuatro vidas,
> y que ésta era la quinta edad.
> (León-Portilla 1986, 7)

[It was referred to, it was said
That there had been four other eras before this one
And that this was the fifth era] (my translation)

The poem proceeds to state that each era had existed with its own Sun. The First Sun featured the sign of water (4-Water), and a great inundation swept away everything in its path, and humans were converted into fish. The Second Sun bore the sign of 4-Tiger and was called Sun of the Tiger. In this era, the Sun lost its trajectory, and without the Sun, the earth was enveloped in darkness (possibly the Ice Age). Under the cover of this eternal night, the tigers began to attack the people and devour them. During this era, after the disappearance of human beings, the giants returned and took over the earth. The Third Sun, known as the Sun of Rain or Sun of Fire (Sun that rained fire), was characterized by a fiery rain that poured down on the people below, decimating everything in its wake; everything on earth was burned in the inferno. One can imagine this as an era of erupting volcanoes. Molten red rocks, lava, and sand rained on the people and destroyed them; this is how the era of the Third Sun ended. The Fourth Sun was the Sun of Wind, and within the ferocious gales and windstorms, everything was swept away, and once again, all perished. This period can be imagined as incredibly powerful hurricanes or tornadoes sweeping the earth. During this era, humans were turned into monkeys. The present era, that is, the Fifth Sun, bears the sign of 4-Movement. It is known as the Sun of Movement of the Earth (earthquakes perhaps). When the earthquakes appear, humans will once again be extinguished; they will disappear from the face of the earth once more (León-Portilla 1986, 7–8).

Jalamanta expounds repeatedly throughout the narrative about how we are living in the era of the Fifth Sun. The corrupt city controlled by oppressive authorities who had forced Jalamanta into exile is the Seventh City of the Fifth Sun. Seventh City has an intertextual link to the Seven Cities of Cíbola, which Spanish conquistadores had frantically sought in the sixteenth century, particularly Fray Marcos de Niza and Francisco Vásquez de Coronado (see Bannon 1964, 86–95). In addition, according to Aztec mythology, the original tribe lived in seven caves before arriving to the Lake Texcoco area, where they eventually founded their empire. Bernardino de

Sahagún (1981, 76) cites the seven caves from whence the Náhuatl-speaking people originated: "Las gentes *nahuas,* que son las que entienden la lengua Mexicana también se llaman *chichimecas* porque vinieron de las tierras ya dichas donde están las siete cuevas" (The Nahua people, who understand [speak] the Mexican language, are also known as Chichimecas because they came from the lands cited already where the seven caves are located). And he names the caves: tepanecas, acolhuacas, chalcas, tlateputzcas, tlaxcaltecas, huexotzincas, and chololtecas (book 10, chapter 24, fragments).

Jalamanta saw the Fifth Sun era as soon disappearing, since the novel was written during a transitional period (1996), and it was thought that the Sixth Sun was fast approaching. At the turn of the century, from the twentieth to the twenty-first, the whole world was apprehensive about what to expect for the year 2000. Many persons anguished over whether the year 2000 would precipitate a catastrophic end of the world. The Spanish proverb "A dos mil años no ha de llegar, ni ha de pasar" (We will not reach the year 2000 nor will we pass it) was invoked for many decades previous and had an ominous, mysterious ring to it. Even scientists feared that catastrophic events would befall the world, particularly with respect to the late twentieth-century computer industry. It was feared that the change from 1999 to 2000 would cause computers to crash worldwide. All gave a sigh of relief when 2000 appeared and nothing happened.

It is interesting to note that although Jalamanta characterizes the Sixth Sun as one of peace and harmony, the biblical description of the Sixth Seal of the Book of Life is described as a violent end to an age:

> The **sixth seal** is catastrophic. When He broke the sixth seal there was a great earthquake; the sun became black as sackcloth; the whole moon became like blood; the stars of the sky fell to the earth; the sky was split apart like a scroll when it is rolled up, and every mountain and island were moved out of their places (6:12–14). But the people of the world were not scared of these natural disasters, for they hid in the caves and among the rocks of the mountains and said to the mountains and to the rocks. (Niekerk 2012, n.p.)

Another date linked to an "end of the world" mystique was December 21, 2012. According to many people around the world, the end of the world was near, a belief due to what anthropologists believed was an erroneous reading and interpretation of Mayan calendar predictions, that the world would end on that date because of the special position of the Milky Way galaxy (see Hundley 2010).

Jalamanta, nevertheless, is optimistic that the new era will be a positive one, characterized by love and understanding. The protagonist often expresses hope for a better future, which was in keeping with the 1960s counterculture belief regarding the new Age of Aquarius. According to popular culture, this "New Age" that the world was approaching would be a better era. The song "Aquarius/Let the Sunshine In," written for the 1967 musical hit *Hair* by James Rado and Gerome Ragni (lyrics) and Galt MacDermot (music), became a number one hit in 1969 when performed by the pop group the 5th Dimension. The concept of the Age of Aquarius and the beliefs inscribed in the lyrics stemmed from astrological readings that indicated to some that the world would be entering a new age, the Age of Aquarius, and that this new age would bring love, peace, and understanding to the world. The lyrics describe this new age and the astrological signs of its coming:

> When the moon is in the Seventh House
> And Jupiter aligns with Mars
> Then peace will guide the planets
> And love will steer the stars
> ("Aquarius Song Lyrics" 2014)

Then the chorus chimes in, announcing the "dawning of the Age of Aquarius." The third verse cites the splendid events that will come with the Age of Aquarius: harmony, understanding, sympathy, trust, liberation of the mind, and so forth. The second part of the song is the verse, which is repeated eleven times:

> Let the sun shine,
> Let the sun shine in
> The sun shine in.
> ("Aquarius Song Lyrics" 2014)

Jalamanta obviously shares the world vision as described in the lyrics of this song, which no doubt greatly influenced Anaya's philosophical thinking regarding the coming of a new age.

Returning to Mesoamerican religious thought, the Aztecs worshiped the sun and saw it as their main deity. Although when asked, Jalamanta denies worshiping the sun, there is a strong emphasis on the relationship between the sun and what he calls the Universal Spirit, or God (46). Jalamanta speaks about the Path of the Sun and of the Sun's light aiding humans in achieving clarity and bringing them closer to the Universal Spirit. The Sun is also seen as a reflection of the Universal Light, and Jalamanta explicitly calls it the Parent Sun (42) and Father Sun (46).

Mayan religious teachings are also evident in Jalamanta's emphasis on human beings and their connections to one another. The Mayas believed that we are reflected in the Other, that is, the other person, or more broadly, other human beings. Their belief expressed in the phrase "in lak'ech" has been translated as "You are my other me" by Luis Valdez as exemplified in his poem "Pensamiento Serpentino." Valdez informs us, "The meaning of the phrase is affiliated with the Mayan definition of the human being which they called 'huinik'lil' or 'vibrant being.' In this regard, we are all part of the same universal vibration." The English phrases of the poem state:

> In Lak'ech
> You are my other me.
> If I do harm to you,
> I do harm to myself.
> If I love and respect you,
> I love and respect myself.
> (Valdez and Paredes 2014, n.p.)

The concept of "huinik'lil," or "vibrant being," is closely related to the human soul described by Jalamanta as being "pure energy" and pertaining to the overall energy of the universe. Thus our individual energies, or souls, are all linked to the energy of the universe.

Hindu Religious Influences

Hindu religious thought also appears repeatedly in *Jalamanta*, as the title of the narrative and the name of the principal protagonist indicate. The veil blinding humans stems from the Vedic concept of Maya:

> The one is reality. Multiplicity is illusion. This illusion of multiplicity is created by the veiling power of the one (the Supreme Consciousness). This veiling power is called Maya Shakti, or Maya.
>
> This power creates the illusion of me and mine, or thee and thine, which creates ignorance in the individual consciousness. Those who realize this ignorance call it avidya (a = no; vidya = knowledge: thus ignorance or absence of knowledge). So maya is also called avidya by yogis. (Johari 2014, n.p.)

The veil in *Jalamanta* is a leit motif that appears repeatedly throughout the narrative, especially at those times when Jalamanta exhorts the people who gather daily to hear his teachings to rid themselves of the veils of illusions that their egos have created to their soul's detriment.

American Indian Influences

American Indian beliefs are evident in the ecological precepts articulated by Jalamanta throughout the narrative, such as the strong belief in the sacredness of nature and in animism, the belief that natural elements are alive. The close connection between humans and animals is also indicative of the American Indian religious influence in *Jalamanta*.

ECOLOGICAL DISCURSIONS
Life on Earth

For Jalamanta, the universe is alive, and all that is within it is also alive. In chapter 2, both Jalamanta and Fatimah are transfixed, observing nature in all its splendor; the omniscient narrator states in wonder at the spectacle of life transpiring: "The river reflected the light and shimmered like diamonds. The stone mountain and the fleet deer, tree and stone, man and woman, the fish and the river and the sea, the birds of the air, all were filled with light, the dance of life" (16). Like humans, all entities in the universe possess a soul (138). This is easy to understand if we conceive of the soul as pure energy. All things in the universe, whether animate or inanimate, are constituted of atoms, which are joined together by energy. Jalamanta explains: "Earth and the universe have a soul, they are alive with the same energy that fills each person" (140). Later, in chapter 20, "Love of the Earth," Jalamanta reiterates this concept when asked by members of his community if the earth has a soul. The response was yes, that since the time of the First Creation, energy has flowed throughout the universe, and the earth and all on it indeed have a soul (154–55).

From the very inception of the *Jalamanta* narrative, the reader is made aware of the importance of the environment surrounding human beings. Fatimah, one of the principal characters and Jalamanta's partner, lives a simple existence by the river. She has her goats, which live off the land and provide her with milk and cheese as well as wool for weaving clothing and blankets. She adds figs from her fig tree to her simple diet, but basically she lives a self-sufficient life, taking very little from the earth. As we say in today's jargon, she has a small footprint.

When Jalamanta addresses the exiled community, he speaks about the Four Sacred Directions and invokes the desert, the river, the animals of the earth, and the trees. He exhorts the people to feel connected to the earth, for "each person has the power within to join the essence of the soul to the essence of the earth" (33). For Jalamanta, the veils humans have constructed around themselves blinds them and keeps them from seeing and experiencing our connection to the earth and its ecological systems that surround us.

Humanity's Kinship to the Animal World

In chapter 21, "Kindra, the Witch," Jalamanta expounds explicitly on the nature of humanity's connection to the animal world. In this chapter, he explores the Mesoamerican indigenous belief system known as *nahualismo*, or *nagualismo*, also connected to *tonalismo*, which posits the belief that all humans have an animal counterpart who looks after them. Kindra is a woman, a healer and shaman; knowing Jalamanta has returned, she decides to visit the couple at their home. She conveys to them the discomfort she feels and her unhappiness at being pejoratively characterized as a witch by the community, for she does not feel she is one. Kindra exemplifies the close relationship to the animal world that humans used to have and have now lost. According to Kindra, people need to be more sensitive to the animal world, and instead of perceiving animals as enemies or as inferior to humans, we should view them as guardian spirits. Jalamanta is saddened at how people have become separated from the animal world and lost their kinship and connection to these fellow earth beings. Instead of exploiting animals and nature, people need to reconnect to the animal world as well as to the mineral world, since everything and everyone is all part of the Universal Spirit.

Jalamanta continues to discuss the power of the witch and how she is able to take the form of animals, such as coyotes, owls, jaguars, and so forth. In nahualismo, there is a belief that each human being is closely connected to one specific animal, who watches and helps the person. This belief in *nahuales* has been expressed in other works by Anaya, particularly in *Bless Me, Ultima*. Kindra, in this case, resembles the wise healer Ultima of Anaya's famous novel.

POLITICAL PERSPECTIVES

Jalamanta, aside from its philosophical discursions, is a deeply political document. Jalamanta was exiled by the moral authority for his "heretical" viewpoints. Ingrained in the novel is a strong critique of the curtailment of freedom of speech and freedom of thought. The moral authority is presented as an oppressive form of government, which has taken over the lives of the people of the Seventh City of the Fifth Sun. The moral authority has appropriated the city and rules with an iron fist. They have spies infiltrating the exiled community, whose members live outside the city limits but are still under the domain of this corrupt government. They can be taken prisoner if they are deemed to be violating the ruling government's moral or political precepts. Any deviation from the central authority's rules and regulations, even thinking freely, is severely castigated, as Jalamanta experienced in the past and likely will in the future for his teachings.

Freedom of thought is deemed particularly dangerous in the purview of the moral authority. The insignias they wear are a skull and crossbones, indicating death. The moral authority represents death of the body, of the mind, and of the soul. Jalamanta's teachings related to finding clarity of the soul and thinking for oneself are viewed as blasphemous. Likewise, seeking to connect with one another within the community is perceived as dangerous and seditious. Even the teachings related to developing trust in themselves and in each other are also deemed dangerous by the over-zealous authorities.

Jalamanta's political discussions can be perceived as thinly veiled critiques of our contemporary political system. The "moral authority" can be linked to the "moral majority," or the conservative movement that came to power during President Richard Nixon's years and thereafter. A strong conservative movement overtook the United States as a backlash to the counterculture of the 1960s. The backlash also included opposition to civil rights demands from minority groups, the feminist movement and the gay and lesbian movement. The "free speech" and "free love" movements also eventually contributed to the backlash, giving rise to the moral majority, as did the opposition from the political left to the Vietnam War in the 1960s and 1970s.

CONCLUSION

Critics have not been kind to the novel *Jalamanta*, and therefore little has been written about it, and it is not one of Anaya's better known works. One critic states, "Anaya's preachy New Age parable is a sharp departure from the yeasty realism that won him a large readership for novels like *Bless Me, Ultima* and *Alburquerque*. Wise, gray-haired, cotton-robed heretic Jalamanta, returning from 30 years of politically enforced exile in the desert, rejoins his faithful wife, Fatimah, and attracts new followers with his teachings" (Steinberg 1996, 58). The critic proceeds to provide a summary of the novel and ends with a caustic: "Jalamanta's pronouncements freely synthesize Christian, Hindu, Islamic, Buddhist, Native American, gnostic and shamanic traditions to present a universal message of fellowship. Like all lofty sentiments, these become somewhat platitudinous with repetition" (ibid.). A review from the *Library Journal* is more kind to *Jalamanta*:

> Thirty years ago, Jalamanta and his people were exiled in the desert, banished from the Seventh City for challenging the monolithic dogmas of the Central Authority. Now, Jalamanta returns to his wife, Fatimah, and to his village full of new wisdom about the oneness of humankind and nature and about the nature of love. Jalamanta's teachings about the Path of the Sun challenge the sterile religious institutionalism of the Central Authority and encourage his villagers to seek their own spiritual paths. Anaya (*Bless Me, Ultima*, Warner, 1994) has fashioned a New Age Joshua in which Jalamanta is a kind of Christic guru preaching an exotic blend of ego psychology, Christian theology, and Hinduism. Recommended for libraries where Anaya's books are in demand. (Carrigan 1996)

Both critics totally missed one of the most important issues articulated in the novel, the ecological concerns clearly expressed in it and detailed in this chapter. *Jalamanta* is a robust repository of Anaya's philosophical, religious, and ecological belief systems; it is written in an elegant and readable literary style. The novel greatly enhances our understanding of this Chicano's spiritual connections and influences, which are evident in his other works. *Jalamanta* provides us with a glimpse of the literary works that influenced the mind of a brilliant author.

REFERENCES

Allen, Reginald E. 1991. *Greek Philosophy: Thales to Aristotle*. 3rd ed. New York: Free Press.

Anaya, Rudolfo A. 1972. *Bless Me, Ultima*. Berkeley, CA: Quinto Sol.

———. 1996. *Jalamanta: A Message from the Desert*. New York: Warner Books.

"Aquarius Lyrics." 2016. Metro Lyrics. Accessed January 18. www.metrolyrics.com/aquarius-lyrics-5th-dimension.html.

Bannon, John Francis. 1964. *Bolton and the Spanish Borderlands*. Norman: University of Oklahoma Press.

Campbell, Joseph. 1973. *The Hero with a Thousand Faces.* Princeton, NJ: Princeton University Press.

Carrigan, Henry, Jr. 1996. Review of *Jalamanta: A Message from the Desert,* by Rudolfo Anaya. *Library Journal* 121 (2): 64.

Clute, John. 2000. *The Book of End Time: Grappling with the Millennium (Destruction of the World as We Know It).* New York: Harper Prism.

Doody, Margaret Anne. 1996. *The True Story of the Novel.* New Brunswick, NJ: Rutgers University Press.

Gennep, Arnold van. 1909. *Les rites de passage.* Paris: Nourry.

Holy Bible [KJV]. 1978. Nashville, TN: National Publishing Company for the Gideons International.

Hundley, Raymond. 2010. *Will the World End in 2012?: A Christian Guide to the Question Everyone's Asking.* Nashville, TN: Nelson.

Johari, Sangeetha. 2014. "Maya or Illusion in Hinduism Philosophy." Sanatan Society. Accessed April 20. www.sanatansociety.org/yoga_and_meditation/ hinduism_philosophy_maya_illusion.htm.

León-Portilla, Miguel, ed. 1986. "Ciclo de los mitos cosmogónicos. Los Soles o edades que han existido." In *Literatura del México Antiguo,* 7–9. Caracas: Biblioteca Ayacucho.

MacKay, Marina. 2011. *The Cambridge Introduction to the Novel.* New York: Cambridge University Press.

Martínez, José Luis, ed. 1981. *Bernardino de Sahagún: El México antiguo.* Caracas: Biblioteca Ayacucho.

Mendivil Capaerth, Carlos. 2014. *El Imperio de los Inkas: The Story of the Inkan Empire.* Lima, Peru: n.p.

Niekerk, Andries van. 2012. "Overview of the Seven Seals." *Revelation by Jesus Christ.* October 27. http://revelationbyjesuschrist.com/2012/10/27/ overview-of-the-seven-seals-2.

Sahagún, Bernardino de. 1981. "Pueblos y señores. Los Primeros Pobladores: Los Mexicanos." In *Bernardino de Sahagún: El México antiguo,* edited by José Luis Martínez, 76. Caracas: Biblioteca Ayacucho.

Steinberg, Sybil S. 1996. Review of *Jalamanta: A Message from the Desert,* by Rudolfo Anaya. *Publishers Weekly* 243 (1): 58.

Valdez, Luis, and Domingo Martinez Paredes. 2014. "In Lak'ech: You Are My Other Me." *Vue: Voices in Urban Education,* Annenberg Institute for School Reform at Brown University. Accessed September 7. http://vue.annenberginstitute.org/ perspectives/lak%E2%80%99ech-you-are-my-other.

Niekerk, Andries van. 2012. "Overview of the Seven Seals." *Revelation by Jesus Christ.* October 27. http://revelationbyjesuschrist.com/2012/10/27/ overview-of-the-seven-seals-2.

Watt, Ian. 1957. *The Rise of the Novel: Studies in Defoe, Richardson, and Fielding.* Berkeley: University of California Press.

5

Land, the Southwest, and Rudolfo Anaya

Robert Con Davis-Undiano

In *The Revolt of the Cockroach People* (1973), Oscar Zeta Acosta captures the spirit of the 1970s Chicano Renaissance in regard to land and land use. In a court scene in this novel, a Mexican American lawyer argues that northern New Mexico was the actual site of the famous Aztlán—the legendary homeland of the ancient Aztecs, which predates México's founding. He claims that Mexican Americans, heirs to the Aztecs on their Mexican side, live in Aztlán by virtue of living in the U.S. Southwest. "We are not Mexicans," he asserts. "We are Chicanos from Aztlán. We have never left our land. Our fathers never engaged in bloody sacrifices. We are farmers and hunters and we live with the buffalo" (161). Taking the American Southwest to be the original homeland of the "cockroach people"—Mexican Americans socially and economically marginalized—is presented as comic. And yet this scene from Acosta's novel expresses the Mexican American belief, dating from the late 1960s, which says that the American Southwest belonged not only to México as recently as 1848 but was the traditional homeland of the ancient Aztecs and their heirs—modern-day Mexican Americans.

Acosta also advances that communities "belong" to their homeland and derive a sense of identity and culture from that tie. Such a belief is not always evident in twentieth-century America, where land is often stripped of cultural associations and reduced to its market value. As part of the Aztlán claim, Acosta is promoting land, as Mexican Americans did throughout the 1960s and 1970s, as a necessary cultural relationship. In the twentieth century, the tie to land, as Rudolfo Anaya comments in his role as land activist, gets subverted in "the hands of world markets and politics" (2009a, 90). Anaya comments that land still remains a part, whether always recognized or not, of what makes culture work, one of the "healing power[s]" in the world that "the epiphany of place provides" (2009c, 145). In the promotion of Aztlán in the 1960s and 1970s, Mexican Americans were making such claims to refocus on this dimension of land's cultural and communal importance.

According to legend, the Aztec homeland was located north of Tenochtitlan (the early site of Mexico City), possibly as far north as Santa Fe, New Mexico. As the story goes, the Mexica god of war Huitzilopochli told his people to leave Aztlán and search for Tenochtitlan. When found, Tenochtitlan became their new homeland, but the Aztecs always wanted to return to their original place. As part of the 1960s Chicano Movement, Mexican Americans capitalized on the importance of the homeland idea and saw themselves as fulfilling a historical destiny by living in the Southwest, which they took to be the site of their original homeland. The Aztlán idea told Mexican Americans that by choosing to live in the Southwest, even if they were immigrants, and even if they were undocumented, they were a people claiming rights to an ancient ancestral inheritance.

As Richard L. Nostrand (1972) notes, the traditional homeland relationship has "three basic elements: a people, a place, and identity with place. . . . People must have lived [in a homeland] long enough" to make "their impress in the form of a cultural landscape" (214). "Having developed an identity [in connection] with the land," they will have developed social customs and cultural practices uniquely tied to land. They will also have developed "emotional feelings of attachment, desires to possess, even compulsions to defend [their land]" (214).

The contemporary conception of a "homeland" seems more complex than such traditional practices can describe. Indigenous peoples in the Américas, Israelis, Palestinians, Mexicans, Syrians, Yazidis, and victims of political upheaval everywhere typically make broader claims for what a homeland could be. Sara Ahmed and her colleagues (2003) reference the contemporary experience of homeland as necessarily convoluted and paradoxical, involving a "reclaiming and reprocessing of habits, objects, names and histories that have been uprooted [owing to frequent] migration, displacement or colonization" (9). The homeland may not be a place where one's community actually lived in the past but could be a claim based on *"making* [a] home . . . about *creating* both pasts and futures through inhabiting the grounds of the present" (9, italics added). Established by "returning to" and by "repossessing" but also by *recreating* a lost place, the "homeland" is now as much a cultural construction as an actual place. The contemporary sense of a homeland is as likely, as Anaya comments, the product of the interaction of "place, imagination, and memory" (2009c, 142).

The promotion of Aztlán as the Mexican American homeland is precisely such a complex claim, with Mexican Americans having a cultural relationship to a place that may or may not have existed. There are mythic elements of the Aztlán concept and only a few indications of any historical validity whatsoever. But if Aztlán *were* in the U.S. Southwest, even as a mythical reference, then Mexican Americans are not exiles or illegals hiding in the U.S. shadows, not interlopers trying to gain property and social advantages that are not theirs. They are a people making a claim on their *own* home. Supporting this idea in the 1960s became an expression of Mexican American hope for the future. The Southwest actually *was* a part of México until 1848, making the homeland claim in one sense actually true, but the Aztlán idea became a broader reference to *all* prior Mexican American cultural ties to the United States.

How does the Mexican American focus on traditional ties to land contribute to Mexican American and U.S. national culture? Valuing land for its cultural associations instead of its commercial value reinvigorates communities and helps to counter the loss of traditions. Mexican American writers and land activists have made this case about U.S. land and land use. During the 1960s, no other activity of the Chicano Movement, asserts Anaya, was as "important" as the cultural relationship to the American Southwest of a Mexican American homeland (1989, 232). Reframing such a relationship was promoted in *El Plan Espiritual de Aztlán* ([1969] 1989), which countered the modern debasement of land and supported land activists striving to protect traditional lands that had rich cultural and historical significance. As Chicano sociologist Devon G. Peña comments, this battle was over cultural "paradigms." Anaya, Reies López Tijerina, María Varela, and other land activists opposed the "bureaucratic model of state and capitalist control of nature as a commodity" and preferred, as Peña explains, "the indigenous model of sustainable local stewardship of the homeland" (1998, 274).

Land activists from this period joined forces, sometimes unwittingly, with American cultural geographers. Carl O. Sauer, the godfather of U.S. cultural geography, weighed in against the nineteenth- and twentieth-century U.S. shift away from a communal model centered on ties to land "where different ways and ends of life went on side by side" (1962, 47). He lamented the modern framing of land primarily as a commodity with demonstrated market value. Mexican American writers and American cultural geographers united in believing that national social ills tied to the loss of shared communal values were intensified through the loss of traditional land ties. Hence American geographer James J. Parsons (1985) advocated protecting "geographic and cultural diversity, the sacredness of the Earth, and the responsibilities of local communities to it," calling for a broad reassessment of how the recognition of cultural attachments to land hold communities together (4). Only when we honor social and cultural land ties, as ecofeminist Vandana Shiva (1998) argued recently, can we "resist the culture of economic organization that destroys both cultural diversity and biodiversity by promoting and nurturing monocultures and monopolies" (viii). Only when communities commit to sustaining cultural and social land ties, as Shiva concludes, do they sustain their appreciation of issues pertaining to "gender, class, ethnicity and other constructions of difference, identity politics, and the environmental movement" (viii).

Chicana philosopher Laura Pulido (1996) adds to Shiva's comment that "social injustice, growing inequality, and a looming environmental crisis," problems appearing in the wake of losing traditional ties to land, are "the greatest threats facing the global community as we enter the twenty-first century" (210). For their part, Mexican American writers have actively promoted the debate over these issues and have argued for maintaining traditional land ties to support a sustainable national culture.

The Chicano Movement's Aztlán declaration in the 1970s was basically a vehicle for advancing all these separate issues. When the Aztlán claim was first made in the 1960s, there were few archaeological or historical arguments for locating Aztlán in New Mexico, or any real support, other than folklore, for making this claim. Even so, for Mexican Americans, the effect of claiming that the homeland was in the American Southwest was catalytic, another step toward turning the United States into a "home," in this case a place where Mexican Americans felt they belonged and could stay no matter what. The claim was even better in that it asserted historical priority from that time "before" the colonial interlopers took over what was originally theirs. This claim stoked a Mexican American sense of pride in ancestral roots and a newfound Mexican American identity.

Once the assertion was made, Mexican Americans were no longer outsiders in a foreign land but were a "first people" with their own land claims. After the Aztlán declaration circulated in literature, social texts, and the arts, many Mexican Americans no longer thought of themselves as marginal, as Mexican exiles; they were now a separate "nation" with unique ties to a place. Especially for a community that intensely sought ethical and religious guidance from *los antepasados*, the ancestors, there was a special significance, a sacredness, in "knowing" that they were living in their ancestral homeland.

The homeland idea has a mixed history, some of it surprising and ironic. Several sixteenth-century texts reference the Aztec migration to México from their original home, the earliest being Fray Diego Durán's *Historia de las Indias de Nueva-España y Islas de Tierra Firme* ([1581] 1994). The claim for Aztlán as the *original* Mexican homeland came from Fray Bernardino de Sahagún (1499–1590), the Franciscan friar who is recognized today as a forerunner of modern-day anthropology. In *Historia General de las Cosas de Nueva España* ([1582] 1981), he recorded that the Aztecs relocated from Aztlán to Tenochtitlan, which became the capital of the Aztec empire (1:288–89). These intriguing references to a historical, and yet likely still mythical, Aztlán lay dormant as a concept not to be refound until the modern era.

Assertion of the Aztlán claim in modern times came amid a climate of conflict and debate about land in the New Mexico Territory. Before

New Mexico became a U.S. territory in 1850, both Spain and México had awarded many large tracts of land—"grants"—across the Southwest to individuals and groups to encourage the establishment of more ranches and villages. By 1850, after having lived under Spanish and Mexican rule, New Mexico was a patchwork quilt of complicated land grants, with names like Tierra Amarilla, Taos Pueblo, Sangre de Cristo, Río Chama, Atrisco, among many others. Subsequent land issues of every sort in New Mexico were played out in relation to these land grants, with litigation and decades, even centuries, of legal disputes, some of them extending *into the present*, over water and land rights connected with the land grants.

At the heart of the legal problems is that land in New Mexico was awarded under two systems of law, Spanish and Mexican, and they often conflicted with each other. To make matters worse, after 1848, land policies and litigation fell under a third legal system, U.S. law, and a completely different approach for establishing and protecting land ownership. We can add to this state of general confusion the fact that New Mexico's fragile ecology, with many arid regions and little water, made the just distribution of land and water even more pressing and difficult. Also, during the years of territorial status (1850–1912), before statehood in 1912, commercial developers bought many New Mexico mineral and agricultural lands in hopes of making huge profits as New Mexico assimilated into the U.S. national economy, and this commercial capturing of land brought even greater complexity and conflict to this region.

The result was that the history of land-grant disputes in New Mexico has at times been a sordid "legacy of bitterness" (Briggs and Van Ness 1987, 4), caused by what Sylvia Rodríguez calls a "collective trauma of massive land loss" (1987, 382). Pueblo peoples, mestizos, and Hispanics had owned land titles in some cases for centuries, and since 1848, many of those lands have been lost through fraud, vigilante action, and aggressive corporations litigating to gain the land in U.S courts. Over the last 150 years, a major historical development in New Mexico has been the transfer of traditional lands to corporations and commercial interests who have little or no concern for New Mexico culture and traditions, with the exception of "the [strategic] marketing of ethnicity" in New Mexico as a commodity often connected with the promotion of Taos, Santa Fe, and Albuquerque (Rodríguez 1987, 387).[1]

Land issues in New Mexico have often focused on the *ejidos*, or communal lands, owned by families and groups (Acuña 2000, 369). Common to Spanish and Mexican law, the *ejido* referenced "common lands . . . owned by the community" that "could not be sold" (Ebright 1987, 24). The stricture against selling *ejidos* was protected by Spanish and Mexican law, but not by U.S. courts after 1850. Under U.S. jurisdiction, "community grants," more common in the nineteenth century, have not fared well in the twentieth century and have all but disappeared (23).

This was the land environment in New Mexico that gave rise to the Aztlán idea on two different occasions. The first resurfacing of Aztlán happened in the nineteenth century, through William G. Ritch's slim volume entitled *Aztlán: The History, Resources and Attractions of New Mexico* (1885). This book was a promotional tract designed to highlight the "territory's mineral wealth" and its readiness for outside investors to promote ranching and land development. The book pitched New Mexico as the historical Aztlán and described it as an exotic locale that could attract investors for the "superb profits" that could be theirs. "This beautiful country," the book boasted, was "destined to be known as the true El Dorado" (137).[2] It promoted New Mexico as the perfect real-estate deal and highlighted Santa Fe especially as the original site of the Aztlán capital in the "land of enchantment," creating an exotic aura with commercial attractions that still persists in popular media today—what Sylvia Rodríguez calls the practice of "ethnophilia" (1987, 386). There was, of course, some distant reason for believing the Aztlán claim, but the goal in Ritch's book was never anything but commercial development. This book was part of a public relations campaign depicting New Mexico as a new, exotic place for investment.

With this new identity, the New Mexico Territory was open for business, with an attraction calculated to work for outside investors. In effect, New Mexico took on the identity of fertile primitivism, dark and malleable—a desirable place ready to be shaped by new commercial interests. As Ritch promised all who came, an enterprising "white" person in New Mexico could easily be situated *"on top of the ladder"* of economic and commercial success (1885, 117).

Ramón Gutiérrez has shown how investors in New Mexico promoted the territory as the land of kindly, noble savages, whose presence demonstrated an evolutionary theory then current in the late nineteenth century and attributable to Lewis Henry Morgan's *Ancient Society* ([1877] 1964). Morgan's book framed New Mexico with Eurocentric standards of culture and society, but with the added exotic appeal of a foreignism—essentially, the traditional recipe for tourism. The book held that ancient societies moved through predictable stages to reach the pinnacle of "modern" development, and New Mexico displayed all the developmental stages simultaneously. A primitive phase happened during "settlement of the country by the Pueblo Indians' ancestral kin" (Gutiérrez 1989, 178). Another period of modern progress began when Francisco Vásquez de Coronado explored the region, and the Spanish and the Mexicans brought in new levels of development and robust economic growth. The last "epoch of history," the fully "civilized" phase, came under the United States, with the "hallmarks of liberal progress," that is, fresh opportunities for venture capital (ibid., 180). The enhanced cultural legitimacy granted at each stage of development matched the incremental movement away from the land's indigenous community.

While the territory's promoters wanted new investors, they were not looking for more Hispanics. In 1850, the territory was sparsely populated with only sixty thousand people. Toward century's end, all knew that New Mexico would soon become a state, and as more people came into the territory, the Hispanic populace would possibly outnumber whites, and a majority of Hispanics could end up governing New Mexico. They would oversee the agricultural and industrial bases of investment that Ritch and others had worked so hard to achieve. On the other hand, an influx of white investors could ensure economic profitability and continued commercial development, and Gutiérrez argues that encouragement of "white" investors into the state was intended to keep the mestizo community from ever governing.[3]

The Aztlán idea surfaced again in the 1960s in the U.S. Southwest. The Chicano Youth Conference in March 1969, in Denver, Colorado, affirmed that Mexican Americans in the Southwest were, in fact, living in Aztlán. These young people critiqued the civil and economic injustices Mexican Americans had faced since 1848, the year of the Treaty of Guadalupe Hidalgo, and called for land reform to begin solving the land-grant disputes in New Mexico.

This focus on land was owing to the influence of reclaim-the-land guru and maverick community organizer Reies López Tijerina, who understood "the resentment that village-dwelling farmers [in New Mexico] held towards those who usurped their lands" (Rosales 1996, 157–58). Addressing a range of land-grant issues, Tijerina advocated recapturing Mexican American land and reasserting Mexican American land rights, which the Guadalupe Hidalgo Treaty was never designed to protect (ibid.). Tijerina's organization, La alianza federal de Mercedes, with the motto "tierra y libertad!" (land and liberty), argued that vigilante violence and the U.S. courts had taken traditional lands in New Mexico from their rightful owners (Acuña 2000, 370). The Alianza and *El Plan Espiritual* jointly argued for returning lands to traditional people in the Southwest and reasserted that justice should guide the reclaiming of a long-forgotten homeland (Anaya and Lomelí 1989, 1).[4] Most important in these calls was the promotion of land-based nationalism. *El Plan Espiritual* said that "*we, the Chicano inhabitants and civilizers of the northern land of Aztlán from whence came our forefathers, reclaiming the land of their birth and consecrating the determination of our people of the sun, declare that the call of our blood is our power, our responsibility, and our inevitable destiny*" ([1969] 1989, 1). This call to action concluded that "we are a bronze people with a bronze culture. Before the world, before all of North America, before all our brothers in the bronze continent, we are a *nation*, we are a union of free pueblos, we are *Aztlán*" (1). This link between land and identity addressed the underlying struggle for social justice, which had land, economic, and cultural dimensions.[5]

From 1969 onward, the idea of Aztlán as a Mexican American place of origin drew attention even outside the Southwest. To keep this momentum, the Chicano Movement pushed for changes in Mexican American strategies of self-determination by creating new businesses and jobs. The net effect in 1969 was that Mexican American unemployment hovered somewhere between 6 and 8 percent, but Mexican Americans were still entering the professions behind whites by 60 percent (Acuña 2000, 384). The Chicano Movement wanted to reposition the Mexican American community by reforming schools so that students could successfully compete for jobs. Rodolfo Acuña notes that while Mexican Americans "made some gains during the period of 1968–74, after this point they slipped backward" with a return to high dropout rates when the first phase of exuberance for the Chicano Movement waned (413).

The movement's intense triple focus on protecting civil rights for individuals, enhancing the business atmosphere for communities, and reclaiming land explains much about its success as a cultural and social phenomenon—all despite huge areas of Chicano life changing little at all. Even so, claiming a "homeland" in the American Southwest signaled a new direction on many fronts for a community that was rethinking its place in the United States. Rafael Pérez-Torres comments in *Mestizaje* (2006) that "in many ways, land lies at the heart of the Chicano movement" (115). "The coalescence of land and body [was] part of a new visioning of identity and subjectivity" for Mexican Americans (124). He adds that "a profound sense of dislocation was at the dark heart of Chicano identity" (197). The homeland idea redefined and deepened such recognition of the relationship between land and identity, and this was a huge step forward.

A few Chicano and Chicana writers during this time continued to assert that the southwestern United States was once the literal and actual Aztlán, the "innocent" place, in the face of considerable evidence to the contrary. Most, however, like Mexican American poet Alurista, were beginning to see "Aztlán as borderless and belonging to those who work, who toil for the wealth that, presently, others who own the means of production enjoy" (Alurista 1991, 227). Along the same line, Genaro M. Padilla (1989) analyzed the Aztlán phenomenon in light of Franz Fanon's *The Wretched of the Earth* to discuss how a group goes about mending a "threatened or even shattered cultural psyche" (113). He argued that for subjugated cultures to triumph over adversity, they must "reject the colonial structures that distort, devalue and seek to destroy their history." The homeland claim worked as such a strategy for cohesively bringing together the damaged traditions of the past and projecting a favorable future as Mexican Americans' destiny (113). The homeland idea was a powerful instrument for repairing a "shattered cultural psyche" and was important to Mexican Americans trying to alleviate the cultural and social residue of racism and lack of participation in mainstream American culture.

The Chicano Movement worked through various land perspectives in its early history in the 1960s and 1970s. The 1969 *El Plan Espiritual*, focusing on the loss of land grants and the injustices perpetrated after the signing of the Treaty of Guadalupe Hidalgo, called for lost lands to be reclaimed, as Tijerina had urged. This declaration was typical of 1960s radicalism in calling for the complete transformation of relations between the local community and the larger culture to establish "social, economic, cultural and political independence" for Mexican Americans ([1969] 1989, 2). The Mexican American need for Aztlán to exist, and the recognition that the claim received, signaled a momentum that carried forward into the Chicano Renaissance, as Luis Valdez, Rudolfo Anaya, Tomás Rivera, Rodolfo Gonzáles, Rolando Hinojosa, Estela Portillo Trambley, Ester Hernández, and Lorna Dee Cervantes, among others, began developing a distinct Chicano and Chicana voice and identity that referenced the homeland concept as a basis for seeking economic and social reform.

Twenty years later, Rudolfo Anaya's important essay "Aztlán: A Homeland Without Boundaries" (1989) signaled a new Mexican American approach to land as the next step in this evolving story. Anaya valued Aztlán as a concept but wanted to create something new, what he called the "New World," an approach referencing confiscated lands across the Américas as well as racial and cultural issues connected with the conquest. In some ways supplanting the homeland idea, this new, expansive notion contextualized the cultural agenda that Mexican American writers, artists, and cultural critics had been moving toward since the middle 1980s.

In the essay, Anaya refers to Aztlán as a useful fiction and acknowledges recent scholarship from the early 1980s that undercut the notion of a historical Aztlán in the U.S. Southwest. The historian John R. Chávez had analyzed sixteenth-century Spanish colonial codices that referenced Aztec and Spanish attempts to find Aztlán. Texts from that period argued that the homeland was but a short four hundred miles northeast of Mexico City, in Nayarit (1989, 51) or, more likely, as came out later, in the Mexican states of Guanajuato, Jalisco, and Michoacán (Matos Moctezuma 1988).[6]

Anaya's basis for displacing Aztlán as a concept was direct and pragmatic. He writes that after the Chicano Movement, the Mexican American community was still in great jeopardy, as it was being assimilated into "mainstream American culture" at an alarming rate. This process, owing to melting-pot pressures, "was occurring so quickly that unless we re-established the covenants of our ancestors[,] our culture was threatened with extinction" (1989, 236). The Aztlán ideal—specific, elegant, and plausible, a direct link to the past—worked instantly to crystallize the social and cultural goals that Mexican Americans were beginning to imagine for themselves. But if Aztlán was not an actual place in the Southwest, then Mexican Americans might need a larger, more sophisticated frame for contextualizing land and the residue of colonialism, which was still having repercussions in the Américas (ibid., 236).

Anaya's New World script—not a single place but a network of cultural and historical connections—could reframe and contextualize the geographically grounded Aztlán. Even those who did not adopt the New World terminology were nonetheless moving in this direction of depending less on the concept of the literal Aztlán in the Southwest. As the Chicano Renaissance succeeded on several fronts in the 1980s, especially economically and culturally—with, for example, the winning of labor contracts from grape and lettuce growers in California—the Chicano Movement's ongoing critique needed to match the wide expanse of how Mexican Americans were viewing their lives, so the focus on the New World concept was far sighted and constructive.

In this approach, Anaya addressed how colonization of the Américas had caused amnesia about the ancient peoples of the New World in relation to mestizo identity, so that the Américas' ancient cultures were covered over by the devastation of the Spanish conquest, even though their "soul" was still connected to the land (1989, 358). Aligned with the thinking of Victor Raul Haya de la Torre, José Martí, José Vasconcelos, Gloria Anzaldúa, and Aníbal Quijano, Anaya saw indigenous identity and land as threads present in the "substratum of [all] my writings" and as voicing part of "the indigenous American perspective, or New World view" that focused on Native cultural origins in the Américas (358). He adds that "we must know more of the synthesis of our Spanish and Indian nature, and know more of the multiple heritages of the Americas" (358).

This "multicultural perspective" (363) and "the New World view" needed to be "syncretic and encompassing" (364), since the New World concept, as Aztlán had before it, turned away from the Spanish tradition—not to oppose it as European but to embrace the New World's hybrid complexity. With this distinction, he was referencing the Américas' ancient history, the conquest, and the contemporary cultural and political reality of living in the United States. Mestizos needed a land-based culture, but that land did not have to be Aztlán. All of this created a different direction for the mestizo recognition of a homeland. In an interview during this time, Anaya remarked that the mestizo is "a person that is not known in this country," and that this "unique person" needs a sustainable New World context within which to affirm relations among land, culture, and mestizo identity—all of which restates the urgent need for the Chicano Movement to begin with (Jussawalla and Dasenbrock 1992, 255).

The Chicano Movement's various land claims were helpful, and the movement's remarkable success since the 1960s has yet to be fully recognized—in part because of its complex social and cultural dimensions, but also because the Chicano Renaissance and its aftermath are still being felt. The designations "Chicano" and "Chicana" point with dramatic force socially, economically, and aesthetically not only to a Mexican American association with Native lands but to an evolving culture that did not exist in any practical sense before the middle 1960s. There is still a need for Mexican Americans to consolidate the gains they have made since the 1960s and make greater strides in the areas of education, jobs, and political representation. As they and other Latinos gain more confidence about mestizo culture and their place in it, especially as they become America's majority community no later than 2050, they will make progress in the process of coming home that began with reclaiming their homeland.

Anaya brings together and focuses these homeland and land issues in the novel *Shaman Winter* (1999). Much of his work makes the case for elevating land's importance and not reducing land to its commercial value, an act of resistance against exploitation and economic, cultural, and racial oppression—a powerful articulation for claiming cultural and historical legitimacy. Probably owing to this commitment to save traditional lands in New Mexico from commercial development, *Shaman Winter* and many of his other novels, stories, poems, and essays focus on land's importance and point toward the possibility of a new, revitalized relationship to land in the American Southwest and in the Américas as a whole.

Shaman Winter at century's end reflects a new awareness of the New World hemispheric staging of the Américas. In what amounts to a second large-scale proposal in Anaya's work (the first being the embrace of indigenous beliefs and cultural patterns in *Bless Me, Ultima*), in this novel, Anaya focuses on land, the homeland, and the significance of a New World perspective. *Shaman Winter* acknowledges the new framing of the homeland idea that had emerged over the previous forty years with a north/south orientation that connects the United States with the whole of the Américas, in place of the east/west orientation that foregrounds the British in the more narrow view of North America's British and French colonization.

Much of *Shaman Winter's* power and appeal comes from a focus on the specifics of why Mexican American culture *needs* a homeland and should promote a broad, hemispheric view of mestizo life in the Américas. Like *Zia Summer* (1995), *Rio Grande Fall* (1996), and *Jemez Spring* (2005), the other Anaya detective novels, *Shaman Winter* unfolds with detective Sonny Baca's struggle with his archrival Raven—the sorcerer villain whom Sonny faces in epic combat to protect the lands of the Américas throughout this series of books.

An ex-schoolteacher who has become a private detective, Sonny Baca is, in many ways, unremarkable. He is a regular guy, footloose in Albuquerque, except that his ancestor and alter ego is Captain Andrés Vaca, a soldier in the Spanish army of Juan Pérez de Oñate y Salazar (1550–1626), the Spanish conquistador who in 1598 conquered New Mexico. In dramatic fashion, this novel opens with Sonny Baca awakening one morning after traveling back through a dream channel, which Raven had opened for him, to 1598 and the Spanish entrada into New Mexico.

The novel follows the present action in Albuquerque through Sonny's eyes, and when the text frequently switches to the 1598 historical drama in New Mexico, we see the story through the eyes of Sonny as Andrés Vaca. Sonny is both people—himself when he is awake, and his ancestor Andrés Vaca when he is asleep and dreaming. As Sonny's awareness of his double consciousness increases, the reader moves back and forth more rapidly between Andrés in the sixteenth century and Sonny in the twentieth, in a split-screen perspective and narrative.

The situation in 1598 is that Oñate's army is preparing to travel from Santa Barbara (Nueva España) to what will become Albuquerque and Santa Fe in El Nuevo México. Anaya builds dramatic tension when the Spanish army crosses into New Mexico to embark on this late phase of the conquest and the probable closing of the northern colonial frontier. Like Keats's Hernan Cortéz in "On First Looking into Chapman's Homer," who contemplates his entrance into the Américas with a moment of pomp, Oñate's army in Anaya's novel contemplates its own "vision of the vast land to the north" and the "throbbing" of a "new time being born" as soon as their feet touch the northern lands (14). Their journey will transform the land before them, and as they move into New Mexico, an already convoluted world in the Américas will become ever more complicated as the Spanish conquer and colonize New Mexican Pueblo peoples.

Anaya does two things to frame this 1598 historical moment dramatically. In regard to the preparation for entering New Mexico, he foregrounds the subplot of one of Oñate's officers, who marries an indigenous woman. Captain Andrés Vaca marries the indigenous Owl Woman on the eve of the entrada, and their union provides a human-scale contrast to the epic drama taking place in the conquest. Whereas the New Mexico conquest is part of the Spanish invasion and empire building, Andrés Vaca and Owl Woman's union represents a counter history of coexistence, union, and community, which at one time may have seemed possible but ultimately was not meant to be.

Second is that Owl Woman is the bearer of the Calendar of Dreams, a bowl on which Toltec priests etched the history *and* the future of the Américas (a focus that I will return to later). The bowl's calendar tells about the Américas' ancient peoples and how the conquest unfolds, the fated meeting of Andrés and Owl Woman, and even Sonny's exploits in Albuquerque in the twentieth century. The couple brings the Calendar of Dreams to New Mexico to provide a macroperspective on these events of the New World, hoping to inspire peaceful coexistence, a potential modeled on their union, instead of the conquest's violent and bloody scenario.

It is clear from *Zia Summer* (1995), first of the Sonny Baca novels, that Raven does not cause the impasses in Sonny's personal life, especially his tendency to be directionless. Distracted by modern life and culture, and with only a weak sense of his New Mexico heritage, Sonny has been a used-car salesman, a schoolteacher, and a detective, otherwise floating through his life and culture, trying to stay clear of commitments and live in the *vato loco* style.

Zia Summer, Rio Grande Fall, Shaman Winter, and *Jemez Spring* progress along the same path as the United States in constructing important cultural milestones of identity—starting with the "melting pot" reference from the past, a reference that loosely reflects Walt Whitman's idea of a composite "American" moving down an "open road" that is the wide expanse of America. This sequence also includes the multicultural phase in the present and the emergence of an as-yet-little-examined era of ethnic identification, which we can call the "see through your own eyes" perspective. This last view suggests Anaya's understanding of other perspectives from a vantage point grounded in ties to land, a sense of place, cultural identity, and personal commitment.

In *Zia Summer* and *Rio Grande Fall*, there are Mexican American versions of these three ways America has thought about cultural identity in relation to land. In *Zia Summer*, Frank Dominic exemplifies the melting-pot version of American identity. Dominic is a candidate for mayor with a plan to develop Albuquerque as the Venice of the Southwest, with an extensive canal system and various expensive tourist attractions. This familiar American type has lost all traces of ethnic identity and ties to land and is motivated primarily by economic pragmatism and greed. Implicit in Frank Dominic's identity is the assumption that America is the neutral meeting ground for people who have shed their ethnicity, especially in their ties to land, to become new, composite "Americans"—everyone and no one in particular. Frank Dominic is an anonymous citizen-investor, a creature of both the modern cityscape and America's large-scale urbanizing and corporatizing of culture.

In *Zia Summer* and *Rio Grande Fall*, Anaya projects contemporary multiculturalism, characterized by an appreciation of the "interesting" differences that make up the "mosaic" of America's many cultures, but with no personal perspective; Sonny's own perspective at this point exemplifies the multicultural movement. This perspective is evident when Sonny has no sense of his past or his own culture. With no standards by which to judge anything, he encounters indigenous cultures and mainstream cultural infatuations in his detective work in Albuquerque, and his inability to judge critically or to discriminate is the weakness that his enemy Raven eventually exploits.

Reacting against the loss of an ethnic orientation in the melting-pot space, the multicultural movement that Sonny exemplifies promotes leaving no ethnicity behind and regarding all ethnic identities as equal in a kind of democratic vision of cultural parity. For a communal or individual identity to be viable, however, one must take ownership of the distinctions and traces from the past that shape the present. The multicultural approach, however, postulated no preference for any particular ethnic perspective but encouraged a "democratic" appreciation of everything existing in the cultural mosaic.[7] This appreciation was supposed to establish a universal viewpoint from which to regard all ethnic identity.[8] The flaw in this conception is the attempt to view approaches to ethnicities, traditions, and cultures without weighing their merits. Everyone alive has an ethnic history and a social station that color and shape a specific worldview, and the view from nowhere, the completely nonbiased view, is not actually possible.

Anaya satirizes the view from nowhere in the Sonny Baca series as a New Age enthusiasm for supposedly exotic cultures, as seen with Tamara in *Zia Summer*, a white woman passionate about indigenous culture but personally ungrounded in her "appreciation" of anything. She belongs everywhere but can claim nothing of her own. Sonny himself moves through all three phases: melting-pot person (as a used-car salesman), multiculturalist (when he teaches high school), and then person embracing his past to discover his destiny (as a detective).

In *Shaman Winter*, melting-pot contradictions and multiculturalism give way to a new space of ethnicity, which is personal and yet connects to land and the world. As Sonny and Raven struggle, Anaya describes these two titans battling over a stolen nuclear reactor core as fighting for the spirit of modern culture and the world's very existence. In Sonny's struggle with Raven, to be able to fight at all, Sonny needs to understand Raven's and his own historical ties to the Américas, his own attempts to recover the past and Raven's efforts to erase it. Without that knowledge, Sonny is defenseless. To gain that knowledge he must immerse himself ever more deeply in New Mexican and the Américas' history, both sixteenth-century New Mexico during the Spanish entrada and contemporary urban society in Albuquerque in his Sonny-as-Sonny and Sonny-as-Andrés perspectives.

Sonny learns about his past by imaginatively traveling there but also by doing archival and historical research. He begins to understand ancient and contemporary ties to land and culture in the Américas. Only when he can see the past in its present manifestation, the "presentness" of the past, as it collides with his conception of cultural space in his contemporary, fragmented life, can he find out who he is. Only by reconciling his Andrés and Sonny worlds can he avoid the modern chaos of personal and cultural amnesia that Raven encourages in the Américas as a cultural plague (Raven's name can be seen as an anagram for *never* as in the radical canceling of history, memory, and identity). Sonny's strength to fight Raven depends directly on the connections he can make between land, culture, and identity—the mestizo tradition in relation to a homeland legacy he is heir to.

As a *cultural* detective, in other words, Sonny saves the world by learning about his own and the Américas' past, and in this novel, he demonstrates how that knowledge about the Américas as a historically complex and multilayered place is essential for confronting present urban land-use issues and environmental challenges. Only an exploration of history in relation to a specific place provides the keys to understanding how the present came to be and how it can be changed. Even more clearly than in the previous two novels, Sonny—a combination of bumbling detective and the Mexican matinee idol Pedro Infante, socially awkward but savvy—can be effective as a detective only when he learns to view his life as existing against the backdrop of the complex cultural history that arises in the connection between land and culture in the Américas. Only the retrieval of the past and a reconnection with land/place in the present can save him and the world.

Sonny learns that a viable approach to affirming ethnic identity begins with a preference *for* a particular place, an ethnic perspective tied to land—also, a preference *for* one's own history with an ancestral and cultural past, however conceived. This approach is suggested not only in the knowledge that Sonny Baca gains about being a Mexican American but in his subsequent commitment to embracing the paradoxes of identity and in what don Eliseo, his curandero/teacher, teaches him about taking an active role in directing his dreams and his life.

In *Zia Summer*, don Eliseo is a minor character with little effect on Sonny Baca, but in *Shaman Winter*, when Sonny has evolved and is capable of moving to the next level of knowledge, don Eliseo is revealed to be a major source of information about the Américas' cultures, an authority on curanderismo, and knowledgeable about cultural change. In touch with the knowledge that Sonny needs, don Eliseo encourages Sonny to embrace his own ethnic and cultural identity and avoid the "view from nowhere," the view that is a forgetting of the past and effectively the downfall of modern culture.

Don Eliseo explains that the critical time and place for being a mestizo in the Américas is *now*. Legacies from the past carry the promise of helping "the human dream" to be "born again," but people must participate most fully in the human adventure by claiming a personal legacy and living it as robustly as possible in the present moment (Anaya 1999, 130). This approach says that other cultural perspectives can be known through the lens of one's own heritage, but one must first take possession of that heritage, based in history and ties to a place of origin, as completely as possible. This perspective involves coming to terms with one's past and developing a critical sense of the present and one's tie to the land and culture native to that place. This deep sense of identity comes with actively using knowledge of the past to participate in shaping the present and, by extension, the future. The personal perspective, seeing through your own eyes, limited as it may seem initially, is the only valid viewpoint from which to explore other perspectives.

A strong image for the cultural space that this book projects is that of Sonny living in modern-day Albuquerque and (through the open dream channel) exploring the Américas' history, the traces of which, once they are identified, are evident everywhere around Sonny in present-day Albuquerque. The message says that the Américas and their cultures have created the cultural underpinning and space of Mexican American life and community. Only with an adequate acknowledgment of history and one's complex "home" space and land can the Mexican American community fully sustain itself into the future.

Shaman Winter details Sonny's movement between the past and the present, as he tries to understand the modern world of Albuquerque as revealing the inheritance of the Américas' colonizing *and* colonized cultures. The many reflections of the New World as a double cultural space in *Shaman Winter*, especially the split-screen perspective of Sonny/Andrés, suggest the ways in which Mexican American culture can be innovative and continually responsive to change. The particular achievement of *Shaman Winter* is its formal acknowledgment of the multiple perspectives required to focus on the Américas' important cultural traditions. Anaya's perspective in this novel is what Gloria Anzaldúa was beginning to describe as "mestiza consciousness," with a strong indigenous appreciation of paradox (*nepantla*) and nonoppositional scenarios (235). This was also Rodolfo Gonzáles's concept of "Chicano" as a hybrid term of identity in "I Am Joaquin." *Shaman Winter* creates the split-screen view of Sonny/Andrés and explores strategies for bringing their worlds into a single hybrid perspective with a renewed sense of culture.

This novel is an important document, as it offers a perspective on the legacy of the Chicano Movement's achievement, especially with its blended past/present perspectives, which reveal Anaya's version of being a mestizo in the Américas. The Mexican American concept of a homeland, which *Shaman Winter* clarifies in some detail, points to characteristics of the homeland idea that are gradually enriching the American national experience in the twenty-first century. *Shaman Winter* vividly reflects a Chicano realignment of culture following a tremendous shift toward recognizing the Américas as a single staging for culture in this hemisphere. In so doing, this novel projects the possibility of realizing a potential for community in the Américas that has scarcely been glimpsed. In its affirmation of mestizo history and identity, it signals that Mexican American culture since the 1960s has been looking ahead to an ethnically diverse and expanding world that will outlast the legacy of colonialism.

Shaman Winter also shows that the role of the New World person is to be not only a product of Western colonialism but also a mestizo change agent, a citizen who is an active explorer of the Américas as a homeland. At the leading edge of a development defined by Martí, Haya de la Torre, Vasconcelos, Quijano, and Anzaldúa, Mexican American writers and artists are chronicling, as *Shaman Winter* does, the cultural changes that are affecting the cultures of the Américas in the twenty-first century.

What Mexican Americans are creating in the New World as they make a home for themselves has the potential to challenge the reigning ideologies of the postcolonial Américas. *Shaman Winter*'s argument is that establishing a mestizo homeland will further drive back and reduce the colonial legacy's effects. Those involved in reclaiming the homeland will continue to foster an emerging reality of the Américas, as in the early decades of the twenty-first century, many aspects of Anaya's New World vision come forward to embolden those making the Américas their home.

Shaman Winter still has more to reveal, and we can go a step further to examine the persistence of colonial influence in Mexican American culture by exploring the relationship between public and private spaces in the novel. Henri Lefebvre's monumental *The Production of Space* ([1974] 1991) provides a perspective for examining how public and private life in the Américas intersect. This pioneering analysis of cultural space in cultural theory and critical geography argues that the relations between public and private spheres of culture can reveal much about a community's orientation and its manner of distributing power. For example, the mestizo homeland is a hemispheric cultural "space," what Anaya calls the New World, but what does it mean to talk about the Mexican American homeland as a cultural "space"? Discussions of cultural space in literary and cultural criticism tend to foreground complex cultural and social situations connected to land and place, as Yi-Fu Tuan demonstrates in *Space and Place: The Perspective of Experience* (1977).

Take the Mexican American depictions of communal order in *Shaman Winter*. This novel displays highly stylized depictions of space that are circulated publicly, for example, the documents and texts that Sonny consults in his research. These are examples of what Lefebvre calls "conceived space," models and crafted depictions of the culture—sometimes actual pictures and paintings but also diagrams, histories, illustrations, and city plans. Conceived spaces are produced by a culture's architects, urban planners, commercial illustrators, artists, and engineers. These texts are the models of how the culture, or parts of the culture, work, and how social and cultural forces relate to each other. Such "conceptualized [or conceived] space" is the handiwork of all who deliberately construct models or facsimiles of the culture, whether the result is a scientific inventory, a blueprint, or an artistic rendering of a neighborhood (Lefebvre [1974] 1991, 38). Conceived spaces can also be verbal and even numerical texts that reflect the order and ordering principles that make up a community's social and cultural relations. Taken as a whole, the conceived spaces of the Mexican American community depict how potentially everything in the community relates to everything else at a particular moment.

It is this dimension of conceived space that Rafael Pérez-Torres analyzes in *Mestizaje* (2006) when he discusses Chicano murals and posters and explores the connections they make between land and identity. He writes that "in relation to land, the thematic representation of mestizaje offers an insight into simultaneous feelings of alienation and home. Land becomes, in these visual texts, something both familiar and strange" (152). Because such conceived spaces—in this case, mural depictions of land—are shared publicly, a defining characteristic of conceived spaces, they tend to carry official status as representing the culture, or large parts of the culture, at a particular moment. People endlessly discuss blueprints, mural art, art in museums, and photographs and paintings of landscapes in professional and other kinds of publications.

Another revealing example of a conceived space would be Alma López's computer collage *La Linea*. This picture shows a rugged landscape on the border between México and the United States, and on this tough terrain, a young Mexican American girl walks along a wall trying to find her footing in the dangerous space between cultures. As a Mexican American and a female living on the U.S.-México border, she is reliant on her own ability to navigate the difficult terrain between cultures. López's work is addressing what it is like to navigate two worlds, especially where one culture is the "dominant space" (Lefebvre [1974] 1991, 39).

Such artworks mark a moment of cultural and social understanding and are "conceived" spaces in the sense of bringing together ideas and values that map complex cultural relations—in this case, cultural connections between México and the United States. In mainstream culture, photos and paintings of national parks and famous monuments fulfill this task as well, as Ken Burns and Dayton Duncan show in the PBS documentary *The National Parks: America's Best Idea* (2009). Such spatial practices unite the larger community around complex depictions of nature, culture, and the "commonwealth" that those conceived spaces draw from.

If we look across Mexican American homes, neighborhoods, workplaces, and community centers, we see the social and idealized projections of "conceived" (public) order located within picture frames on walls and sprawled across desks as blueprints, city plans, fashion designs, floor plans, and municipal project proposals. These representations reflect images drawn from Mexican American culture as well as from the national culture. Images presented in this way act as mooring points for a community at a particular moment, and a gallery of such images and designs would reveal the style, identity, and official values of Mexican American culture in relation to the dominant culture.

There are also the private spaces of Mexican American culture that are not official representations of anything. These are the areas of "representational space," or "lived space," in Lefebvre's term, spaces that are lived in "directly . . . through [their] associated images and symbols" ([1974] 1991, 39). These lived spaces are the intimate, even hidden, spaces of Mexican American life that people inhabit and retreat to—bedrooms, living rooms, bathrooms, family rooms, lawnmower sheds, altars, utility rooms, storage cabinets, and even the highly personal spaces of drawers and closets. These spaces—even the body's hidden zones, folds, and cavities—are conventionalized and a part of culture, too, but their depictions are not circulated publicly, and their noncirculated status as private and intimate spaces defines them.

These lived-in spaces "tend towards more or less coherent systems of nonverbal symbols and signs" (Lefebvre [1974] 1991, 39). They embody "complex symbolisms, sometimes coded, sometimes not," and however personal they are, their intelligibility exists in relation to the official "conceived spaces" in the documents, paintings, murals, city plans, and so on that circulate prominently in a public display of culture (33). "Lived" spaces are often "passively experienced" and are taken for granted and even "forgotten" when not attended to (33).

In *Shaman Winter*, the existence of Sonny's open channel to another time in the Spanish colonial era presents him with a conceived space that does not exist in his own day in contemporary Albuquerque. That conceived space is the Calendar of Dreams, the etched bowl belonging to Owl Woman, which tells her story and that of Andrés, Sonny, Raven, and potentially everyone else in the Américas. The Calendar of Dreams' perspective is that of the north/south orientation of the Américas (as opposed to the east/west orientation of European settlement) and includes the life of the Américas' ancient peoples and *everything* that has transpired in the New World.

As a conceived space for the Américas, the Calendar of Dreams depicts the history of indigenous people, the Spanish, and African Americans. Unlike British accounts of North America as the privileged trek of European colonists, who methodically marched westward and destroyed tribal peoples as they crossed the continent, or the Spanish story about the conquest, the ascension, and eventual fall of Spanish colonialism in the New World, the Calendar of Dreams starts with an indigenous perspective and tells about all who have come to the New World.

The Calendar of Dreams is not an ideal view of everyone, but it presents the *interested* perspective of the person who views it, the antithesis of the view from nowhere. Always tracking a specific person's journey and showing where it leads, the Calendar of Dreams' perspective is the potential of a personal, engaged view of life in the Américas. Not in itself a repository of stories but a potential for stories to be articulated, the Calendar of Dreams is an open view of the Américas as a staging ground that has always existed as a possibility but only in this creation has become a reality.

Over the last fifty years, the broad goal of the Chicano community has been to change the lived spaces of everyday life—to make life better for

Mexican Americans in their workplaces, houses, schools, and community centers. The 1960s Chicano Movement tried to support those changes by advancing and promoting a revitalized conceived space, the sacred space of a once-lost homeland, Aztlán. Those attempts to model an indigenous future when people could come back to their homeland were influential and effective. We can see the success of those efforts in the changes that took place in Mexican American literature, social texts, communal reinvestment, mural art, painting, popular design, and in the images on lowrider cars, tattoos, and so forth. And like all hybrid spaces, Aztlán canceled the social prestige of a dominant legacy, in this case, the Spanish colonial legacy. Aztlán was a hybrid strategy within Mexican American culture that helped to reframe the power relationships of actual life in the Mexican American community, and to a significant degree this initiative has succeeded.

The New World as depicted in the Calendar of Dreams is another challenge and a new conceived space for the Américas in the twenty-first century. The mestizo homeland projected on a broad scale, the Calendar of Dreams is an image designed to match the expansive mestizo sense of land and place across the Américas. As the hybrid space that houses mestizo stories, the Calendar of Dreams also contains Spanish and British chapters, too, but the New World story is no longer their exclusive possession. The Calendar of Dreams is a larger story that incorporates the history of the mestizaje along with the stories of the Spanish, the British, the Portuguese, and the French.

Since the 1960s, Mexican Americans have promoted a new understanding of land and the potential for incorporating cultural ties to land through the recognition of long-standing traditions focused on communal needs. That initiative to define a relationship to land different from that of mainstream culture has been a strategy for connecting Mexican Americans to U.S. culture and hybrid identity as they come home to the United States. Their redefining of a relationship to land has also connected them with national concerns about the loss of cultural ties to land and of the cultural richness that depends on an identification with land and the spirit of place. This championing of land's importance has helped to make the United States a receptive home for Mexican Americans and has energized an argument for retaining traditional ties to land that can help to create a better future for America as a whole.

Oscar Zeta Acosta's assertion of Aztlán as a Mexican American home in the United States is accurate, even though that story is complex and still evolving. This story could not be told until the modern era, when the possibilities for cultural change opened up, and Mexican Americans became the people who can tell their own story. The Calendar of Dreams, with its perspective on the Américas, is a powerful concept that provides a way to talk about the retelling of such stories. The Calendar of Dreams suggests that in the recognition of mestizo identity and in the reclamation of the mestizo homeland, Mexican Americans in the twenty-first century have discovered the stories that need retelling, stories about land, race, and mestizo peoples. Such stories tell about remaking connections to *los antepasados*, through land and the cultural relationships that land makes possible.

There is a mandate in *Shaman Winter* to seize the opportunity of perspective and knowledge when it is available and to carry it forward, as don Eliseo says, to help "the human dream" to be "born again" (139). The Mexican American exploration of the relationship of land and mestizo identity, an unpacking of Acosta's statement that "Chicanos [are] from Aztlán," is another important piece in the strategy for turning the United States into a home for the Mexican American community. Acosta's work and Anaya's novel suggest that Mexican Americans have always been where they belong but since the 1960s have been learning to resee their connection to the land around them.

NOTES

1. See Wilson, *The Myth of Santa Fe* (1997). For a valuable overview of land problems in New Mexico, see Briggs and Van Ness, *Land, Water, and Culture* (1987).
2. An insightful discussion of Ritch's books, which I am generally following here, is Gutiérrez, "Aztlán, Montezuma, and New Mexico" (1989).
3. It is the overriding thesis of Gutiérrez's "Azlán, Montezuma, and New Mexico" that the drive to associate the Territory of New Mexico with Aztlán was politically and commercially motivated.
4. *El Plan Espiritual's* focus on Mexican American life and land, new and liberating,

advanced that "EDUCATION must be relative to our people, i.e., history; culture, bilingual education, contributions, etc. Community control [is needed] of our schools, our teachers, our administrators, our counselors, and our programs" ([1969] 1989, 3). Following this call to action, in March 1968, one thousand students walked out of Lincoln and Garfield High Schools (among others) in East Los Angeles, and a bloody "blow-out" confrontation followed in a seven-month standoff between the Chicano community, the police, and the Los Angeles Unified School District Board of Education (Rosales 1996, 184–85). Such protests and the concern for educational reform in *El Plan* argued for the institution of bilingual education and student-oriented curricula in Latino schools across the country. Such protests also led to the startup of Chicano studies programs in colleges and universities nationally and even worldwide, an initiative advanced in detail in *El Plan de Santa Barbara* ([1969] 1989).

Key to *El Plan Espiritual de Aztlán* was economic development to serve the Mexican American community. A Mexican American "economic program" could "drive the exploiter [white investors] out of our community" and bring about "a welding together of our people's combined resources to control their own production through cooperative effort" (*El Plan Espiritual* [1969] 1989, 4). The community had to be willing to "make its own decisions" on "the taxation of goods" and "the profit of our sweat" (4). If needed, "Chicano defense units"—Brown Berets—could enforce economic and other transformative measures essential for advancing the Mexican American cause (2). An armed paramilitary unit had weak support over time, but it was initially based on 1960s optimism about social protest, inspired by successes such as that of César Chávez (though nonviolent) in organizing the National Farm Workers Association and the United Farm Workers in Delano.

5. In 1979, Joseph Sommers wrote that the Aztlán idea was nothing more than a "harkening back in sadness and nostalgia for a forgotten, idealized, and unobtainable past," an empty cultural abstraction (Sommers and Ybarra-Frausto 1979, 38). Others worried that the Aztlán movement was just another appropriation of Native culture for non-Native cultural capital and gain. But within the Mexican American community, the Aztlán claim's effect was electric and helped to bring about a renaissance in Chicano culture, art, and social life. Aztlán was a constructed "place," if not a real location, and the early debunkers of Aztlán seemed to miss this larger picture and the significance of claiming a Mexican American homeland in the United States as a validating act in itself.

6. The irony in this correction of a tradition is that, as linguistic analysis shows, the "Cochise culture of southern Arizona" probably *was* the origin of peoples as diverse as the Utes in Colorado and the Aztecs around Mexico City (Chávez 1989, 51). Tribes from México, New Mexico, California, Texas, and Colorado spoke the Uto-Aztecan languages of the Cochise people, who were native to the southwestern United States (51–52). So though the American Southwest

was probably *not* Aztlán, at least not *literally* Aztlán, "the earliest evidence of a clearly distinguishable [Cochise] culture"—in southern Arizona, as early as 8000 B.C.—indicates that the Aztec home, long before the purported Aztlán, may well have been in what is now the U.S. Southwest after all (51).

7. For a variety of perspectives on the multicultural approach to education and identity, see Giroux, *Border Crossings* (1992); Anyon, "Social Class and the Hidden Curriculum of Work" (1980); Apple, *Ideology and Curriculum* (1979); and Sleeter, *Empowerment through Multicultural Education* (1991).

8. I fully understand that educational theorists and actual teachers are not intending to distance their students from racial issues by taking the broad view of ethnic cultures and races. David Hursh, for example, in "Multicultural Social Studies" (1997), would seem to be arguing the opposite of multiculturalism as I describe it when he says the aim of multiculturalism is "to recognize, draw out, and analyze with students, the diversity of their own lives and society." "The school becomes a public arena," he goes on," where teachers, students, and others use history, political science, and other social sciences to make sense of their lives" (119). These are laudable aims, clearly. It simply is not evident to me that multiculturalism as it has been theorized and advanced can actually accomplish such aims. Multiculturalism is the beginning of a good idea. It simply needs to be thought out completely.

REFERENCES

Acosta, Oscar Zeta. 1973. *The Revolt of the Cockroach People*. New York: Vintage Books.

Acuña, Rodolfo. 2000. *Occupied America: A History of Chicanos*. New York: Longman.

Ahmed, Sara, Claudia Castañeda, Anne-Marie Fortier, and Mimi Sheller. 2003. *Uprootings/Regroundings: Questions of Home and Migration*. Oxford: Berg.

Alurista. 1991. "Myth, Identity and Struggle in Three Chicano Novels: Aztlán . . . Anaya, Méndez, and Acosta." In *Aztlán: Essays on the Chicano Homeland*. Eds. Rudolfo A. Anaya and Francisco Lomelí, 219–29. Albuquerque: University of New Mexico Press.

Anaya, Rudolfo A. 1991. "Aztlán: A Homeland Without Boundaries." In *Aztlán: Essays on the Chicano Homeland*, eds. Rudolfo A. Anaya and Francisco Lomelí, 230–41. Albuquerque: University of New Mexico Press.

———. 1995a. "The New World Man." In *The Anaya Reader*, 353–65. New York: Warner Books.

———. 1995b. *Zia Summer*. New York: Warner Books.

———. 1996. *Rio Grande Fall*. Albuquerque: University of New Mexico Press.

———. 1999. *Shaman Winter*. New York: Warner Books.

————. 2009a. "Mythical Dimensions/Political Reality." In *The Essays*, 89–94. Norman: University of Oklahoma Press.

————. 2009b. "Sale of Atrisco Land Grant Means Loss of History, Tradition." In *The Essays*, 131–34. Norman: University of Oklahoma Press.

————. 2009c. "The Writer's Landscape: Epiphany in Landscape." In *The Essays*, 141–46. Norman: University of Oklahoma Press.

Anaya, Rudolfo A., and Francisco Lomelí, eds. 1991. *Aztlán: Essays on the Chicano Homeland*. Albuquerque: University of New Mexico Press.

Anyon, Jean. 1980. "Social Class and the Hidden Curriculum of Work." *Journal of Education* 162:67–92.

Anzaldúa, Gloria. 1987. *Borderlands/La Frontera: The New Mestiza*. San Francisco, CA: Aunt Lute Books.

Apple, Michael M. 1979. *Ideology and Curriculum*. London: Routledge and Kegan Paul.

Briggs, Charles L., and John R. Van Ness. 1987. Introduction to *Land, Water, and Culture: New Perspectives on Hispanic Land Grants*, 3–13. Albuquerque: University of New Mexico Press.

Chávez, John R. 1989. "Aztlán, Cibola, and Frontier New Spain." In *Aztlán: Essays on the Chicano Homeland*, edited by Rudolfo A. Anaya and Francisco Lomelí, 49–71. Albuquerque: University of New Mexico Press.

Chicano Coordinating Council on Higher Education. 1969. *El Plan de Santa Bárbara*. Oakland, CA: La Cause Publications.

Durán, Fray Diego. (1581) 1994. *The History of the Indies of New Spain (Historia de las Indias de La Nueva-España y Islas de Tierra Firme)*. Translated by Doris Heyden. Norman: University of Oklahoma Press.

Ebright, Malcolm. 1987. "New Mexican Land Grants: The Legal Background." In *Land, Water, and Culture: New Perspectives on Hispanic Land Grants*, edited by Charles L. Briggs and John R. Van Ness, 15–64. Albuquerque: University of New Mexico Press

El Plan Espiritual de Aztlán. (1969) 1989. In *Aztlán: Essays on the Chicano Homeland*, edited by Rudolfo A. Anaya and Francisco Lomelí, 1–5. Albuquerque: University of New Mexico Press.

Giroux, Henry A. 1992. *Border Crossings: Cultural Workers and the Politics of Education*. New York: Routledge.

Gonzáles, Rodolfo. 1997. "I Am Joaquin." In *Literatura Chicana, 1965–1995: An Anthology in Spanish, English and Caló*, edited by Manuel De Jesús Hernández-Gutiérrez and David William Foster, 207–22. New York: Garland.

Gutiérrez, Ramón A. 1989. "Aztlán, Montezuma, and New Mexico: The Political Uses of American Indian Mythology." In *Aztlán: Essays on the Chicano Homeland*. Rudolfo A. Anaya and Francisco Lomelí, 172–90. Albuquerque: University of New Mexico Press.

Hursh, David. 1997. "Multicultural Social Studies: Schools as Places for Examining and Challenging Inequality." In *The Social Studies Curriculum: Purposes,*

Problems, and Possibilities, edited by E. Wayne Ross, 107–19. Albany: State University of New York Press.

Jussawalla, Feroza, and Reed Way Dasenbrock. 1992. "Rudolfo Anaya." In *Interviews with Writers of the Post-Colonial World*, 243–55. Jackson: University Press of Mississippi.

Keats, John. 1973. "On First Looking into Chapman's Homer." *John Keats: The Complete Poems*, 72. London: Penguin.

Lefebvre, Henri. 1991. *The Production of Space*. Translated by Donald Nicholson-Smith. Oxford: Blackwell. Originally published as *La Production de l'espace* (Paris: Anthropos, 1974).

Matos Moctezuma, Eduardo. 1988. *The Great Temple of the Aztecs: Treasures of Tenochtitlan*. Translated by Doris Heyden. New York: Thames and Hudson.

Morgan, Lewis Henry. (1877) 1964. *Ancient Society*. Cambridge, MA: Belknap Press of Harvard University Press.

Nostrand, Richard L. 1972. *The Hispano Homeland*. Norman: University of Oklahoma Press.

Padilla, Genaro. 1989. "Myth and Comparative Cultural Nationalism: The Ideological Uses of Aztlán." In *Aztlán: Essays on the Chicano Homeland*, edited by Rudolfo A. Anaya and Francisco Lomelí, 111–34. Albuquerque: University of New Mexico Press.

Parsons, James J. 1985. "'Bioregionalism' and 'Watershed Consciousness.'" *Professional Geographer* 37 (1): 1–6.

Peña, Devon G., ed. 1998. *Chicano Culture, Ecology, Politics: Subversive Kin*. Tucson: University of Arizona Press.

Pérez-Torres, Rafael. 2006. *Mestizaje: Critical Uses of Race in Chicano Culture*. Minneapolis: University of Minnesota Press.

Pulido, Laura. 1996. *Environmentalism and Economic Justice: Two Chicano Cases from the Southwest*. Tucson: University of Arizona Press.

Ritch, William G. 1885. *Aztlán: The History, Resources and Attractions of New Mexico*. Boston: Lothrop.

Rodríguez, Sylvia. 1987. "Land, Water, and Ethnic Identity in Taos." In *Land, Water and Culture: New Perspective on Hispanic Land Grants*, edited by Charles L. Briggs and John R. Van Ness, 313–403. Albuquerque: University of New Mexico Press.

Rosales, F. Arturo. 1996. *Chicano!: The History of the Mexican American Civil Rights Movement*. Houston, TX: Arte Público Press.

Sahagún, Fray Bernardino de. (1582) 1981. *Historia General de las Cosas de Nueva España*. 4 vols. Mexico City: Editorial Porrúa.

Sauer, Carl O. 1962. "Homestead and Community in the Middle Border." *Landscape* 20 (2): 44–47.

Shiva, Vandana. 1998. "Subversive Kin: A Politics of Diversity." In *Chicano Culture, Ecology, Politics: Subversive Kin*, edited by Devon G. Peña, vii–ix. Tucson: University of Arizona Press.

Sleeter, C., ed. 1991. *Empowerment through Multicultural Education.* Albany: State University of New York Press.

Sommers, Joseph, and Tomás Ybarra-Frausto, eds. 1979. *Modern Chicano Writers: A Collection of Critical Essays.* Englewood Cliffs, NJ: Prentice-Hall.

Tuan, Yi-Fu. 1977. *Space and Place: The Perspective of Experience.* Minneapolis: University of Minnesota Press.

Wilson, Chris. 1997. *The Myth of Santa Fe: Creating a Modern Regional Tradition.* Albuquerque: University of New Mexico Press.

PART 2
Anaya's Poetics of the Novel

6

Rudolfo Anaya's *Bless Me, Ultima*

A NUEVOMEXICANO CONTRIBUTION
TO THE HEMISPHERIC GENEALOGY OF THE
NEW WORLD BAROQUE

Monika Kaup

In this chapter, I seek to demonstrate that Rudolfo Anaya's acclaimed first novel, *Bless Me, Ultima* (1972), rightfully belongs within a cultural and artistic context in which it hasn't been widely noted—the hemispheric continuities of the New World baroque. The baroque arrived in the Américas on the ships of the conquistadores; that is to say, the baroque's original arrival in the New World was the result of European colonialism. Its offspring is the New World baroque, the baroque that grew up in Spain and Portugal's colonies in the Américas. The material culture of the New World baroque, however, offers widespread evidence that the Iberian colonial baroque was transformed through idiosyncratic mestizo and local adaptations in the seventeenth and eighteenth centuries. Such alterations can be found across the visual arts as well as in colonial literature (mostly authored by criollos), but it is predominant in rural religious architecture and painting. In pioneering studies in the 1920s, culminating in the 1940 magnum opus *Redescubrimiento de América en el arte*, Argentine art historian Ángel Guido was the first to suggest that the American baroque was a new, rebellious baroque, which contested the European baroque's original function as a repressive tool of colonialism and the Counter-Reformation. Guido's works in turn inspired a post–World War II generation of Latin American intellectuals, foremost among them Cuban writers Alejo Carpentier and José Lezama Lima. Carpentier and Lezama Lima popularized the notion of a transculturated, or syncretic, and "anticolonial" New World baroque. They argued that the official European baroque was adapted and transformed at the hands of indigenous and mestizo artisans, whose labor created most of the monuments of baroque art in the Américas. These artists inserted pre-Columbian symbols into the iconography of the Catholic baroque, undoing the colonial negation of their world and at the same time deforming and re-creating the European expression that had been imposed on them. Guido, Carpentier, and Lezama Lima claimed that New World artists had stolen the colonizer's art and turned it into an expression of their own: the historical baroque, imposed "from above," was transformed "from below"; somehow, the colonizer was in turn colonized. In Lezama Lima's words, the American baroque was an instrument not of the Counter-Reformation, but of *contraconquista* (counterconquest).

Since initial publication of these ideas—Lezama Lima's essay "Baroque Curiosity" appeared in the 1958 collection *La expresión americana*, and Carpentier's essays "Questions Concerning the Contemporary Latin American Novel" and "The Baroque and the Marvelous Real" appeared in print in 1964 and 1981 respectively—these claims have been widely influential. The post–World War II period saw the publication of a series of revisionist Latin American art histories by Pál Kelemen, Manuel Toussaint, Teresa Gisbert, Carolyn Dean, Gauvin Bailey, and many others; revisionist art histories are still being published, confirming the substance of Carpentier's, Lezama Lima's, and Guido's claims about the modification of Catholic art at the hands of indigenous and mestizo artists and artisans. Kelemen's early assessment is paradigmatic:

> Colonial art in Spanish America is far from a mere transplantation of Spanish forms into a new world; it grew out of the union of two civilizations which in many ways were the antithesis of each other. Non-European factors were at work also. Thus it incorporated the Indian's preferences, his characteristic sense of form and color, the power of his own heritage. . . . The baroque style lent itself amazingly well to the fusion of these influences. A full-blooded baroque spread to even the less accessible regions of Latin America and with its register of variations developed such regional expressions as the "Andean mestizo" and the "Mexican *poblano*" style. ([1951] 1967, 1:22)

Lezama Lima and his predecessor Ángel Guido both offer excellent detailed illustrations of how, on the façades and in the interiors of New World baroque churches, indigenous sacred and profane symbolism shares space with the Catholic iconography of angels, saints, and virgins. Lezama's describes the transculturated iconography on the façade of the Church of San Lorenzo in Potosí, Bolivia—the work of the Quechua Indian sculptor José Kondori:

> The Indian Kondori succeeds in inserting the Inca symbols of the sun and the moon, abstractly rendered, and Inca mermaids, oversized angels whose Indian faces reflect the desolation of their exploitation in the mines. . . . The supports of his columns flaunt a powerful abstraction of Inca suns, whose opulent energy cascades over the plaintive face of the *mitayo* mermaid playing a native guitar. . . . How did [the Jesuit fathers] view the unsought bonus that equated American leaves with Greek trefoils, the Inca half-moon with the acanthus foliage of Corinthian capstones, and the music of the *charangos* [a native musical instrument] with the sound of Doric instruments and the Renaissance viola da gamba? ([1958] 2010, 236)

One of the masterpieces of the so-called Andean mestizo style, Kondori's façade of San Lorenzo (figure 6.1) is an outstanding example of the deformation and transculturation of the colonial Spanish baroque "from below." In central México, the other main area of the mestizo New World baroque, such work is known as tequitqui art (*tequitqui* is a Náhuatl term for tributary), art created by the usually anonymous indigenous and mestizo artisans who built, sculpted, and painted the monuments of the New World baroque (see figure 6.2). A Cuban poet and writer who during his adult life traveled little outside Havana, Lezama Lima was indebted to Ángel Guido's pioneering art historical studies of the New World baroque iconography of San Lorenzo. The first to identify indigenous elements in New World baroque iconography, Guido listed items in a wide range of categories: native flora (such as corn and thistle flowers), native fauna (such as hummingbirds and monkeys), human figures, native cultural artifacts (such as the charango), and native astrology and myth (the Andean sun, moon, and stars).[1]

6.1. José Kondori, façade, Church of San Lorenzo, 1728–44, Potosí, Bolivia.
(Photo by Lois Parkinson Zamora)

The argument that I am making here is about continuities between the mestizo cosmovision of Anaya's *Bless Me, Ultima* and the New World baroque. Like the façades and interiors of New World baroque churches, Anaya's novel delineates a hybrid sacred and profane cosmology, in which the symbols and icons of the dominant colonial Catholic culture are subjected to deformation and mongrelization "from below." As critics have noted, *Bless Me, Ultima* is a Mexican American bildungsroman, narrating Antonio's spiritual maturation. Anaya's novel presents Mexican American spirituality as a conundrum, a mystery that the young Antonio is tasked to solve. Part of Antonio's spiritual pilgrimage takes place outside of external social reality, through a series of eight mystical or visionary dreams. As

6.2. Detail of interior wall, Church of Santa María Tonantzintla (1690–1730), State of Puebla, México. (Photo by Lois Parkinson Zamora)

Juan Bruce-Novoa has observed, "Antonio is not torn between an Anglo and a Chicano world, but between two ways of being Chicano"—the colonial Hispanic heritage on the one hand, and the Native heritage indigenous to the Américas on the other (1996, 183). The offspring of a mestizo culture fractured along multiple fault lines, Antonio is presented with a cultural inheritance in a chaotic state of disorder. Everywhere Antonio turns, he encounters conflict and struggle between opposing forces: the rivalry between his paternal and maternal ancestors, the free-roaming vaquero clan of the Márez and the sedentary agricultural clan of the Luna; the dichotomy between Hispanic Catholicism and Native pantheism, the duality of creation and destruction, the battle of good against evil, and the conflict between the contemporary reality of post–World War II modernity and the timeless reality of the sacred. Guided by his mentor, the curandera Ultima, Antonio embarks on a spiritual journey into his nuevomexicano mestizo religion and mythology that seeks to put chaos into order and reconstruct a hypothetical underlying cosmic harmony. And indeed, Antonio experiences many epiphanic moments of revelation that seem to promise the fulfillment of this goal, where conflict seems to cease and peace to reign. Examples are the initial moment when Ultima takes Antonio's hand and awakens his spiritual vision to a revelation of a mystical union with the universe: "the four directions of the llano met in [him]" (Anaya 1972, 10). Another instance is the moment at the end of Antonio's dream of an apocalypse prophesied by Native myth, when at Ultima's command, the cosmic forces cease to battle, and Ultima subsequently settles the dispute between the Márez and Luna clans by proclaiming that the sea water of the ocean (associated with the Márez) and the sweet water of the rivers (with the Luna) are one and the same water: "*You have been seeing only parts, Antonio,* she finished, *and not looking beyond into the great cycle that binds us all.* Then there was peace in my dreams and I could rest" (113).

Yet, such visions of cosmic reconciliation and harmony do not last. They are invariably displaced by renewed outbreaks of conflict. Even Ultima's death at the end as a pharmakos (as Roberto Cantú [1990, 41] has noted)—atoning for the blood she has spilled in selfless battle against evil, to save Antonio's uncle Lucas's life from the curse of the Trementina sisters—only puts to rest a finite and human-scale episode of conflict. Antonio receives Ultima's blessing before her death, but this blessing is nothing but an injunction to continue the quest for cosmic harmony, by taking Ultima's place and continuing her work, as a mediator of opposites. For at the macrocosmic scale, the conflict between Catholic monotheism and Native pantheism *within nuevomexicano* Catholic spirituality continues unabated. Further, there are deaths and cruel injustices that remain unredeemed, such as the death of Florence, posterior to his lapse into atheism because of the senseless destruction of his family. In short, *Bless Me, Ultima*'s ending is really just another beginning, for the task of reconstructing cosmic order out of chaos remains ahead, a task Antonio is now ready to assume as an adolescent, after graduating from Ultima's apprenticeship.

Despite its powerful drive for closure and integration, *Bless Me, Ultima* terminates on a note of the absurd rather than the logical, on the fragmentary rather than the unified whole. This is the formula of the baroque. In the words of Catalan critic Eugenio d'Ors, the baroque is characterized by "inner fragmentation" and division; the baroque is "broken, *absurd*, like nature . . . not logical and unitary, like reason" (2010, 88). Further, as d'Ors points out, the characteristic discontinuity, mobility, and dynamism of the baroque expresses the idea of unfinished becoming rather than of static being (87). This is very much the state of nuevomexicano Mexican American culture in Anaya's novel. Despite the antiquity of this culture, and even though, as Anaya has suggested, Antonio recovers, in Jungian fashion, the collective memory and ancestral myths of his culture, going back to pre-Columbian times, nuevomexicano culture is a culture in motion.[2] It is a culture still undergoing transformation under the continuing impact of opposing forces. Carpentier adapted d'Ors's theory to claim baroque as essentially Latin American, as the organic expression of the continent's sociohistory of cultural, racial, and artistic mestizaje by way of the dialectical process of conquest and rebellious counterconquest. The baroque, writes Carpentier, "arises where there is transformation, mutation or innovation" ([1981] 1995a, 98): "America, a continent of symbiosis, mutations, vibrations, *mestizaje*, has always been baroque: the American cosmogonies, where we find the *Popol Vuh*, where we find the books of the *Chilam Balam* . . . correspond to the baroque" (98).

D'Ors—as well as Carpentier, who follows him in this respect—thought of the baroque and its antithetical counterpart, the classical, as ahistorical styles, as timeless opposing forces of the human spirit that recur at any period and in any culture. (D'Ors famously listed twenty-two baroques, including a Nordic, a Buddhist, and a fin de siècle baroque.) But historically, the baroque first arose in seventeenth-century Europe as a cultural and aesthetic response to early modern religious and scientific upheavals—the Counter-Reformation and the rise of modern science.

The baroque's characteristic exuberance and excess resulted from cosmological schism and crisis—the destabilization and loss of established

worldviews caused by the Copernican revolution and the breakup of
the unity of the Christian church. The artistic response to early modern
scientific and religious crises, baroque art stages "a theater of ceaseless
conflicts" (Braider 2004, 8). The baroque impulse is to portray powerful
forces in combat, to disrupt and deform, to subject the overall composition
to contrary stresses and tensions. Good architectural illustrations of this
principle are the undulating and twisted walls of the Roman baroque and
its closest analogue in the Américas, the churches of Brazilian mulatto
architect and sculptor Antônio Francisco Lisboa, known as O Aleijadinho, who together with José Kondori figures as the most emblematic

6.3. Francesco Borromini, San Carlo alle Quattro Fontane (1634–38), Rome,
Italy. (Author's photo)

New World baroque artist in Guido's and Lezama Lima's works (figures 6.3 and 6.4).

Cosmological revolution is also the source of the baroque's paradigmatic "horror of the void," which is emblematic in Pascal's famous exclamation about the eternal silence of the infinite spaces that know nothing of, and terrify, him. The discovery of infinity; the expansion of the cosmos (as a result of new technologies, the telescope and microscope); the decentering of the Ptolemaic universe by Copernican theory and Kepler's subsequent discovery that the heavenly spheres moved not in circular but in elliptical orbits; and the disintegration of the Christian

6.4. Aleijadinho (Antônio Francisco Lisboa), Church of San Francisco de Assisi (1766–94), Ouro Preto, Brazil. (Author's photo)

church into warring partisan factions—all these centripetal scientific and religious forces exploded the confines of the unity and balanced harmony of Renaissance classicism into the loose, open, dynamic forms of the baroque. In Heinrich Wölfflin's 1915 study *Principles of Art History*, the Swiss art historian argued that the strict norms of Renaissance classicism gave way to a freer conception of art in the baroque, replacing closed, self-contained, and symmetrical compositions with decentered, asymmetrical, dynamic ones. In what he called the "painterly" baroque, the focus shifts from essence to appearance, from "being" to "seeming," as theatricality and the shifting play of appearances newly come to dominate. As Wölfflin said, the baroque depicts things not as they are but as they seem to be. Mexican writer Carlos Fuentes, in an essay on William Faulkner, explained the baroque's stylistic abundance as actually an expression of insufficiency:

> The baroque, Alejo Carpentier once told me, is the language of peoples who, not knowing what is true, desperately seek it. Góngora, like Picasso, Buñuel, Carpentier, or Faulkner, did not know; they discovered. The baroque, language of abundance, is also the language of insufficiency. Only those who possess nothing can include everything. The *horror vacui* of the baroque is not gratuitous—it is because the vacuum exists that nothing is certain. The verbal abundance of Carpentier's *The Kingdom of this World* or of Faulkner's *Absalom, Absalom!* represents a desperate invocation of language to fill the absences left by the banishment of reason and faith. (2010, 543)

Fuentes's comments identify the content of the form of the baroque's horror of the void. Indeed, his phrase "not knowing what is true, [they] desperately seek it" also perfectly describes Antonio's quest in *Bless Me, Ultima*. Like many other baroque and neobaroque works—including the Mexican baroque poet Sor Juana's masterpiece, *Primero Sueño* (1692; *First Dream*), *Bless Me, Ultima*—to adapt Octavio Paz's observation on Sor Juana's poem—affirms the passion for knowledge in the absence of knowledge.[3] *Bless Me, Ultima* is quintessentially baroque in staging force and counterforce in combat, something that many critics have noted in discussing the novel's many "binary oppositions" and the mediating function of Ultima and Antonio (Bruce-Novoa 1996, 188; Lamadrid 1990, 106), though without relating the novel's dramatization of deeply entrenched dualisms to the baroque and the New World baroque. To appreciate Anaya's recourse to baroque style in the narration of Manichaean struggle between antagonistic cosmic forces, it is helpful to point out transhistorical parallels with John Milton's depiction of the cosmic battle between heaven and hell in *Paradise Lost* (1667). Satan's heroic stature had constituted a persistent problem for readers of Milton's epic, who were unable to square Milton's unquestionable loyalties as a Christian and Puritan artist with his positive figuration of the arch adversary: as William Blake memorably put it, whereas Milton should have been on the side of God, he was "of the Devil's party without knowing it" (Roston 1980, 53). As Murray Roston has shown, Satan's charisma and elevated stature in Milton's epic makes sense once one considers *Paradise Lost* in a baroque context, as an epic in the baroque "grand style," albeit by a Protestant writer. Given that the "baroque impulse is on displaying mighty forces in combat," Satan's heroism in *Paradise Lost* ceases to appear as a "literary failing," instead coming into sight as an "essential ingredient in the overall design" (62–63)—the "vital baroque counterforce required to demonstrate God's might" (65). Recognizing the older Milton's status as a baroque writer requires considering the universal European appeal of baroque style in the seventeenth century, beyond the familiar partisan and regional uses of the baroque in Counter-Reformation southern Europe, as both Roston and Peter Davidson (2007) have urged. Far from being confined to a specific religion, class, or period, the baroque's appeal reached across social, historical, and geographical barriers, to become a versatile, transnational—and eventually transhistorical—mode for the dynamic representation of crisis and transformation.

Compared to the obstacles to be overcome in accepting the existence of a Protestant British baroque in Milton and elsewhere (that is, the ingrained British prejudice against accepting the term), the baroque stylization of cosmic battle in *Bless Me, Ultima* is easy to recognize, and much easier to accept.[4] Who is God, Antonio asks: the man on the cross, or the golden carp, a pantheistic deity? Who is more powerful, the all-forgiving

Virgin, the brown Virgin of Guadalupe, or the black bass, a pantheistic destroyer deity? "If the golden carp was a god, who was the man on the cross? The Virgin? Was my mother praying to the wrong God?" (Anaya 1972, 75). Ultima is a figure steeped in Native knowledge and is barred from entering a Catholic church. Yet she—not the priest, who is helpless— possesses the power to save Uncle Lucas's life, by lifting the curse placed on him by the Trementina sisters and to exorcise the harmful pagan spirits at the Téllez homestead. And who or what exactly is Ultima? A hybrid being—part human, part supernatural—Ultima's soul is incarnated in her owl; she is said to be like a saint ("una mujer que no ha pecado" [a woman without sin]; 96), but the implication here is that she is a bruja, a witch. Opposites blend into each other and change places. Further, at Antonio's first communion on Easter Sunday, his prayer for an answer from the Catholic god remains unfulfilled: "I called again to the God that was within me, but there was no answer. Only emptiness. I turned and looked at the statue of the Virgin. She was smiling, her outstretched arms offering forgiveness to all" (211).

In striking contrast to the Christian god's nonresponsiveness, the pagan deities, the golden carp and the black bass, reveal themselves in the flesh to Antonio and his friend Cico.

> Then the golden carp came. . . . The huge, beautiful form glided through the blue waters. I could not believe its size. It was bigger than me! And bright orange! The sunlight glistened off his golden scales. He glided down the creek with a couple of smaller carp following . . . I could not have been more entranced if I had seen the Virgin, or God himself. . . . Then the golden carp swam by Cico and disappeared into the darkness of the pond. . . . I knew I had witnessed a miraculous thing, the appearance of a pagan god, a thing as miraculous as the curing of my uncle Lucas. And I thought, the power of God failed where Ultima's worked; and then a sudden illumination of beauty and understanding flashed through my mind. This is what I had expected God to do at my first communion! If God was witness to my beholding of the golden carp then I had sinned! (105)

The source of the myth of the golden carp is Jasón's Indian, the only Indian living in Antonio's hometown, Guadalupe; Jasón's Indian passes the myth on to the friends Cico, Samuel, and Florence. More to the point, the American Indian spirits in Anaya's novel appear in the mode Carpentier dubbed the American marvelous real. In his famous 1949 prologue to *The Kingdom of This World*, Carpentier drew a categorical distinction between the artificiality of the supernatural in European surrealism, fabricated in the writer's laboratory, and the supernatural in Latin American literature, which is found "at every turn" of ordinary Latin American reality and history ([1949] 1995b, 87). Carpentier's examples are Mackandal's lycanthropic powers; Henri Christophe's invincible citadel La Ferrière, constructed with the blood of bulls; the quest for El Dorado, which was still being sighted in the twentieth century—hence the reference to the real in the term "American marvelous real." Carpentier explains that the marvelous real is faith based, affirming the "irrational" popular beliefs of premodern and non-Western mythology as valid knowledge: "To begin with, the phenomenon of the marvelous requires faith. Those who do not believe in faith cannot cure themselves with the miracles of saints" ([1949] 1995b, 86). The many fantastic episodes in *Bless Me, Ultima*—Antonio's two sightings of the golden carp and the black bass; the mermaid on the lakes; the rocks falling from the sky on the Téllez homestead; the magic hairball vomited up by Uncle Lucas; Ultima's clay dolls, which are live embodiments of the evil Trementina sisters and crumple as they in turn die; not to mention the numerous lesser miracles—all exemplify this Latin American folk magic, which has the status of the real and requires faith. Nonbelievers cannot see the golden carp, as Cico explains in response to Antonio's worry that fishermen might kill him (Anaya 1972, 108). This, of course, returns us to the problem of the Catholic god's silence *despite* the fact of Antonio's deep faith—the purely European nonmestizo elements of nuevomexicano religion seem to be excluded from manifesting as "marvelous real" in Anaya's novel.

My overall claim in this chapter has been that the nuevomexicano mestizo cosmovision that is revealed to Antonio during his spiritual apprenticeship under the tutelage of Ultima is part of the genealogy of the New World baroque, the mestizo rearticulation of the colonial European baroque. This is true in two distinct respects. First, in terms of *subjective* experience, Antonio's spiritual vision is a "tormented vision," to borrow art historian Robert Harbison's characterization of the "lurid depiction of religious emotion" characteristic of baroque religious art, including mysticism, with its mixture of pleasure and pain (2000, 33, 52). Like other baroque and neobaroque artists, Anaya depicts his young protagonist in the throes of inner conflict and emotional upheaval, tossed this way and that by powerful forces beyond his control. Since Anaya's subject is spirituality, a comparison with baroque religious art seems appropriate: baroque saints such as Bernini's Saint Teresa, as well as their neobaroque secular adaptations, such as Frida Kahlo's self-portraits, are (or depict) heroes who *suffer*—individuals caught in the act of (heroic) suffering. The "baroque iconography of sanctified suffering," in Lois Parkinson Zamora's apt phrase (2006, 182), epitomized by what John Rupert Martin (1977, 112) calls the "furious martyrdoms" of the Counter-Reformation baroque, encodes a subjectivity that is based on the conversion of agony into agency: the *cause* for which the saint is suffering makes the suffering glamorous. Although Frida Kahlo was not religious, she, as Lois Parkinson Zamora has shown, "routinely engaged the baroque iconography of sanctified suffering" (2006, 182) to create an autobiographical and secular mythology of her personal suffering.[5] Anaya's case is both parallel to and different from Kahlo's—parallel in constituting a twentieth-century neobaroque appropriation of seventeenth-century baroque religious iconography, but different in that it does not secularize the baroque but remains within the orbit of spirituality. Harbison's observation seems most apt in capturing Antonio's spiritual education:

> The most characteristic seventeenth-century contribution to devotional imagery is a class of scene allied to martyrdom but milder, the saint in prostration or ecstasy, a moment once dynamic and passive. Like a martyrdom it is something the hero-subject *undergoes*, completely beyond his control though he has probably prepared for it, using methods like those Ignatius popularized, which are best carried out by the solitary sufferer. (2000, 52)

The term "undergoing" identifies the way in which—as in baroque saints' mystical visions of God—eight visionary dreams are visited on Antonio from the outside, by supernatural forces. At the same time, his fortitude in enduring their effects is shaped by Ultima in her role as spiritual guide. It is significant that Antonio's visionary dreams do not begin until *after* the arrival of Ultima; Antonio's ecstatic experience and his access to spiritual tutelage coincide.

The second aspect of my claim about *Bless Me, Ultima*'s neobaroque nuevomexicano mestizo cosmovision relates to the overall composition of Anaya's cosmology beyond Antonio's subjective experience. *Bless Me, Ultima*'s mestizo cosmology is the fictional prose analog of the flamboyant

6.5. Cupola, Tonantzintla. (Author's photo)

mestizo iconography of New World folk baroque altarpieces. Examples would be the façade of the San Lorenzo in Potosi, Bolivia, or the Church of Santa María Tonantzintla, near central México, where Catholic angels and saints mix with indigenous figures, flora, and fauna. Notice the profuse ornamentation of Santa María Tonantzintla, an incomparable example of the baroque principle of the "horror of the void": no empty space is left unfilled (figures 6.2 and 6.5). On the interior walls of Tonantzintla, tropical fruit and vegetation carved in stucco, gilded, and colored in polychrome climb up all the way to the apex of the cupola, setting the stage for images of Counter-Reformation worship—the cult of Mary, of saints and martyrs, and so forth (fig. 6.5).

The cupola of Tonantzintla depicts a vision of the heavens and of paradise, but it is a celestial vision whose dominant Catholic elements have been set into variation by indigenous myth and beliefs. In the four spandrels below the cupola are the four evangelists Matthew, Mark, Luke, and John (see figure 6.5). Farther up, in the upper circle alternating with the windows, are early theologians Saint Augustine, Saint Jerome, Saint Ambrose, and Saint Gregory the Great. At the apex is the white dove, symbol of the Holy Spirit.

But one has to look hard to find these Christian figures in the tangle of the carved forest of thick local vegetation, from where Indian bodies and faces are also seen to peer out, feeding on the fruits of the land (figure 6.6). "The marvelous chapel at Tonantzintla," writes Carlos Fuentes,

is one of the most startling confirmations of syncretism as the dynamic basis of postconquest culture. What happened here happened throughout Latin America. The Indian artisans were given engravings of the saints and other religious motifs by the Christian evangelizers and asked to reproduce them inside the churches. But the artisans and masons of the temples had something more than a copy in mind. They wished to celebrate their old gods as well as the new ones, but they had to mask this intention by blending a praise of nature with a praise of heaven and making them indistinguishable. Tonantzintla is in effect a re-creation of the Indian paradise. White and gold, it overflows with plenty as all the fruits and flowers of the tropics climb up to its dome, a dream of infinite

6.6. Detail of interior wall (carved forest), Tonantzintla. (Author's photo).

abundance. Religious syncretism triumphed as, somehow, the conquerors were conquered. (1999, 146–47)

This interartistic comparison between eighteenth-century Mexican folk baroque architecture—Tonantzintla's indigenized Christian cosmology—and contemporary Chicano literature—*Bless Me, Ultima*'s nuevo-mexicano spirituality—illustrates the principle of New World baroque cosmovision, which can be defined as the decentering of the sacred. As Carpentier explains in "The Baroque and the Marvelous Real," the baroque mode of "proliferating nuclei" related to the principle of horror vacui—both of which epitomize baroque excess—generate an expansive energy that breaks down limits and decenters hierarchies and order within the composition:

The baroque . . . is characterized by a horror of the vacuum, the naked surface, the harmony of linear geography, a style where the central axis, which is not always manifest or apparent (in Bernini's Saint Teresa it is very difficult to determine a central axis), is surrounded by what one might call "proliferating nuclei," that is, decorative elements that completely fill the space of the construction, the walls, all architecturally available space: motifs that contain their own expansive energy, that launch or project forms centrifugally. It is art in motion, a pulsating art, an art that moves outward and away from the center, that somehow breaks through its own borders. ([1981] 1995a, 93)

Carpentier's claims about baroque decentering and its links to transculturation in the New World have been elaborated by other Latin American and Caribbean theorists and writers, such as Martinican writer Édouard Glissant. In essays collected in *Poetics of Relation* (1997), Glissant elaborates a cross-cultural poetics founded on processes rather than essences, in which the baroque figures prominently as a mode that enables the becoming-other and hybridization of existing cultural identities. The essay "Concerning a Baroque Abroad in the World" elaborates on the important role of baroque decentering and proliferation:

> Baroque art mustered bypasses, proliferation, spatial redundancy, anything that flouted the alleged unicity of the thing known and the knowing of it. . . . The "historical" baroque constituted, thus, a reaction against so-called natural order, naturally fixed as obvious fact. As conceptions of nature evolved and, at the same time, the world opened up for Western man, the baroque impulse also became generalized. The baroque, the art of expansion, expanded in concrete terms. . . . This evolution reached its high point in *métissage*. Through its vertiginous styles, languages and cultures hurtled the baroque will. The generalization of *métissage* was all that the baroque needed to become naturalized. From then on what it expressed in the world was the proliferating contact of diversified natures. (Glissant 1997, 78)

Glissant's claim about the "naturalization" of the de-centering of the baroque in the New World sociohistory of mestizaje derives from Carpentier, who was the first to establish the link:

> And why is Latin America the chosen territory of the baroque? Because all symbiosis, all *mestizaje*, engenders the baroque. The American baroque develops along with *criollo* culture, with the meaning of *criollo*, with the self-awareness of the American man,

be he the son of a white European, the son of a black African or an Indian born on the continent. . . . : the awareness of being Other, of being new, of being symbiotic, of being a *criollo*; and the *criollo* spirit is itself a baroque spirit. ([1981] 1995a, 100)

Anaya's novel illustrates the powerful social and transformative repercussions of baroque proliferation and decentering indicated by Glissant and Carpentier. The centripetal momentum of the baroque effects the dethroning of the single center of Christian theology—the Christian god. If Tonantzintla offers a compelling visual illustration of the mechanism of proliferation, *Bless Me, Ultima*'s mestizo cosmovision goes even further in displacing the Christian god from the center of the mestizo pantheon of deities and spirits that he still occupies in Tonantzintla, at the apex of the cupola. In Anaya's mestizo New World baroque cosmovision—to adapt Ramón Gutiérrez—when Jesus came, the corn mothers did *not* go away, but were transformed into New World articulations of the Virgin Mary.[6] Furthermore, as Carpentier ([1981] 1995a) explains, the baroque principle of decentering and rebellious rearticulation intersects with the American marvelous real, which—like the baroque—is based on the coexistence of opposite logics or beliefs (American folk beliefs and modern Western concepts). As such—again like the baroque—it is a decentered "open form."

Why is it that the baroque becomes the instrument of the rebellious deformation of a cultural norm—ironically, the same norm that was imported to the Américas to serve as the vehicle of colonization? As Roberto González Echevarría explains, unlike Renaissance classicism, the art of symmetry and homogeneity, the irregular baroque is in principle an aesthetics of difference:

The new American sensibility found in the baroque an avenue for the different, the strange, that is to say, the American. . . . The baroque allowed for a break with Greco-Latin tradition by allowing the fringes, the frills, as it were, to proliferate, upsetting the balance of symmetry, displacing the centrality of renaissance aesthetics. . . . Through its capaciousness and proliferation the baroque inscribed the American. The speech of blacks in Góngora's poetry is like the presence of Inca or Aztec deities on church friezes. (1993, 198)

In other words, the New World baroque could both follow in the footsteps of the European baroque and set out for a new direction—by compounding the formalist deformation in elite baroque art such as Góngora's with the transcultural deformations of the American folk baroque.

I conclude with a brief discussion of two major contributions by Latin American theorists who have recently taken the postcolonial analysis of the New World baroque popularized by Lezama Lima and Carpentier to a more abstract level, placing it within the global history of modernity, framing the baroque as Latin America's alternative modernity. Brazilian critic Irlemar Chiampi, in *Barroco y modernidad* (2000), and Ecuadorian Mexican philosopher Bolívar Echeverría, in *La modernidad de lo barroco* (1998), both argue that the baroque constitutes an alternate—eccentric and hybrid—modernity that is historically rooted in Latin America and related to its past colonial condition and subsequent anticolonial developments. Discussion of the baroque is inevitably tied to the question of modernity: the baroque is a modern phenomenon. But the way the baroque operates, as seen in *Bless Me, Ultima*—hybridizing, connecting and expanding rather than purifying, dissociating and segregating—indicates that the baroque represents an alternative model of the modern that departs from Enlightenment rationalism. Indeed, Enlightenment rationalism stigmatized the baroque under the pejorative label "baroque," meaning "bizarre," leading to the baroque's effective erasure from artistic canons at the beginning of the eighteenth century. After nearly two centuries "in purgatory," baroque came back at the beginning of the twentieth century: a crisis of Enlightenment modernity opened the way for rediscovery of the alternative modernity of baroque; this stimulated a series of baroque revivals across the arts (literature, visual arts, and architecture) in Europe as well as in the Américas, which we know as neobaroque. Writing from a Latin Americanist standpoint, Irlemar Chiampi (2010) argues that the twentieth-century rediscovery of the baroque via the neobaroque enabled

> an archaeology of the modern, one that allows us to interpret Latin American experiences as a dissonant modernity. . . . The baroque, crossroads of signs and temporalities, aesthetic logic of mourning and melancholy, luxuriousness and pleasure, erotic convulsion and

allegorical pathos, reappears to bear witness to the crisis or end of modernity and to the very condition of a continent that could not be assimilated by the project of the Enlightenment. (508)

She later concludes,

It is no accident, then, that the baroque—pre-Enlightenment, pre-modern, prebourgeois, pre-Hegelian—should be reappropriated from this periphery (which enjoyed only the leftovers of modernization) as a strategy for subverting the historicist canon of the modern. The recovery of the baroque is both an aesthetics and a politics of literature, an authentic paradigmatic shift in poetic forms that implies, among other consequences, the abandonment of the silent presence of the eighteenth century in our mentality. (522)

The framework of the baroque as Latin America's alternative modernity further helps situate Anaya's *Bless Me, Ultima*: it is a Latino neobaroque contribution from north of the U.S.-México border, which documents Latin American difference in the trajectory toward the modern as described by Chiampi. Like many other Latin American neobaroque works of art and literature (by Lezama Lima, Carpentier, Severo Sarduy, Gabriel García Márquez, José Donoso, Diamela Eltit, Édouard Glissant, and others), Anaya recovers the New World baroque—a formation distant in time—for his contemporary novel to articulate a uniquely Latino and Latin American sensibility.[7] Nonetheless, there are also connections to Europe, via the extended transhistorical and transcultural network of the baroque, New World baroque, and neobaroque, as I have shown in the brief comparison with *Paradise Lost*. But Anaya shares with other Latin American baroque and neobaroque works the appropriation of the exuberant, antidissociative baroque for the purposes of rebellious transculturation and mestizaje against the grain of the European colonial legacy.

In his study *La modernidad de lo barroco*, Ecuadorian philosopher Bolívar Echeverría sheds further light on what he calls the baroque ethos (*ethos barroco*), a historical strategy of adaptation to colonial Spanish culture on the part of the colonized. Inspiring the popular indigenous and mestizo syncretism "from below" that sets out to Indianize Christianity,

the baroque ethos is a minor strategy of deformation and appropriation
that fulfills the task of living *within* the belly of the beast, as it were, of
making the official colonial culture habitable for the conquered. Echeverría explains that this was an effort to recreate the dominant European
civilization on the part of "the most abject social strata of the colonial
social pyramid" (1998, 181):

> It is the *criollos* of the lower strata, mestizos of Indian and African
> heritage, those who, without knowing it, would end up doing what
> Bernini had done to the classical canons: *they would re-make the*
> *most viable, the dominant civilization, the European.* They would
> awaken and later reproduce its original vitality. In so doing, in
> nourishing the European codes with the ruins of the pre-Hispanic
> code (and with the residues of African codes of the slaves that had
> been violently imported), they would soon construct something
> different from what they had planned; they would create a Europe
> that had never existed before them, a different, "Latin American"
> Europe. (82; my emphasis)

Echeverría clarifies that, while transformative, the baroque is *not* a revolutionary strategy:

> A strategy of radical resistance, the baroque *ethos* is, however, not a
> revolutionary ethos in and of itself: its utopia is not in the "beyond"
> of an economic and social transformation, in a possible future,
> but rather in the imaginary "beyond" of an economic and social
> transformation, in a possible future, but rather in the imaginary
> "beyond" of an intolerable *hic et nunc* threatrically transformed.
> (16)

Like other theorists of New World baroque, Echeverría argues that the
baroque ethos effected subversive modifications of the official colonial
culture, limited to the realm of the everyday and unofficial practices,
rather than outright rebellion. Anaya's novel *Bless Me, Ultima* presents a
small portion of this rich archive of baroque popular culture of the New
World.

NOTES

All unacknowledged translations are mine.

1. On Guido's inventory of indigenous symbolism in the Andean mestizo style, see Bailey (2010, 18). Bailey's list is incomplete; I modified it.

2. In "An American Chicano in King Arthur's Court," Anaya explains: "Was she [Ultima] the anima, a woman of wisdom, the collective mothers of the past, or a reflection of the real curanderas I had seen do their work? I know she became a guide and mentor who was to lead me into the world of my native American experience. . . . Do not fear to explore the workings of your soul, your dreams, your memory. Dive deep into the lake of your subconsciousness, your memory!" (1995, 298).

3. *First Dream* imagines the soul's ascent to the summit of creation in quest of knowledge while dreaming, a quest that fails as her understanding is overwhelmed; she recoils and awakens. Paz (1988) explains that "*First Dream* is not a poem about knowledge as a vain dream, but a poem about the act of knowing. . . . A confession that ends in an act of faith: not in learning but in the desire to learn" (380).

4. Davidson's study is an impassioned plea to overcome British prejudice against the baroque as inherently Catholic and, thus, the "style of the enemy" (2007, 29), which, he argues, has obscured recognition of a British baroque in literature and the visual arts (including, for example, the so-called metaphysical poets, as well as architects Christopher Wren and Nicholas Hawksmoor): "Britain has never been enthusiastic about describing its cultural production as a part of an international phenomenon, an unease which extends to Modernism almost as thoroughly as it does to Baroque" (65).

5. See Lois Parkinson Zamora's *The Inordinate Eye* (2006) for a discussion of Frida Kahlo's secular appropriation of baroque religious art in her self-portraits (167–232).

6. Gutiérrez (1991) explains that, after the Spanish conquest of New Mexico (settlement beginning in 1581), the Franciscan friars set about Christianizing Pueblo culture and spirituality by transforming certain of its aspects. For example, they allowed Pueblo Indians "to continue their worship of the Corn Mother, albeit transmogrified as the Blessed Virgin Mary" (78). This is an excellent example of what one might call syncretism "from above," a strategy for which the Jesuits in particular were famous. According to Octavio Paz,

> [T]he tabula rasa had been supplanted by what one might call a policy of linkage, which endeavored to establish a bridge of communication, more supernatural than natural, between the native and Christian worlds. This new syncretism, in contrast to the popular syncretism of the Indians, proposed not to Indianize Christianity but, rather, to seek prefigurations and signs of Christianity in paganism. (1988, 35)

In the process of transculturation underpinning the New World baroque, it is important to point to the tension between these opposite ends of a two-pronged process of attempts at mutual co-optation. Absent such official policies of toler-ance for syncretic forms, popular Indianizing syncretisms "from below" would likely not exist.

7. For a discussion of some of these works, see Zamora's *The Inordinate Eye* (2006) and my *Neobaroque in the Americas* (Kaup 2012).

REFERENCES

Anaya, Rudolfo A. 1995. "An American Chicano in King Arthur's Court." In *The Anaya Reader*, 293–303. New York: Warner Books.

———. 1972. *Bless Me, Ultima*. Berkeley, CA: Quinto Sol.

Bailey, Gauvin Alexander. 2010. *The Andean Hybrid Baroque: Convergent Cultures in the Churches of Colonial Peru*. Notre Dame, IN: University of Notre Dame Press.

Braider, Christopher. 2004. *Baroque Self-Invention and Historical Truth: Hercules at the Crossroads*. Burlington, VT: Ashgate.

Bruce-Novoa, Juan. 1996. "Learning to Read (and/in) Rudolfo Anaya's *Bless Me, Ultima*." In *Teaching American Ethnic Literatures: Nineteen Essays*, edited by John Maitino and David Peck, 179–91. Albuquerque: University of New Mexico Press.

Caminero-Santangelo, Marta. 2004. "'Jasón's Indian': Mexican Americans and the Denial of Indigenous Ethnicity in Anaya's *Bless Me, Ultima*." *Critique* 45 (2): 115–28.

Cantú, Roberto. 1990. "Apocalypse as Ideological Construct: The Storyteller's Art in *Bless Me, Ultima*." In *Rudolfo Anaya: Focus on Criticism*, edited by César A. González-T., 13–63. La Jolla, CA: Lalo Press.

Carpentier, Alejo. (1981) 1995a. "The Baroque and the Marvelous Real." In *Magical Realism: Theory, History, Community*, edited by Lois Parkinson Zamora and Wendy Faris, 89–108. Durham, NC: Duke University Press.

———. (1949) 1995b. "On the Marvelous Real in America." In *Magical Realism: Theory, History, Community*, edited by Lois Parkinson Zamora and Wendy Faris, 75–88. Durham, NC: Duke University Press.

———. (1964) 2010. "Questions Concerning the Contemporary Latin American Novel." In *Baroque New Worlds: Representation, Transculturation, Counterconquest*, edited by Lois Parkinson Zamora and Monika Kaup, 259–64. Durham, NC: Duke University Press.

Chiampi, Irlemar. 2000. *Barroco y modernidad*. Mexico City: Fondo de Cultura Económica.

———. 2010. "The Baroque at the Twilight of Modernity." In *Baroque New Worlds: Representation, Transculturation, Counterconquest*, edited by Lois Parkinson Zamora and Monika Kaup, 508–28. Durham, NC: Duke University Press.

Davidson, Peter. 2007. *The Universal Baroque*. Manchester: Manchester University Press.

Dean, Carolyn. 1999. *Inca Bodies and the Body of Christ: Corpus Christi in Colonial Cuzco, Peru*. Durham, NC: Duke University Press.

d'Ors, Eugenio. 2010. "Excerpts from 'The Debate on the Baroque in Pontigny.'" In *Baroque New Worlds: Representation, Transculturation, Counterconquest*, edited by Lois Parkinson Zamora and Monika Kaup, 78–92. Durham, NC: Duke University Press.

Echeverría, Bolívar. 1998. *La modernidad de lo barroco*. Mexico City: Ediciones Era.

Fuentes, Carlos. 1999. *The Buried Mirror: Reflections on Spain and the New World*. New York: Houghton Mifflin.

———. 2010. "The Novel as Tragedy: William Faulkner." In *Baroque New Worlds: Representation, Transculturation, Counterconquest*, edited by Lois Parkinson Zamora and Monika Kaup, 531–53. Durham, NC: Duke University Press.

Gisbert, Teresa. 1980. *Iconografía y mitos indígenas en el arte*. La Paz: Gisbert y Cía.

Glissant, Édouard. 1997. *Poetics of Relation*. Translated by Betsy Wing. Ann Arbor: University of Michigan Press.

González Echevarría, Roberto. 1993. *Celestina's Brood: Continuities of the Baroque in Spanish and Latin American Literature*. Durham, NC: Duke University Press.

Guido, Ángel. 1940. *Redescubrimiento de América en el arte*. Rosario: República Argentina.

———. 2010. "America's Relation to Europe in the Arts." In *Baroque New Worlds: Representation, Transculturation, Counterconquest*, edited by Lois Parkinson Zamora and Monika Kaup, 183–97. Durham, NC: Duke University Press.

Gutiérrez, Ramón A. 1991. *When Jesus Came, the Corn Mothers Went Away: Marriage, Sexuality, and Power in New Mexico, 1500–1846*. Stanford, CA: Stanford University Press.

Harbison, Robert. 2000. *Reflections on Baroque*. Chicago: University of Chicago Press.

Kaup, Monika. 2012. *Neobaroque in the Americas: Alternative Modernities in Literature, Visual Art, and Film*. Charlottesville: University of Virginia Press.

Kelemen, Pál. (1951) 1967. *Baroque and Rococo in Latin America*. 2 vols. New York: Dover.

Lamadrid, Enrique R. 1990. "Myth as the Cognitive Process of Popular Culture in Rudolfo Anaya's *Bless Me, Ultima*: The Dialectics of Knowledge." In *Rudolfo Anaya: Focus on Criticism*, edited by César A. González-T., 100–12. La Jolla, CA: Lalo Press.

Lezama Lima, José. (1958) 2010. "Baroque Curiosity." In *Baroque New Worlds: Representation, Transculturation, Counterconquest*, edited by Lois Parkinson Zamora and Monika Kaup, 212–40. Durham, NC: Duke University Press.

Martin, John Rupert. 1977. *Baroque*. New York: Harper and Row.

Paz, Octavio. 1988. *Sor Juana; or, The Traps of Faith*. Translated by Margaret Sayers Peden. Cambridge, MA: Harvard University Press.

Roston, Murray. 1980. *Milton and the Baroque*. London: Macmillan.

Toussaint, Manuel. (1948) 1967. *Colonial Art in Mexico*. Translated and edited by Elizabeth Wilder Weismann. Austin: University of Texas Press.

Wölfflin, Heinrich. (1915) 1950. *Principles of Art History: The Problem of the Development of Style in Later Art*. Translated by M. D. Hottinger. New York: Dover.

Zamora, Lois Parkinson. 2006. *The Inordinate Eye: New World Baroque and Latin American Fiction*. Chicago: University of Chicago Press.

Zamora, Lois Parkinson, and Monika Kaup, eds. 2010. *Baroque New Worlds: Representation, Transculturation, Counterconquest*. Durham, NC: Duke University Press.

7

Chican@ Literary Imagination

TRAJECTORY AND EVOLUTION
OF CANON BUILDING FROM THE MARGINS

Francisco A. Lomelí

Chican@ aesthetics has had an inauspicious durability within American letters, because the canon had to be redefined for it to be accepted as part of the general literary landscape.[1] In the contemporary period, during the 1960s and 1970s, Chicano literature had a difficult time fitting in because its focus, language, and subject matter were at odds with mainstream literatures from both the United States and México. Besides, its often messianic mission did not seem proper for some scholars of literature because of its extraliterary exigencies. In essence, some considered it a bastard child, since its contemporary manifestations were closely linked to barrio lifestyle, oral tradition, and protest pamphleteerism along with considerable mythifications and, heaven forbid, a social conscience. Naysayers tended to emphasize its decentralized optics of possible subversion and an insistent heterodoxy in terms of thematics and worldview. In fact, some even questioned whether it was literature at all. Besides, what bothered purists most was the free mingling of two languages into an original mix of interlingualism rarely seen before—although not altogether unprecedented—but especially now because it aspired to be aesthetically driven and relevant. How could it be classified or categorized if it defied many of the literary paradigms set by national literatures or traditional measures? More conventional critics sometimes resented it because they found themselves at a disadvantage for not possessing the necessary tools to evaluate and assess such an expression. Independent of such doubts and perceptions, the literature created its own mytho-space, thus advancing a unique identity that acquired a face of its own. It evolved to a high degree of academic and artistic legitimacy that is today undeniable and irrefutable, thanks in great part to its overwhelming presence and impact. In the 1970s, that was not the case. It was necessary to search, dig, excavate, identify, and catalog old and new works to prove to a suspicious jury (often not too anonymous in English, Spanish, Comparative Literature, and American Studies Departments) that such a literature even existed. Because of this resistance, traditional departments took some time to diversify their curricula and, from there, begin to accept the onslaught of a "new" literary expression that expanded their disciplinary purview.

In a short time this literature went from being invisible—much like Chicanos themselves—to gaining some perceptibility, even notoriety in some cases, for it provoked curiosity and raised eyebrows. I pondered these questions in 1975 with a presentation titled "A Synthesis of Chicano Literature for Academics" as part of a graduate student panel that temerariously aimed to define Chicano literature as well as reflect on its autochthonous qualities at a time when a lot of misconceptions prevailed.[2] It was well received by a smallish crowd of forty people at the University of New Mexico, who mulled over our methods on proving the literature's existence and validity. The panel of graduate students from the Modern and Classical Languages Department, along with the distinguished Spanish poet Angel González, set out to offer a panoramic but critical summary of Chicano literature through the various genres as a way of proving our claims that such a literature could be discussed within the vein of traditional and nontraditional literary constructs.[3] Plus, the panel members made a bold proclamation: that such a literature contained much of the substance of other literatures; that is, it could be analyzed, measured, and, yes, criticized for its literary content and intrinsic quality.

I distinctly remember the inquisitive faces in the audience that night, including Rudolfo and Patricia Anaya. The audience heard explanations, proposals, claims, and justifications, but they were especially hungry for empirical evidence. Once the panel members provided concrete examples of each genre, you could see the nods of approval in the crowd, almost sighing: "It's about time someone unfolded the magic carpet to let us see what it contained." Apparently, no collective group of critics had gathered before to assemble such a panoramic view of what works had been published in recent times and in the past. Literature by Chicanos and Chicanas was being produced, oftentimes in isolation, but no one seemed to know its contours, its multiple contexts, or its intertextual connections. That is, few recognized it as a body of literature because most assumed that the dispersed single works were isolated exceptions that would eventually die out. Yet, we quickly discovered that the production of actual works was growing by leaps and bounds in unknown corners of the Southwest and Midwest, although only scattered lists of unreliable documented sources were available, proving that the literature still very much existed in the margins or alien to the mainstream. One year later, Donaldo Urioste and I published *Chicano Perspectives in Literature: A Critical and Annotated Bibliography*, consisting of 127 titles as well as critical reviews of a wide gamut of works from all genres, including some that were not commonly included in literature departments, such as oral tradition in print and a controversial section we deliberately labeled "Literatura Chicanesca."[4] Our main criteria embodied a broad sense of inclusiveness regardless of the venue or quality of publication (that is, a garage production, a mimeograph copy, a university subsidy, or a non-Chicano publisher), the region, or the historical period (meaning before the watershed year of 1965). With this modus operandi in mind, we were able to include in our findings such early works as Eusebio Chacón's *El hijo de la tempestad; Tras la tormenta la calma: dos novelitas originales* (1892), Felipe Chacón's *Obras de Felipe Maximiliano Chacón, "el cantor neomexicano": Poesía y prosa* (1924), Vicente Bernal's *Las primicias* (1916), and *Breve reseña de la literatura hispana de Nuevo México y Colorado* (1959), by José Timoteo López, Edgardo Núñez, and Roberto Lara Vialpando, plus we daringly discussed John Rechy's *City of Night* (1963) and Fabiola Cabeza de Baca's *We Fed Them Cactus* (1954). Some critics considered our approach a form of appropriation because we were "imposing" the Chicano identity on authors from previous eras, but again we restated our premise: these authors were of Mexican descent regardless of the label they adhered to during their lifetime. In other words, their genealogy was pivotal for grouping them into a long-standing literary legacy that went beyond national and ethnic identities (Spanish→Mexican→American→Chicano).

Librarians in the Southwest received the book with positive reviews because it helped them classify and categorize works that had been unclassifiable, unknown, or questionable. In some cases, it assisted them in justifiably creating for the first time a Chicano section in the library stacks.[5] Not all reviews were glowing, particularly from Juan Rodríguez's influential *Carta Abierta*, a sporadic and informal collection of critical reviews on recent works, usually filled with humor and tongue-in-cheek commentaries.[6] His main contention was that our criteria superficially divided works according to the authors' origins instead of their thematic thrust. He considered our nationalistic measuring stick deterministic and evasive of what the literature was attempting to communicate polit-ically. But Urioste and I felt compelled to determine a work's inclusion in the body of Chicano literature according to who created it and not under what conditions, nor the work's elusive inherent value or, even less relevant, the author's ultimate objective, which could be driven by subjectivity. We claimed that we could not impose a single criterion to the writings themselves except for the ethnic origins of the writers; not-withstanding, we gathered bibliographical data in order to collectively assess what Chicanos were producing, and from there, we attempted to make general hermeneutic assessments along with specific critical anal-yses. Plus, we considered it important to distinguish between Mexican (or Latin American) writers and Chicano authors, which other critics, in their desperation to identify Chicano works, did not do, consequently confusing one for the other.[7]

In addition, we tackled the thorny and unsavory subject of misappro-priation by certain Anglo writers who produced Chicano topics, such as Frank Waters's *People of the Valley* (1941), Frank Bonham's *Viva Chicano* (1970), Eugene Nelson's *The Bracero* (1972), William Cox's *Chicano Cruz* (1972), and John Nichols's *The Milagro Beanfield War* (1976).[8] We attempted to distinguish between Chicano writers and others without necessarily judging the quality of the writing per se. John Nichols's work is an excellent example of that, but we intimated the need to set the stage for dealing with such extreme cases as Daniel James, who in 1983 used the name Danny Santiago for his *Famous All Over Town* to hide that he was

Anglo. Ours was not the most pleasant of tactics, but one we considered necessary and crucial to define the parameters of an emerging literature, while pointing out with equanimity that the literature corresponded only to its creators and not masqueraders. It was not an issue of denouncing non-Chicanos, but of simply underscoring that the lived experience of having a Mexican background—without regard to percentages of miscegenation or blood count—were fundamental to the literature's definition. We detected an opportunism by certain individuals to pass their writings off as Chicano when they were outsiders to any kind of Chicano social experience.[9] Urioste and I contended that such writers in the mid-1970s muddied the waters for those who had yet to crystallize a clear concept of what Chican@ literature could be back then. Some critics later accused us of being dogmatic, narrow, and circumscribed in our ethnic scope, but the opposite meant dilution, vagueness, and imprecision. Our working definition was based on understanding Chicanos as a people of Mexican descent who had lived some kind of American experience, instead of someone who crossed the border yesterday or suddenly turned the switch to become Chicano. We were not in favor of DNA tests, and we avoided claiming that birth in the United States was a requirement. In other words, we depended on some of the same criteria usually used to define other national literatures, consequently avoiding some of the dogmatism we were accused of.

There was another front we had to face. We did not perceive Chicano literature as strictly a contemporary phenomenon after 1965 as many others did. We were not only open to traditional genres and transgeneric compositions, but we sided with the view that such a literature had an identifiable background and actually extended into a far past, without knowing how far back. That's when we came across Luis Leal's seminal article "Mexican American Literature: A Historical Perspective," which confirmed some of the important roots unknown to us previously.[10] We soon realized don Luis depended greatly on a Hispanic-Mexican historical backdrop to make his assertions and claims, while confirming that much of the literature traced back to Mexican literature, through colonial chronicles, memoirs, accounts, and other writings, clearly affected what became the American Southwest. He set the challenge and the bar quite high: locate and document old works to untangle the complicated issue of a literary history. He also hinted that Chicano literature had much of its origins in the interplay between a Mexican backdrop and an Anglo social context, from which its hybridity, biculturalism, and bisensibility all made sense. That became one of my mantras, and I have attempted to pursue this line of research through many of my writings, books, and bibliographies.

One of my central aims has entailed expanding the parameters of the existence of Chicano literature through a method of identifying works from a far past, even though the general perception is that more lacunae exist than a steady stream of works. This is more relative than one can initially imagine. To answer such a question, we need to retrace our steps through the Hispanic colonial period, the American conquest, and the settling of the American Southwest until more contemporary times, when a string of works can be identified. The main issue rests on stating that Chicanos did not spring up like mushrooms, nor were they hatched suddenly when Anglo-America took notice. If such works are not foundational, the argument could be made that they are at least viable—some would call them undeniable—antecedents to establishing a literary lineage, or genealogy, for a subsequent body of literary expression that took some time to jell because of multiple historical, political and social circumstances. The recorded production of works has persisted in varying degrees since colonial times in such early works as *Relaciones,* by Alvar Núñez Cabeza de Vaca from 1542; chronicles such as Pedro de Castañeda's (on behalf of Francisco Vásquez de Coronado) *Relación de la jornada de Cíbola, poblados, ritos y costumbres* (1596); Fray Marcos de Niza's *Descubrimiento de las siete ciudades por el Padre Fray Marcos de Niza* (1539); Fray Gerónimo de Zárate Salmerón's *Relaciones de todas las cosas que en el Nuevo México se han visto y sabido de 1538 hasta 1626* (1856); Fray Francisco de Escobar's *La relación de Fray Escobar de la expedición de Oñate a California (1605)*; firsthand accounts by Fray Junípero Serra; poetry by Miguel de Quintana; and many others.[11] Aside from chronicles and fictionalized accounts, poetry, ballads, dramas, and other mixed literary genres from the nineteenth century also abound, including during the time of the American conquest after 1848, as evinced widely in regional newspapers spread from Texas through New Mexico and California. Anselmo Arellano, Julián Vigil, Doris Meyer, Gabriel Meléndez, and others became steeped in unearthing a considerable body of literary expression in the hundreds of Hispanic newspapers that dotted the entire Southwest landscape, especially in New Mexico.[12] To locate such texts, critics have had to make concerted efforts as literary archaeologists and detectives as well as archivists, bibliographers, and folklorists. The odds of finding such texts were at times mind-bogglingly low, requiring sifting through boxes and other uncataloged materials, but even so, works resurfaced thanks to serendipity and the careful grooming of collections and depositories. The challenge has been daunting, however, as Cleve Hallenbeck poignantly notes:

> Most of the provincial material dealing with the Spanish period in New Mexico [and by extension, other regions] has forever disappeared. Complete records once existed in the archives at Santa Fe. . . . All the archives in the province . . . were destroyed in the Great Pueblo Revolt of 1680. Then most of the archives covering the period 1693 to 1846 were burned or otherwise disposed [of] by the early Anglo-American officials, who could not read Spanish.[13]

In other cases, leather or paper archives suffered the indignity of serving as wrapping paper or packing material, even toilet paper, consequently minimizing their value as historical documents—in great part because they were written in Spanish, a language seen as a threat to Anglocentrism. The fact is that most of the early literature has been innocently, surreptitiously, or systematically overlooked, dismissed, or ignored because of the subjectivity of cultural bias and linguistic blindness. When it has not been relegated to oblivion in these ways, Hispanic literary production has been put into the category of oral tradition or unclassifiable mixed genre, or simply been considered "subliterary." Indeed, the odds have been against many of these texts, thus undermining their possible literary significance.

Fortuitously, through references found in more reliable materials or the discovery of empirical evidence, numerous literary samples have resurfaced and survived the long odds associated with hostility or indifference. That's how the epic *Historia de la Nueva México* from 1610, by

Gaspar Pérez de Villagrá, reappeared and has now become a basic staple of colonial studies, oftentimes favorably compared to Alonso de Ercilla's well-known *La Araucana*. That is also how *el poeta negrito* from the nineteenth century survived alongside other popular troubadour compositions, thanks to the *décima*; ballads of intrigue, romance, and military conflicts; *cuentos*; *inditas*; and *alabados*, forming the backbone of Hispanic writings during the times of geographical isolation and subsequent cultural marginalization, but also highlighting its uniqueness vis-à-vis materials derived from English.[14]

The fundamental myth to dispel is that peoples of Mexican descent were this mass of swarthy, uneducated, illiterate mongrels, as portrayed by Anglo sources up through the nineteenth century just because they supposedly looked and acted "too Indian." Quite the contrary, they created networks of literary societies and debate clubs, forums for reciting poetry, writing workshops, and of course the ample editorials and other writings proper to the nature of newspapers. A convincing example is the number of participants (such as Manuel C. de Baca, Porfirio Gonzales, José Inés García, Eusebio Chacón, and others) involved in producing and disseminating literary works of various genres during the 1890s in northern New Mexico, in what I have termed an early Hispanic renaissance, forming what we can designate as the first ethnic literary renaissance predating the valuable accomplishments of the Harlem Renaissance in the 1920s. Models of cultural determinism, however, reigned in American social circles, in part out of convenience and opportunism—to usurp Latinos' resources—but also to ensure that they would remain an indentured sector of American society, supposedly predestined to serve in daily activities that made life much easier for Anglo-Americans. Plus, segregation and discrimination would wield their ugly sides, fostering institutional racism to further justify and reinforce the conquest of 1848. The price was land and resources, a diminishing social and cultural clout, and a grip on all institutions (educational, health, and so forth). One of the central ulterior motives was to propagate a low self-esteem as well as promote not so subtle signs of an inferiority complex, knowing full well such a psychological war could have long-lasting effects on the Mexican American populace.

But Mexicans have been a resilient people, capable of overcoming long campaigns of smear tactics and stigmatization. They negotiated the overthrow of the life they knew in the nineteenth century by creating literary societies, centers of journalism, and publications to maintain an intellectual edge, regardless of the work being mainly in Spanish and thus unacknowledged by the new American settlers. Slowly, Mexican Americans carved out a parallel society that permitted the development of their communities. There is not enough time to re-create all the literary history that emerged in various parts of the American Southwest, but it is clear that peoples of Mexican descent struggled and persevered to obtain and retain a degree of literacy and social autonomy against the odds of an enveloping American society, which slowly took over everything that had been Mexican: mines, ranches, land, basic resources (e.g., water rights), churches, local governments, and other institutions. Businesses, banks, and education were converted into English-speaking enterprises, and Mexicans became more and more cornered, marginalized, and to some degree dependent.

Despite such developments, writers of Mexican descent continued to create and produce, even clandestinely, writings as a means to symbolically dialogue with their milieu.[15] María Amparo Ruiz de Burton wrote about the takeover of California in the 1870s and 1880s, and Eusebio Chacón, from New Mexico, addressed the changing times in the 1890s, both authors dealing with the internal upheaval of violence and social friction. Now, these two are considered some of the earliest authors writing from a vantage point that marked a dialogic relationship with those who were in charge of the changing of the guard. The twentieth century was greatly affected by immigration after the Mexican Revolution, as the United States developed its agricultural industries and other services. Mexicans became a good part of the backbone of the American economy in the Southwest, particularly in periods after the two world wars, the Korean conflict, and the Vietnam War. Their labor through the Bracero Program (1942–1964) was required and became essential to maintaining a middle-class boom. These Mexicans became Chicanos in the 1960s, but even before this, some wrote about their communities (in the 1920s, Daniel Venegas, Adolfo Carrillo, and Jorge Ulica from San Francisco; in the

1930s and 1940s, Américo Paredes from Austin; in the 1940s and 1950s, Mario Suárez from Tucson, Fray Angélico Chávez and Cleofas Jaramillo from Santa Fe, and Fabiola Cabeza de Baca from Albuquerque; from the 1950s on, José Antonio Villarreal from Santa Clara, California, and others). But the civil rights era of the 1960s stirred a new consciousness about identity politics, social rights, and recognition of the roles Chicanos could play and were playing in American society, given the opportunity. New voices came together to formulate a literary canon of struggle, cultural affirmation, and ethnic pride as never seen before, thus forging an identity out of the shadows of mainstream American society.

My book *The Chican@ Literary Imagination: A Collection of Critical Studies by Francisco A. Lomelí* (2012), edited by Julio Cañero and Juan F. Elices, from the University de Alcalá de Henares in Spain, aims to target some of these points and other significant referential material of Chican@ creativity. In the process, I attempt to develop a paradigm of foundational constants that appear to manifest themselves through a good portion of Chican@ literature, which helps partly explain the literary motives as well as the thematics and constructs used. The following examples come together to form important links of Chican@ experiences by which we can assess a broad framework of intersectional lines of contact and dialogue. The complexity of the dialogic relationship between topics and authors clearly illustrates how Chican@ literature cannot be defined by a single ideological tenet. The literature has become broad in scope, overarching in perspective and optics, and expansive in its coverage of human experience. Some precepts worth considering:

1. A search for a unique expression and worldview that encases popular issues of concern related to validation, legitimacy, cultural credibility, historicity, and voice (e.g., Jimmy Santiago Baca, Alurista, Sandra Cisneros, Rudolfo Anaya, Denise Chávez, José Montoya, Montserrat Fontes, Luis Omar Salinas)

2. A poetics of moral and political overtones that encompass power relations, self-affirmation, and belonging (Luis J. Rodríguez, John Rechy, Michael Nava, Oscar Zeta Acosta, Graciela Limón, José Antonio Villarreal, Abelardo Delgado, José Antonio Burciaga)

3. An aesthetic practice grounded on forms of mestizaje that fuse Mexican styles with Anglo-American nuances as modified by different Chican@ experiences (Juan Felipe Herrera, Alberto Ríos, Ron Arias, Lucha Corpi, Alejandro Morales, Ricardo Sánchez, Estela Portillo Trambley, Pat Mora, Gary Soto, Alma Villanueva)

4. A literature more focused on a collective protagonist in contrast to an individual one, with resonating epic qualities even when an individual protagonist does appear (Víctor Villaseñor, Sandra Cisneros, Tomás Rivera, Miguel Méndez, Erlinda Gonzales-Berry, Rolando Hinojosa-Smith, Margarita Cota-Cárdenas, Américo Paredes)

5. An emanation of a cultural self that persists, whether to reaffirm that self or to resist it in terms of gender and sexual orientation (Cherríe Moraga, Gloria Anzaldúa, Arturo Islas, Ana Castillo, Alicia Gaspar de Alba, Richard Rodríguez, Michael Nava)

6. A dialectic framework of social forces (Rolando Hinojosa-Smith, Rodolfo "Corky" Gonzales, Reyna Grande, Luis Valdez, Ixta Maya Murray, Rudolfo Anaya, Miguel Méndez, Ana Castillo)

7. A local reality used as a microcosm to understand the outside world (Estevan Arellano, Víctor Villaseñor, Rolando Hinojosa, Norma Cantú, Helena María Viramontes, Sabine Ulibarrí, Irene Beltrán-Hernández, Luis Alberto Urrea, Miguel Méndez)

8. A contrast of fantasy and social realities (Rudolfo Anaya, Ron Arias, Celso de Casas, Juan Felipe Herrera, Rosaura Sánchez, Beatrice Pita, Cecile Pineda)

9. Personal willpower versus external structures (Josefina López, Rudolfo Anaya, Alicia Gaspar de Alba, Gloria Anzaldúa, Alfredo Véa, Reyna Grande, Alurista)

10. A literary voice of intuition, struggle, and vindication (Ana Castillo, Gloria Anzaldúa, Miguel Méndez, Alicia Gaspar de Alba, Benjamín Alire Sáenz, Cecilio García-Camarillo, Demetria Martínez, Rodolfo "Corky" Gonzales)

To highlight some of these referential markers, I focus on literary history extensively in five articles, some of which focus on New Mexico as a sample to better understand and assess the kind of literary production found in the rest of the American Southwest. Here, in certain cases, I concentrate on the origins and background of Chican@ literature and criticism in large oversweeping treatments. The intent is to establish periodizations, much as Luis Leal does, by filling in gaps, trends, and developments, accompanied by concrete examples and some critical commentary. In an effort to recapture and refocus our imagination as a viable form of liberation, I outline a literary legacy that has identifiable roots dating back to the early northwest of México, which surreptitiously in 1848 became the American Southwest. The issue of a historiographical black hole in the Southwest before 1965 comes up in different forms because only México remained as a viable reference point of our being. The central idea revolved around a "quantum leap from limbo to center stage in order to reclaim a rightful place in modernity by bringing into question our long-standing invisibility and second-class status."[16] It was strategic and necessary to address such a gap because that is what Anglo-America remembered, as if we only constituted part of a static past. Octavio Romano in 1969 had already stated with tremendous conviction, "[T]he historical and intellectual presence of Mexican-Americans depends exclusively on us because no one else is going to do it."[17] That cue was pivotal and therefore motivated the subsequent articulation and development of a regional case model, using New Mexico as a basis by which to reconstruct an early Hispanic framework of specific works and characteristics:

> [T]he regional case model's distinction lies in being both diachronic and synchronic, eclectically dealing with written and oral sources. Concentrating on a single geographical area allows for a view of a complex network of interfacing data that provide a three-dimensional representation of a regional society. The cross-sectional stratification offers a more complete picture of trends, happenings and ideas. It encompasses historical revisionism, cultural anthropology partisan politics and literary theory.... Region functions as an immediate identifier, a cultural matrix or as an insular feature to which people relate. In other words, region becomes the outer visible crust of what we study from within,

providing the cultural elements of what is filtered through the creative literary act. Region is the *patria chica* (homeland) within all of us that somehow captures our essence or synthesizes what we believe ourselves to be.[18]

It is not by coincidence that Rudolfo Anaya represents an optimum example of someone whose region plays a central role in his writings. He grew up in rural and later urban New Mexico (his *patria chica* comprised two complementary spheres), capturing a mythic past greatly influenced by an indigenous sensibility that always rubbed elbows with a Hispanic presence. Anaya captures not only the terrain and landscape but also its people, who internalize the seasons as well as its rituals and beliefs. Anaya is living proof of a New Mexican mestizo who shares a double worldview as well as a bisensibility. He forms part of the land with some of the oldest myths and legends in the United States, where the quotidian can be magical real, and where the unbelievable can be ordinary. He simply taps into this world of the incredible because, much like Gabriel García Márquez, he does not have to invent the inconceivable, given that some of New Mexico offers the unreal as real. He considers himself not a "creator" of stories but a conduit or medium for storytelling, where myth fuses with history, or where the writer connects with an energizer of uncontainable tales. He describes his storytelling inspiration in these terms:

> The storyteller tells stories for the community as well as for himself. The story goes to the people to heal and establish balance and harmony, but the process of the story is also working the same magic on the storyteller . . . who must be free and honest, and . . . must remain independent of the whims of groups. Remember, the shaman, the curandero (folk healer), the mediator[,] do their work for the people, but they live alone.[19]

The storyteller, then, becomes the oracle of Chican@ imagination, and creating such stories becomes the means by which authors give meaning to their surroundings. As they reach these moments of epiphany, they in turn provide the mirror by which the Chican@ community sees itself and wonders about its place in time and space. Anaya stands out as one of those visionaries who taps into various realms of human existence.

The Chican@ Literary Imagination also delves into a series of philosophical and theoretical inquiries about Chicano culture, the problems and interrogations with respect to essentialism, works that symbolically deal with internal exile, Chicanas creating fictive voices in the early 1980s, the idea of remapping a post-barrio through a postmodern lens, and the ubiquitous and thorny subject of the U.S.-México border and its literary manifestations. In addition, there are eight articles devoted exclusively to monographic examinations of single authors: Tomás Rivera, Sabine Ulibarrí, Alejandro Morales, Josefina López, Cecile Pineda, Miguel Méndez, Raymond Barrio, and Fray Gerónimo Boscana. Each essay attempts to extract meaning from rereadings of their respective works, and from that I propose a kind of constellation of critical thinking about these variegated authors to gain a deeper sense of Chican@ literary imagination, what makes them tick or what makes them unique. Some of the authors are well known, but others are obscure or simply understudied. The most obscure and unexpected example is Franciscan Fray Gerónimo Boscana, a Spanish priest who in the middle 1820s composed the first California indigenous ethnography, generally known by the single title *Chinigchinich*, having first appeared in translation in 1846 as a section in Alfred Robinson's *Life in California: During a Residence of Several Years in That Territory*.[20] The same text appeared in a subsequently revised translation in 1978, titled *Chinigchinich: A Revised and Annotated Version of Alfred Robinson's Father Gerónimo Boscana's Historical Account of the Beliefs, Usages, Customs and Extravagances of the Indians of This Mission of San Juan Capistrano Called the Acágchemen*, thanks to anthropologist and linguist John P. Harrington, who provided extensive annotations with insightful clarifications. In dealing with such an elusive text, I came to realize that the context was just as elusive, defying classification because of its transgeneric form, and thus serving as a model example of how critics have to expand their approaches, methodologies, and paradigms. If not, the result could be disastrous, by forcing a square into a round hole. Such a revelation is quite useful to approach Chican@ writings in general, to see and appreciate them on their own terms, which, though uncanny, can unveil nuggets of meaning and signification. The other question that remains is, what other texts might be discovered to further expand and solidify the literature's reputation within literary circles to establish once and for all the value and unique position the literature has played in unveiling "American" experiences that otherwise would continue to be obscured and forgotten?

In sum, many of the texts and philosophical parameters mentioned in this chapter support the idea that a Chicano@ literary imagination has been operating for quite some time, although it has taken years for this literature to gain general acceptance. For some of the time, it remained outside the radar screen of what was regarded as mainstream literary production, but that has been properly challenged and, I hope, overcome. Now we can count on a significant body of works from which critics can discuss and evaluate the responsibilities of creating an ethnic canon, even if it means speaking from the margins. Operating from the margins has taught us many valuable lessons in the form of accountability, by turning relative privilege into obligation and duty. Then again, much work remains as a challenge for all. If this study does not lead us to championing a theory of Chican@ creativity and imagination, perhaps it will aid in the groundwork for other critics to undertake the task.

NOTES

1. Chican@ represents a recent way of encompassing gender equity by suggesting both female and male instead of privileging one over the other.
2. This presentation was published in Spanish many years later under the title "Síntesis para los académicos," in *Ventana Abierta* 6, no. 23 (2007): 30–32.
3. The members of the panel included Donaldo Urioste, who spoke on the Chicano novel and theater; Marcela Aguilar-Henson on poetry and Chicana poetics; Erica Frouman on the essay; and Angel González on short fiction.
4. The work was published in Albuquerque by Pajarito Publications in 1976. After its publication, we were told that the work's success was mainly due to its scope, with its expanded critical reviews versus simple annotations. The label "Literatura Chicanesca" emerged in part while reflecting on what is termed *literatura gauchesca* from nineteenth-century Argentina, when intellectuals, not gauchos themselves, created such a category to indulge in a romantic vein of talking, thinking, and imagining themselves as earthy gauchos who supposedly represented the essence of being Argentine. We detected some parallels worth

pursuing to underscore how an outsider perspective rearticulates and reformulates a particular expression. Argentine intellectuals, such as José Hernández in his famous *Martín Fierro* and others, literally and literarily masqueraded as gauchos, with a confabulated speech that imitated gauchos as bound by a *costumbrista* style and poetics proper within Argentine romanticism.

5. Consequently, it also helped bookstores create sections of ethnic studies and literature stacks that before had seemed inconceivable.

6. The first issue of the journal appeared in 1975 and extended through 1984: first in Seattle, then San Diego, and last in Seguín, Texas.

7. For example, Ernie Barrio's *Bibliografía de Aztlán: An Annotated Chicano Bibliography* (1971) lists nineteen items in the literature section, but only five are actual Chicano monographic works. The rest encompass Mexican authors Octavio Paz, Mariano Azuela, Emilio Abreu, and cultural critic Miguel León-Portilla. Also included in the section are Chicano philosopher Eliu Carranza, plus *chicanesco* writers Frank Waters, William D. Lansford, and Raymond Barrio, in addition to critic Joseph Sommer's *After the Storm: Landmarks of the Modern Mexican Novel* (1968). Among the Chicano writers, we find the first woman in Fabiola Cabeza de Baca, plus Abelardo Delgado, Rodolfo "Corky" Gonzales, Richard Vásquez, and Luis Omar Salinas. As one can surmise, the criteria for inclusion in Barrio's bibliography in 1971 is murky at most and confusing at least, and the literature's definition was still a project in progress. According to the list provided, José Antonio Villarreal's epic novel *Pocho* (1959) is omitted, giving proof that it was "rediscovered" shortly after the bibliography was published.

8. Urioste and I considered placing John Steinbeck's *Tortilla Flat* (1935) in the same controversial category, but we concluded that the author was not appropriating a people's downtrodden experience, because he used it as an early example of inequalities.

9. Some critics' sensibilities were obviously rattled in the 1970s, because some discussion emerged among literary circles about who was best equipped to analyze the literature's content given its uniqueness. Urioste and I stayed out of the fray because we considered it misguided, unfair, and shortsighted to claim that only Chican@s could conduct critical-interpretive work on the literature. An example of outstanding work is Joseph Sommers, among others.

10. The article appeared in *Revista Chicano-Riqueña* 1, no. 1 (Spring 1973): 32–44.

11. Portions of Zárate Salmerón's chronicle were known via oral tradition in its time, but it was not published in its entirety until 1856.

12. Anselmo Arellano's *Los pobladores nuevo mexicanos y su poesía, 1889–1950* (1976) and Julián Vigil's edited works and articles have been instrumental in identifying a series of early authors and writings, plus Doris Meyer's *Speaking for Themselves* (1996); Nicolás Kanellos's *Hispanic Periodicals in the United States* (2000); and Gabriel Meléndez's *So All Is Not Lost* (1997). I have also unearthed the works of eighteenth-century poet Miguel de Quintana and nineteenth-century novelist Eusebio Chacón, both of whom were from New Mexico.

13. Hallenbeck, *Land of the Conquistadores*, viii.

14. *Inditas* are poetic or prose captivity tales of young Hispanic women by American Indians. *Alabados* are traditional hymns closely associated with the religious fervor of the Hermanos Penitentes from New Mexico, who formed a social and religious organization that tried to meet the spiritual needs of the Hispanic people during the withdrawal of the organized church institution in the latter half of the eighteenth and first half of the nineteenth centuries.
15. It is worth remembering that María Amparo Ruiz de Burton did not use her real name on the cover of her books, opting for C. Loyal for *The Squatter and the Don* from 1885 and H. S. Burton for her first novel, *Who Would Have Thought It?*, from 1872.
16. Lomelí, "Po(l)etics of Reconstructing," 223.
17. Romano, "Historical and Intellectual," 35.
18. Lomelí, "Po(l)etics of Reconstructing," 222.
19. Anaya, *Silence of the Llano*, 19.
20. Boscana, *Chinigchinich in* Life in California.

BIBLIOGRAPHY

Anaya, Rudolfo A. *The Silence of the Llano: Short Stories.* Berkeley, CA: Tonatiuh–Quinto Sol International, 1982.

Arellano, Anselmo. *Los pobladores nuevo mexicanos y su poesía, 1889–1950.* Albuquerque, NM: Pajarito Publications, 1976.

Barrio, Ernie. *Bibliografía de Aztlán: An Annotated Chicano Bibliography.* San Diego, CA: Centro de Estudios Chicanos Publication, San Diego State University, 1971.

Boscana, Gerónimo. *Chinigchinich* in *Life in California: During a Residence of Several Years in That Territory* by Alfred Robinson. New York: Wiley and Putnam, 1846.

Cañero, Julio, and Juan F. Elices, eds. *The Chican@ Literary Imagination: A Collection of Critical Studies by Francisco A. Lomelí.* Alcalá de Henares, Spain: Biblioteca de Benjamin Franklin, 2012.

Hallenbeck, Cleve. *The Land of the Conquistadores.* Caldwell, ID: Caxton, 1950.

Harrington, John P., ed. and trans. *Chinigchinich: A Revised and Annotated Version of Alfred Robinson's Father Gerónimo Boscana's Historical Account of the Beliefs, Usages, Customs and Extravagances of the Indians of This Mission of San Juan Capistrano Called the Acágchemen.* Banning, CA: Malki Museum Press, 1978.

Kanellos, Nicolás. *Hispanic Periodicals in the United States: Origins to 1960; A Brief History and Comprehensive Bibliography.* Houston, TX: Arte Público Press, 2000.

Leal, Luis. "Mexican American Literature: A Historical Perspective." *Revista Chicano-Riqueña* 1, no. 1 (Spring 1973): 32–44.

Lomelí, Francisco A. "Po(l)etics of Reconstructing and/or Appropriating A Literary Past: The Regional Case Model." In *Recovering the U.S. Literary Legacy*, edited by Ramón Gutiérrez and Genaro Padilla, 221–39. Houston, TX: Arte Público Press, 1993.

———. "Síntesis para los académicos." *Ventana Abierta* 6, no. 23 (2007): 30–32.

Lomelí, Francisco A., and Donaldo W. Urioste. *Chicano Perspectives in Literature: A Critical and Annotated Bibliography.* Albuquerque, NM: Pajarito Publications, 1976.

Meléndez, Gabriel. *So All Is Not Lost: The Poetics of Print in Nuevomexicano Communities, 1834–1958.* Albuquerque: University of New Mexico Press, 1997.

Meyer, Doris. *Speaking for Themselves: Neomexicano Cultural Identity and the Spanish-Language Press, 1880–1920.* Albuquerque: University of New Mexico Press, 1996.

Romano, Octavio. "The Historical and Intellectual Presence of Mexican Americans." *El Grito: A Journal of Mexican American Thought* 2, no. 2 (Winter 1969): 32–46.

Ruiz de Burton, María Amparo. *The Squatter and the Don.* 1885. Edited and introduced by Rosaura Sánchez and Beatrice Pita. Houston, TX: Arte Público Press, 1992.

8

De vatos y profetas

CULTURAL AUTHORITY AND
LITERARY PERFORMANCE IN THE WRITING
OF RUDOLFO ANAYA

Enrique R. Lamadrid

In a celebrated multifaceted literary career sustained for half a century, Rudolfo Anaya has achieved a deep artistic resonance and cultural authority that continue to inspire and challenge readers and audiences. Since literary criticism alone has been unable to adequately address the magnitude of this phenomenon, anthropological and linguistic framing can offer a more comprehensive estimation. Through writing construed as cultural performance, Anaya may be understood as a cultural leader, not because of celebrity alone. A return to ethnopoetics and performance theory allows a fuller assessment of what may be defined as his mytho-poetics and socio-literary praxis. Anaya's performance as storyteller "consists in the assumption of responsibility to an audience for a display of communicative competence" (Bauman 1975, 203). Ethnopoetic performance is emergent and creates socially symbolic structure through performative action, and by extension literary inscription. In this overview of Anaya's projects, I assess his dialogue with tradition and his vision for the future, as he exercises the role of both *vato* and *vate*, homeboy and seer, for nuevomexicanos and Chicanos.

In the roles of storyteller, mythmaker, and *pícaro*, Rudolfo Anaya presides over the birth of Chicano literature with the foundational coming of age novel *Bless Me, Ultima* (1972), even as he satirizes it later in the mock epic poem *The Adventures of Juan Chicaspatas* (1985). He recasts the search for Chicano identity in the Indo-Hispano philosophical essays of *Jalamanta: A Message from the Desert* (1996), as well in the escapades of *Alburquerque* (1992) and in the sequel tetralogy of detective novels, with hero Sonny Baca, great-grandson of the notorious sheriff of Socorro County Elfego Baca, scourge of renegade Anglo Texans: *Zia Summer* (1995), *Rio Grande Fall* (1996), *Shaman Winter* (1999), and *Jemez Spring* (2005).

A brief scan of recent projects reveals a dynamic nexus of innovation, tradition, and continuity. Replete with the archetypical minimalism of Juan Rulfo, Anaya's recent novel *Randy Lopez Goes Home* (2011) is acclaimed as a picaresque Chicano *Pedro Páramo* (Rulfo [1955] 1959) and requiem for his literary and life partner, Patricia Lawless, who responded to every word of the story in her last days. Time has stopped on the Día de los Muertos, in the canyon of a mysterious desert river, as the reader and the protagonist realize that all the characters are dead but still seeking atonement and the meaning of their lives.

In his latest play, *Rosa Linda* (2013), first conceived thirty years ago but finally produced in 2013 at the National Hispanic Cultural Center in Albuquerque, Anaya has emerged as the García Lorca of the upper Pecos Valley. This tragedy is a bloody dirge for ancestral patriarchy, with whispered allusions to Delgadina, the princess who fatally spurned the incestuous passion of her father, subordinating the divine right of kings to a greater celestial order. Historically known as Turcos in New Mexico, Mexican gypsies, their music and dance, are key characters in the drama.

Anaya's recent children's book, *How Hollyhocks Came to New Mexico* (2012; *Cómo llegaron las varas de San José a Nuevo México*) revisits the folk legends of local encounters with the Santo Niño and his parents in the pine-filled *florestas* of the Sierra de la Sangre de Cristo and in the *valles* and llanos of the upper Río Grande. Facilitating their flight from King Herod's Slaughter of the Innocents, a myopic angel mistakes the sands of northern Egypt for the White Sands of New Mexico, and Jesus spends his formative early years among the Pueblo Indians.

Anaya negotiates his cultural authority on page and stage with *resolanas*, illuminated cultural dialogues on the virtual plazas of the literary commons, enacted through novels, stories, and essays, but without neglecting the liminal space of bilingual children's books, these all but unnoticed by critics. Theater has been his favorite public communal exercise and remedy for the solitude of writing. Recently, the intimate, almost ritual venues of community theater have been cast more broadly into film, with the 2013 release of *Bless Me, Ultima*, directed by Carl Franklin.

The mantle of cultural authority on Anaya's shoulders was not, nor could have been, bestowed on him by publishers or critics dazzled with the first Chicano best seller or the first Chicano author to be honored with the National Medal of the Arts (2002). It is rather a homespun garment, woven with the narrative threads that bind him to New Mexico and lead him beyond its labyrinths into the larger world. In his public life and through his characters, Anaya consistently eschews literary pretention and posturing while he retells with craft and humility the stories of his people, offering them up in service to community.

One such activist project is the *Curse of the ChupaCabra* (2006), a detective novel written for more novice readers that takes on the complex problematics of drug abuse and trafficking. One of the supporting characters is Cristina Molina, an East LA counselor with a bridge program for barrio kids based on introducing them to the hero cycles of ancient literature as a way to understand models for leadership. In her project, students "collected oral histories from their parents and grandparents. They quickly learned from these stories of hard work and survival that their parents had performed heroic deeds. The struggle to immigrate to a new country produced heroes. The hero acted for the good of the family and the community. The hero actually embodied the culture" (97).

As various critics have pointed out (Tessarolo 1988; Taylor 1994; Holton 1995), elements and topoi of the primordial hero myth, both explicit and implicit, are present in almost all of Anaya's narratives. He achieves what Victor Turner identified in ritual drama: "[P]ublic reflexivity takes the form of performance" (1979, 465). Literary drama shares these qualities, the stage where performance becomes a process of transformation for both the group and the individual. This emphasis on process illuminates individual agency, which is often obscured with more structural ideas of culture.

Anaya places his favorite themes in bioregional settings along the Río Pecos and Río Grande, both urban and rural. The themes are now familiar

to his readers—cultural heroes and antiheroes, origin stories, coming of
age, cultural conflict, and the search for identity. Yet he simultaneously
maintains a vast intertextual network in dialogue across cultures, with
what has been written and told before him and with tellings that project
into the future.

Like a Chicano James Joyce, he places epic themes in local settings
through irony and satire. In Joyce's *Ulysses* ([1922] 1934), metempsycho-
sis, or the transmigration of souls and stories, is the central motif. Joyce's
Molly Bloom mispronounces it, "met him pike hoses." The haunting
voices of the dead are everywhere. As Anaya's Randy Lopez (2011c) enters
the valley of the dead, riding on a sway-backed mare, he stops at a cantina
to talk to two old beer-drinking, tobacco-spitting, shit-kicking (Max
Evans style) Anglo cowboys. In a jovial mood, one of them wants to "bet
him Mike's horses" on the spot, in his soliloquy predicting how he would
transform into bear shit:

> A horse is smarter than a man, he said. That mare was a beautiful
> woman in another life. Her husband abused her, so the sway back.
> You believe in—
> Yup. We jus go on becoming something else. Bet-him-Mike's-
> horses. A Greek word. But that knowledge is old as the Hindus.
> Means the flesh dies but the soul moves to a new home. Thas all.
> (Anaya 2011c, 11)

Randy continues his journey and meets key figures from the Bible, world
literature, and local folklore. Like a Chicano Miguel de Unamuno in his
famous "nivola" *Niebla* ([1914] 1982), Anaya explores his own metanovel
and converses with his own characters, who are in turn seeking him
out for clarification of their own identities. In the novel *Alburquerque*
(1992), the protagonist Abrán Gonzales solves the mystery of his multiple
origins—Anglo, New Mexican, Sephardic Jewish—and discovers that
the writer of the novel is his biological father. At the writer's house, Joe,
Abrán's friend, senses the shadows and spirits of the writer's family of
characters. They are more than shadows. Two of them, Juan Chicaspatas
and Al Penco (heroes of Anaya's mock epic) have been visiting the writer,
and his wife waves goodbye to them from her balcony:

Her eyes shone in the dark. She waved at Juan and Al as they disappeared into the dusk, then leaned over the balcony railing and said, "It's sad to see them go, but they'll be back."

Ben Chávez [the writer] nodded. "Yes, once you deliver a soul into the world it enters the cycle of creation."

A curandera, Joe thought, as he looked at the writer's wife. A shaman. Owl eyes shining in the dark. Midwife to the writer who gives birth to his characters. (246–47)

Various characters walk freely between Anaya's novels and stories. Anaya is also in constant dialogue with nuevomexicano and Chicano cultural tradition. Conversations with his whole cast of characters, female and male, are part of the fabric of his stories: La Llorona, La Malinche, la Virgen de Guadalupe, El Coco, El Kookóoee (multiple facets of the Indo-Hispano "boogeyman" El Cucui), San Isidro, and the millennial pícaro Pedro de Ordimalas, boatman on the River of Life and the personified rock with eyes at the gate of heaven. Allusions to classical Greek mythology and the original Ulysses abound in Randy Lopez's conversation with Pedro, who saves him from drowning in the River of Life (even though he is already dead):

You must have pissed off Poseidon.

I have cursed no gods, Randy replied.

Wait a minute, Pedro said thoughtfully. Then he's jealous! He doesn't want you to cross to Sofía! You're a hero, Randy!

I'm no hero. There are no Scylla and Charybdis *here.*

But La Llorona and El Coco live along the river. They eat young souls. And they do whatever Poseidon tells 'em.

Randy was in no mood to discuss old myths. Stories of water spirits and mermaids were a dime a dozen. (Anaya 2011c, 96)

Anaya is also thoroughly versed in the basics of Mesoamerican myth, many aspects of which can be traced in the successive worlds and emergences of Pueblo Indian spiritual traditions, the far northern iteration of the Quinto and Sexto Soles of central México. He joined other Chicano writers in the symbolic recovery of Aztlán as the Chicano homeland in essays (Anaya and Lomelí 1989, 2017 2nd ed. with Lamadrid) and a novel (Anaya 1976). The deep reflections of *Lord of the Dawn: The Legend of Quetzalcóatl* (1987) inform and illuminate readers, many of whom are unfamiliar with *The First Tortilla* (2007), an ingenious telling for children of an episode among many involving the intercultural Mesoamerican corn deity, known as Dhipak to the Mayas and Centéotl to the Nahuas. Corn has been buried and hidden away under the earth in punishment for the ingratitude of humans, who begin to starve until the ants take pity on us and carry the grains up to the surface again to save us from starvation. In *The Legend of La Llorona* (1984), an early short novel also adapted for the stage, Anaya historicizes the story by conflating the ancient Mesoamerican wailing woman with the historical Malinche, iconic mother of mestizos.

Critics immediately noticed the mythic dimensions of *Bless Me, Ultima* but were confused and concerned that the allusions were not true to the usual cast of characters found in Chicano poetry and murals, including Quetzalcóatl, Huitzilopochtli, his mother Coatlicue, Tonantzin, and so forth. The golden carp seemed naïve and idiosyncratic, proof of what they perceived as the apolitical qualities of Anaya's writing, part of the carica-ture of the nuevomexicanos' supposed love of fantasy heritage.

But myth is much more than scholasticism and literary allusion to classical mythologies. Myth is an ancient system of signification, which mediates cultural contradictions, ecological change, and historical conflict (Lamadrid 1985). In *Bless Me, Ultima*, family rivalries between pastoralists and agriculturalists have roots that stretch back into the Neolithic and the rivalry of Cain and Abel. As the protagonist, Antonio Márez Luna, comes to consciousness, he realizes his mediating role as healer of contradictions. The mythopoetic vision of Anaya reconfigures the discourse of myth to invoke its transformative and healing powers. New meanings are generated for difficult new times.

A seasoned mythmaker, Anaya's fascination with etiology and legends of origin led him into the imaginations of his youngest readers and those young in heart. The children of *Bless Me, Ultima* could sense power of the living spirits and beings of the llano and river. The powerful spirit and magma hot springs of Tortuga Mountain brought healing energy to the pro-tagonist of the novel of the same name (Anaya 1979). In mock invocations to Aztec gods in *Juan Chicaspatas* (1985), Anaya directed a playful nod to his *chicanista* readers. And he once and for all reclaimed the *r* of the original spelling of Alburquerque (1992a), with his apocryphal now-gospel tale of the Americano railroad stationmaster who couldn't spell. Another gift to Anaya's home city is the annual tradition of burning El Kookoóee, in Albuquerque's South Valley. In 1990 he assembled a group of Chicano artists, who imagined what the traditional Cucuy boogeyman from greater Mexican folklore might look like, and then they built it, to the delight of neighborhood children. Over the years, in collaboration with local schools, children design the monster in annual art contests and write about him as well. In an exorcist exercise of bibliotherapy, the public is invited to write downs fears and messages on strips of paper, which are gathered, put into a sack, and burned with the monster (Anaya 1992b, 1997a).

Etiology became a constant theme of Anaya's books for children, which also became a showcase for Chicano artists and illustrators like Edward Gonzales, María Baca, Amy Córdova, and Nicolás Otero. The first, *Farolitos of Christmas* (1995), settled the yearly ritual etymological disputes about the little paper lanterns that light the night and the path of the Santo Niño to your house on Christmas Eve, la Noche Buena. Luminarias, as they are called in Albuquerque, had always referred to pitch wood bonfires in the north. Since cheap paper bags first came to New México around World War II, the inventor of the *farolito* lanterns becomes an ailing grandfather who can no longer chop wood. Using the "play within the play," Anaya could not resist the opportunity to insert key scenes of *Los Pastores*, the traditional shepherds' play, nuevomexicano style. The book was staged as an annual play by La Compañía de Teatro de Alburquerque for many years. Almost ten years after *Farolitos of Christmas*, every seventh grader in New Mexico received a copy of *The Santero's Miracle* (2004), whose supernatural character is San Isidro, patron saint of agriculture, courtesy of the state. *La Llorona: The Crying Woman* (2011; see also Anaya 1997b) introduced the omnipresent wandering soul to children by detraumatizing the legend and extracting the terrifying theme of infanticide. The agent of mortality is Señor Tiempo, a monstrous Mayan-looking deity who uses the mask of a benevolent wise man to trick a young immortal mother, the daughter of the Sun, into compromising the immortality of her children. Anaya has aptly demonstrated his skills in reforging, resignifying, and retelling myths. With a nod toward the many bilingual educators of the state, almost all of his children's books appear with parallel English and Spanish versions. Entire scenes of *Los Pastores* were also staged in Spanish in the bilingual *Farolitos* play, with local folk theater groups participating.

Over the years, critical attention to the corpus of Anaya's work has waxed and waned, but national attention to his legacy reached a high point when the National Endowment for the Arts (NEA) selected *Bless Me, Ultima* for its nationwide Big Read Program of community reading events. New readers in places as far flung as New Paltz, New York, in the upper Hudson River valley, were clamoring for more information on Anaya and New Mexico. The clearest window into the cultural landscapes of the Río Pecos, the setting for the novel, is documentary photography. There have been many artistic responses to the writings of Anaya, but most appeared as book illustrations. The first major art exhibit dedicated to Anaya was the photographic tribute of Miguel Gandert, renowned nuevomexicano photographer, who has dedicated his energies to documenting regional Indo-Hispano cultures, the most complete record of their very existence. He contextualized the complexities of mestizo culture in New Mexico for national readers, accompanied by my catalog essays (Gandert and Lamadrid 2007). Gandert drew and expanded on this body of work to produce *Sueños del Valle, Vientos del Llano* (2013), a photo mural public art installation dedicated to Anaya and *Bless Me, Ultima* for the City of Santa Rosa.

The settlement of Pecos Valley in the nineteenth century is a Hispano pioneer story. The settlers hopefully staked their claims in the valley and on the llano, leaving their past behind. The llano became a blank slate, on which more primordial stories could be inscribed. The silence of the llano was filled by many voices:

> Nuevo Mexicano homesteaders headed east from the Río Grande Valley to the great staked plains of the Llano Estacado, bisected and defined only by the Pecos River valley and its low caprock ridges. The plains lie where mountains stood, were washed away and buried. Likewise, the vast, mythic landscape literally swallowed the

people and obscured their history and the Indo-Hispano rituals which memorialize it. (Gandert and Lamadrid 2007, 4)

Growing up, Anaya never saw any of the Indo-Hispano celebrations that commemorate the cultural politics of colonial New Mexico. Only *Los Pastores*, the shepherds' plays of Christmas, were present. He did not discover matachines, Moros y Cristianos, or Comanches celebrations until later in life. He realized that in terms of cultural history, they were "residual traditions," rooted in earlier history, but with a new role in contemporary times. Randy Lopez understands them well:

The hispano village didn't produce an Aeschylus, but they had drama. The sacred dance of los Matachines performed to the lilting tune of fiddle and guitar while two rows of masked figures danced. The little girl dressed in first-communion was the Virgin Mary; for the ancient mexicanos she was Malinche. She danced for the Monarca, Moctezuma, and led him out of the Aztec underworld to lead the twelve tribes again.

The time of the mestizo was at hand.

A boy acted the part of the Bull. Playful, charging the kids in the crowd, but also representing the dark side of the human soul. El Toro had to be controlled by the mayordomos and led away. Thus the ancient struggle between good and evil was portrayed for grateful audiences. (Anaya 2011c, 102–103)

Anaya loves the matachines and could be seen in the crowd for decades at Jemez Pueblo's Guadalupe feast day. He named and dedicated one of his plays to the mestizo themes of the ritual dance in *Matachines* (2011b).

Just like the fiestas that he loves, Anaya's literary projects are crafted as "sites of symbolic social action and cultural signification, where identities and relations are continually being reconfigured" (Guss 2000, 12). The cultural authenticity he observes, creates, and reflects on is based not on essentialist, romantic notions of cultural recovery or preservation, but on what James Clifford defines as "hybrid, creative activity in a local present-becoming-future . . . local structures producing histories rather than simply yielding to History" (Clifford 1987, 126)

Cultural and linguistic hybridity are addressed explicitly by Anaya and his characters in what both declare the "Time of the Mestizo." A great many of Anaya's key characters live their lives between races, cultures, and languages—"coyotes," a low-down term from the mixed caste system of colonial times but still used in contemporary New Mexico (not to be confused with the human trafficker coyotes of the U.S.-México border). Two layers of cultural hybridity coexist in a land twice conquered. What I have called "antiguo mestizaje" was the product of Spanish conquest and the incomplete process of Hispanicization from the late sixteenth to the early nineteenth centuries (García and Lamadrid 2012). From American conquest in 1846 forward emerges what many Chicano writers and critics call the "new mestizaje," the Anglo-Hispano layer that characterizes the world we all inhabit. Anaya's writing bridges the two.

The first agents of Americanization in the life of the author and of Randy Lopez are young female teachers, who worked on the front lines of acculturation and accommodation. Randy honors the memory of one in his life's work, the book entitled *My Life among the Gringos*. In the valley of death he sees his teacher and librarian, Miss Libriana, who of course does not remember him. She remembers:

> I taught for many years, so many kids. When the Presbyterians came to the village they hired me to teach the Mexican children. The Presbyterians thought the kids should learn English and become Anglicized.
>
> Anglicized. That meant to become like Anglos. White. But so many of the hispano kids were brown. How could they give up the color of their skins? Even in a democracy, color still mattered to some.
>
> Of course culture was more than skin. It went deeper. It was a plethora of identity tags. Language. History. Legends. Music. The mythopoetic of a community. It meant pride in the ancestors and honoring their way of life.
>
> Randy had explained Anglicized in his book. It was a euphemism for gringoized. But nobody liked the word gringoized. (Anaya 2011c, 49)

The thorniest issue for Anaya in the international literary community is his choice to use his second language in his writing. His early essay "A Chicano in King Arthur's Court" (Anaya 1995a; originally a lecture he gave in 1984) addresses the contradictions and consequences of adopting English as the creative medium with which to reach Chicano as well as Anglo audiences. Anaya taught creative writing in the English Department of the University of New Mexico, until his retirement in 1993. Randy Lopez, like his creator, also chooses English. Here he warms himself at the fire of Pedro de Ordimalas and notices strange portents in the sky:

> The sweet smoke from the juniper and piñón logs rose into the sky. The Día de Los Muertos clouds were now upside-down exclamation points. Like those in Spanish that tell the reader someone's about to shout or get emotional.
>
> Randy's laptop didn't have upside-down exclamation marks, or if it did, he couldn't find them. Oh well, he would wing it. Use what he had, Chicano-style.
>
> He thought ! looked better. The stem was erect. Upside-down, it looked like it was dripping. !Órale!
>
> What would Quixote say about the strange happenings in the heavens? (Anaya 2011c, 95)

As usual, Anaya shifts into picaresque mode to address the most hotly contested topics in the literary world regarding himself and his characters. Like a Chicano Mark Twain, he effectively immunizes himself and any pretentions he may harbor by using satire and ironies that keep his fiercest critics at bay and his admirers dreaming. Simultaneously a vato and a far-seeing vate, Anaya reaffirms his cultural authority, performs his storytelling, and exercises continuing cultural leadership on the literary stages of New Mexico and the world.

REFERENCES

Anaya, Rudolfo A. 1972. *Bless Me, Ultima*. Berkeley, CA: Quinto Sol.

———. 1976. *Heart of Aztlán*. Albuquerque: University of New Mexico Press.

———. 1979. *Tortuga*. Berkeley, CA: Editorial Justa.

———. 1984. *The Legend of La Llorona: A Short Novel*. Berkeley, CA: Tonatiuh–Quinto Sol International.

———. 1985. *The Adventures of Juan Chicaspatas*. Houston, TX: Arte Público Press.

———. 1987. *Lord of the Dawn: The Legend of Quetzalcóatl*. Albuquerque: University of New Mexico Press.

———. 1992a. *Alburquerque*. Albuquerque: University of New Mexico Press.

———. 1992b. "La Llorona, El Kookoóee, and Sexuality." *Bilingual Review/Revista Bilingüe* 17 (1): 50–55. (Also in Anaya, *The Anaya Reader*, 415–28.)

———. 1995a. "An American Chicano in King Arthur's Court." In *The Anaya Reader*, 293–303. New York: Warner Books.

———. 1995b. *The Anaya Reader*. New York: Warner Books.

———. 1995c. *The Farolitos of Christmas*. New York: Hyperion Books for Children.

———. 1995d. *Zia Summer*. New York: Warner Books.

———. 1996a. *Jalamanta: A Message from the Desert*. New York: Warner Books.

———. 1996b. *Rio Grande Fall*. New York: Warner Books.

———. 1997a. *Ernesto's Encounter with el Kookoóee*. Albuquerque, NM: Serafín R. Padilla.

———. 1997b. *Maya's Children: The Story of La Llorona*. New York: Hyperion Books for Children.

———. 1999. *Shaman Winter*. New York: Warner Books.

———. 2004. *The Santero's Miracle: A Bilingual Story*. Albuquerque: University of New Mexico Press.

———. 2005. *Jemez Spring*. Albuquerque: University of New Mexico Press.

———. 2006. *Curse of the ChupaCabra*. Albuquerque: University of New Mexico Press.

———. 2007. *The First Tortilla: A Bilingual Story*. Albuquerque: University of New Mexico Press.

———. 2011a. *La Llorona: The Crying Woman*. Albuquerque: University of New Mexico Press.

———. 2011b. *Matachines*. In *Billy the Kid and Other Plays*, edited by Cecilia J. Aragón and Robert Con Davis-Undiano, 127–79. Norman: University of Oklahoma Press.

———. 2011c. *Randy Lopez Goes Home*. Norman: University of Oklahoma Press.

———. 2012. *How Hollyhocks Came to New Mexico*. Los Ranchos, NM: Rio Grande Books.

———. 2013. *Rosa Linda*. Play performed April 19–21, Vortex Theatre, National Hispanic Cultural Center, Albuquerque, New Mexico.

Anaya, Rudolfo A., and Francisco Lomelí, eds. 1989, 2017 2nd ed. with Lamadrid. *Aztlán: Essays on the Chicano Homeland*. Albuquerque: University of New Mexico Press.

Bauman, Richard. 1975. "Verbal Art as Performance." *American Anthropologist* 77 (2): 290–311.

Clifford, James. 1987. "Beyond the 'Salvage Paradigm.'" In *Discussions in Contemporary Culture*, edited by Hal Foster, 121–29. Seattle, WA: Bay Press.

Franklin, Carl, dir. 2013. *Bless Me, Ultima*. Dover, DE: Tenaja Productions. Film.

Gandert, Miguel. 2013. *Sueños del Valle, Vientos del Llano*. Public art photo mural commissioned by the City of Santa Rosa, New Mexico.

Gandert, Miguel, and Enrique Lamadrid. 2007. *Rituales de la Tierra y del Espíritu—Rituals of the Earth and Spirit*. New Paltz, NY: Samuel Dorsky Museum of Art in association with State University of New York. Exhibit catalog.

García, Peter J., and Enrique R. Lamadrid. 2012. "Performing Indigeneity in the Nuevo Mexicano Homeland: Multiple Border Zones, Enchantment, and AlienNation." In *Comparative Indigeneities of the Americas*, edited by Lourdes Gutiérrez Nájera, Arturo J. Aldama, and M. Bianet Castellanos, 96–110. Tucson: University of Arizona Press.

Guss, David M. 2000. *The Festive State: Race, Ethnicity, and Nationalism as Cultural Performance*. Berkeley: University of California Press.

Holton, Frederick S. 1995. "'Bricoleur': Christianity and Mythmaking in Rudolfo Anaya's *Bless Me, Ultima*." *Confluencia* 11 (1): 22–41.

Joyce, James. (1922) 1934. *Ulysses*. New York: Modern Library.

Lamadrid, Enrique. 1985. "Myth as the Cognitive Process of Popular Culture in Anaya's *Bless Me, Ultima:* The Dialectics of Knowledge." *Hispania* 68 (3): 496–501.

Rulfo, Juan. (1955) 1959. *Pedro Páramo*. México, DF: Fondo de Cultura Económica.

Taylor, Paul Beekman. 1994. "The Chicano Translation of Troy: Epic *Topoi* in the Novels of Rudolfo Anaya." *MELUS* 19 (3): 19–35.

Tessarolo Bondolfi, Lia. 1988. *Dal mito al mito: la cultura di espressione chicana: dal mito originario al mito rigeneratore*. Milan: Jaca Book.

Turner, Victor. 1979. "Frame, Flow and Reflection: Ritual and Drama as Public Liminality." *Japanese Journal of Religious Studies* 6 (4): 465–99.

Unamuno, Miguel de. (1914) 1982. *Niebla: nivola*. Madrid: Cátedra.

9

How the Gothic
Put Its Whammy on Me

Mario Acevedo

For some reason there is a moat between literary writers and genre writers, so a genre writer such as myself is seldom invited to add his two centavos to any academic discussion unless he's been dead for at least fifty years. By genre writer, I mean that I write commercial fiction. I was educated as an engineer. I don't have an English or literature degree, nor do I have an MFA. I learned my craft from other genre writers, most of them highly accomplished. But like all other writers—genre, literary, essay, poetry—I have to write. I have to express myself through the printed word. What is most important to me is that I have stories to tell. Big, fat stories. Fiction. Lies. As a genre writer my duty is not to educate but to entertain. So if you learn something from reading this chapter, it was purely by accident.

This chapter was originally an essay for the 2014 Conference on Rudolfo Anaya at California State University, Los Angeles. What inspired the topic I chose was this sentence from the conference description: "Anaya's work is thus an illustration of how ethnic literatures can avoid a narrow or naïve realism caught in the personal or local with no reference points to national and global implications."[1] I interpret this connection of *naïve realism to the national and global* as the *whammy*, and I grew up without a whammy. It was the "gothic," the weird and fantastic, that connected my naïve realism to the national and global and thus put the whammy on me, for an appreciation of that gothic led me to my stories and my success as a writer.

As a boy I didn't like vampires. Or zombies. Or ghouls. Or ghosts. I thought all those supernatural monsters were silly. But I was terrified by El Cucuy and La Llorona. They were real. Nobody ever told me to be afraid of vampires, so I wasn't. But if I didn't behave, my mother threatened to lock me outside at night and let El Cucuy make fajitas out of me. I never questioned that threat, whether I was in Las Cruces or Pacoima or Chihuahua. La Llorona would get me too if I wasn't careful. She might have been a five-hundred year-old *viejita,* but that didn't keep her from hustling around on those skinny old-lady legs.

But so what if I believed in El Cucuy and La Llorona? That wasn't enough to put the whammy on me. And the alleged mysticism about the land of my youth—southern New Mexico—certainly wasn't enough. The beauty of New Mexico and the compelling draw of its traditions— none of that impressed me when I was young. A large part of the reason is that northern New Mexico is different from southern New Mexico. When people talk about New Mexico, they usually mean Taos, Santa Fe, the paintings of Georgia O'Keeffe, the santeros.

The people of northern New Mexico go back hundreds, if not thousands, of years, to the Spanish settlers, the comancheros, the Hopis, the Navajos, the Anasazi. The people of southern New Mexico are transient, and after one or two generations, they move on like tumbleweeds. Growing up around Las Cruces caused me to see the land through a perspective of naïve realism and to never appreciate its history, its traditions, its romance. Our past was something to be easily discarded and forgotten.

Most of my ambivalence stemmed from being raised in the Spanish Baptist Church, where I was taught to look down my nose at the Catholics—a major force in the Hispanic community—and to stay clear of their quaint misinterpretations of the Holy Scriptures. Growing up in Las Cruces, I didn't get a sense for the need to value our history and traditions. History belonged in dusty old books and had no place in our lives, especially if it impeded progress—as defined by the developers and contractors who pulled the strings of our local government. To them, tradition was something to be knocked down and paved over.

I watched historic Las Cruces get demolished. I saw the quirky shops, the old hotels, the vintage neon signs, the homey cafés, all torn down to make way for the new and to fatten the wallets of a chosen few. If the destruction of our cultural past—Hispanic, Anglo, or Native—didn't matter to the city, why should it have mattered to me? The heart of old Las Cruces was St. Genevieve's Church, built on top of the original 1859 structure and dedicated in 1887. St. Genevieve's served the largest Catholic congregation between El Paso and Albuquerque. As a *chamaco* I would stand along its iron fence and gaze with awe at this forbidden papist citadel, which was certainly more magnificent than anything we dowdy Protestants worshipped in. Even though the church was off limits to me, I realized that a great wrong had been done in 1967, when the structure was abruptly razed to the ground. In selling the land, the Catholic Church had reneged on several deals, so development of the property was mired in litigation for decades. Where once stood a proud church to rival any other such structure in the Southwest, we were left with a dirt parking lot.

The congregation drifted from cinderblock shack to cinderblock shack until the new St. Genevieve's was built, but the structure was so shabbily constructed that parishioners were advised not to sit in the center pews to avoid having hunks of ceiling plaster fall on their heads. So much for the blessings of progress. The Loretto Academy, founded in 1870 and the first school established in southern New Mexico, met a similar fate.

Under the guise of "urban renewal," almost all of downtown Las Cruces was smashed into rubble and hauled away. The displaced shopkeepers were an eclectic mix of residents typical of the Mesilla Valley: Jewish immigrants; African American descendants of freed Texas slaves; American Indians, who were once again robbed of their property; Oklahomans displaced during the Great Depression; older *paisanos*; younger *veteranos*.

At one time, Las Cruces was replete with that unique early twentieth-century southwestern architecture—thick adobe under a concrete shell, the walls spiked with vigas and decorated with funky art deco flourishes. But that charm mattered little to our government planners. The old city hall, torn down. Local landmarks, torn down. The popular Herndon Hotel at the corner of Griggs and Main, where my mother and father spent their wedding night after taking the bus from Fort Bliss—torn down.

The mission in La Mesilla was spared not by the foresightedness of our elected leaders or the wisdom of the church, but by parishioners who faced down the bulldozers until the authorities flinched and backed away. Few of those marvelous old structures remain, such as the Doña Ana Courthouse. The isolated examples of early Las Cruces architecture are scattered about town like discarded gems from a broken necklace.

After the damage was done, the city tried scheme after scheme to revive what had been a vibrant downtown, but their efforts did more to funnel money into the pockets of the developers than to prevent Main Street from becoming an economic dead zone. Needless to say, you can find plenty of free parking in downtown Las Cruces. There's not much else. This lack of respect for local customs and traditions wasn't limited to the local government. When I was a kid, on the night of Ash Wednesday, we'd watch a procession of torches carried by the faithful as they climbed Tortuga Mountain from the chapel at Tortugas, an enclave south of town. When the federal government built Interstate 25, they—and the local government—made no provisions for the pilgrimage, and another tradition was brushed aside in the name of progress. Even more recent treasures, like our marvelous examples of midcentury neon aesthetic, such as the Triangle Trade Center and the marquees for the Rocket and Fiesta Drive-ins, were demolished and sold for scrap.

In his books, Rudolfo Anaya makes a point of showing us the importance of the Río Grande to the fertility and spiritual vitality of northern New Mexico. At one time, the river as it ran through the Mesilla Valley was so bountiful that the Mansos and Mescaleros used to live on its harvest of fish. But ever since Elephant Butte Dam was built upstream, the river has been stopped for months at a time, so that for much of the year, to us in Las Cruces, the mighty Río Grande wasn't much more than a dry, sandy trough. Certainly there was plenty of natural beauty around me. To the immediate east, the majestic Organ Mountains. Farther east, White Sands. The Lincoln National Forest. To the west, the Gila Cliff Dwellings. But what stood most prominently in my young, impressionable mind was that little in Las Cruces was worth treasuring.

Which brings me back to how the gothic put the whammy on me. One day I decided to write a vampire book. So why did I write about vampires? For the main reasons that an artist creates anything. Out of frustration and desperation. For years I had written novels and tried to get them published. The result? *Nada*. I had penned one manuscript I was certain would get me a contract but then saw that precious hope sink into obscurity without so much as a reply to my heartfelt queries. I decided to say the hell with it. I would write the most ridiculous story I could think of: a detective-vampire investigates an outbreak of nymphomania at a nuclear weapons plant.

Unwittingly, I had veered into territory cultivated by Anaya in his Sonny Baca series, where his nemesis, Raven, compromises the United States government's holiest-of-holies—the nuclear weapons industry. Both Anaya and I put our villains smack inside the nuclear Vatican. That we chose the nuclear weapons industry as subjects for our books is no surprise if you're from New Mexico. The Manhattan Project of World War II consummated its research at Los Alamos, and the first atomic bomb was detonated at Trinity Site, near Alamogordo.

But wait, there's more. Anaya and I couldn't resist throwing our literary lasso around the 1947 UFO crash near Roswell. Think about it: where else would the aliens touch down but the Land of Enchantment? If you would've asked me then if I was writing "gothic" literature, I would've denied it. I worked hard to make my vampires and their world as antigothic as possible.

And what could be more antigothic than tacos and tamales? I figured that for a Chicano vampire, life as an undead bloodsucker was supposed to be a curse, but no barrio *refin?* I could torment my vampires with eternal damnation, but I wasn't so heartless that I could deny them the food that gives us cholos and chicas our famous plump *nalgas*.

Why a Chicano vampire?

Why not? Until then, we might have had plenty of Chicano bloodsuckers—especially in the legal profession—but none that were fanged revenants. With Félix Gómez of southern New Mexico, we finally did.

We Chicanos are starved for representation in this country's pop culture. Fortunately, we've made some progress. The first Latino I remembered on TV was Ricky Ricardo. Then Maria as the Spanish maid with the broken arm on *The Dick Van Dyke Show*. Remember Manolito, played by Henry Darrow, né Enrique Tomás Delgado, from *The High Chaparral*?

And we provided the greatest villain ever.

Khan, the role Ricardo Montalbán chewed into delicious morsels in *Star Trek II: The Wrath of Khan*. But unfortunately, Hollywood couldn't leave well enough alone and had to replace him with an Englishman for the remake.

So we were due for a Chicano vampire. As the hero.

But I was stuck. What business did I have writing about vampires? Remember, I was disconnected from the gothic. The answer to that question came because I gave myself permission for three different reasons.

First, I read Charlaine Harris's *Dead Until Dark*, which was later adapted into the *True Blood* series on television. I admired how Harris deconstructed the gothic legends and reassembled them with humor and new personalities. It turned out there are no commandments about the supernatural. If she could reinvent the vampire and shapeshifter mythos, why couldn't I?

Second, our cultural myths. By this time I was old enough to appreciate that fables could be remolded to spook an ever-changing audience. To a child, the boogeyman is the monster under the bed, the stranger who will try to kidnap you. To adults, the boogeyman might be the Muslim terrorist, the rising tide of south-of-the-border immigration (*para español oprima dos*), or the greatest threat of all: socialized medicine. I could do whatever I wanted with our cultural myths as long as I addressed a current *sentimiento*.

And third, I liked writing fiction—lies, the bigger the better. I've always found that life was more interesting if you could bend the truth. When my mother called me *un mentiroso*, I took that as an honor.

So inadvertently—and not for the first time in my life—I had backed myself into doing something I once had no intention of doing. I was writing about a vampire, and what was more gothic than a vampire?

So I invented Félix Gómez, but before I could write my novel, I needed a way for him to become a vampire.

I made him a sergeant in the U.S. Army. To quote the opening line in my debut novel: "I went to Iraq a soldier: I returned a vampire."

Ten words. Okay, so far, so good. Now what? I needed another eighty thousand.

I liken writing a story to sculpting with clay. You throw a lump on the page and begin to scrape away here, add a little there, and gradually the shape takes a recognizable form. I had the first three lumps: a premise, a protagonist, and an opening line. Now to add more lumps. More characters. Backstory. Setting. Plot twists. The climax. The denouement. *El fin.*

And since I was writing a vampire story, I had to introduce elements of the gothic—the weird and fantastic. For me that meant not just undead bloodsuckers but also choice bits of the modern American gothic: political conspiracies and UFOs.

Being from New Mexico, I realized that at one point I'd have to include the coyote—the trickster—in my pantheon of supernatural characters. About this time I learned that with an *apellido* of Acevedo, it was a good chance that my ancestors included Jews hiding among the conquistadores fleeing the Spanish Inquisition.

From there, it wasn't much of a leap to imagine that a Jewish conquistador had attracted the eye of Hernán Cortés's famous courtesan doña Marina and fathered the first Mexican, who in turn became Coyote in my vampire series. Though including doña Marina would, as former New Mexico governor Bruce King would say, open a whole box of Pandoras.

Doña Marina is the most problematic of our Mexican heroines, and her role in the fall of the Aztec empire feeds well into gothic myth. She probably began as Malinalli, who was taken as a slave by rival indigenous people, and then offered to the newly arriving Spaniards. There she entered history when she became an interpreter for Cortés and was instrumental in his orchestrating an alliance between the various nations chafing under Aztec hegemony. Once Cortés and the conquistadores defeated the Aztecs, then it was a matter of double-crossing their allies to divide and conquer until all of México was under the Spanish heel.

Besides serving as Cortés's interpreter, she was also his courtesan and bore him a son. Malinalli became Marina, then doña Marina. Cortés later passed her off to Juan Jaramillo, whom she married. During this time she became La Malinche and, with that moniker, was branded as México's most notorious traitor.

As La Malinche, doña Marina became the archetypal mother of México. Octavio Paz in *The Labyrinth of Solitude* interprets her relationship with Cortés as a metaphor for the violation that brought about modern

Mexican culture. After her death she was absorbed into myth, and considering her infamous résumé, La Malinche's reputation was further sullied when she was recast as La Llorona. Now she was damned to stalk the waterways as she cried for her lost children, symbols for the subjugated indigenous people she had drowned while a servant of the Spaniards.

Heavy stuff.

But all this was unknown to me when my mother first threatened me with a visit from La Llorona. The La Llorona of my youth was a phantom who prowled the irrigation canals of Las Cruces. We so feared her that when my friends and I returned to our homes at night, we sprinted past the ditches rather than risk attracting her murderous attention. But as I learned about La Llorona, aka La Malinche, aka Malintzin, aka doña Marina, aka Malinalli, I realized that she had been given a raw deal. Not surprising considering that her history was written by men. Why hold legions of men accountable for their crimes when you can scapegoat one woman?

The whammy came to me when I decided that Coyote, the trickster in my story, needed an origin, and what better mother could he possibly have than La Malinche? His father would be a Jewish conquistador, on the lam from the Inquisition, who managed to dip his quill, so to speak, in doña Marina's ink well. Together they helped write another chapter in the supernatural Pan-American gothic. Their bastard son would become the first mestizo, who then morphed into Coyote after he was turned into an immortal bloodsucker by a were-jaguar. Coyote serves as both a mentor and a foil to Félix Gómez. His role is not much different than coyote in other works, such as Anaya's Coyote in *Winter Shaman*.

I looked to Anaya and his take on the gothic in its naturalist form in *Bless Me, Ultima*. I studied his explanations of the cultural forces that had shaped New Mexico and compared them with other works, such as *Empire of the Summer Moon*, by S. C. Gwynne. It was by blending those narratives that I could better reinterpret history to tell my story.

In my forthcoming book, *Rescue From Planet Pleasure*, I decided Félix Gómez would have to battle extraterrestrials. An enemy that powerful required all the supernatural power Félix could muster, so I set my book in northern New Mexico, where the mojo would be strongest. Thanks to Chaco Canyon's myriad overlapping spiritual traditions, I could tap its mystical power by harnessing the vortex centered on the Sun Dagger petroglyph on top of Fajada Butte.

Next I paired Coyote with his mother, La Llorona, and threw in El Cucuy for good measure. But how could anyone write about northern New Mexico and not include the Native peoples?

So I drew upon Navajo skinwalkers and Hopi kachinas. Basically, I think I trampled on enough sacred ground to offend everyone.

The old traditions—the New Mexico gothic—that I had once ignored, I now readily embraced. I had at last connected my naïve realism to the national and global and so allowed the gothic to put its whammy on me.

NOTE

1. Conference on Rudolfo Anaya: Tradition, Modernity, and the Literatures of the U.S. Southwest, held at California State University, Los Angeles, on May 2–3, 2014. Quotation from http://rudyanayaatcalstatela.blogspot.com.

PART 3

History, Ancient Genealogies, and Globalization

10

Rudolfo Anaya's
Historical Memory

Rosaura Sánchez

The fiction of Rudolfo Anaya stands out for its multilevel dialogue with the history of New Mexico, world literature and culture, global political and technological history, and indigenous religious discourses. The multiple discourses embedded in his dialogic creations are ultimately concerned with cultural change, loss of historical traditions and beliefs, and spiritism. Elements that once defined New Mexican Chicanos are seen to be at risk of fading away with modernization, urbanization, gentrification, loss of land and displacement, and opportunism. A study of Anaya's work necessarily involves an analysis of his configuration of history and memory in his fiction. This chapter focuses on the figuration of time and space in Anaya's highly popular detective narrative series: *Zia Summer* ([1995] 2008), *Rio Grande Fall* ([1996] 2008), *Shaman Winter* ([1999] 2009), and *Jemez Spring* (2005).

The study of history and memory in literature is especially intriguing and revealing, precisely because it involves rewriting or restructuring prior historical texts or ideological subtexts, according to Frederic Jameson (1981, 76). Dialogic texts that include multiple discourses and refer to various temporalities necessarily call for a reading or rereading of antagonistic relations. Exploring how these contradictions are figured in a popular genre like that of the detective novel leads necessarily to the examination of form and genre. The detective genre is fast becoming a central component of Chicano/a literature. In Latin America detective stories have been popular since the nineteenth century, but in the last four decades, the *novela negra* genre has attracted a great deal of critical attention. Perhaps the most well-known author of the novela negra is the Mexican Paco Ignacio Taibo II. In Taibo's work, set primarily in Mexico City streets and colonias, the criminal is the state or capital. In Anaya's work, Albuquerque is the key space, a city that has undergone rapid change since World War II. It is now part of a large metropolitan statistical area with nearly a million in population. This large urban center has been subject to a culture of tourism, attracting artists and New Age groupies, and has seen the development of high technological industries, often related to the nuclear labs in the state, as well as the establishment of casinos by indigenous communities. With this growth have also come violence, police brutality, poverty, and homelessness. I would not, however, place Anaya's work within the novela negra genre, for despite his critical commentary on several social and political issues, his detective novels ultimately deal with spiritual and psychological concerns, placing causality elsewhere. The criminal in Anaya's novels is not capitalism or the state, but evil itself, an ethical and moral construction rather than a political or social one. In his novels, evil assumes human form and allies with the state, capital, or criminals whenever convenient and possible; otherwise evil functions on its own, as it seeks to destroy its antithesis and the planet.

What especially defines Anaya's work is a cyclical perspective of time and history, which leads to a definite tension in these novels between historical and ahistorical, and between social reality and a dimension beyond the real. By historical I am referring to the multiple references to New Mexico history that abound in Anaya's works, and by ahistorical, I am referring not only to the time of shamanism but also to the particular way in which history is inscribed in his novels. This tension, I want to argue, is evident in the intersection of multiple temporalities that are configured in the work. Here I am drawing on the work of Jameson, for whom intersection is not a conjuncture, but a dissonance, a contradiction, as I discuss shortly (Jameson 2009).

Critics like Paul Ricoeur have posited that time can be divided into objective and subjective.[1] Objective time would be the time of the cosmos, the movement of the earth around the sun, and in Anaya, the changing seasons. Objective time can also refer to the time of a sequence of events, changes in modes of production, technological developments, and political shifts. In Anaya's detective novels, time covers the pre-Oñate colonization period, the period of Spanish settler colonialism, the U.S. invasion in 1846, and the twentieth and twenty-first centuries. Subjective time, on the other hand, is existential time, the characters' lived experience of time. Though time itself is not representable, we become aware of its passing in the movement of characters, the blossoming of trees, the being born and the dying. In a work of fiction, time appears as traces of particular moments that are identifiable when they intersect other temporalities and—importantly—the time of others. Time is written and rewritten as narrative.

Through narrative and the construction of multiple temporalities, Anaya takes hold of and reworks history in his four detective novels. Characters in Anaya's works become aware of the passage of time in their stories of cultural loss and loss of historical memory. The older characters lament that the younger people are no longer concerned with their past. As the detective Sonny Baca notes, some individuals, especially the old people, yearned for a simpler time, measured by the sun's course, the cyclical time of seasons, because now "time was measured by the stock market, multinational corporations earnings, and banks that took interest from the third world's economies. A false time, setting its imprint on the human psyche, sure to pervert human nature beyond repair" (Anaya 2005, 101). I argue that in Anaya's work, postmodern time and premodern time intersect as temporalities in dissonance.

How do we, Anaya's readers, approach these various temporalities? Since time and space are inseparable, and since these temporalities are produced within particular narrative spaces marked by modes of production, we can begin by focusing on the cultural mode of literary production, that is, on the formal processes that make up a narrative. These formal processes, or genres, can be seen as the cultural logic of a particular moment and—notably—a particular economic mode of production. Different historical periods and different modes of production will then, understandably, generate different types of narratives. Folktales, for example, were prevalent in precapitalist peasant societies. Today, in the period of late capitalism, the postmodern novel prevails, with its incorporation of multiple genres. A study of literary genre or subgenres can thus open the door to formal processes linked to different temporalities. Multiple generic forms and multiple temporalities are clearly at play in the wide-ranging work of Anaya—at some level, incompatible forms—some of which are residual, some emergent modalities, that speak to the scope and variety of Anaya's literary production over the span of fifty years.

What interests me especially here is the figuration of time through a variety of genres and subgenres. Anaya's detective novels share aspects of the hard-boiled novel, the romance genre, the gothic story, the realist novel, the modernist novel, mythic tales, speculative fiction stories, and cinematography. As I noted earlier, each generic mode of production is marked by its own cultural logic and attendant temporalities, which in turn intersect. The romantic genre is most evident in the binary structure of the four detective novels. At one level, the main conflict is between what we could call the forces of evil and the forces of good or light. The villain, or personification of evil, is Raven, also called Anthony Pájaro, a force that cannot be killed, and a man that detective Sonny Baca will discover is both his double and his nemesis. Sonny's friend on the police force, Howard, says the FBI has a list of Raven's aliases, including John Worthy, Worthy John, Jean Bearman, and John Black Crow. Raven is said to have been around since the beginning of time; he was there in the Spanish colonization of New Mexico and thereafter in every period, always bringing down destruction and violence and seeking to create chaos. Romantic narratives of this kind are not the only ones to be marked by these binary entanglements; preromantic tales can be binary as well, as evident in the folktales, fairy tales, and myths of many cultures. The perspective in romantic narratives is often portrayed in terms of a struggle between individuals, but in earlier folktales, the forces of evil could be dragons, witches, or sorcerers. Much like in popular fiction, such as stories of Superman, Batman, or even Sherlock Holmes, in the romantic genre, there is necessarily a nemesis, the negative other of the central protagonist, and in each of Anaya's detective novels, Raven seeks to destroy Sonny and the world. It goes without saying that the fight between Sonny and Raven is a constant unending battle, since the force of evil cannot be killed. This continuous conflict is in fact inscribed in the novel's time and in its very equilibrium of things.

This binary, Manichean formulation stands in direct contradiction with a highly critical presentation and analysis of today's pressing issues and problems, which are also very much present in the detective quartet. The threats posed by drugs, ecological disasters, dispossession, gentrification, nuclear contamination, murders, and kidnappings occur within a space of constructed social reality. This space is intersected by what Alejo Carpentier would call the "marvelous real," *lo real maravilloso* (2007). The marvelous is configured in the maintenance of precapitalist belief systems among villagers and others, while the "real" is found in the insertion of present-day events and issues. These two planes represent two temporalities that intersect in the novels. I want to emphasize, however, that as I note above, the intersection is not a conjuncture but is grounded in dissonance and contradiction. These various time intersections, along with the multiplicity of genres, are also characteristic features of postmodernist literary works. Other binary structures are likewise constitutional to the works. Historically, the detective Sonny is aware of ethnic divisions going back to 1846: "The split would be *we* versus *them: we* the Mexicanos and our way of life threatened by *them* the Americanos. In the middle were the once great Indian pueblos of the Río Grande, which had seen the arrival of both great tides of immigrants onto their land. They cast a pox on both houses" (Anaya [1999] 2009, 166). This history which "festered and grew into the bone, blood and soul" (160) is said to inhabit the memory of all nuevomexicanos. Sonny is also aware of class divisions:

> The Chicanos in the city, those workers who lived in the mobile-parks where they could afford the rent, those same workers who often appeared as "quaint" background fodder in videos taken by tourists, paid no attention to the psychic-phenomena ladies, whores of the New Age, whom nobody blamed for making a living because usually they had four or five snotty kids to feed, were behind on the rent, and the ex was not paying the alimony. (2005, 233)

These binary class and ethnic divisions, however, are mostly an afterthought in the novel, in which Chicanos and Hispanos are part of the ruling class, and most of the characters, with the exception of some indigenous figures, are landowners, business owners, or professionals.

The view of history as cyclical in Anaya's detective series is a theme often remarked on by the evil character Raven: "Time is a continuum, a cycle repeating itself, like the snake swallowing its own tail" ([1999] 2009, 192). This ahistorical, marvelous, and cyclical view of history leads the characters to sense that while things change, evolve, and are transformed, they also remain the same in fundamental ways. The struggle between good and evil is said to be constant across time. Life itself is cyclical. Reincarnation is posited by several characters, who see themselves as recapitulating and reproducing previous lives. Other types of repetition and restagings are also alluded to. Social stratification of the past, for example, is said to parallel that of today. Power differentials have indeed been around from time immemorial, and yet clearly the feudal system and the capitalist system are not one and the same. And the social contradictions and sites of tension in each system are markedly different. But in Anaya's novels, Sonny, who is able to travel across different times, mostly perceives similarities and the constant presence of evil.

This focus on past periods is marked by nostalgia, another distinctive feature of postmodern texts. There is much of the nostalgic novel in Anaya. Images of the past, as noted by Jameson, can be transformed into commodities, false memories of the past that seek to compensate for what is perceived to have been lost (1990, 137). Anaya's novels are full of this nostalgia for a lost culture and especially a nineteenth-century historical past, in an era in which, again to borrow from Jameson, "genuine historicity or class traditions have become enfeebled" (137). The affect of nostalgia is central and in turn leads to a generational narrative form of images and simulacra of the past. The generation of don Eliseo and his friends Toto and Concha remembers a time when "the community was a vecindad in which people took care of each other" (Anaya [1995] 2008, 240). Sonny, acutely aware of land loss and dispossession, remembers a childhood when the valley used to be full of vineyards and cornfields, land that has now been gentrified and filled with insipid housing developments.

Don Eliseo had warned Sonny: "Lose the language, the threads of history, and the traditions and the ways of your ancestors will disappear from the earth of La Nueva Mexico" ([1999] 2009, 180). This nostalgia is linked to a premodern or pre-1846 past, before foreigners arrived and fenced the land, a time of communal land that is now private property. But the yearning for a time of memory, of sheepherding paisanos, is intersected by an awareness of metropolitan reality, of urban space marked by privatization and problems. The lived contradictions of the present do not allow for an idealization of the barrio, as noted by Sonny: "The surface of [today's] barrio [could be] pastel colors bright with sunlight, friendly sounds, and the smiles of the people. [But] beneath that surface lay the danger" (226). The danger beneath the façade is that of poverty, drug traffickers, cults, corrupt politicians, and evil forces.

This nostalgia is also linked to the current of what in Latin American literature is the romantic costumbrismo, the portrayal of quaint, picturesque sketches of manners and nature. As in Latin American costumbrista novels, in Anaya there are ample descriptions of the valleys, rivers, canyons, mountains, clouds, rain and thunderstorms, as well as the roads, highways, and bridges. Descriptions also abound of celebrations at the churches or cultural centers as well as of kachinas and saints, which still figure in the culture of the old folks. Local New Mexican color and flavors, especially food, sights, smells, textures, and tones, all produce the affect of nostalgia, that is, the production of a specific feeling: the ache and longing for something lost.

SONNY AS SHAMAN AND SHAMUS

As in other novels of the detective genre, in Anaya's works we find the individual private investigator, here former high school teacher Sonny Baca, who navigates the streets of not only a contemporary urban space, in this case, Albuquerque, but also the villages of northern New Mexico, where old Hispano families still hang on to what are now diminutive ranches, and where indigenous pueblos still struggle to survive. Sonny Baca is described as a handsome man, about thirty years of age, drawn to and sought after by—of course—beautiful women; he is impetuous and oftentimes unwilling to listen to the advice of his mentors. Yet despite his impulsiveness, he always manages to get out of the scrape, generally (but not always) physically intact. Although the novels are not procedural police stories, the private detective somehow finds assistants everywhere, whether it be his girlfriend, Rita; his neighbor, don Eliseo, who is a shaman, and don Eliseo's friends, don Toto and Concha; the curandera/shaman Lorenza Villa, who often functions as a sidekick; or others he meets and befriends. His distrust of government officials, be they police officers or CIA or FBI agents, is palpable throughout the works; his one friend at the police station is Howard, the medical examiner, an African American who faithfully provides Sonny with information. He also has a good friend at the library, Ruth, who does research for him, and later in the library, Sonny meets a teenager, Cyber, who can hack into CIA and FBI files for him. Most of these characters reappear intertextually in all four novels, as do Sonny's mother and twin brother, Mando. With a little help from his friends, Anaya's detective investigates worldly crimes but also takes on supernatural forces of evil, which assume human form, as he comes to accept, with the help of don Eliseo and Lorenza, that he too is a shaman. I am arguing that this marvelous, or supernatural, temporality defines these novels, beyond the overriding detective premise.

Sonny, the great-grandson of Elfego Baca, a historical nineteenth-century lawman and hero in the Socorro area, will, in time, learn from don Eliseo and Lorenza how to deal with supernatural forces. At first he is not aware of these forces nor of what is to be his fated role in combating them. The main crimes Detective Baca deals with are murder, kidnapping, and nuclear threats, but the ecological threat and potential loss of the water supply are also running threads in all four detective novels, as well as in the novel *Alburquerque* (1992). In *Zia Summer*, Sonny has to contend with Raven's cult of Zia women, or brujas, ostensibly worshippers of the sun and the Zia sun symbol, who kill the detective's cousin, Gloria, when she tries to leave the cult. As in Anaya's other works, women in his detective novels appear mostly in traditional roles: as *curanderas*, mothers, lovers, temptresses, victims, friends who admire him, and evil corrupt women who conspire with Raven or the police or CIA and FBI to kill him. Even when women appear in key positions, they are rapidly dispensed with as they assume the traditional roles. The female mayor, Marisa Martínez, for example, is cast in *Alburquerque* in the role of temptress in her interaction with the main character, Abrán; and the famous artist/potter, Naomi, appears in *Jemez Spring* to tempt Sonny, but she is quickly murdered to keep her from saying what she knows about the governor's murder and the corrupt plot of the capitalist Frank Dominic. The main female characters in the detective novels are Rita and Lorenza, both described as beautiful mestizas, both there to support and serve the needs—professional and personal—of Sonny.[2]

Investigating the death of Gloria in *Zia Summer* gets Sonny involved in a much larger issue: he discovers that Raven is attempting to blow up a truck transferring high-level plutonium waste from Los Alamos to the WIPP, the Waste Isolation Pilot Plant, a nuclear waste dump near Carlsbad. Raven, here calling himself Anthony Pájaro, not only is responsible for Gloria's death but is also the leader of an antinuclear group who speaks with zeal about the dangers of toxic contamination of the planet. Having the activist who denounces the dumping of radioactive waste into the Río Grande be at the same time the villain and the epitome of evil is of course problematic in that it functions to discredit environmental movements. Raven is correct in arguing that the nuclear storage facilities are seeping nuclear waste and contaminating the water table and causing cancer. The government of course assures the public that there is no risk involved in moving these storage tanks, but as Rita notes, "People are fed up with government lies" ([1995] 2008, 292). This very "real" conflict serves to illustrate the dissonance between the two temporalities in the text, the historical and the ahistorical, or supernatural, operating in tandem.

Political struggle is enacted and then undermined by Raven, when he twists a "politically correct" environmental movement to bring about an apocalypse. As Sonny notes, "Raven had another agenda, a darker, more evil plan. Chaos was his god. Violence his end. Raven envisioned the end of the world and his cult coming into power in the new world" (308). For that reason Raven plans to dynamite the truck as it goes down the highway. It falls to Sonny, Rita, and a rancher friend, Escobar, to find where the explosives are being placed, since the police as well as the National Guard prove useless. Sonny and his two friends discover that Raven has set the explosives under the Arroyo del Sol Bridge. Naturally, the three get there just in time; a fight ensues between Sonny and Raven, but Rita intervenes to save Sonny. Raven, in his attempt to strike Sonny down, falls into the rain-swollen creek and is carried off, disappeared but not destroyed.

Thus a fictional account of a contemporary historical issue, the radioactive contamination of the planet, is intersected in Anaya by a supernatural temporality. Through this encounter, Sonny comes to acknowledge that he will need to develop his shaman powers (his fate and purpose) if he is to combat Raven effectively. The supernatural temporality now becomes dominant in the melodrama. Don Eliseo begins to teach him about the Señores and Señoras de la Luz, but for Sonny, the old man's practices are simply spiritual. It is only later, when Sonny is in need of a *limpia* to cure him from *susto*, that the curandera Lorenza, who herself practices a kind of indigenous shamanism, will initiate Sonny into the realm of the supernatural and enable him to discover his *nahual*, the coyote. The playing field of his conflict with Raven will thus be leveled, or raised, perhaps, to the plane of the supernatural.

Lorenza reveals to Sonny that he will only be able to deal with Raven in his dreams. "You see, the world of nature is our world. We think entering this age of technology erases the past. It doesn't. Our nature is linked to that of our ancestors, to their beliefs. The surface changes for us but we know that beneath the surface lies the true world, the world of spirit" ([1996] 2008, 114). Dreams in the novels are psychological and magical spaces, in which violent encounters take place and the revelation occurs that "the real enemy is within" (2005, 224). Dreams connect Sonny to the spirit world and to the spirits of his ancestors and the indigenous kachinas. That indigenous religions in México and New Mexico were persecuted and driven underground yet still survive is a historical fact, but that the world of spirits is the "true world" is an affirmation of the primacy of the supernatural and metaphysical in Anaya's novels. Hereafter, Sonny acquires the power to shape-shift into his nahual. As a coyote, Sonny is a trickster with his own set of powers, which he will need to use to battle Raven. Within this metaphysical horizon, this atemporal, transcendent, cyclical, and spiritual time, the conflict with Raven will now take place in the four novels. The contemporary historical setting notwithstanding, the plot and premise of the novels take place on another plane altogether.

The second novel, *Rio Grande Fall*, centers on Albuquerque and its International Balloon Fiesta, which draws many visitors annually and is a big moneymaker for the city. Sonny receives a call from the medical examiner, Howard, telling him that one of Raven's followers, the one who had killed Gloria and tried to kill Sonny, has fallen from a balloon and died. This report will draw Sonny into an investigation of the Balloon Fiesta, especially after the city director of the event, Madge Swenson, enlists his help, hoping to spin the death as a tragic accident and not a murder to assuage the fears of would-be ballooners. The investigation will lead Sonny to check out three names on the list of hundreds of participants at the festival who plan to ride a balloon. Here we return to the realm of social reality and a concrete historical temporality: one of the participants is an Italian involved in the distribution of South American cocaine; one, an ex-CIA agent involved in the past with the Nicaraguan Contras and the distribution of drugs in the United States; and one, an exiled Colombian journalist whose husband was killed after she wrote an exposé on the Cali cartel.

This case will endanger Sonny's life, not only at the hands of Raven but also at the hands of ex-CIA agents. His discovery is that a million-dollar transfer of cocaine to New Mexico is being organized by the ex-CIA agents in collusion with balloon festival director, Madge Swenson, who in turn is in cahoots with a surgeon whose project is to transplant baboon hearts in humans. The unmasking of the requisite detective novel drug plot is accompanied by critical remarks from Howard on the government's involvement in the drug trade. Here the novel offers a realist account of the motives and deceptions behind the scene of these historically grounded topics, but this socio-political plot is a mere backdrop to the search for Raven, who has kidnapped Sonny's lover, Rita, along with a young girl. Sonny's desperate search leads to a series of near-death episodes. While checking out a black balloon, Sonny and Madge will be shot at and attacked by Raven and his men; Sonny and Lorenza will almost asphyxiate while tied up and launched in a balloon that they are unable to control; at another moment, he will have a knife fight with Raven in a hotel; still later, he will almost be burned to death in a drug dealer's warehouse in Juárez by Raven and his associates; and finally, with the help of Lorenza, Sonny will be able to rescue Rita and the girl after battling Raven at his former camp in the woods, but only by taking the form of his nahual, the coyote. The novela negra plot that has the detective exposing state and city collusion with drug traffickers is neutralized by the power of the supernatural, for Raven has a hand in everything that happens and is in collusion with the ex-CIA agents, the surgeon, the city festival manager, and the drug suppliers, as he seeks money to obtain a plutonium kernel for the making of a bomb. In the end, when the detective discovers the multilevel plot, the surgeon knocks him out and begins to torture and electrocute Sonny in his laboratory. Sonny suffers near death but is saved at the last minute by the arrival of his friends. The electrocution, however, leaves Sonny partly paralyzed.

In his third novel, *Shaman Winter*, Anaya is at his creative best, blending elements of speculative fiction with elements of the marvelous. This is also Anaya's most historically grounded account of New Mexico's past, which serves as the basis for dream exploration. By now we know that Raven is a shapeshifter with great powers, including the ability to fly. He cannot be killed and thus is a constant presence throughout history. What makes *Shaman Winter* stand out is that here, through dreams, Raven will attempt to alter the space-time continuum, as he sets out to destroy Sonny. By killing Sonny's ancestral grandmothers from different historical periods, Raven diabolically seeks to obliterate Sonny's bloodline and retroactively eliminate his very existence. Time travel through dreams takes place in a temporality of virtual reality. Dreams, like myths, can serve as socially symbolic acts to enable individuals or collectivities to resolve their problems or differences (Jameson 1981, 76). But in Anaya, these dreams are memory spaces for reclaiming a forgotten past as well as battlegrounds for combating the forces of evil. In effect, the past becomes a perpetual present, continually reenacted in dreams. Here Sonny and Raven, two rivals with powers, challenge each other, each trying to destroy the other, not only in the material sphere, but in the realm of dreams, positing a certain materiality to the dream sphere with consequences in real time. In fact, Sonny finds, to his surprise, that dreams can be materialized when he discovers his ancestral Owl Woman's Bowl of Dreams in real life, a bowl used by Raven to hide the "plutonium pit." Yet the bowl was an image, an artifact from a dream that had taken Sonny back to 1598. Later don Eliseo will explain that the glyphs on Owl Woman's bowl point to the cycles of time and the dreams of the Américas, dreams that Sonny can read and interpret (Anaya [1999] 2009, 132). Sonny Baca is thus not only the traditional gumshoe who follows clues, interviews people, visits different sites, does research, and consults and relies on assistants, but he is also a shaman, a good brujo, with powers, struggling to save his past (and history itself) by saving his great-grandmothers and time as a whole since Raven wishes "to end time because he realizes that in time we are perfecting our souls" (134). The novels thus posit a parallel reality, akin to cyberspace and cyberdream ([1999] 2009, 262), a spiritual space wherein a universal consciousness can be attained.

In *Shaman Winter* Sonny has recuperated most of his motor skills and his mind, but his legs are still weak, and he has to use a wheelchair. By now, Sonny has come to accept his shamanistic powers and, following don Eliseo's advice, begins studying his dreams. These dreams take the reader through New Mexico history, dating from the initial Spanish colonization to the early twentieth century, with Pancho Villa and Sonny's great-grandfather Elfego Baca. Learning that it is important to write down one's dreams, Sonny notes that in his earliest dream, he was a Spanish soldier, Andrés Vaca, in Oñate's colonization expedition of 1598. In the dream, before entering New Mexico, he (as Andrés) falls in love with Owl Woman, a Pueblo Indian, and he decides that he wants to give up soldiering and settle down, have children with this woman, work the land, and raise cattle and sheep. Vaca goes with her to the river, where they make love; there she shows him the dark tripod bowl with symbols engraved on the outside, those of an owl and the horns of a bull, the symbol of Vaca. This Bowl of Dreams, which will later materialize, speaks to the idea of fated encounters. In this episode, the marriage, agreed to by the chiefs and shaman of Owl Woman's tribe, will be erased from history when someone kidnaps Owl Woman. The kidnapper is none other than the Bringer of Curses, Raven himself, who appears in Sonny's dream, snatching her away, leaving his signature four black feathers on the marriage bed. Raven aims to disappear Owl Woman and take her into the underworld of spirits to destroy Sonny's past and therefore his future/present. In this way, the past, generally seen as irrevocable, can in fact be altered through time travel. We are now in the realm of speculative fiction.

Within the work's cyclical perspective of time, Sonny comes to understand that four hundred years ago, Raven was already here. His reverie is interrupted by a phone call from Eloisa Romero from Santa Fe, asking for Sonny's help because her daughter has disappeared from her bedroom; Sonny finds out that four feathers were left on the child's bed, confirming Raven's continued presence in the present. In subsequent episodes, Raven kidnaps four young ladies participating in Christmas posada plays. Sonny comes to discover that the four girls are distantly related to him, as are the four women from the past that he sees being kidnapped by Raven in his dreams. Not fully convinced about his bloodline or ties to Andrés Vaca, Sonny does some historical and genealogical research and in the process finds that there was in fact an Anthony Pájaro (one of Raven's aliases) in the Oñate 1598 expedition. Don Eliseo explains that Raven, having failed to murder Sonny on this plane of existence is now trying to kill him in his dreams. Raven knows that Owl Woman is one of Sonny's original abuelas, and if he kills her and changes the time line, Sonny will cease to exist. Don Eliseo tells Sonny that by entering his dreams, "Raven can travel to [Sonny's] past and destroy it" ([1999] 2009, 35). The disrupted space-time continuum premise is laid clear: "If Raven can kill four maternal grandmothers, he kills [Sonny] by killing [his] history" (36). Dreams, says don Eliseo, connect one to history (37). In *Shaman Winter*, evil forces, not historically situated power relations nor control of historiography, are what can erase an individual's history and threaten both memory and being.

In the temporality of the present, Sonny realizes that the moments staged in his dreams are in some way connected to his intensive reading of history. His dreams are thus a way to access the past. A dream, says don Eliseo, "is a way to enter the world of spirits. It is also a way to enter history" (21). According to don Eliseo, Sonny's soul has been shattered by his being electrocuted (in the previous novel), and since the valley where he lives is the place of his ancestors, it is here, in this particular space, through his dreams, that he can be restored and reborn (23).

Sonny's historical research at the university library will not only confirm past episodes in his dreams but also provide new input that will be staged in his dreams. Historiography within the material world thus becomes a source for the creation and projection of dreams and the establishment of a supernatural dimension. With the help of Lorenza, who drives the paralyzed Sonny to different sites where young women have been kidnapped, Sonny is able to continue reading his library books in the van. He reads that the first migrants onto the land of New Mexico were the Anasazi, the ancestors of the Pueblo peoples (53). We are made to recall that when the Spaniards came, the friars tried to Christianize the Indians, destroying their ceremonial kivas; burning masks, fetishes, and other paraphernalia; and prohibiting dances and the handling of snakes. The Inquisition also beat and hanged the medicine men who resisted conversion. With the Spanish conquest came diseases, including smallpox and measles, as well as the oppressive encomienda system, requiring the Indians to work for the Spaniards and pay tribute in corn and blankets. The Pueblos, however, would not abandon their kachinas and traditions, nor did they wish to be the slaves of the Spaniards, so in 1680 they rebelled. The inclusion of this history is merely anecdotal, and it only marginally figures in the plot of the novel. The rebellion scene in Sonny's dream is the site for a second kidnapping, again of a young Spanish girl, who was to marry another of Sonny's ancestors, Hernán Vaca. What at one level is a justified uprising of the Pueblos against the Spanish settlers becomes a narrative device to stage another kidnapping of Sonny's distant grandmothers by Raven.

In subsequent dreams, Sonny is unable to save a third grandmother, kidnapped by Raven during the 1846 invasion of New Mexico led by Colonel Stephen W. Kearny. Epífana Aragón, who was to marry Lisandro Jaramillo, another grandfather in Sonny's past, is abducted in Las Vegas by Raven, disguised as one of Kearny's army soldiers. In 1881 after meeting Billy the Kid, who is riding to the side of Rosa, the love of his life, Sonny is unable to save Billy but does save the girl; in a subsequent dream, Sonny rides with his great-grandfather Elfego Baca to Columbus, New Mexico, where in 1916 Pancho Villa enters with his men to free his lover, Soledad, jailed by the gringos to draw Villa to the town. Although Villa is able to free Soledad, Sonny is not able to rescue her from Raven, who kidnaps a fourth grandmother.

Dreams are thus a way to review historical moments that are not central to the novel's plot, but that open up the novel to a series of adventures,
where Sonny more often than not fails to save the day. Dreams also enter
Rita's life when, the night of her miscarriage, she reports having had a
dream about her Navajo, or Diné, ancestors, who were rounded up by
Kit Carson in 1864 and forced to march to the reservation called Bosque
Redondo near Fort Sumner. The forced march in the middle of winter
killed many women and children and caused a number of miscarriages.
Events of the past are thus seen to be reenacted in the present by evil
policies and evil men, and we discover that Rita's miscarriage of Sonny's
offspring is also caused by Raven.

The erasure of Sonny's history through the kidnapping of his four
grandmothers is only one of the narrative plots. The main plot involves a
conspiracy to produce a nuclear bomb, by bringing a Ukrainian physicist
to Los Alamos. Raven is behind this plot too, as he is in possession of a plutonium kernel, although he will rely on the support of an antigovernment,
white supremacist militia group, the Avengers, that seem to be behind
the building of the bomb. Vehemently xenophobic, especially against
the "brown hordes from Latin America" (Anaya [1999] 2009, 74), the
Avengers are all set on detonating a nuclear explosion that will topple the
government and then establishing a military dictatorship. It is revealed
further that the top echelons of the militia group are in the government, in
the military, in research labs, in the Pentagon, and in Congress. Perhaps
even the director of the FBI is part of the militia. The implications are
nasty: a fascist state, a race war, a class war, and so on. The way Sonny
reads it, for this militia, the important thing is to destroy the very spiritual
center of the country, and that means destroying New Mexico (77).

This episode in *Shaman Winter* is part thriller, but ultimately, the antigovernment plotting is directly linked to Raven's evil machinations and
his objective to destroy the planet and Sonny Baca. The dangers of nuclear
research and nuclear waste, as well as the threat of an ebola virus breakout,
like the militias and government coverups, serve as background for explaining the struggle between darkness and light, between Raven and Sonny.

The plotline is further complicated by the personal when Sonny subsequently discovers that Rita's miscarriage has been caused by Raven.

Concerned with not only his past forebears but also with his future descendants, Sonny fears for his bloodline and needs to defend the spirits of his unborn child or children; he becomes even more determined to find Raven and kill him, although at some level, Sonny knows that Raven cannot be killed. Two additional girls, both related to him, will be kidnapped, with one search provoking a chase scene and crash that restores Sonny's mobility and use of his legs. In *Shaman Winter*'s denouement, the metaphysical once again is foregrounded as it becomes the dimension in which the final struggle takes place. As the hour of the winter solstice approaches, don Eliseo warns Sonny that Raven will kill the girls, take their spirits, and bring down the sun. To get to Raven, Sonny must go into the dream world, but it is important that he control the dream and be the master of his own destiny. With a gigantic dreamcatcher built by don Eliseo for defense, Sonny enters the dream accompanied by don Eliseo and his dog, Chica. In a detailed dream sequence, Sonny, as is his wont, is impetuous and does not listen to don Eliseo's warnings, giving Raven the opportunity to get him into his circle to kill him. Don Eliseo intervenes to save him and is killed instead. Ultimately, Sonny will be able to suck Raven through the hole in the dreamcatcher and set the grandmothers and young girls free. At novel's end, carrying don Eliseo, who has sacrificed his life to save Sonny's, the detective walks out of the dreamworld; space-time continuum having been righted, Sonny and Raven are poised to meet and do battle again.

In Anaya's last novel in the series, *Jemez Spring*, the issues of water, dispossession, and gentrification are central problematics as again is the nuclear energy issue, taken up here with a timely and topical Al Qaeda terrorist twist. Again, the high-ranking directors in the CIA and FBI are in collusion with Raven, right-wing militias, drug traffickers, multinational corporations, and politicians, all ready to blame Al Qaeda for planting a bomb on Jemez Mountain. When the governor changes his mind about participating in Dominic's water scheme, he is killed, as are those, like the artist Naomi, who know too much. Again the distortion of history plays a role as Raven joins Dominic, whose water plans include not only privatizing water rights but also rewriting history by planting an ancient Caucasian skull in the Santa Fe Mesa to erase Pueblo claims to being First

Peoples in the region. Water had become "the gold of the desert and he who controlled the supply could make the rules" (Anaya 2005, 18). The indigenous group, the Green Indians, which organizes against Dominic's plan to privatize the water, is accused of being connected to Al Qaeda terrorists, especially the leader, known as Bear, who is Naomi's lover. In an effective narrative compression of time and space, all the action in this novel takes place in one day.

Sonny's main concern, however, is not the planet's destruction nor the issue of water rights, all of which are merely background for encounters between Sonny and Raven, but his personal loss, the loss of his unborn children, now assumed to have been twins, whom he sees as spirits within Raven's web. The spirit world is now not only accessible through dreams, but present in daily life, as it intersects waking reality, such as when the spirits of the past march down the street amid the revelers who await the end of the world once the bomb on Jemez Mountain explodes. Sonny's mentor, don Eliseo, who had died saving Sonny in the third novel, now accompanies Sonny daily as spirit. The dream world, previously compared to cyberspace, now is presented as virtual reality, akin to laser-produced images found in the theater-in-the-round where Sonny is summoned to meet Raven, who argues, echoing Pedro Calderón and William Shakespeare, that life itself is a dream: "You see, my dear boy, we are images in the movie of life. We are projections who strut and fret our hour upon the stage and then are heard no more. The light will go out, Sonny, the movie will end. You will disappear into a void far beyond virtual reality" (2005, 225–26).

Illusions and the use of images to control the masses now become key sites of struggle. Time itself is presented as "the final illusion," as past, present, and future all blend into one temporality. As Sonny explains, "The tenses of time blended into each other, not only in the dream time, but also in that time known as ordinary time" (279). The materiality of the world disappears as the dream world, the spiritual world, explains it all. In this idealist interpretation, the dream dimension is said to be the realm of the unconscious, of the soul (163–64), and it is here where the real struggle, the spiritual struggle, takes place. Recognition of this sphere brings enlightenment and transcendence. Raven, however, distinguishes between illusion and the spiritual sphere, and in his discussion of Sonny's obsession with his unborn children, he makes clear that Sonny has deluded himself, thinking that the images of his daughters are real; they are mere illusions, he says, images that he could keep with him forever, although he could never bring his unborn daughters back. In the dream world, however, Sonny could conjure up his past ancestors and free them from Raven's grasp. In the middle of this metaphysical discussion—tellingly at the Barelas Bridge—reality enters the scene again, for as Raven prepares to kill Sonny with his raised scimitar, Bear, the murdered Naomi's lover, crashes through the trees and knocks Raven into the Río Grande, where he disappears once again, at least for the time being.

Evil, and the struggle against it, has always existed, argues the Sonny Baca detective quartet. And Raven is that evil. Is he a symbol of imperialism? Of capitalism? Of fascism? No, this is not an evil that emerges from economic, political, and social tensions and struggles, although Raven is quick to manipulate and benefit from any of these. Evil, it is said, resides, ahistorically, in the hearts of men, in the DNA (2005, 105), and especially in the soul of Raven. The four Anaya novels are thus full of very specific historical references and short synopses of what occurred in the Southwest after the U.S. invasion, with the land loss, the privatization of land, and the new laws of the U.S. occupation, but the historical setting is just that, a backdrop, and the events are (in the truest sense of the word) circumstantial and not central to what is taking place in the novels nor to what concerns Sonny. Even the fight for water rights in *Jemez Spring* is not primary, despite the recognition that without water, the Indians' fields would die and they would "become the West Bank Palestinians" (133). In all four novels, then, the heart of the matter is the metaphysical dimension. There are those who scoff at the idea of ghosts and spirits, say the old Hispanos and say Anaya's novels, but the spirits of the ancestors, that is, the historical past, are here (178). With this spirit dimension comes the character's recognition that evil is universal and transcendent, that it resides in the hearts of men, and that it has always existed and always will exist. That this ahistorical mindset in Anaya is intersected by a range of pressing and topical historical concerns creates a dissonance between the material and the spiritual that is not resolved. Admittedly, at one point, don Eliseo suspects that it is man that creates both gods and demons. But Raven is presented not as a figment of New Mexicans' imagination, but as a real evil force capable of destroying the city of Albuquerque and the planet itself. It falls to readers to take up Sonny's constructed dreams and illusions as socially symbolic acts to be unmasked, demystified, and thus recoded and rewritten. Perhaps therein reside the power and purpose of both dreams and fiction: the power to imagine and the power (and will) to discern. Anaya's works speak to this dual potential with both purpose and power.

NOTES

An earlier version of this chapter was read at the Conference on Rudolfo Anaya: Tradition, Modernity, and the Literatures of the U.S. Southwest, held at California State University, Los Angeles, on May 2–3, 2014, organized by Roberto Cantú on Rudolfo Anaya.

1. Discussed by Jameson in *Valences of the Dialectic* (2009, 502).
2. No one would doubt that Anaya would be hard pressed to pass the Bechdel test or the Mako Mori test.

REFERENCES

Anaya, Rudolfo. 1992. *Alburquerque.* Albuquerque: University of New Mexico Press.

———. (1995) 2008. *Zia Summer.* Albuquerque: University of New Mexico Press. Page citations from 2008 edition.

———. (1996) 2008. *Rio Grande Fall.* Albuquerque: University of New Mexico Press. Page citations from 2008 edition.

———. (1999) 2009. *Shaman Winter.* Albuquerque: University of New Mexico Press. Page citations from 2009 edition.

———. 2005. *Jemez Spring.* Albuquerque: University of New Mexico Press.

Carpentier, Alejo. (1949) 2007. *Prólogo a El reino de este mundo.* Madrid: Alianza Editorial.

Jameson, Frederic. 1981. *The Political Unconscious. Narrative as a Socially Symbolic Act.* Ithaca, NY: Cornell University Press.

———. 1990. *Signatures of the Visible.* New York: Routledge.

———. 2009. *Valences of the Dialectic.* London: Verso.

11

Imagining the Local
and the Global in the Work of
Rudolfo A. Anaya

Horst Tonn

Two trips to Spain in 1980 and 1988 led Rudolfo Anaya to reflect on his position in relation to Old World/New World entanglements. Toward the end of his essay "The New World Man," Anaya observes: "I could walk anywhere in the world and feel I was a citizen of the world, but it was Nuevo México that centered me; it was the indigenous soul of the Americas that held my secret."[1] This statement connects a stance of cosmopolitanism with a commitment to a region and an affiliation with the pre-Columbian traditions of a hemisphere. On the one side of this equation stands the traveler, who moves comfortably at his own pace and leisure in various parts of the world. On the other side, we find the author reliably rooted in New Mexico, the state where Anaya has lived throughout his life.

Although Anaya has traveled widely in Europe, Asia, and the Américas, New Mexico continues to be the place he feels deeply connected to in a way that goes clearly beyond local attachment and mere familiarity. New Mexico, he claims, provides a center and much-needed stability. Beyond that, a transcendent affinity, a deep, only intuitively grasped mutual intelligibility is said to characterize the relationship between the writer and his place. It is this particular constellation of the local and the global that interests me in this chapter. Most obviously, the local and the global are not polar opposites nor mutually exclusive options. In Tom Lutz's seminal study of American regionalism, he argues for a third space between the local and the global for what is generally considered regionalist writing.

According to Lutz, much regionalist writing follows an "ethic of cosmopolitanism" whereby cultural differences are neither enshrined nor off-handedly dismissed. Instead, "these texts promote a superior cultural position that comprehends all difference, and though not quite dismissing difference as atavistic, they suggest that a literary overview will make cultural differences not so much the basis for different identities, as the many elements of a larger, *literary* identity based precisely on such accumulated representations."[2]

In this chapter, I make a similar claim for the work of Rudolfo Anaya. Cultural differences—whether they are based on ethnicity, region, history, class, or any other relevant category—are not foundational, but relational. They constitute a field of interrogation rather than a set of alternatives. Thus, to juxtapose the local and the global sets up a false opposition. Instead, our attention might focus on the ways in which these texts explore the ongoing calibrations of one's relationships to nation, region, local spaces, and so forth.

Rudolfo Anaya's work is deeply embedded in the culture and topographical space of his native New Mexico. At the same time, the author persistently reflects on the complications of the regional and local, and he seeks to relate this to broader formations of the transnational and the global. Anaya grew up in a Spanish-speaking home in Santa Rosa, New Mexico, from which it seemed "the whole world spoke Spanish."[3] One of the early windows to a larger world beyond Santa Rosa was the town's modest public library, about which Anaya has touchingly written. By his own account, he spent many Saturday afternoons roaming the dusty shelves of that library, generously guided by the local librarian, who appreciated the curiosity of the young boy. Some forty years later, the enclosures of his early upbringing have given way to the perception of a pervasively relational world system: "More than ever we live in an age of interdependence. Groups within nations, as well as nations within the international arena, have moved into a fragile but exciting state of interdependency. The world is in a fluid state, and our most simple actions reverberate in far and distant places."[4] This quotation captures well the trepidations and ambivalences about the current state of globalization that many of us share. The newly emerging interdependencies are exciting and promising because they open up new ways of relations and encounters. At the same time, we realize how our consumer habits deplete resources in other parts of the world, and how the regime of Western capitalism causes destitution and inhumane working conditions elsewhere. Before we go on, a few passages on the current debates about cosmopolitanism may be in order here.

ON COSMOPOLITANISM

Cosmopolitanism is typically associated with certain urban settings, such as Los Angeles, Berlin, New York, Lagos, Mumbai, Mexico City, and so on. Variants of the cosmopolitan subject appear to be the alienated expatriate, the restless drifter or nomadic professional who seems numbed by excessive mobility and exudes a sophisticated world weariness. Most generally, cosmopolitanism entails an attitude of self-assured worldliness combined with the ability to connect and interact in different countries and cultures. Further, cosmopolitanism may be viewed as a cultural practice, as, in Ulf Hannerz's words "a mode of managing meaning" across spatial and cultural distances.[5] It can be seen as a particular optic that is receptive to polyphonies, the fluidity of boundaries and the mutual resonances between the universal and the culturally specific. As German sociologist Ulrich Beck has pointed out, it requires "inner mobility"—that is, the ability to recognize the equally valid claims of universality and difference. It is marked by a specific sensibility and dialogic skills, which are continuously shaped.

"I am a citizen of the world." The sentence is commonly attributed to Diogenes, Greek philosopher of the fourth century B.C., and it has become the foundational statement of a set of convictions that have been robustly resonant in Western contexts for twenty-four centuries since. To some this statement may sound impossibly vague. How could one possibly claim a mutually committed relationship of citizenship with an entity as expansive and complex as the world? For others, however, Diogenes's vast gesture may articulate the kernel of a radical utopian promise of achieved universality. From a Western point of view, cosmopolitanism may seem intuitively congenial and attractive. From a non-Western perspective, it is frequently associated with all the ailments typically attributed to the West, such as rootlessness, moral shiftlessness, materialism, arrogance, decadence, superficiality, and so forth.[6] As Walter Mignolo and others have argued, cosmopolitanism is an integral part of the project of Western modernity: "[T]hat cosmopolitan razor is trying to mold the planet according to the subjectivity, desires, comfort, satisfaction, and security of those who embrace, theorize and push cosmopolitanism." And in the process it has been "complicitous with the formation of European imperial powers and of European expansion in America, Africa, and Asia, as well as with the continuation of Europe in the United States."[7]

Debates about cosmopolitanism have thrived recently in the context of transnationalism and globalization studies, in particular since the 1990s. Most likely, these debates have been significantly energized by Western triumphalism after the presumed end of the Cold War some twenty-five years ago. Cosmopolitanism is frequently invoked as the possibly happy outcome of an otherwise very uncertain itinerary of the future course of globalization. It has been taken up in a number of different ways and by many academic disciplines.[8] Kwame Anthony Appiah considers the ethical demands of cosmopolitanism and emphasizes its potential to reconcile universality and difference. Appiah proceeds from the basic ethical mandate that others matter as much as we do, which as a consequence must reject all fundamentalisms as well as the absolute truth claims of some ethnic and religious groups.[9] Rudolfo Anaya has argued in a similar direction when he envisions "an integrated world based on mutual respect."[10] Jacques Derrida stresses the legal and political dimensions of cosmopolitanism when he turns to issues of refugee rights and international law, urging us to adapt the universal right to hospitality to contemporary migrations across the globe. Ulrich Beck finds that what he calls "realistic cosmopolitanism" is the most promising way to deal with issues of "otherness" and "boundaries" in an increasingly globalizing world.

Although cosmopolitanism has generated tremendous amounts of research, it remains an elusive term. Gertrude Himmelfarb has observed that the idea of cosmopolitanism has "a nice, high-minded ring to it."[11] Cosmopolitanism suggests progressive ideas and ideals of a world beyond nationalisms, of a new global age promising yet unimaginable possibilities of citizenship, mobility, and cultural hybridity, all facilitated by a commitment to universal rights and principles. Moreover, cosmopolitanism resonates with ethical imperatives such as tolerance, openness, hospitality, and appreciation of otherness. Anthony Giddens emphasizes tolerance of cultural diversity and a commitment to democratic values as the prime attributes of a cosmopolitan outlook: "In a globalising world, where information and images are routinely transmitted across the globe, we are all regularly in contact with others who think differently, and live differently, from ourselves. Cosmopolitans welcome and embrace this cultural complexity."[12] Cosmopolitanism rejects the narrowing perspectives of cultural hierarchies and exclusivities. Instead, it values culture and appreciates the relational productivity of cultures.

THE TRANSCULTURAL REACH OF ANAYA'S WORK

Let me begin here with a comment by Ishmael Reed, which he made in an interview with Rudolfo Anaya in 1976:

> Ishmael Reed: You know, you talk very much about national identity and mythology and all this, but I used *Bless Me, Ultima* in Buffalo, and these kids have probably never seen many Latino people or Chicano people. Polish working-class kids. They loved the book. They thought it was the best book. It does have universal . . . well, I hate to say that, but it does seem to cut across class and cultural lines.[13]

Ishmael Reed's anxiety about a possible universal dimension in *Bless Me, Ultima* speaks to the cultural moment of the 1970s. The well-marked pause after the word "universal" suggests that Reed is approaching something almost unspeakable. In James Clifford's more recent formulation, Reed is up against "the repressive alternatives of universalism and separatism."[14] To claim that an "ethnic text" has universal relevance may weaken the power of that text to articulate cultural difference. It might have undermined the efficacy of Anaya's novel to contribute to a distinct canon of Chicano literature, which was still in a fledgling stage at the time this conversation took place.

Today Ishmael Reed's anxieties concerning universality are more of a historical reminiscence. For one, Rudolfo Anaya's work and its broad international reception are proof that both are possible—writers can energize their own culture and resonate with audiences outside their own group. The many translations of Anaya's work are one kind of evidence for the transnational reach of his writing. Anaya's novels have been translated into Japanese, French, Polish, German, Spanish, and Italian.[15] Readers from highly diverse cultural backgrounds resonate with the issues articulated in his work: identity conflict, coming of age, and acculturation; spiritual (dis-)orientation; cultural and physical displacement; and forced migration. Much of this writing is informed by what Tom Lutz has described as an "antihegemonic strain."[16] Anaya attempts to be diagnostic and counterhegemonic at the same time. He seeks to excavate and circulate subjugated knowledges. At its core, his writing is partly driven by an antimodernist agenda, which has been described by T. Jackson Lears for the period 1880 to 1920:

> The antimodern impulse stemmed from revulsion against the process of rationalization first described by Max Weber—the systematic organization of economic life for maximum productivity and of individual life for maximum personal achievement; the drive for efficient control of nature under the banner of improving human welfare; the reduction of the world to a disenchanted object to be manipulated by rational technique.[17]

A CHICANO IN CHINA

A Chicano in China is a book mostly characterized by wit, playfulness, and utopian exuberance. It emphasizes the transformative power of self-staging and foregrounds practices of travel that in many ways depart from those of conventional Western tourism. Some moments on the trip are rendered in such an outrageously preposterous way that they have to be read as self-deflating irony. Take as one example the moment of arrival in Beijing:

> We touch down at the Bejing airport in the early afternoon. *El Tercer Mundo! He llegado, con una canción en mi corazón.* Peking, land of

my grandfather's dreams. I rush to embrace the Chinese. Brown brothers, Raza! Can you imagine a billion new souls for *La Raza?* We could rule the world. But immigration stops me. I cannot pass. *La Migra* has been stopping Chicanos at the border for a long time. Chinese sounds fill the air. I cannot speak my brother's language.[18]

This passage is reminiscent of some of the more rambunctious passages in Oscar Zeta Acosta's self-dramatizations. It is more stream of consciousness than revelatory of an obvious ideological agenda regarding colonization. Its exuberant conflation of peoples, borders, and fantasies speaks to the ambivalences of arrival in a distant place. The trepidations of welcoming the unknown converge with the longing for the familiar. Moreover, in its shift from joyful familiarity to speechlessness, it strikes a more serious note not altogether uncommon in intercultural encounters. The euphoria of arrival is hampered by the technicalities of immigration procedures. The vibrancy of foreign sounds is followed by exasperation with not having a shared language.

In May 1984 Rudolfo Anaya and his wife, Patricia, traveled to China as part of a group of fellows of the Kellogg Foundation. Clearly, the mode of travel has a significant effect on the experiences of the travelers. In this case, a select group of artists and academics accompanied by a Chinese guide followed a rather full schedule of tourist attraction visits and arranged meetings with professional peers and other representatives of China's elites. Along the way, the group enjoyed Chinese opera, museums, scenic sites, and local cuisine. That is one part of the story. Some critics have remarked that Anaya's encounter with China remains within an orientalist frame.[19] According to this argument, Anaya freezes the "other" of Chinese culture and turns it into an object that is to be conquered, thus perpetuating a colonialist paradigm under the guise of Chicano liberation. The argument is based on Edward Said's conception of orientalism "as a Western style for dominating, restructuring, and having authority over the Orient."[20]

If one considers the self-reflexivity, humor, and playfulness of *A Chicano in China*, then Anaya's approach to China appears to be (self-)transformative rather than possessive. The journal is not so much about China as it is about the author's engagement with China. There is very little to be learned about China from this book. In his self-professed "myopic foreign-ness," Anaya wants to know what China will do to him, how exposure to China will affect his own world knowledge.[21] As a traveler he wants to find an adequate "lens" (35), and his approach to the foreign culture is rather spontaneous and intuitive.[22] Anaya is keenly aware of the likely limits of intercultural encounters, as they have been candidly described by Appiah: "I am urging that we should learn about people in other places, take an interest in their civilizations, their arguments, their errors, their achieve-ments, not because that will bring us to agreement, but because it will help us get used to one another."[23] Several times in the book, Anaya refers to his trip to China as a "pilgrimage"—a spiritual or secular journey aimed at self-transformation. The idea of pilgrimage is clearly not an innocent fantasy, as it is deeply embedded in the colonization of the Américas. On the other hand, the moral and ideological frames that emerge as constants throughout Anaya's writings seem to preclude interpretations suggestive of complicity with colonialist/imperial ideological agendas. As a traveler Anaya appears to be guided by chance and intuition:

> Over the years my wife Patricia and I have traveled many places, and generally our way as pilgrims is to wander, to let our sense of adventure and intuition lead us into back streets, museums, mer-cados where the people buy and sell their goods, and especially into the ancient ruins of lost civilizations. We have always been rewarded by chancing upon ceremonies of life meaningful and poignant enough to change us forever. A pilgrim should remain open to those unexpected moments of change travel provides, which are the fulfillment of life on the road.[24]

The best way to travel, then, is to be meditative and explorative, suscepti-ble to the contingent encounters of the moment. In this mode one aspires toward a quality of observation somewhat reminiscent of the convergence of "wandering" and "wondering," as articulated in the poetry of British romantic writers, for example, William Blake's "London" and William Wordsworth's "Daffodils." The traveler aims to grasp the uniqueness of the moment of encounter. To travel is an opportunity "to learn to see."[25] Anaya keeps a distance from the perceptions of his fellow travelers. About a briefing at the U.S. embassy in Beijing, he comments: "Our questions all reflect a United States quick-fix mentality. Our group is a group of instant experts. I am put to sleep by the drone of questions, the complaints of how things don't work in China as they do in the U.S."[26] By contrast he feels exhilarated by the encroaching mist on the drive back to the hotel. The immediacy of a poetic moment takes precedence over the exchange of routinely shared cultural attitudes at the embassy.

Writers like Rudolfo Anaya and many others have transformed representations of the American Southwest from what Audrey Goodman has called aesthetic regionalism:

> By 1930 a region had become an aesthetic space where premodern traditions resisted social and technological change, culture took precedence over economics, local relationships were more important than national policies and international treaties, and concern for the natural environment outweighed the forces of development. Such aesthetic regionalism was nostalgic to the extent that it specified—and longed for—an older social organization, but it also provided a means of imagining local alternatives to the systemic expansion of the capitalist order.[27]

The vibrancy of Rudolfo Anaya's work can be partly attributed to his being equally attentive to the region of New Mexico as to the world at large. His writing effectively dispels common assumptions about the regional and the local. Much of his work can be read as "a means of resisting the pressures of modernization."[28] By reimagining the past as circular, he seeks to maintain some measure of continuity in the face of the accelerated unidirectionality of modernity. At the same time he has been very candid in his assessment of the combined forces of globalization, militarization, and corporate capitalism, as well as the disturbing simultaneity of tradition and modernity: "We set up bingo games as we pray for rain, and we train our children to take care of tourists as they forget to take care of the old ones. We begin to see the elemental landscape as a resource to be bought and sold."[29] While Anaya often asserts the epiphanic potential of nature, he also calls attention to the profound disruptions and displacements of our time. As he recognizes the communal depth and reliability of family and village life, he remains alert to the incontrovertible forces of mobility, dispersal, and economic flight. In Anaya's work, the mapping of physical and geographical spaces contributes to the fleshing out of moral, emotional, and cognitive landscapes that are equally local and global.

NOTES

1. Anaya, "New World Man," 364.
2. Lutz, *Cosmopolitan Vistas*, 36.
3. Anaya, *Shaman Winter*, 18.
4. Anaya, "Light Green Perspective," 27.
5. Hannerz, *Transnational Connections*, 102.
6. Buruma and Margalit, *Occidentalism*, 8, 11.
7. Mignolo, *Darker Side*, 253, 270.
8. For recent contributions to the field, see the essays in Brock, *Cosmopolitanism Versus Non-Cosmopolitanism*; Skrbis and Woodward, *Cosmopolitanism*; and Beck, *Cosmopolitan Vision*.
9. See Appiah, *Cosmopolitanism*.
10. Anaya, *Chicano in China*, x.
11. Gertrude Himmelfarb, "The Illusion of Cosmopolitanism" (1996), quoted in Skrbis and Woodward, *Cosmopolitanism*, 5.
12. Giddens, *Runaway World*, 4f.
13. Dick and Sirias, *Conversations*, 8.
14. Clifford, *Routes*, 11.
15. Moreover, many other Chicano/a writers have been translated into German. Among them are Rolando Hinojosa, Sandra Cisneros, Sheila Ortiz Taylor, Cecile Pineda, and most recently, Salvador Plascencia, author of *People of Paper*.
16. Lutz, *Cosmopolitan Vistas*, 25.
17. Lears, *No Place of Grace*, 7.
18. Anaya, *Chicano in China*, 17.
19. See, for example, Cass, "White Man's Fantasies." See also Renato Rosaldo's argument about "imperialist nostalgia" in *Culture and Truth*.
20. Said, *Orientalism*, 3.
21. Anaya, *Chicano in China*, 100.
22. Ibid, 35.
23. Appiah, *Cosmopolitanism*, 78.
24. Anaya, *Chicano in China*, vi.
25. Ibid., 202.
26. Ibid., 49.

27. Goodman, *Translating Southwestern Landscapes*, xv.
28. Goodman, *Lost Homelands*, 56.
29. Anaya, "Mythical Dimensions," 28.

BIBLIOGRAPHY

Anaya, Rudolfo A. *A Chicano in China*. Albuquerque: University of New Mexico Press, 1986.
———. "The Light Green Perspective: An Essay Concerning Multi-Cultural American Literature." *MELUS* 11, no. 1 (1984): 27–32.
———. "Mythical Dimensions/Political Reality." In *Open Spaces, City Places: Contemporary Writers on the Changing Southwest*, edited by Judy Nolte Temple, 25–30. Tucson: University of Arizona, 1994.
———. "The New World Man." 1989. In *The Anaya Reader*, 355–65. New York: Grand Central, 1995.
———. *Shaman Winter*. Albuquerque: University of New Mexico Press, 2009.
———. "What Good Is Literature in Our Time?" *American Literary History* 10, no. 3 (Autumn 1998): 471–77.
Appiah, Kwame Anthony. *Cosmopolitanism: Ethics in a World Of Strangers*. New York: Norton, 2006.
Beck, Ulrich. *Cosmopolitan Vision*. Cambridge: Polity Press, 2006.
———. "The Truth of Others: A Cosmopolitan Approach." *Common Knowledge* 10, no. 3 (2004): 430–49.
Brock, Gillian, ed. *Cosmopolitanism Versus Non-Cosmopolitanism*. Oxford: Oxford University Press, 2013.
Buruma, Ian, and Avishai Margalit. *Occidentalism: The West in the Eyes of Its Enemies*. New York: Penguin, 2004.
Cass, Jeffrey. "A White Man's Fantasies: Orientalism in Rudolfo Anaya's *A Chicano in China*." In *Hispanic American Writers*, edited by Harold Bloom, 17–27. New York: Chelsea, 2009.
Clifford, James. *Routes: Travel and Translation in the Late Twentieth Century*. Cambridge, MA: Harvard University Press, 1997.
Derrida, Jacques. *On Cosmopolitanism and Forgiveness*. London: Routledge, 2001.
Dick, Bruce, and Silvio Sirias. *Conversations with Rudolfo Anaya*. Jackson: University of Mississippi Press, 1998.
Giddens, Anthony. *Runaway World: How Globalisation Is Reshaping Our Lives*. London: Profile Books, 2002.
Goodman, Audrey. *Lost Homelands: Ruin and Reconstruction in the 20th-Century Southwest*. Tucson: University of Arizona Press, 2010.
———. *Translating Southwestern Landscapes: The Making of an Anglo Literary Region*. Tucson: University of Arizona Press, 2002.

Hannerz, Ulf. *Transnational Connections*. London: Routledge, 1996.

Lears, T. J. Jackson. *No Place of Grace*. Chicago: University of Chicago Press, 1994.

Lutz, Tom. *Cosmopolitan Vistas: American Regionalism and Literary Value*. Ithaca, NY: Cornell University Press, 2004.

Meléndez, A. Gabriel, M. Jane Young, Patricia Moore, and Patrick Pynes, eds. *The Multicultural Southwest*. Tucson: University of Arizona Press, 2001.

Mignolo, Walter D. *The Darker Side of Western Modernity*. Durham, NC: Duke University Press, 2011.

Rosaldo, Renato. *Culture and Truth*. Boston: Routledge, 1993.

Said, Edward. *Orientalism*. New York: Random House, 1979.

Skrbis, Zlatko, and Ian Woodward. *Cosmopolitanism: Uses of the Idea*. London: Sage, 2013.

Temple, Judy Nolte, ed. *Old Southwest/New Southwest*. Tucson, AZ: Tucson Public Library, 1987.

———. *Open Spaces, City Places: Contemporary Writers on the Changing Southwest*. Tucson: University of Arizona, 1994.

12

Transnational Tales

A MILLENNIUM OF INDIGENOUS
CULTURAL INTERACTION BETWEEN
THE UNITED STATES AND MÉXICO

John M. D. Pohl

Standing outside the Church of San Miguel Analco, in Santa Fe, New Mexico, for the first time, I was fascinated by the National Park Service sign that identified it as having been constructed by the Tlaxcalteca Indians of México in 1610.[1] "I think my family is descended from these Nahua settlers rather than what is identified as the Spanish culture here in New Mexico," remarked Kurly Tlapoyawa, an Albuquerque filmmaker, public historian, and indigenous rights activist with whom I had been corresponding. Kurly had expressed interest in my ideas concerning the Tlaxcalteca among other indigenous peoples of southern México who have been the subject of my research over the past thirty years, and we agreed to meet at San Miguel when I was invited to Santa Fe to give a lecture for the Archaeological Institute of America.

Between A.D. 1200 and 1600, the Tlaxcalteca together with a score of kingdoms across the plain of Puebla formed a confederacy, the Children of Quetzalcóatl (Children of the Plumed Serpent), which dominated much of southern México before the Aztec empire. Recent research that my colleagues and I conducted indicates that the Eastern Nahuas, Mixtecs, and Zapotecs, along with more than fifteen other language groups across southern México whom they dominated, had composed a significant part of a late postclassic economic system that extended from Central America up the Pacific coast to Oaxaca, Jalisco, and Nayarit, then northeast to Zacatecas, Chihuahua, New Mexico, and Arizona. These populations

The Church of San Miguel Analco, Santa Fe, New Mexico, was reputedly
constructed adjacent to a more ancient Ancestral Pueblo kiva, a practice that
was very common with the construction of churches adjacent to pre-Columbian
temples in Tlaxcala, Puebla, and Oaxaca, sponsored by the Franciscan and
Dominican orders working together with indigenous noble leaders. San Miguel
became a patron saint of Tlaxcala when he made his miraculous appearance to a
Nahua named Diego Lázaro de San Francisco and opened a spring of water that
had the ability to cure the sick. (Author's photo)

maintained barrios within one another's kingdoms, intermarried to
form monopolies over resources, and enriched themselves through trade
in exotic commodities, such as textiles, dyes, turquoise, copper, gold,
shell, and the feathers of exotic tropical birds (Pohl, Fields, and Lyall
2012). Nevertheless, historians and archaeologists have overlooked their
achievements in favor of the focus on the Aztec empire as the dominant

political and economic power of the late postclassic period. There are several reasons for this, not the least of which is the politics of history in constructing national identities.

The indigenous peoples of the United States and México are regarded in very different ways. Separation by the 1848 Treaty of Guadalupe Hidalgo led to some profound distinctions being made between "our Indians" versus "their Indians." By the end of the nineteenth century, the U.S. Southwest had become endowed with a kind of natural antiquity—mysterious cliff dwellings and other ancient human remains set within titanic rock formations conveyed a larger-than-life sense of antiquity and national entitlement at the same time Europeans were moving classical statuary to London, Egyptian obelisks to Paris, and Babylonian temple gates to Berlin. The effect, however, was to view the American Indian people themselves, both the hunting tribes and the pueblo-dwelling peoples, together with the colonizing Spanish and indigenous peoples from México, as a vestigial population largely detached from their natural surroundings.

México, on the other hand, invested heavily in the legacy of the Aztec empire and promoted it as the official heritage of all Mexican people. Emphasis was placed on the celebration of ancient achievements to promote a developing twentieth-century nation-state (Pohl 2002). To characterize ancient Mexican civilization, as part of greater Mesoamerica, archaeologists defined a specific set of traits, including the domestication of maize, the use of writing systems, an accurate 365-day calendar, and sophisticated forms of art—particularly monumental sculpture; large-scale architecture featuring stepped pyramids, palaces, and plazas; among other significant features (Pohl 1999, 3–11). An evolutionary chronology was developed, which defined a classic period extending between A.D. 200 and 900, a time of astounding feats, such as the construction of the Pyramid of the Sun at Teotithuacan, the extraordinary Zapotec acropolis of Monte Albán, and the majestic Maya temples of Palenque and Uxmal. The term "classic" was adapted from its use by Western European historians to define what they regarded as the height of civilizational ideals in Greco-Roman culture. It seemed only appropriate, therefore, to cast the preceding millennium as a Mexican preclassic period (1500 B.C.–A.D.

200), during which the Olmec chiefdoms rose to prominence. The subsequent postclassic (A.D. 950–1521), on the other hand, was perceived as a time of "collapse," comparable to Europe's late antiquity. This perception of the postclassic period in México is of society becoming fragmented, and cities overrun by hunting tribes from the desert wastelands of the north. Mexican civilization was only redeemed with the rise of the Aztec empire, its capital becoming Tenochtitlan, or what is today Mexico City, a city that boasted a population of more than 250,000, making it one of the largest cities in the world by 1500 (Willey and Phillips 1958).

The apparent dichotomy between the tribes in the north and the Aztec empire in the south led to more than a century of debate about what, if any, influences these cultures may or may not have had on one another (Lekson 2008). Early southwestern archaeologists recognized similarities in the geometric designs in pottery and the practice of maize agriculture. Large-scale architecture suggested connections with the Gran Chichimeca to the south, from which the Aztecs claimed to have originated in myth (Di Peso 1974). Southwestern peoples such as Hopis, Pimas, and Papagos spoke Uto-Aztecan languages and maintained oral traditions that related their origins to México. These similarities and connections appeared to suggest a direct link with Mesoamerica, and yet no evidence indicated that the Aztec empire had ever "reached" that far north of the Basin of Mexico (White 1960). Therefore, differences in interpretations remain inherently biased by the development of two different archaeologies, one oriented to the understanding of the rise of states in Mesoamerica from 1500 B.C. to A.D. 1521, and the other oriented to the emergence of tribes and complex chiefdoms in the Southwest from A.D. 1000 to 1540 (Coe and Koontz 2013; Lekson 2008; Pohl 1999). In fact, the Society for American Archaeology still distinguishes between the two fields by sponsoring two different journals, *American Antiquity* and *Latin American Antiquity*, which essentially brings us right back around to "our Indians" versus "their Indians." Recognizing the limitations in regional approaches to the rise of Ancestral Pueblo societies versus the danger of overextending the evidence for highland Mexican cultural influence, several scholars have proposed theories that consider both factors. Most notable is the observation that the emergence of the first large-scale Ancestral Pueblo society, the Anasazi of Chaco Canyon around A.D. 950, coincides with the rise of the Toltec capital of Tula. At this time, turquoise was playing a significant role in the development of a macroeconomy across the Southwest and into northern México. Regarded as a gemstone, turquoise was used as a form of ritual currency that bound diverse peoples into systems of symbolic reciprocity through articulated wealth and staple finance economies (Hull et al. 2014; Pohl 2001; D'Altroy and Earle 1985). One highly valued source, located in the Cerrillos Hills, east of Santa Fe, New Mexico, was controlled by the ranking Chaco ceremonial center of Pueblo Bonito, where tens of thousands of individual pieces of the blue stone have been recovered archaeologically. Significantly, Cerrillos Hills is the source of the majority of turquoise recovered from the Toltec capital of Tula, in central México, suggesting that Pueblo Bonito and Tula were engaged in exclusive long-distance trade (Harbottle and Weigand 1992; Taube 2012). But just how intense were these exchanges, and what role did the peoples collectively known as Chichimecas, who lived in the intermediate areas of northern and western México, play in this trade?

Anthropologists studying the complex relationships among tribes, chiefdoms, and states have observed that they engage in mutually beneficial relationships that capitalize on their respective environmental and cultural adaptations (Leach 1973; Friedman 1998; Fried 1975; Helms 1993). Mutualism was fundamental to the success of Ancestral Pueblo peoples; for example, it enabled them to maintain a higher standard of living by integrating subsistence strategies that would otherwise be unattainable to any single group deploying any single strategy alone (Spielmann 1991; Spielmann and Eder 1994; Wilcox 1991). The idea was originally conceived in the simple advantages of exchanging the carbohydrates in maize, beans, and squash for the protein in wild game procured by nearby tribal hunting populations. Hunters were adept at supplying more than simply meat, however. Because they negotiated vast distances over formidable terrain, they possessed a unique ability to exploit widely dispersed resources of many different kinds (Earle 2005; Reyman 1995; Scharlotta 2014). Once hunters identified some product that was attractive to farmers within their migration circuit—anything from turquoise to shell or peyote, for example—they could easily incorporate its exploitation into their foraging strategy and transport it back to farmers for even greater gain. Once farmers, in turn, made a product useful to a state, the effect could lead to social transformations as both societies began to engage in exclusive trade relationships (Pohl 2001, 90). Monopolies over resources were formulated through intermarriages, a fundamental form of social and economic integration. The discovery of the chemical residue of cacao in Anasazi drinking vessels, a ritual beverage associated with royal marriage rituals in México, suggests that elite kinship bonds were an essential part of the Anasazi-Toltec exchange system (Washburn et al. 2014; Pohl 2003d).

As the Anasazi engaged with the Toltecs, the leaders responsible for directing the acquisition and processing of materials like turquoise clearly began to affect certain forms of Toltec political behavior, leading to an intensification of social stratification (Weigand 1992). Artifacts of precious turquoise, shell, and copper associated with burials at Pueblo Bonito, for example, are indicative of individuals who were clearly attributed paramount rank, and many religious stories related by contemporary Pueblo peoples through their oral traditions suggest that they possessed formidable powers of control over their people, subverting traditional systems of exchange that led to indebtedness and even enslavement (Lekson 2008, 200–201). Some scholars have proposed that Anasazi paramounts should be compared to Mesoamerican "kings" (Lekson 2015). Kingship is a complex issue in Mesoamerican scholarship. The seventh- and eighth-century kings of the classic Mayas, like the divine Pacal of Palenque or Hasaw Chan Kawil of Tikal, were clearly masters of all they surveyed and ruled through institutionalized systems of descent that dated back centuries. The Toltecs emerging at the outset of the postclassic appear to have maintained more diversified administrations, rooted in corporate forms of behavior administered by multiple kin groups, who focused on specialized commercial endeavors (Kowalski and Kristan-Graham 2011). Tula's rise and fall recounted in early colonial histories suggest that its priests and kings probably maintained a governmental system more along the lines of Tula's successor, the late postclassic Tolteca-Chichimeca ceremonial center of Cholula (Pohl 1999, 162–72).

Tula was abandoned around A.D. 1150. Indigenous histories attribute its collapse to violent internal factionalism among its administrators, the priests Quetzalcóatl, Tezcatlipoca, and Huitzilopochtli in myth. Disruptions of this kind appear to be confirmed by the extraordinary amount of intentional burning of architecture and defacement of monumental art within the main ceremonial center (Pohl 1999, 159–60). Significantly, the Anasazi center of Chaco Canyon was abandoned around the same time, and Pueblo religious stories attribute its demise to comparable forms of behavior (Lekson 2008, 200–201). Whether the two phenomena are directly related is still unknown, but considering that their paramounts were so closely connected through trade and specialized forms of social, economic, and political organization during the previous century, it seems likely.

From the eleventh through the twelfth century, the Toltec economy had moved along Chichimec hunting trails, and it was inevitable that some Chichimec tribes would be attracted to the prosperity of their Toltec trading partners. By the end of the ninth century, many Chichimecs were migrating into southern and central México, where the two groups intermarried after the fall of Tula. These new confederations of Tolteca-Chichimeca spoke Náhuatl and organized themselves into small independent city-states. Their descendants became the Eastern Nahua peoples of the plain of Puebla and the Tehuacán Valley and the Western Nahua peoples of the Valley of Mexico, who eventually founded the Aztec empire and adjacent regions of Morelos and Guerrero.

The Eastern Nahuas established a new ceremonial center at Cholula, Puebla, where the cult of Quetzalcóatl was centered. Quetzalcóatl was revered by more than a dozen different ethnic groups throughout southern México, who claimed that the penitent hero had traveled through their kingdoms to establish his presence as a devotional figure (Pohl, Fields, and Lyall 2012). Cholula, the new Tollan, was venerated as a major market, pilgrimage center, and source of religious and political cohesion. The foundation of this theocratic power was a religious ceremony dedicated to Quetzalcóatl whereby a prince was required to journey to Cholula to meet with two of the god's high priests. After several days of prayer and penitence, the ears, nose, and lips of the initiate were pierced with sharpened eagle and jaguar bones, and a turquoise ornament was inserted. In this way the prince was declared a tecuhtli, or lineage head, and was thereby granted, by Quetzalcóatl's divine authority, the rulership of a royal estate, or tecalli. The appeal of the cult of Quetzalcóatl and the tecuhtli ceremony was that they transcended all local religious

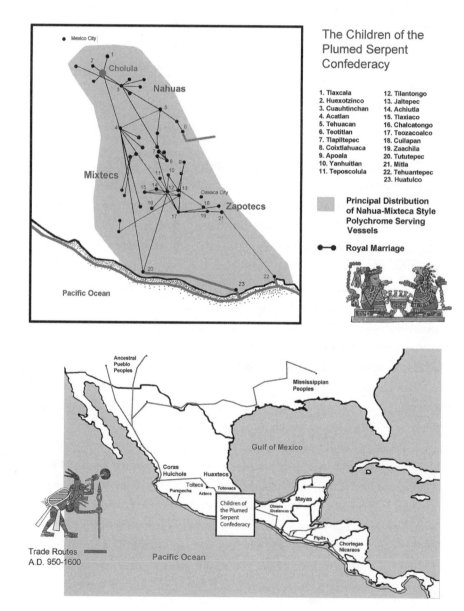

The Children of the
Plumed Serpent
Confederacy

1. Tlaxcala
2. Huexotzinco
3. Cuauhtinchan
4. Acatlan
5. Tehuacan
6. Teotitlan
7. Tlapiltepec
8. Coixtlahuaca
9. Apoala
10. Yanhuitlan
11. Teposcolula
12. Tilantongo
13. Jaltepec
14. Achiutla
15. Tlaxiaco
16. Chalcatongo
17. Teozacoalco
18. Cuilapan
19. Zaachila
20. Tututepec
21. Mitla
22. Tehuantepec
23. Huatulco

Principal Distribution
of Nahua-Mixteca Style
Polychrome Serving
Vessels

Royal Marriage

Trade Routes ▬▬
A.D. 950-1600

customs and bound ethnically diverse peoples together into homogenous social and political units, thereby facilitating elite alliance and economic exchange among city-states throughout the central and southern highlands (Pohl 1999, 169–70; 2003a, 62–63). By A.D. 1250, the Eastern Nahuas were engaging the Mixtecs and Zapotecs in royal marriages documented in colonial texts, maps, *lienzos,* and painted books called codices (Pohl 2003d). Some describe a legendary odyssey from Cholula by noblemen, the Children of Quetzalcóatl, who later founded kingdoms throughout southern México and beyond.[2] Similar intrusions have been documented for the Coatzacoalcos region of Veracruz and the Soconusco region of coastal Chiapas. Nahua peoples of coastal Guatemala and El Salvador claimed that their communities were founded by these same Tolteca-Chichimeca. Calling themselves Pipil, they spoke an Eastern Náhuatl dialect and claimed Quetzalcóatl as their god (Pohl 2003c).

A unique pictographic communication system and art style was adopted throughout central and southern México at this time, termed Nahua-Mixteca after the two cultures most responsible for its development in southern México between Puebla and Oaxaca. Some scholars also call it the Cholula, international, or postclassic religious style. It is characterized by an almost geometric precision in line. The figures are representational, even cartoon-like in their proportions, and painted in vivid primary colors. Tenth-century dates for Cholula polychrome pottery indicate that the style was largely conceived by Cholula artisans, although

(*facing*) The Children of Quetzalcoatl (Plumed Serpent) confederacy was dominated by the Eastern Nahuas, Mixtecs and Zapotecs, together with more than fifteen other language groups with which they were allied between A.D. 1250 and 1600. Marriage alliances consolidated power and ensured monopolies over both the wealth and staple economies of southern México. The trade map depicts the indigenous exchange corridors that linked México with what is now the United States during this period. Following the conquest of Tenochtitlan, indigenous rulers of southern México supplied troops and directed the Spaniards to reorganize first on the Pacific coast of Oaxaca for the conquest of Central America and the exploration of the Gulf of California, using these traditional routes of economic and cultural exchange. This was followed by the subjugation of the Purépecha and Aztatlán kingdoms of Michoacán, Jalisco, Nayarit, and Sinaloa, and ultimately an expansion into the Gran Chichimeca with the discovery of vast silver deposits throughout the north. (Author's illustration) it certainly incorporated influences from other production centers as it evolved, including lower Central America. Eventually it was employed by some fifteen different language groups as a primary communication system, even replacing earlier writing systems in southern and eastern México that dated back to the first millennium B.C. (Pohl 2003b).

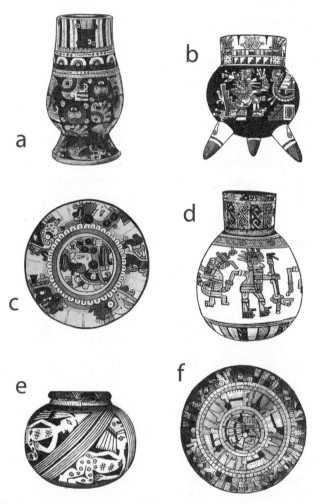

Polychrome ceramics: (a) Nahua, (b) Mixtec, (c) Zapotec, (d) Aztatlán-Cora, (e) Mogollon-Paquime, and (f) Huaxtec. The late postclassic world system witnessed the introduction of a unique pictographic communication system that was deployed by peoples throughout southern and northern México, with painted books called codices and ceramic ornamentation to facilitate social, political, and economic interchange. (Author's illustration)

THE LATE POSTCLASSIC WORLD SYSTEM

Research over the past twenty years has forced us to reevaluate traditional evolutionary models for the late postclassic period (Smith and Berdan 2003). The shift toward political decentralization after the abandonment of Tula is often equated with notions of "collapse" or "fall," when in fact we know that many social institutions actually became more complex. One problem has been the tendency by cultural anthropologists to employ political centralization as a measure of sophistication in state organization, and by archaeologists to concentrate their research on sites that boast large public buildings. Rather than focusing on centralized systems, we now find that the postclassic is better characterized by decentralized political structures and the emergence of new economic systems that served as primary integrative mechanisms for Mesoamerica (Pohl 2003a, 2003b, 2003c, 2003d). The explanation for this phenomena may very well lie in the advantages in organizational principles on which chiefdoms were predicated. If chiefdoms can adopt systems of social stratification to make them more effective producers of raw materials, like turquoise, that are consumed by states, then states might just as easily appropriate aspects of the segmentary systems of chiefdoms to reorganize themselves more effectively across wider geographical ranges than their classic predecessors had (Fargher, Espinoza, and Blanton 2011). One need look no further than the Chicomoztoc creation accounts to see how careful the Tolteca-Chichimeca were to invoke "tribal" organizational principles in the formulation of their confederacies while seating a state ideology of centrality in the pilgrimage and market center of Cholula (Pohl 2001, 2003a; Carrasco and Sessions 2007; Kirchhoff 1961; Knab 1983). The accounts invoke Chichimec deer hunting trails collectively as the "Road to Tula" in poetic metaphor, but in reality, these trails were major routes of commercial transport for the turquoise and shell trade. The mutualism essential to desert subsistence strategies also produced commodity specialists, like the Huichol of Nayarit, whose acquisition of peyote, an intoxicant with commercial value, continues to be likened to a sacred deer hunt even today (Pohl 1999, 89; Weigand 1975; Wilcox 1986).

Comparable systems of organization are found in Central America, where chiefdoms were organized into small villages but maintained a remarkable degree of social integration through shared ritual beliefs, manifested in the production of highly sophisticated forms of cast gold jewelry along with a complex iconographic system manifested in poly-chrome ceramics (Helms 1988; Quilter and Hoopes 2003). Large-scale cacao production necessitated widely distributed settlement systems in the coastal areas of Chiapas, Guatemala, Honduras, El Salvador, and possibly much of lower Central America as well (Voorhies and Gasco 2005). The ability to double up commodities by harvesting the deer, jaguar, and exotic bird species that favored cacao ecosystems created an extraordinarily prosperous livelihood, which promoted decentralization as an optimal economic strategy as well as trade networks along systems of trails in ways directly comparable to those of northern México and the American Southwest (Sheets 2009).

The resulting late postclassic world system witnessed the introduction of a social package of new forms of wealth, including finely crafted works of art; manufactured gold, copper, silver and turquoise, as well as jade and shell jewelry in unprecedented quantities; the feathers of tropical birds; lavish polychrome pottery; and specialized foods like cacao, used to make chocolate; maguey, used to ferment pulque; and even hallucinogenic mushrooms to make drinks even more intoxicating.

Historical codices, accounts of social affairs as southern Mexican nobles themselves perceived them, rarely depict a marketplace sign, and never portray the kind of behavior that we would recognize as trans-actional within them. Rather, the behavior we associate with trade or exchange appears with unparalleled frequency between men and women seated before royal palaces and engaged in gift giving and feasting. The evidence indicates that the royal feast was as the primary setting for the elite transactions that characterized late postclassic southern Mexican exchange systems (Pohl 2003c).

With decentralization came free enterprise, as Tolteca-Chichimeca palaces were transformed into highly competitive craft houses, each seeking to buy their way into more lucrative alliances through systems of bridewealth, dowry, and other forms of gift exchange. Women not only supplied the lifeblood of the alliance system through exogamous marriage but also became the principal producers of artworks (Pohl 2003c, 177).

Competition became so pronounced that royal traders and craftspeople were driven to seek out the rarest and most exotic materials to maximize the value of their gifts. Noble families were quick to see that the greater a royal house's ability to acquire these exotic materials and to craft them into exquisite jewels, textiles, and featherwork, the better marriages it could negotiate. The better marriages it could negotiate, the higher rank a royal house could achieve within a confederacy and, in turn, the better access it would have to more exotic materials, merchants, and craftspeople. In short, royal marriages promoted monopolies over both access to rare commodities and the skill sets of highly trained artisans to transform them into the currency of social relations. By A.D. 1300, many of these social innovations were emulated by the suppliers as well.

Just as the Eastern Nahuas of the plain of Puebla invested in Cholula as the new Tula to coordinate the social, political, and economic agendas of their constituent city-states, a comparable center was established in the north at Paquime, Chihuahua, which in turn succeeded Pueblo Bonito (Pohl 1999, 201–10; Lekson 2015). The archaeological culture of the region is called Mogollon, and it is characterized by the production of intricate figurative and geometric design work in ceramic. Originally developed among groups of small villages settled in southern New Mexico and Arizona between A.D. 1000 and 1150, ceramic bowls depict images of birds (including macaws), mountain sheep, and deer, among other animals as well as people participating in ritual dances and even playing musical instruments.

Significantly, ocean fish were also a popular theme, and notably, many representations can be identified as species associated with the Guaymas area of the Sea of Cortez, more than five hundred miles south of the Mimbres region (Jett and Moyle 1986). This suggests that the Mimbres were originally functioning as intermediaries between the Anasazi and peoples of western México to the south along the Pacific coast. Confirmation is found in recent DNA studies that connect Mimbres populations to contemporary Tarahumara, Huichol, and Nahua populations of Chihuahua, Zacatecas, Nayarit, and Jalisco. The fact that certain vessel forms associated with marriage feasts were used by both ancient Mimbres and contemporary Tarahumara are indicative of precisely the kinds of long-distance relationships we might envision for the broader systems of exchange at this time (Snow, Shafer, and Glenn Smith 2011; Shafer 2012).

By A.D. 1300, Paquime had become a significant Mesoamerican trading center, uniting many of the attributes of the Mogollon tradition with those of highland México. Particularly notable was the construction of a late postclassic Mesoamerican ballcourt, with nearby artifacts of cast and hammered west Mexican copper and the remains of scarlet macaws, whose natural habitat otherwise extended no farther than Oaxaca and Veracruz. Although today, much of the site is heavily eroded from severe exposure, a sixteenth-century visitor reported seeing the ruins of houses up to seven stories high, with white plastered walls painted with colorful designs, colonnades of heavy timber pillars, and plazas surfaced with jasper-like stonework, indicating that the community was occupied up to the late fifteenth century (Pohl 1999, 201–209).

Archaeologists have concluded that Paquime emerged as a late Mogollon response to dramatic population movements following the abandonment of Anasazi and Mimbres communities to the north, followed by a significant restructuring of social, political, and economic organization in Chihuahua, to the south. One of the principal characteristics of the new order was the construction of platform mounds surmounted by residential structures, mirroring the scores of palaces identified archaeologically throughout southern México at this same time, with their networks of small courts and rooms; notably, such architectural innovations were accompanied by the production of polychrome ceramics and typical Mesoamerican jewelry forms, such as ear spools, nose ornaments, and pectorals, suggesting a direct engagement with Mesoamerican peoples, including reciprocal exchanges in kinship titles among nobles (Lekson 2008; Pohl 2001, 2003c). Designs on Casas Grandes polychrome suggest that certain forms of Mesoamerican ritualism were being adopted as well (Pohl 2001, 93–95). Some vases depict entire narrative scenes in which a cultural hero wearing the headdress of a scarlet macaw interacts with plumed serpents and black painted priests. To the Eastern Nahuas, Mixtecs, and Zapotecs, the scarlet macaw was the personification of a solar maize god named Seven Flower–Xochipilli (Pohl 1994b). Seven Flower was the patron of royal palaces and craftspeople. Festivals held in his honor were celebrated by lords and ladies with bacchanal-like banquets, during which participants lavished gifts of woven garments, feathers, and jewels on one another. Seven Flower was the patron of royal marriages and sexual procreation, and as father of the gods, he presided over the thirteenth, or highest, heaven where only the royal born were admitted after death. It is not surprising therefore that he was also the patron of rituals involving hallucinogenic plants, during which participants believed that they could actually visit the royal paradise to discuss matters of utmost importance, such as marriages, inheritance, and land distribution, with their deceased ancestors. The cult of Seven Flower–Xochipilli essentially embodied the ideology of elite gift giving and reciprocity that was the focus of postclassic southern Mexican alliance networks (Pohl 1994b). The political ideology of a new Mesoamerican elite embodied in the symbolism associated with ritual commodities, like the scarlet macaw, would have had tremendous appeal for the emerging Pueblo peoples of northern México and the American Southwest, where the bird's plumage was exchanged for precious turquoise. Testament to the successful introduction of this new form of ritualism in association with feasting is found in continuing narrative traditions associated with the Pueblo cultural heroes Sun Youth and Maize Boy (Mathiowetz 2011).

Archaeologists often focus on the exchange of material goods without considering the wider context of cultural interaction. This is especially true of the symbolism and ideology manifested in art and ritual. People seldom trade for goods within a wealth finance system on the basis of rarity or aesthetic appeal alone. They are just as concerned with developing an appreciation of the ritual context for display, and therefore they apply formal mechanisms for absorbing new symbols and ideas into their culture to facilitate consumption. This is achieved by most North American Indian peoples either through visions conveyed to charismatic leaders by supernatural forces in dreams, or through barter with foreigners who possess a ritual that is deemed valuable enough to imitate. Acquisition strategies are then incorporated into legends, the ritual context for trade, and values as expressed in commercial equivalency; even social ideology could be conveyed through traditional songs, rituals, and stories (Pohl 2001).

The principal source for the late postclassic influences in Paquime ritualism was the Aztatlán region of Sinaloa, Jalisco, and Nayarit, where their descendants, the Cora, Huichol, and Tepehuan peoples, live today. By A.D. 1250, Aztatlán nobles had established an extensive network of city-states located upland from the Pacific coast, where each controlled a separate river valley that provided access to the Gran Chichimeca and the Huaxteca. Using Chacala and Puerto Vallarta as ports, they maintained a trading system extending from Zacatecas in the north to Oaxaca in the south (Pohl 2001, 2012a, 2012b). The Aztatlán production of Mixtec codex-style polychrome ceramics proves that the rulers of these kingdoms intermarried with Mixtec noble families, no doubt through the kingdom of Tututepec, the principal destination for the turquoise that was shipped from the mines in the American Southwest and northern México, through west México, for distribution throughout Oaxaca and Puebla (Pohl 2001, 2003c).

What is so curious about the postclassic economy is that it was adopted in North America so many centuries after it had first been introduced in South America. The Moche of Peru, for example, created artistic wonders in turquoise mosaic together with ornaments in gold, silver, and copper. Many were executed in a unique international style, derived from the narrative imagery appearing on magnificently painted ceramics as early as the first century A.D. There are several reasons archaeologists have been so reticent to consider long-distance trade and cultural exchange between North America, Central America, and South America, not the least of which was the backlash to theories of global diffusionism propagated by astounding feats of seamanship like the Kon Tiki expedition (Heyerdahl 1950). It would be half a century before scholars returned to the issue and determined that the balsa sailing raft had been ingeniously adapted to the effective exploitation of spondylus shell between Ecuador, Michoacán, and Nayarit (Pillsbury 1996).

Despite a basic understanding of who might be moving goods, we know little about what kinds of other sea craft propelled the new economy, or how they were used together in conjunction with ports of trade. Seagoing Maya canoes were first observed by Columbus transporting large quantities of trade goods off the Atlantic coast of Central America, a tradition that continues with Chibchan peoples like the Kuna of Panama today. Fray Marcos de Niza reported on Pacific commercial traffic between Sinaloa and Baja California. These may have been canoes or sailing rafts, but we know that consumption in abalone shell was significant in late postclassic México as well as in the southwestern United States. Much of it appears to be varieties native to southern California, which the Chumash were famous for exploiting, using an extraordinary seaworthy vessel known as the tomol. Ritual and religious veneration for the sea among Pacific coastal populations needs more research. Scholars have been fascinated by the Huichol's ritual pilgrimages into remote northern México to acquire peyote, but in fact the Huichol associate just as many of their creation stories with the Pacific Ocean, which they pray to as "Our Mother the Sea."

Contrary to the assumption that Mesoamerican peoples were simply "slow" to introduce certain technological innovations from Central and South America, it appears that the new elite economy was intentionally adopted, along with a package of related social traits, only after the intensification of Pacific coastal trade during the late postclassic (Anawalt 1998). The fact that Mogollon, Aztatlán, Mixtec, and Zapotec peoples were trading through Guaymas, Chacala, Puerto Vallarta, Tututepec, and Tehuantepec points to the critical role of sea travel in the symbiotic relationships established between suppliers and consumers in the postclassic world economic system. Linguistic studies, in turn, reveal some surprising connections between the coastal peoples of Oaxaca and remote regions of the American Southwest as well as Central America (Sapir 1949). The Chontal of Huatulco, the port for the Mixtec city-state of Tututepec, for example, speak a Hokan language connected with southern California and Arizona as well as Honduras (Kaufman 2007). Ethnohistorical sources suggest that they were engaged in commercial importation of cacao from coastal Chiapas by seagoing canoes. Some also speak of travelers from "Peru," a name originally associated with lower Central America. Huave, spoken by people occupying the area of the ancient Zapotec port of Tehuantepec, is remarkable for its extraordinarily complex vocabulary for shell, suggesting that these people had been shell acquisition specialists. Indeed, ethnohistorical sources describe them as having been accomplished seafarers, traveling as far south as Nicaragua. Evidence of this kind suggests that the acquisition and transport of elite matériel was managed by a mosaic of competitive trading specialists, of multiple ethnicities, who maintained extraordinary long-distance relationships with related "home" cultures elsewhere along the Pacific coast. Eventually, they were either patronized through mutualistic arrangements or subjugated by city-states within Nahua-Mixtec-Zapotec–dominated confederacies, who in turn pumped the wealth into the highland Mexican economy, up from the Oaxaca coast, in quantities comparable to, if not surpassing, those transported on overland routes from Veracruz and Chiapas. By 1480, rival systems had emerged. The Purépecha (Tarascans), for example, founded a state composing much of what is today Michoacán and were known to have engaged balsa-sailing-raft traders of Ecuador at the mouth of the Zacatula River (Pohl 2001, 194). Having founded a capital at Tzintzúntzan on Lake Pátzcuaro, the Purépecha were attempting to conquer the Aztatlán kingdoms of Jalisco and Nayarit, when they were attacked by an Aztec imperial army, under the command of Emperor Axayácatl. When the Purépecha inflicted a devastating defeat on Axayácatl, the Aztecs were forced to rethink their Pacific coast strategy, and they turned south to subjugate the Tlapanec spondylus shell traders, who controlled the port of Acapulco, Guerrero. The Tlapanec language is related to Subtiaba of Nicaragua, indicating that the traders of Acapulco were functioning in much the same way as the Chontal and Huaves of Tututepec and Tehuantepec to the east.

INDIGENOUS CONQUISTADORES

For two centuries the Children of Quetzalcóatl confederacy remained the dominant cultural, political, and economic force throughout southern México, until a rival emerged in the Basin of Mexico: the Aztec Empire of the Triple Alliance among the Western Nahuas. In 1458, the Aztecs conquered the Mixtec kingdom of Coixtlahuaca with an imperial army of no fewer than three hundred thousand men. Having thereby severed the primary trade and alliance corridor at its most critical link, the Aztecs then turned on other confederacy members, destabilizing the internal relationships that bound royal houses into systems of mutual obligation, and eventually dominated nearly all of central and southern México. By 1519, only the Eastern Nahuas of Tlaxcala remained independent, while ranking noble families of the Mixtecs and Zapotecs had withdrawn to their coastal centers of power at Tututepec and Tehuantepec respectively. It was then that Hernán Cortés landed in Veracruz and, over the following two years, waged war with the Aztec Empire at the head of an allied army of Spaniards and indigenous troops, composed of Eastern Nahuas and Mixtecs, as well as with disaffected city-states within the Basin of Mexico itself.

In August 1521, Cortés, with an army of more than one hundred thousand men, besieged Tenochtitlan and captured the last Aztec emperor, Cuauhtémoc, but only after what is regarded as the longest continuous battle in military history (Pohl 2002). Within a year, the Children of Quetzalcóatl confederacy had enthusiastically allied itself with the Spaniards and contributed thousands of troops for the conquests of the Isthmus of Tehuantepec, Chiapas, Guatemala, and west México, extending as far as California, Arizona, and New Mexico (Matthew and Oudijk 2007). Coastal Oaxaca became the initial staging area because of its strategic importance to the economy of southern México throughout the late postclassic.

Confederate members were seeking to not only regain what they had lost to the Aztecs but actually expand their control into primary sources of production with Spanish assistance. Under the control of caciques, colonial indigenous rulers, southern México became a land of opportunity. Traditional forms of production, marketing, trade, and tribute collection thrived. Maize, bean, and squash cultivation was supplemented with European domesticated plants and animals, and the region became integrated into the Hapsburg "world" economy. Textile production thrived as a regional specialization, especially with the addition of wool and silk to the native cotton already in use. Dyed with the local scarlet cochineal, garments were unsurpassed in quality and workmanship. Eventually, the dye would rival even gold on the European commodities market. Caciques capitalized on the colonial economy by engaging in lucrative

(a) Portrait of Don Juan Cortés from the Lienzo de Guevea. Cortés was the Zapotec cacique of Tehuantepec and a descendant of the twelfth-century Oaxacan dynastic founder and warlord Eight Deer. Don Juan changed his name from Cocijoeza to Cortés following baptism, appropriating a fictive kinship title to confirm his alliance with the conquistador. The cacique supplied the labor, resources, and navigational intelligence necessary for the construction of the first fleet of ships to explore the Gulf of California, in 1527, using an indigenous coastal trade route that linked Guaymas with coastal Oaxaca. (b) An illustration from the Relación de Tlaxcala depicts an Eastern Nahua cacique ministering to the Zunis with a rosary and a bible during the Coronado expedition in 1542. Images of this kind were created by Tlaxcalteca artists as official forms of indigenous documentation to the Spanish crown in the tradition of pre-Hispanic codices. (Author's illustration)

long-distance trading ventures, gaining monopolies over the transporta-tion of international goods from Manila to Spain, via the overland routes through México that they had dominated during the late postclassic (Terraciano 2001). Many ports that had served traders for centuries, like Huatulco, Acapulco, Puerto Vallarta, and Chacala, became home ports for the vigorous Manila Galleon trade.

By the middle of the sixteenth century, Tlaxcalteca caciques and other Eastern Nahua, Mixtec and Zapotec cacicazgos across the plain of Puebla and Oaxaca were sponsoring pioneer expeditions of settlers into northern México and the American Southwest (McEnroe 2009; Simmons 1964; Swadesh 1974). A report, originally composed for Phillip II, depicts a Tlaxcalteca cacique ministering with a bible and a rosary to the Zunis during the 1542 Coronado expedition (Acuña 1984).

The discovery of and exploitation of silver deposits in northern Méx-ico became a priority for the viceroyalty, but there was no fully residential population to exploit them. In 1591, four hundred families from Tizatlán, Tepeticpac, Ocotelulco, and Quiahuiztlán were sent to found communities throughout the Gran Chichimeca, including Nueva Tlaxcala de Saltillo, Durango, Aguascalientes, Coahuila, Zacatecas, Nuevo León, and San Luis Potosí. A surviving census bears testimony to the degree with which they still valued their Nahua identities, with names like Diego and Isabel Quauhtli, Miguel and María Mixcóatl, Juachín and Isabel Ocelotl, and Bartolomeo and María Coatl. The Tlaxcalteca who subsequently settled in Santa Fe, New Mexico, founded the barrio of Analco, where the church dedicated to San Miguel is regarded as the earliest Christian sanctuary in the United States. Significantly, when one "googles" San Miguel Analco today, one is directed to a barrio of Nativitas, Tlaxcala, where San Miguel was believed to have made his first miraculous appearance as patron saint of Tlaxcala. Although Tlaxcalteca settlements have not been documented to the same extent, they were soon joined by other Eastern Nahua, Mixtec, and Zapotec families, who founded settlements in the north. For example, Mixtec and Zapotec populations from Oaxaca moved to Salvatierra, Guanajuato, and, with the opening of the silver mines, San Luis Potosí, while the barrio of Atrisco in Albuquerque, New Mexico, is named for the former Eastern Nahua kingdom of Atlixco, Puebla.

Having been engaged through trade with the peoples of the Gran Chichimeca since the thirteenth century, the Tlaxcalteca in particular acted as intermediaries, by negotiating treaties for routes of transport, forming militias for protection, and establishing communities to facilitate permanent settlement of the hunting and foraging populations (McEnroe 2012, 2014). This was largely accomplished by developing mutualistic relationships, not unlike those that had been established by their ancestors centuries before. In return, the viceroyalty extended rights that were equivalent to those of Spanish colonists. The Tlaxcalteca were entitled to ride horses, carry firearms, own cattle, and manage oxcart trains. They negotiated their own trade agreements with the Pueblo populations and intermarried but maintained their Nahua identity. Náhuatl, an Uto-Aztecan language related to many Chichimeca languages, including Tepehuan, Tarahumara, Papago, Pima, and Hopi, was used as a lingua franca.

The Tlaxcalteca continued to write their wills and testaments in Náhuatl as late as the eighteenth century. When called on to testify before vice-royal officials, Chichimec caciques and *gobernadores* communicated with government officials through Nahuatlacos, Náhuatl translators in Mexico City, indicating that this had become the common language of social exchange on the northern frontier (Kessell 2002, 140–41).

Eastern Nahuas, Mixtecs, and Zapotecs introduced the European economy to the pueblos of the southwestern United States, where sheep raising and wool blanket weaving, as well as metal working, were combined with traditions in polychrome ceramic that extended back to the

A CHIMAYO WEAVER AT HIS LOOM

A popular tourist postcard of 1922 portrays a Chimayó, New Mexico, weaver producing a Saltillo serape. The tradition was introduced by pioneering Eastern Nahua populations, along with sheep and the production of wool. It then influenced local indigenous traditions, such as those of the Navajos. Early serapes preserved in museum collections are woven in precious materials reflective of the ancient palace economy of southern México. Thread was produced from gold and priceless cochineal dye, supplied by the Mixtec and Zapotec cacicazgos of Oaxaca, probably through their pioneering populations, who settled first in Guanajuato and later in northern México beginning as early as the mid-sixteenth century. Textile production and its raw materials had value equivalencies in the manufacture of jewelry as well. For example, a Santo Domingo Pueblo necklace of shell and green stone, preserved in the collections of the Amerind Foundation in Dragoon, Arizona, was valued at two hundred sheep when it was acquired in 1924. (From the author's collection) fourteenth century, when Pueblo peoples moved south to found Paquime and to engage the city-states of the Aztatlán tradition in Sinaloa, Nayarit, Jalisco, and, by coastal trade, Oaxaca (Pohl 2001; Mathiowetz 2011).[3]

Acting as mediators between Spanish and Indian officials, the Tlax-calteca opened turquoise and copper mines, despite these materials making little direct contribution to the broader imperial economy, which was rooted in silver and gold. What had once been a pre-Columbian palace-based economy, which linked the southwestern United States to southern México, was transformed into the frontier economy of New Spain. Feasts so critical to the exchange of goods continued to be cele-brated, with an annual ritual calendar shared between Pueblo Indian rituals and Eastern Nahua rituals, such as the Danza de Matachines, first sponsored by the Tlaxcalteca (McEnroe 2009; Harris 2000). Significant landscape features throughout northern México and the southwestern United States were given Nahua names and endowed with Nahua spirit forces, such as Moctezuma and Malinche, and myths associated with the legends of conquest were performed in the dances, the traditional way of constructing a Nahua territorial narrative. It is surely no coincidence that the identification of Chicomoztoc, the legendary Tolteca-Chichimeca place of origin, eventually became associated with each of the major silver-mining regions as they were discovered, from San Luis Potosí to Zacatecas (Levin Rojo 2014).[4]

It seems that Eastern Nahuas saw themselves as having originated in the north in pre-Hispanic times and now as simply returning to it (McEn-roe 2012, 127). While caciques throughout southern México sent popula-tions to invest their labor in lucrative viceregal frontier enterprises, like the mining industry, it is equally notable that many of the strategies adopted by the leaders of indigenous revolts mirror comparable Eastern Nahua, Mixtec, and Zapotec millenarian movements as well. Among the captives whom Governor Antonio de Otermín interrogated to determine how the 1680 Pueblo Revolt had been so effectively planned were two messengers from Tesuque, who stated that the revolt was being directed by a repre-sentative of Pohe-yemu, a deity closely associated, if not actually equated, with Moctezuma in Pueblo religious stories. Another captive whom Oter-mín interrogated was Pedro Naranjo, an eighty-year-old resident of San

Felipe Pueblo (Hackett 1942, 245–49). Naranjo said that the insurrection had been planned for many years, and that the Pueblos, who spoke five separate languages, communicated through pictographs painted on deer hides or what sound like southern Mexican codices. Naranjo identified the leader as a resident of San Juan Pueblo named Popé and related how the sorcerer was directed by three fiery demons associated with a sacred underground place of origin, Lake Copala (Simmons 1980, 130)

A little more than a century earlier, disaffected caciques across the plain of Puebla found themselves threatened by the seemingly limitless powers of the encomenderos (conquistadores and others given lands for their services to the Crown). When their appeals to the Franciscans to intercede proved ineffectual, they began to engage with indigenous priests who were calling for insurrection. Martin Ocelotl was the son of a pre-Hispanic Eastern Nahua merchant and a renowned sorceress of Oaxaca. Following the conquest, Ocelotl became a wealthy entrepreneur, who organized trading ventures from Tlaxcala to Guatemala and amassed a considerable fortune through his dealings with the most powerful caciques in southern México. Eventually he began to advocate for a return to the traditional ways of life by holding festivals in honor of the patron god Camaxtli-Mixcóatl, who had led the first Chichimec tribes out of the caves of Chicomoztoc. He then began to incite the caciques to insurrection by claiming that two demons had appeared to him, warning of a great famine that would ravage the countryside and eventually lead to the overthrow of the Spaniards. Ocelotl was captured, and he died shortly after his trial and conviction. He was then succeeded by his followers, including Andrés Mixcóatl and Juan Coatl, among others who carried on the sorcerer's vision well into the seventeenth century, when the Pueblos began to agitate for revolt in the north, using many of the same strategies (Pohl 1994a, 106–108). The Spanish administration had much to fear from these prophecies. In 1550, an armed revolt erupted in Coatlan, a cacicazgo of mixed Nahua, Mixtec, and Zapotec populations in Oaxaca, after indigenous leaders mobilized their people with a prophecy of the return of the god Quetzalcóatl. The revolt was only suppressed after two years of fighting and a considerable loss of life (Pohl, Fields, and Lyall 2012, 45).

The fact that Copala, the place associated with Popé's demons, is the Náhuatl for "place of copal," a tree resin incense essential to Nahua ritualism, is certainly significant as well as the fact that Popé's associates, like Alonso Catití, were identified as being coyote, a viceregal casta term for persons of mixed Mexican Indian and Pueblo Indian ancestry on the northern frontier. Some of these individuals would have been the descendants of disaffected Tlaxcalteca who had participated in the Coronado campaign but chose to remain behind in 1542 (Castañeda de Nájera 2002). Other Tlaxcalteca had been recruited by Juan de Oñate, from among the original four hundred families who had been sent to pioneer the northern frontier in 1591. Following the Acoma revolt of 1598, Governor Oñate punished the Acoma population with mutilations and slavery sentences for hundreds. Appalled by these ruthless acts, one faction of Tlaxcalteca moved away to join the Zuni Pueblo (Pérez de Villagrá 1992). In fact, Otermín's informant, Pedro Naranjo, may have been of Tlaxcalteca or Tepeyacac Puebloan ancestry (Chávez 1967).

The causes for the Pueblo Revolt were complex. Spanish rule was severe and largely directed by administrators motivated more by the prospect of quick profit than by fostering long-term economic, political, and social development strategies. By the 1660s, Franciscan missionary efforts were increasingly directed against indigenous religious beliefs as well. Dances were forbidden, and hundreds of sacred objects, including masks and ritual dress, were seized and burned in their efforts to eliminate what they saw as the pagan kachina "cult." Pueblo Indian populations had dwindled by more than half since Oñate had established the first settlements in New Mexico, largely because of disease and famine. Much of the misfortune had been caused by the introduction of Spanish systems of governance and economy, intended to facilitate the direction of indigenous labor and taxation. Although they lived in multistory dwellings and used systems of intensive agriculture that supported dense populations, Pueblo communities could never function in the same way as the *congregaciones* that characterized the cacicazgos of southern México, nor were they intended to.

Pueblos had to be far more flexible in the arid environment of the American Southwest, using both terrace and canal systems, each in different ways year by year, to take advantage of scarce or inconstant water resources over widely dispersed areas of cultivation. Agricultural intensification on the level of what had evolved in Mesoamerica was nearly impossible to maintain over the long term, and when faced with regional degradation in climate, Pueblos would simply relocate to more favorable areas, which made them difficult to govern. The introduction of livestock, on the other hand, would have far more dramatic consequences (Liebmann 2014). Pueblo settlements could function effectively only with the support of tribal hunting populations, through interdependent systems of mutualism that enabled both groups to enjoy a level of prosperity unavailable to any one group using any single strategy alone. Decreasing agricultural production with the reduction in Pueblo population, together with the introduction of livestock among both indigenous and Spanish settlements, left hunting tribes with little alternative but to take what they needed from settlements through raiding. Having fought a protracted war against the Chichimec tribes of northern México throughout the sixteenth century, the viceroyalty now found themselves facing an even more formidable threat. With the introduction of the horse, entirely new forms of tribal organization emerged among the Comanches, Apaches, and Navajos, who dominated the surrounding wilderness and could attack at virtually any time with impunity.

The need for increased protection led to demands for a frontier army (Chartrand 2011, 14; Naylor and Polzer 1986). By the 1780s, militia units across North America had grown from a few hundred to more than eighteen thousand men. At first the viceroyalty required that these troops be drawn largely from the Spanish population, being apprehensive of the loyalties of mestizo or Indian casta troops. When they realized that they lacked sufficient numbers, however, individuals simply identified themselves as Spanish on the rolls to fulfill the requirement, which in effect signaled the end of casta identification on the frontier, since these men were also the heads of households (Gutierrez 2014; Restall 2005). Eventually a sizable and stable community of mixed-race people with no claims of being either Amerindian or Spanish appeared and would contribute enormously to the spirit of self-determination underlying the Independence movement of 1810. Nevertheless, many northern families continued to conduct their personal affairs, such as the composition of wills, in Náhuatl (Offutt 2001).

By the nineteenth century, the indigenous identities of southern México became subsumed under both the "Spanish" and the Pueblo populations, the latter having withdrawn into their traditional territories after securing treaties with the viceroyalty that would ensure much of their autonomy. While some tribes like the Comanches and Apaches continued to raid both Spanish and Pueblo settlements, other tribes like the Navajos began to act as intermediaries, adopting a semisedentary existence to become sheepherders as well as traders with the tribes of the Great Plains. In so doing, they promoted the traditional economy in textiles, polychrome ceramic, shell, turquoise, copper, and eventually silver, until by the end of the nineteenth century, the Santa Fe railway was introducing tens of thousands of Atlantic American tourists to the art and craftwork fashioned by Navajo as well as Zuni, Hopi, and Río Grande Pueblo artisans.

Today, markets such as the Santa Fe Indian Market showcase work from about 1,200 leading American Indian artists. The market features pottery, jewelry, textile weavings, painting, sculpture, beadwork, basketry, and other traditional work. The economic effect of the market has been calculated at nearly $20 million. Artists display their work in booths around the Santa Fe town plaza and adjacent streets, selling directly to the general public. To participate, all artists must provide proof of enrollment in a federally recognized tribe, and their work must meet strict quality and authentic materials standards. When the Santa Fe railway partnered with the National Mexican railway to open México to American tourism, Mexican secretary of public education José Vasconcelos Calderón used the American Indian market model to foster Indigenismo programs, by which indigenous communities in Puebla and Oaxaca elevated craft production in ceramics, textile weaving, and jewelry production to pre-Columbian levels of sophistication. Increased production and sophistication in ceramic, textile, and jewelry arts are fueled not only by tourism but also by accelerated demand to stock the shelves of chain stores like Cost Plus and Pier 1, not to mention the lobbies of Marriot, Hilton, and so many other hotels who display such works for the ambiance of authentic indigenous craftsmanship.

The new prosperity has in turn reinvigorated many traditional social and political forms, as southern Mexican communities perceive tremendous value in promoting their indigenous identity (Stephen 1993). This has reactivated many ritual forms. The stakes are high, and families rely on kin group endogamy to maintain production standards; to monopolize access to resources, such as dyes, wool, clay sources, and so forth; and to brand specific forms and styles. Bridewealth exchanges between families are evaluated by the truckload, returning the significance of this form of exchange to values equivalent to those of the palace economies of the pre-Columbian past. Aspirants to high office in the Zapotec weaving community of Teotitlán compete for the privilege of feast sponsorship through Guelaguetza, dancing for days at a time while wearing ritual dress that can demand months of production time and cost thousands of dollars to produce. Comparable processes of social empowerment are documented for the U.S. Southwest, not to mention the Mata Ortiz phenomenon, a revitalization of the Paquime tradition of Chihuahua as well.[5]

The Aztecs continue to dominate our perspective of cultural dynamics during the postclassic period. The Aztec identity is recognized as an essential part of the national identity of México as well as that of the Chicano indigenous movement in the United States. Yet if all Mexican citizens can point to their flag and their magnificent monuments and therefore claim official Aztec heritage, what is the status of the millions of people of actual Indian heritage who continue to live on traditional lands, preserve so many of their customs, and speak more than twenty-five indigenous languages? The fact is that the Aztec Empire was only part of the story of cultural development in the Mexican highlands prior to the Spanish conquest. While the fall of Tenochtitlan in 1521 may have signaled the official end of one Indian civilization, it heralded the rise of another, whose legacy continued throughout the colonial period and persists to the present day.

As we walked back down the street from the church of San Miguel to the central plaza of Santa Fe, Kurly Tlapoyawa remarked, "I recently spoke

The poster for a 2013 conference on transnationalism and indigenous rights held at the University of California, San Diego, depicts a group of indigenous women of Oaxaca. There are more than a million and a half Nahua speakers, five hundred thousand Mixtec speakers, and five hundred thousand Zapotec speakers, together with fifteen other different language groups living in México and the United States. These peoples maintain dual identities as both national and indigenous citizens on both sides of the border today, just as they have for a millennium. (From author's collection; permission for publication courtesy of the Center for U.S.-Mexican Studies, University of California, San Diego)

to a relative who claims the Spanish ancestry of New Mexico, and I asked him how he knew he was Spanish. He told me it's because his family has the names of the cities in Spain from which they originated. When I asked him if he knew one of the cities, he said, Acatzinco!" Kurly and I both smiled at the irony in this. Acatzinco was a powerful Eastern Nahua–Mixtec kingdom of the plain of Puebla, closely allied with both Cholula and Tlaxcala. That a New Mexican family of today would advocate a Spanish heritage, while preserving the identity of an indigenous cacicazgo of southern México as their place of origin, bears testament to the enduring vitality of the millennial legacy of transnational indigenous history that continues to characterize both the United States and México today.

NOTES

1. This work benefited greatly from discussions with several colleagues, including Roberto Cantú, Alberto Diaz-Cayeros, Xóchitl Flores Marcial, Janine Gasco, Daniela Gutierrez, Timothy Knab, Stephen Lekson, Dana Leibsohn, Matthew Liebmann, Michael Mathiowetz, Sean McEnroe, Ronald Spores, Lynn Stephen, David Wilcox, Kurly Tlapoyawa, and Danny Zborover.

2. As a result of marriage alliances, most of the kingdoms of the plain of Puebla were composed of mixed Mixtec, Popolocan, and Nahua populations, while the kingdoms of the Valley of Oaxaca were composed of Zapotec, Mixtec, and Nahua populations. Many of these peoples continue to reside on traditional lands throughout the region today.

3. While Eastern Nahuas introduced wool through sheep raising, both gold and cochineal were supplied by the Mixtec and Zapotec cacicazgos of Oaxaca, who had been introduced to the treadle loom by the Dominican bishop Juan López Dezárate around 1535.

4. The recounting of Chichimec origins during the sixteenth century in Nahua pictorial maps and lienzos coincided with the discovery of major silver sources in the north, suggesting that caciques were using the foundation legend to establish traditional claims to the precious metal before sending pioneering populations into the north to act as mediators with the Guachichiles, Caxcanes, Pames, Tecuexes, Zacatecas, and Guamares, among other tribes of the Gran Chichimeca.

5. Dances of the Conquest, or the Matachines, originated in both Tlaxcala and Oaxaca during the 1520s. They represent a conflation of historical events, ranging from the commemoration of the Spanish Reconquista, the fall of Tenochtitlan, to wars between rival indigenous noble families during pre-Hispanic times. In so doing, many of the characters, such as Moctezuma, Malinche, Cortés, and Santiago, portrayed by the dancers may become syncretic indigenous beings entirely separate from the historical personages for which they are named. By the seventeenth century, much of Tlaxcala, Puebla, and Oaxaca had witnessed a dramatic decline in population. European diseases like smallpox had taken its toll, as had emigration to the northern provinces. Indigenous peoples of southern México resided in thousands of small villages socially and politically isolated from the rest of the country, until the twentieth century, with the introduction of the tourist economy under government-sponsored Indigenismo programs and the return to levels of craft production that today nearly match those of the late postclassic palace economies.

REFERENCES

Acuña, René. 1984. *Relaciones Geográficas del Siglo XVI*. Tlaxcala, México: UNAM.

Anawalt, Patricia. 1998. "They Came to Trade Exquisite Things: Ancient West Mexican-Ecuadorian Contacts." In *Ancient West Mexico: Art and Archaeology of the Unknown Past*, edited by Richard F. Townsend, 233–49. Chicago: Art Institute of Chicago.

Carrasco, Davíd, and Scott Sessions. 2007. *Cave, City, and Eagle's Nest: An Interpretive Journey through the* Mapa de Cuauhtinchan No. 2. Albuquerque: University of New Mexico Press.

Castañeda de Nájera, Pedro de. 2002. *Narrative of the Coronado Expedition*. Chicago: Donnelley.

Chartrand, René. 2011. *The Spanish Army in North America, 1700–1793*. Oxford: Osprey.

Chávez, Angélico. 1967. "Pohe-Yemo's Representative and the Pueblo Revolt of 1680." *New Mexico Historical Review* 42 (2): 85–126.

Coe, Michael D., and Rex Koontz. 2013. *Mexico: From the Olmecs to the Aztecs*. London: Thames and Hudson.

D'Altroy, Terence N., and Timothy K. Earle. 1985. "Staple Finance, Wealth Finance and Storage in the Inka Political Economy." *Current Anthropology* 26 (2): 43–57.

Di Peso, Charles C. 1974. *Casas Grandes: A Fallen Trading Center of the Gran Chichimeca*. Vols. 1–3. Amerind Foundation Publication 9. Flagstaff, AZ: Northland Press.

Earle, David D. 2005. "The Mojave River and the Central Mojave Desert: Native Settlement, Travel, and Exchange in the Eighteenth and Nineteenth Centuries." *Journal of California and Great Basin Anthropology* 25:1.

Fargher, Lane F., Vernice Y. Heredia Espinoza, and Richard E. Blanton. 2011. "Alternative Pathways to Power in Late Postclassic Highland Mesoamerica." *Journal of Anthropological Archaeology* 30:306–26.

Feldman, Marion H. 2007. *Diplomacy by Design: Luxury Arts and an "International Style" in the Ancient Near East, 1400–1200 BCE*. Chicago: University of Chicago Press.

Fields, Virginia M., John M. D. Pohl, and Victoria I. Lyall. 2012. *Children of the Plumed Serpent: The Legacy of Quetzalcoatl in Ancient Mexico*. London: Scala.

Fried, Morton H. 1975. *The Notion of Tribe*. Menlo Park, CA: Cummings.

Friedman, Jonathan. 1998. *System, Structure, and Contradiction: The Evolution of Asiatic Social Transformations*. Walnut Creek, CA: Alta Mira.

Gutierrez, Daniela. 2014. "Casta in Colonial Alta California." Paper presented at Conference on Rudolfo Anaya: Tradition, Modernity, and the Literatures of the U.S. Southwest, California State University, Los Angeles, May 2–3.

Hackett, Charles Wilson. 1942. *Revolt of the Pueblo Indians of New Mexico and Otermin's Attempted Reconquest, 1680–1682*. Albuquerque: University of New Mexico Press.

Harbottle, Garman, and Phil C. Weigand. 1992. "Turquoise in Pre-Columbian America." *Scientific American* 266 (2): 78–85.

Harris, Max. 2000. *Aztecs, Moors, and Christians: Festivals of Reconquest in Mexico and New Spain*. Austin: University of Texas Press.

Helms, Mary W. 1988. *Ulysses' Sail: An Ethnographic Odyssey of Power, Knowledge, and Geographical Distance*. Princeton, NJ: Princeton University Press.

———. 1993. *Craft and the Kingly Ideal: Art, Trade, Power*. Austin: University of Texas Press.

Heyerdahl, Thor. 1950. *Kon-Tiki*. New York: Rand McNally.

Hull, S., M. Fayek, F. J. Mathien, and H. Roberts. 2014. "Turquoise Trade of the Ancestral Puebloan: Chaco and Beyond." *Journal of Archaeological Science* 45:187–95.

Jett, S. C., and P. B. Moyle. 1986. "The Exotic Origin of Fishes Depicted on Prehistoric Mimbres Pottery from New Mexico." *American Antiquity* 51:688–720.

Kaufman, Terrence. 2007. "Hokan." In *Atlas of the World's Languages*, 52. 2nd ed. London: Routledge.

Kessel, John L. 2002. *Spain in the Southwest: A Narrative History of Colonial Arizona, Texas, and California*. Norman: University of Oklahoma Press.

Kirchhoff, Paul. 1961. "Se Puede Localizar Aztlán?" *Anuario de Historia*. Año 1. Facultad de Filosofía y Letras, Universidad Nacional Autónoma de México.

Knab, Timothy. 1983. "En Qué Lengua Hablaban Los Tepalcates Teotihuacanos? (No Era Náhuatl)." *Revista Mexicana de Estudios Antropológicos* 29 (1): 145–58.

Kowalski, Jeff Karl, and Cynthia Kristan-Graham. 2011. *Twin Tollans: Chichén Itzá, Tula, and the Epiclassic to Early Postclassic Mesoamerican World*. Rev. ed. Washington, DC: Dumbarton Oaks.

Leach, Edmund. 1973. *Political Systems of Highland Burma: A Study of Kachin Social Structure*. London School of Economics Monographs on Social Anthropology 44. London: Bloomsbury Academic.

Lekson, Stephen H. 2008. *A History of the Ancient Southwest*. Santa Fe, NM: School for Advanced Research.

———. 2015. *The Chaco Meridian: Centers of Political Power in the Ancient Southwest*. Walnut Creek, CA: Alta Mira.

Levin Rojo, Danna A. 2014. *Return to Aztlán: Indians, Spaniards and the Invention of Nuevo Mexico*. Norman: University of Oklahoma Press.

Liebmann, Matthew. 2014. *Revolt: An Archaeological History of Pueblo Resistance and Revitalization in 17th-Century New Mexico*. Tucson: University of Arizona Press.

Mathiowetz, Michael Dean. 2011. "The Diurnal Path of the Sun: Ideology and Interregional Interaction in Ancient Northwest Mesoamerica and the American Southwest." Ph.D. diss., University of California at Riverside.

Matthew, Laura E., and Michel R. Oudijk. 2007. *Indian Conquistadors: Indigenous Allies in the Conquest of Mesoamerica*. Norman: University of Oklahoma Press.

McEnroe, Sean Francis. 2009. "Spain's Tlaxcalan Vassals: Citizenship and State Formation on Mexico's Northern Frontier." Ph.D. diss., University of California at Berkeley.

———. 2012. "A Sleeping Army: The Military Origins of Interethnic Civic Structures on Mexico's Colonial Frontier." *Ethnohistory* 59 (1): 109–39.

———. 2014. *From Colony to Nationhood in Mexico: Laying the Foundations, 1560–1840*. Cambridge: Cambridge University Press.

Milford, Homer. 1995. *Turquoise Mining History*. Santa Fe, N.Mex.: Abandoned Mine Land Bureau Reports.

Naylor, Thomas, and Charles W. Polzer. 1986. *The Presidio and Militia on the Northern Frontier of New Spain: 1570–1700*. Tucson: University of Arizona Press.

Offutt, Leslie S. 2001. *Saltillo, 1770–1810: Town and Region in the Mexican North*. Tucson: University of Arizona Press.

Pérez de Villagrá, G. 1992. *Historia de la Nueva México, 1610*. Albuquerque: University of New Mexico Press.

Pillsbury, Joanne. 1996. "The Thorny Oyster and the Origins of Empire: Implications of Recently Uncovered Spondylus Imagery from Chan-Chan, Peru." *Latin American Antiquity* 8 (1): 313–40.

Pohl, John M. D. 1994a. *The Politics of Symbolism in the Mixtec Codices*. Vanderbilt University Publications in Anthropology 46. Nashville, TN: Vanderbilt University.

———. 1994b. "Weaving and Gift Exchange in the Mixtec Codices." In *Cloth and Curing: Continuity and Change in Oaxaca*, edited by Grace Johnson and Douglas Sharon, 3–13. San Diego Museum Papers 32. San Diego, CA: San Diego Museum of Man.

———. 1999. *Exploring Mesoamerica*. Oxford: Oxford University Press.

———. 2001. "Chichimecatlalli: Strategies for Cultural and Commercial Exchange between Mexico and the American Southwest, 1100–1521." In *The Road to Aztlán: Art from a Mythic Homeland*, edited by Virginia Fields and Victor Zamudio Taylor, 86–101. Los Angeles: Los Angeles County Museum of Art.

———. 2002. "Aztecs: A New Perspective." *History Today* 52 (12):10–17.

———. 2003a. "Creation Stories, Hero Cults, and Alliance Building: Postclassic Confederacies of Central and Southern Mexico from A.D. 1150–1458." In *The Postclassic Mesoamerican World*, edited by Michael Smith and Frances Berdan, 61–66. Salt Lake City: University of Utah Press.

———. 2003b. "Ritual and Iconographic Variability In Mixteca Puebla Polychrome Pottery." In *The Postclassic Mesoamerican World*, edited by Michael Smith and Frances Berdan, 201–206. Salt Lake City: University of Utah Press.

————. 2003c. "Ritual Ideology and Commerce in the Southern Mexican High-lands." In *The Postclassic Mesoamerican World*, edited by Michael Smith and Frances Berdan, 172–77. Salt Lake City: University of Utah Press.

————. 2003d. "Royal Marriage and Confederacy Building among the Eastern Nahuas, Mixtecs, and Zapotecs." *The Postclassic Mesoamerican World*, edited by Michael Smith and Frances Berdan, 243–48. Salt Lake City: University of Utah Press.

————. 2012a. "The Odyssey of the Plumed Serpent." In *Children of the Plumed Serpent: The Legacy of Quetzalcoatl in Ancient Mexico*, edited by Virginia M. Fields, John M. D. Pohl, and Victoria L. Lyall, 94–107. London: Scala.

————. 2012b. "La tradición Aztatlán de Nayarit-Jalisco y el estilo nahua-mix-teca de Cholula." *Arqueología Mexicana* 20 (115): 60–65.

Pohl, John M. D., Virginia M. Fields, and Victoria L. Lyall. 2012. Introduction to *Children of the Plumed Serpent: The Legacy of Quetzalcoatl in Ancient Mexico*, edited by Virginia M. Fields, John M. D. Pohl, and Victoria L. Lyall, 15–49. London: Scala.

Quilter, Jeffrey, and John Hoopes. 2003. *Gold and Power in Ancient Costa Rica, Panama, and Colombia*. Washington, DC: Dumbarton Oaks.

Restall, Matthew 2005. *Beyond Black and Red: African-Native Relations in Colonial Latin America*. Albuquerque: University of New Mexico Press.

Reyman, Jonathan E. 1995. "Value in Mesoamerican-Southwestern Trade." In *The Gran Chichimeca: Essays on the Archaeology and Ethnohistory of Northern Mesoamerica*, edited by Jonathan E. Reyman, 271–80. Aldershot: Avebury.

Sapir, Edward. 1949. "Central and North American Languages." In *Selected Writings of Edward Sapir in Language, Culture and Personality*, 5th ed., 169–78. Berkeley: University of California Press.

Scharlotta, Ian. 2014. "Trade Routes and Contradictory Spheres of Infuence: Movement of Rhyolite Through the Heart of the Western Mojave Desert." *California Archaeology* 6 (2): 219–46.

Shafer, Harry J. 2012. "Classic Mimbres Social Field and Drinking Buddies: What DNA Evidence and Large Pots May Tell Us About Mimbres Ceremonies and Feasts." Paper presented at the 17th Biennial Mogollon Archaeology Conference, Western New Mexico University Museum, Silver City, NM, October 4–6.

Sheets, Payson. 2009. "When the Construction of Meaning Preceded the Meaning of Construction: From Footpaths to Monumental Entrances in Ancient Costa Rica." In *Landscapes of Movement*, edited by Clark Erickson, James Snead, and Andrew Darling, 158–79. Philadelphia: University of Pennsylvania Press.

Simmons, M. 1964. "Tlascalans in the Spanish Borderlands." *New Mexico Historical Review* 39 (2): 101–10.

————. 1980. *Witchcraft in the Southwest: Spanish and Indian Supernaturalism on the Rio Grande*. Lincoln, NE: Bison Books.

Smith, Michael, and Frances Berdan, eds. 2003. *The Postclassic Mesoamerican World*. Salt Lake City: University of Utah Press.

Snow, Meradeth, Harry Shafer, and David Glenn Smith. 2011. "The Relationship of the Mimbres to other Southwestern and Mexican Populations." *Journal of Archaeological Science* 38:3122–33.

Spielmann, Katherine, ed. 1991. *Farmers, Hunters, and Colonists: Interaction between the Southwest and the Southern Plains*. Tucson: University of Arizona Press.

Spielmann, Katherine, and James F. Eder. 1994. "Hunters and Farmers: Then and Now." *Annual Review of Anthropology* 23:303–23.

Stephen, Lynn. 1993. "Weaving in the Fast Lane: Class, Ethnicity, and Gender in Zapotec Craft Commercialization." *Crafts in the World Market: The Impact of Global Exchange on Middle American Artisans*, edited by June Nash, 59–83. Albany: State University of New York Press.

Swadesh, F. L. 1974. *Los Primeros Poladores*. Notre Dame, IN: University of Notre Dame Press.

Taube, Karl A. 2012. "The Symbolism of Turquoise in Postclassic Mexico." In *Turquoise in Mexico and North America: Science, Conservation, Culture and Collections*, edited by J. C. H. King, Max Carocci, Carolyn Cartwright, Colin McEwan, and Rebecca Stacy, 117–34. London: British Museum.

Terraciano, Kevin. 2001. *The Mixtecs of Colonial Oaxaca: Ñudzahui History, Sixteenth through Eighteenth Centuries*. Stanford, CA: Stanford University Press.

Voorhies, Barbara, and Janine Gasco. 2005. *Postclassic Soconusco Society: The Late Prehistory of the Coast of Chiapas, Mexico*. Albany: Institute for Mesoamerican Studies, State University of New York.

Washburn, Dorothy K., William N. Washburn, Petia A. Shipkova, and Mary Ann Pelleymounter. 2014. "Chemical Analysis of Cacao Residues in Archaeological Ceramics from North America: Considerations of Sample Size and Systematic Controls." *Journal of Archaeological Science* 50:191–207.

Weigand, Phil C. 1975. "Possible References to La Quemada in Huichol Mythology." *Ethnohistory* 22:15–20.

———. 1992. "The Macroeconomic Role of Turquoise within the Chaco Canyon System." In *Anasazi Regional Organization and the Chaco System*, edited by David E. Doyel, 169–73. Anthropological Papers 5. Albuquerque: Maxwell Museum of Anthropology, University of New Mexico.

White, Leslie A. 1960. "The World of the Keresan Pueblo Indians." In *Culture and History: Essays in Honor of Paul Radin*, edited by Stanley Diamond, 53–64. New York: Columbia University Press.

Wilcox, David R. 1986. "A Historical Analysis of the Problem of Southwestern-Mesoamerican Connections." In *Ripples in the Chichimec Sea*, edited by F. J. Mathien and R. H. Mcguire, 9–44. Carbondale: Southern Illinois University Press.

―――. 1991. "Changing Contexts of Pueblo Adaptations, A.D. 1250–1600." In *Farmers, Hunters, and Colonists: Interaction between the Southwest and the Southern Plains*, edited by Katherine Spielmann, 128–54. Tucson: University of Arizona Press.

Willey, Gordon R., and Philip Phillips. 1958. *Method and Theory in American Archaeology*. Chicago: University of Chicago Press.

13

And It Was Good

THE MESTIZO CREATION STORIES
OF RUDOLFO ANAYA

Spencer R. Herrera

People need five basic elements to survive: air, water, food, fire, and shelter. To create a community of people surviving together, the basis for a civilization, we need one more thing: stories. The first list of items protects and nourishes the body. Stories nourish the soul. For this reason, people have been telling stories since the dawn of humanity. This is especially true for myths, which are stories that interpret "natural events in an effort to make concrete and particular a special perception of human beings or a cosmic view" (Holman and Harmon 1986, 317). But what happens when we stop making myths, or at least to the degree that we once did during earlier civilizations? The act of creation is a powerful gift that enables us to reach the pinnacle of our thinking. Storytelling, specifically mythmaking, is a vital part of our genetic code, designed to help us survive. Once we stop making myths, we can no longer consider ourselves creative beings. For without mythmaking, we cease to create our world and re-create new ways of living in it.

Rudolfo Anaya, the premier Southwest author of our time, understands that the creation of a cosmic view is just as important as the natural phenomena that generate myth. Through his more than two dozen fiction books, Anaya has been re-creating myths by telling stories of how the natural world came to be. For him, re-creating our sense of the cosmos and how life and the natural world began is a responsibility that we must continue to develop and nurture. Anaya himself stated in an interview, "I see myself more in the process of re-creation. Because I'm not interested in telling or adhering to any myth and being truthful—in the sense that you research and really try to understand the myth. Man is a myth-making animal and this is one of our failures as modern man. We're not making myths anymore" (Johnson and Apodaca 1998, 39). Anaya has taken it on himself, not solely as a celebrated author, but as an elder, to rekindle the flames around the communal fire, retelling our stories and teaching us how to reinvent myth.

Anaya does not explain in detail why the decline of mythmaking is a failure of modern man. However, the philosopher Friedrich Nietzsche believed that "myth functioned as the standard for measuring the 'health' of society" (Mangion 2015, 1). According to Nietzsche, "The value of myth was that of bringing together a people: with myth, a culture had a common foundation from which it could draw the strength to overcome the limitations and fragmentation produced by the branches of knowledge" (2). As someone who throughout his career has sought to challenge commonly accepted beliefs by recreating myths, Anaya would undoubtedly agree with Nietzsche's belief that "every culture that has lost myth has lost, by the same token, its natural healthy creativity" (5). Without heavy doses of healthy creativity, it is almost impossible to create common bonds to unite a people and its culture. This being the case, Anaya is right: our inability to make myths would be one of our biggest failures, and it needs to be corrected before we lose our capacity to do so, or worse, devolve from being a creative people to those who also suffer from a lack of culture.

The peril of waiting too late in our lives to start learning how to create myths or of not doing so as a society is that we slowly lose our capacity to envision new worlds and possibilities for the real one we live in. It is no wonder that Anaya begins his lessons early by teaching the next generation how to make myth. This is one reason Anaya's Antonio character in *Bless Me, Ultima* (1972) is a young boy who questions the myths he has been taught, mostly by the Catholic Church. Anaya must have realized this later in his career, as he turned much of his artistic attention to writing children's literature.[1] If we are to learn the magic of creation and mythmaking, then we must begin early at developing this craft.

To facilitate this process, Anaya wrote four children's books that deal directly with mythmaking and creation stories: *Roadrunner's Dance, The First Tortilla, How Hollyhocks Came to New Mexico,* and *How Chile Came to New Mexico.*

Bloom's taxonomy, which orders the hierarchy of higher-order thinking, shows the act of creation, such as generating new ideas, products, or ways of viewing things, as the highest form of thinking ("Bloom's Digital Taxonomy" 2015). In this sense, Anaya's interview response, quoted earlier, about mythmaking is powerful and raises the question as to why modern society does not make myths anymore, or at least to the degree that earlier generations did. Through creation, not only do we become strong, independent thinkers, we also generate knowledge. This is especially true when we re-create creation myths. This does not mean we are challenging belief systems to discredit their core tenets or their explanations for the genesis of humanity, or even to validate one explanation of the cosmos over another. Our effort here is to complicate our understanding of the universe and provide different versions of its origins and future potential. In the end, strong critical thinking is beneficial to the human experience, even for those ideas that require faith. This process must begin with children, and this is what Anaya accomplishes with these children's books.

The most recognizable creation story in Western society is found in Genesis, the first book in the Bible. In this narrative, God creates the heavens, earth, light, sky, land, sea, plants, trees, sun, moon, stars, all the animals, and the first male and female within a period of six days. Six times in Genesis 1, the phrase "It was good" is stated. This phrase follows a pattern: God commands an act of creation, and it becomes so. Then God examines His work and pronounces it "good." Following the creation of human beings, male and female, made in His own image, God looks at all that He has made and says, "It is very good." After the six days of creation, God rested, blessed the seventh day and made it holy.

Although many origin stories conflict with the Bible's version, others align with it. This is the beauty of mythmaking. It fills the gaps of knowledge about natural phenomena and can neither be completely proved nor disproved. In his children's books, Anaya does not attempt to compete with the Bible through validation or contradiction—he simply wants to reinvent. In fact, most of Anaya's mythmaking in children's books is not about creation but about the origins of something, be it a plant or food item, and its introduction into a local community. *Roadrunner's Dance*, the sole nonbilingual book discussed here, is the exception, which I explain at the end of this chapter.

The ability to tell a new and different story about the origin of something that belongs to all of us enables us to avoid what Nigerian novelist Chimamanda Ngozi Adichie calls "the danger of the single story." To write a singular narrative is to "show a people as one thing, as only one thing, over and over again, [until] that is what they become" (Adichie 2009, n.p.). She argues that a single story robs people of dignity. It alienates us from our equal humanity. Rather than allow us to feel connected to our fellow human beings, the single story emphasizes our differences. According to Adichie, children in particular are impressionable and vulnerable in the face of a story. This is why access to diverse stories has the potential to be life changing.

Having lived in New Mexico, among centuries-old Pueblo civilizations and generations of Hispanic tradition, and after traveling to numerous diverse countries, Anaya is knowledgeable about many different ways of understanding the world and can appreciate various interpretations of how life began. The Bible teaches one creation story, which does not even involve the possibility of evolution.[2] And unfortunately, once Adam and Eve are exiled from the Garden of Eden, we, as human beings, are never able to return to our biblical genesis. But herein lies the power of embracing mythmaking: "When we reject the single story, when we realize that there's never a single story about any place, we regain a kind of paradise" (Adichie 2009, n.p.). In support of Adichie's ideas, the importance of mythmaking for children is that it allows them to understand that "in the real, messy world of creativity, giving away the thing you don't really understand for the thing that you do is an inevitable tradeoff" (Gladwell 2011, 18). The mystery behind biblical creation is unfathomable, but children can appreciate a story about things culturally relevant to them that make sense in their world, such as foods and animals.

Within the trilogy of Anaya's bilingual creation stories, *The First Tortilla*, *How Hollyhocks Came to New Mexico*, and *How Chile Came to New*

Mexico, there is a fair amount of thematic commonalties. Anaya's first bilingual origin story, *The First Tortilla,* is about the introduction of corn and the creation of the tortilla. The second bilingual origin story is about the arrival of hollyhocks in New Mexico, in *How Hollyhocks Came to New Mexico.* The third bilingual origin story explains the introduction of chile in New Mexico, in *How Chile Came to New Mexico.* Of these three bilingual books, the second title is of particular importance because its Spanish version is necessary for the story to make sense. The first published book in the group of four, *Roadrunner's Dance,* is unique for several reasons and thus I analyze it last. It is written entirely in English. It also describes the actual creation of the roadrunner, which according to the story is a new being that did not previously exist. In contrast, the other books introduce a new plant or seed into a region but do not create a living creature.

It is understandable why Anaya chose the introduction of corn and the creation of the first tortilla as his first bilingual origin story. After all, corn is the main staple and basis for most indigenous diets of the Western Hemisphere. Notably, however, Anaya does not attempt to create or re-create the myth of corn's actual emergence into the world. He is not interested in reinventing the cosmos for children, especially for things as sacred as corn and the related symbolic figure, the Corn Maiden, who is the mother of many indigenous peoples. This is too sacred a subject for Anaya to treat within a children's story. It deserves a much deeper, complex read, such as with the golden carp and Jesus analogy found within *Bless Me, Ultima.*

In *The First Tortilla* (2007) corn already exists in the natural world, so this book is not about the creation of corn, but about its introduction to people. In this story an indigenous village in México is experiencing great drought and must relocate to find food, since their crops are not yielding produce. Jade, a young village girl, learns that the Mountain Spirit has not sent them rain because he is upset with the people for forsaking him. Jade decides to go on a perilous trip to visit the Mountain Spirit and take him an offering of beans and squash sprinkled with chiles. The Mountain Spirit is pleased with Jade's offering, and as a reward, he brings rain to the area so that the people can grow their crops and remain in their homeland. He also gives her an additional gift—corn kernels that the ants store away for food. She takes the kernels to her family, and her mother makes masa and then cooks it over a hot stone. Jade calls the delicious corn masa product a tortilla, the first one ever made. Soon they plant the kernels, which grow into corn, and they teach the other women in the village how to make tortillas. Now they have corn, beans, squash, and chiles, the main staples that today still make up a large percentage of the indigenous diet in México.[3] In this story the reader learns not about the creation of corn, but about its introduction to the people by the Mountain Spirit.

How Hollyhocks Came to New Mexico (2012) is the only children's book by Anaya that requires a dual-language text. The Spanish title of this bilingual book, *Cómo llegaron las varas de San José a Nuevo México,* is essential for the myth's message to make sense. This story comes from the Bible, but with a distinct Nuevo México twist, before this land ever came to be known by this name.

Anaya's story speaks of the birth of Jesus to Mary and Joseph in Bethlehem, as well as Jesus's broad recognition in the land of Judea-Israel and surrounding areas as the King of Kings. At the time of Jesus's birth, during the Roman occupation, King Herod ruled in Jerusalem. The king was angry and jealous that this newborn child was also considered a king. In Anaya's version, King Herod orders his soldiers to kill all the children in Bethlehem to ensure that the newborn king would be among them. To save Jesus from this fate, an angel named Sueño descends from heaven and offers to fly the Holy Family to Egypt, where they will be safe. True to his name, Sueño falls asleep along the journey, and when he awakes, they are flying over New Mexico. Mistakenly, he believes that White Sands is the Egyptian desert and that the Río Grande is the Nile.

As the Holy Family makes their way north, to distance themselves from Herod's reach, they become immersed in Pueblo culture. They eat the Pueblo food staples, corn, beans, squash, and chile; they learn to make adobe homes; Mary learns about indigenous folk healing and how to grind corn and make tortillas with a metate; and the Holy Family enjoys the unleavened bread she makes. The two desert peoples share stories and influence each other in ways that will last until the present time. At one point, the Holy Family comes across a village that reminds them of home, a place that would one day be called Belén. At another village, called Chimayó, the people tell the Holy Family that they are sad because the village elders are sick. Jesus blesses the dirt in the arroyo, and the sick rub themselves with the blessed dirt and become cured. Both places still exist today, and the people carry on traditions related to their Christian history. Belén hosts an annual pastorela that tells about the birth of Emmanuel, and every Good Friday, thousands of people participate in a pilgrimage to Chimayó to receive the holy dirt.

After traveling from the southern border of what is present-day New Mexico to the northern end, during what appears to be several years, the young Jesus tells his father, Joseph, that it is time to return home. As planned, with the help of the Pueblo men, they build a tall ladder that reaches heaven so that Sueño can see it. He does and climbs down the ladder to take the Holy Family back home to Israel. But before they leave, Joseph (José) plants his shepherd's staff in the ground as "A gift to the people of this wonderful country" (Anaya 2012, 36). After the summer rains arrive, colorful hollyhocks sprout from José's staff. The creation myth continues: "That fall the flowers' dark seeds spread across the land. The following season every home enjoyed the graceful and lovely flowers" (38). Anaya closes the story by explaining, "In Spanish hollyhocks are called Varas de San José, because they grew from St. Joseph's staff" (38).

In the biblical version of this story, Herod orders the murder of all male children two years of age and under. Although the total murdered is fewer than what Anaya states, it is still a historical infanticide of great proportion and sadness. Also, in the Bible, an angel of the Lord comes to Joseph in a dream to warn him of the impending danger. The angel advises him to take his family to Egypt. The angel later tells Joseph about Herod's death and of the time to return home. Once again, in Anaya's version, the angel Sueño carries them to safety, which is the only way they could have magically crossed such a long distance to New Mexico. But rather than affirming the validity of myths, Anaya reinvents them.

In *How Chile Came to New Mexico* (2014), Anaya explains the myth of how chile seeds were introduced to the Pueblo people who lived along the Río Grande. In the story, Young Eagle, a young Pueblo man, falls in love with Sage, a beautiful young Pueblo woman, and wants to marry her. Young Eagle and his parents decide to visit Sage's home to meet with her parents. Chronologically, we know that this myth takes place after the introduction of corn as a food source because when Young Eagle and his parents arrive at Sage's home, her mother welcomes them with roasted corn kernels and chokecherry tea. Thus, corn had already traveled from México and made its way north into the Pueblo diet.

Sage's father understands that the purpose of their visit is to ask for his daughter's hand in marriage. He states that he is old, and for this reason, the corn and meat he eats has no flavor. He makes them a proposition: "Friends who come from the south tell us the Aztecs have chile, a fruit that makes food taste good. If Young Eagle brings me chile seeds, I will let him marry my daughter" (4). Young Eagle's parents do not like this idea because they know that such a journey would be long and perilous. But Young Eagle loves Sage and accepts the challenge, despite the eminent dangers that lie ahead.

During his journey, Young Eagle encounters several obstacles. A river monster disguised as a whirlpool tries to drown him. Young Eagle quickly appeases the river spirit with cornmeal, and it lets him pass. Days later he finds himself in a punishing desert without any water left in his gourd. As Young Eagle bends down to drink water from a pool, a vulture swoops down to attack him. Young Eagle throws some corn kernels to the ground, and as the vulture stops to gather them, he shoots it with an arrow. The bird falls to the ground and then disappears in a puff of smoke. The oasis and vulture were mirages placed there by the jealous spirits that his parents had warned him about.

After finding fresh water, Young Eagle arrives at a copper canyon in present-day Chihuahua. When he descends into the canyon, a large boulder with evil eyes and sharp teeth tries to crush him. Young Eagle holds up Sage's turquoise necklace for protection, and the boulder rolls away from him and falls off a cliff. Soon he encounters a large eagle, who carries him on its back and flies over the canyon. Young Eagle encounters many tribes along his journey and eventually reaches the valley of the Aztecs. There he meets Parrot Man, an elder who feeds him a meal with sprinkled chiles, which he enjoys very much. Parrot Man fills Young Eagle's sack with yellow chile seeds and makes him promise to "share the seeds with [his] neighbors along the Great River to the north" (26).

With the help of the eagle, Young Eagle's return trip is swift. Upon arrival at the pueblo, he goes with his parents to Sage's home, hands the seeds to her father, and asks for his permission to marry Sage. Her father happily replies, "Good! Now we have chile seeds to plant in the spring. Yes, you may marry my daughter!" (32). By the spring, the pueblo plants the seeds, and by late summer, the entire village is harvesting chiles and cooking them with their food.

Anaya affirms that we can trace the origin of the chile seeds we use in our modern diet back to the seeds Young Eagle brought to New Mexico. So as the myth continues today, so does its relation to origin stories. In Anaya's version, Young Eagle and Sage have many healthy children. And in the Pueblo culture today, during storytelling time, Young Eagle's quest is still told. The origin story of chile in New Mexico lives on.

This myth bears some resemblance to a biblical story. Young Eagle fulfills Sage's father's request and brings back chile seeds from the south. After Young Eagle returns to the village triumphant in his quest, Sage's father fulfills his side of the agreement and grants them permission to marry. Sage's father keeps his word, and the young couple has many healthy children who will pass on their tale.

Unfortunately, the Bible's equivalent love story does not share such an uplifting plot. In Genesis, a young man named Jacob meets Rachel as she tends to her sheep near a well. Similar to Anaya's myth, Jacob sees that "Rachel was beautiful and well favored" (Genesis 29:17). Jacob wants to marry Rachel, but he knows that he has no dowry to offer her family. He meets Rachel's father, Laban, who agrees to give his daughter in marriage if Jacob works for him for seven years. After the seven years are complete, Jacob demands his wife, so Laban hosts a feast during which the bride is covered in a veil. After a night-long celebration, presumably with wine, Jacob takes his new bride to the nuptial tent to be with her. When Jacob awakes in the morning, however, he realizes that Laban has tricked him; Jacob has actually married and spent the wedding night with Laban's older, unattractive daughter, Leah. Jacob's only recourse is to work for Laban another seven years, after which he is able to marry Rachel. The irony is that God sees that Jacob loves Rachel more than Leah, "And when the Lord saw that Leah was hated, he opened her womb: but Rachel was barren" (Genesis 29:31). Leah gives Jacob many children, especially sons, while Rachel is barren until God finally gives her two sons of her own, although she dies during the birth of the second one.

The stories are similar because Young Eagle and Jacob both fall in love with beautiful women, ask for their hands in marriage, and agree to fulfill a mission before they can marry their future brides. The main difference is that the Puebloans keep their word. Young Eagle brings the chile seeds back and shares them with everybody, and Sage's father grants him permission to marry his daughter. Although Young Eagle is successful in his quest, he is only able to complete it with the help of his pueblo. Before the quest, his parents warn him of the jealous spirits that would attempt to thwart his mission. To help him, his mother gives him roasted corn, jerky, and a gourd for water. His father gives him cornmeal and a new bow and arrows. Sage gives him her turquoise necklace for protection, and the entire pueblo gathers to wish him a safe journey. His village supports him. In return, the whole community will benefit from the chile seeds and tastier foods. Together, Young Eagle and Sage create a happy and healthy family, supported by their pueblo.

The biblical story, however, presents a stark contrast. Deception, bitterness, sadness, and pain seem to be the dominant lessons. Although Jacob falls in love with Rachel, he marries Leah first, a plan that involves trickery and surely must include his daughters as coconspirators at some level. Seven years later, he marries Rachel, but because she is unable to have children, she asks her maidservant to serve as a surrogate mother. Jacob afterward marries the maidservant to follow the custom of that time. Not to be outdone, Leah, although already bearing several children for Jacob, also offers her maidservant to Jacob. He takes her as a wife, too. The story and family continue on a downward spiral, powered by deceit and jealousy. Despite their failures, it is only through divine intervention that Jacob's family line prospers.

The biblical version of this love story makes it clear why Anaya sees the importance of telling new myths. Once again, it is not to counter long-held Christian beliefs; it is simply to provide alternative versions of how to interpret the world, love each other, and support one another for the greater good. Myths, like love stories, create new possibilities.

One fascinating common thread in these first three children's books is the symbolism behind the seed motif. Each myth that has been explained to this point is a creation story, underscored by the reference to seeds, a symbolic origin of life. The books' titles do not reference this directly, instead focusing on corn and tortillas, hollyhocks, and chile. But the finished product is not the gift to these people. The gift is rather the potential for future possibilities that will nourish the body and the community, as well as decorating the landscape.

The planting of corn kernels has both a direct and an indirect effect on the community: "The corn plants grew. Corn tortillas became the favorite food of the people," and Jade, her family, and "the villagers did not have to leave home" (Anaya 2007, n.p.). The chiles cultivated by the Mayas, Toltecs, and Aztecs spawn diversity and relationships. The people "share different seeds and now have many kinds of chile" (Anaya 2014, 24). This is a lesson that Parrot Man, the Aztec elder, intrinsically understands. Community sharing enriches the quality of life for all, as evidenced by his instructions for Young Eagle: "You must share the seeds with your neighbors along the Great River to the north" (26). Although Sage's father did not create the seeds, but only received them, he rejoiced in their arrival to his people by exclaiming "Good!" and with him "[t]he entire pueblo rejoiced" (32, 34). In addition to sowing seeds of food, "colorful hollyhocks sprouted from Joseph's staff [and] [t]hat fall the flowers' dark seeds spread across the land[,] [whose] lovely flowers" became known as las varas de San José (Anaya 2012, 38). Seeds, the very lifeblood of all plants and trees, originate from somewhere. Like those of any living being, the seeds' own creation stories are of mythic proportion.

Although a tale of mythic creation, *Roadrunner's Dance* (2000) differs substantially from Anaya's other three children's books. It is the only one of the four books written exclusively in English. This could be because it was published by a New York press several years before the other books were published in the Southwest. This book is also about an animal rather than a seed or plant. Significantly, the book deals with the actual creation of a new creature, who emerges sometime after the development of the natural world and its inhabitants. The new creation is a roadrunner, which is made by a committee of animals rather than by a single god. Such distinctions convey a sharp contrast to the Bible's creation story; the roadrunner is a newly created creature made by a community of stakeholders to help restore balance to the ecosystem.

In this myth, a snake who lives in the desert believes he is the king of the road and hisses and threatens to strike any person or animal who attempts to use the road without his permission. The elders decide to go to Sacred Mountain to speak with Desert Woman, who created the desert animals, to see what could be done to alleviate the problem, since Snake was making travel along the road impossible. She does not like to interfere in the lives of people or animals. Nevertheless, she knows the matter is urgent. She places a rattle on the tip of Snake's tail so that he would warn people when he was nearby. Now he no longer is just a desert snake, but has become a rattlesnake. But the rattle only emboldens Snake to become more aggressive and menacing. Desperate for a solution, the animals also complain of Rattlesnake and ask Desert Woman to take away his fangs and rattle. Desert Woman replies, "What I give I cannot take away" (n.p.). She implores the animals to make him behave, but each one, the quail, the lizard, and the owl, cower at the thought.

Rather than destroy what she made, Desert Woman wants to create something new that might restore the natural balance. Above all, she seeks a collaborative creation: "If you help me, together we can make a guardian of the road. . . . I will form the body, and each of you will bring a gift for our new friend" (n.p.). Desert Woman carefully molds the body from wet clay. Deer brings two slender mesquite branches for legs to run fast. Raven takes one of his long black feathers to offer as a tail for balance. Eagle plucks dark feathers from his wings to make the new creature strong. Heron provides a thin reed from the marsh to serve as a long beak to peck at Rattlesnake. Coyote brings two shiny riverbed stones to make sharp eyes. Last, Desert Woman gives the gift of dance so that the animal is fast and agile and then breathes life into the clay creature. It takes patience and practice, but Roadrunner soon learns how to make his awkward body turn into that of a graceful dancer.

Confident in his abilities, Roadrunner seeks out Rattlesnake. True to his character, Rattlesnake attempts to strike Roadrunner for using the road without his permission. After a battle, in which Roadrunner dances around Rattlesnake and pecks at his tail, the snake surrenders and agrees not to threaten those who want to use the road. Thanks to Roadrunner, and the collaborative effort that it took to create him, the balance of nature is restored. Anaya's story is a good example of how "[c]reation myths suggest models for how people should behave toward each other and the rest of creation" (Leach 2001, 43). Within our imaginations lie the stories to help us create solutions to society's problems. Unfortunately, in today's digital age, we are distancing ourselves from the natural world and the ability to sense the stories around us.

Mythmaking is not just a literary exercise. It is an endeavor to expand and enrich our lives. It allows us to understand how we arrived to our present state by reaching back into the past. Without myths, we have no origin, and thus no place to which we can return. Anaya tells us that the trust his ancestors placed in stories was passed on to him (2009, 53). He in turn passes on the trust in stories to his readers. Through his children's books and creation myths, we can do the same for the next generation. The cycle of re-creation continues, and that is good.

NOTES

1. Anaya has published fifteen books that could be classified as children's literature, representing roughly one-third of his illustrious publication career.
2. The closest exception is when God states in Genesis 3:14 that the serpent will be forced to travel along its belly. Essentially, God removes the serpent's legs as punishment for deceiving Adam and Eve. This is not an evolutionary change, however, since the serpent did not evolve but was forcibly changed in an instant. Note that all biblical quotations in this chapter are from the King James version.
3. With the introduction of corn, American Indians are able to plant corn, beans, and squash together. This ancient farming tradition is called the Three Sisters crop, a popular myth in many indigenous nations.

REFERENCES

Adichie, Chimamanda Ngozi. 2009. "The Danger of the Single Story" (video). TEDGlobal 2009, www.ted.com/talks/chimamanda_adichie_the_danger_of_a_single_story.

Anaya, Rudolfo A. 2000. *Roadrunner's Dance.* New York: Hyperion.

———. 2007. *The First Tortilla.* Albuquerque: University of New Mexico Press.

———. 2009. "Shaman of Words." In *The Essays,* 52–63. Norman: University of Oklahoma Press.

———. 2012. *How Hollyhocks Came to New Mexico.* Los Ranchos, NM: Rio Grande Books.

———. 2014. *How Chile Came to New Mexico.* Los Ranchos, NM: Rio Grande Books.

"Bloom's Digital Taxonomy." 2015. *Educational Origami.* Last modified June 17. http://edorigami.wikispaces.com/Bloom%27s+Digital+Taxonomy.

Gladwell, Malcolm. 2011. "Creation Myth: Xerox PARC, Apple, and the Truth about Innovation." *New Yorker,* May 16. www.newyorker.com/magazine/2011/05/16/creation-myth.

Holman, Hugh C., and William Harmon, eds. 1986. *A Handbook to Literature.* New York: Macmillan.

Holy Bible: King James Version. 1994. Nashville, TN: Thomas Nelson.

Johnson, David, and David Apodaca. 1998. "Myth and the Writer: A Conversation with Rudolfo Anaya." In *Conversations with Rudolfo Anaya,* edited by Bruce Dick and Silvio Sirias, 29–48. Jackson: University Press of Mississippi.

Leach, Alexandra N. 2001. "The Earth's Birthday Story: Creation Myths in Children's Books." *Journal of Children's Literature* 27 (1): 43–48.

Mangion, Claude. 2015. "Nietzsche's Philosophy of Myth." Academia.edu. Accessed January 29. http://www.academia.edu/197368/Nietzsches_Philosophy_of_Myth.

PART 4
Interview

14

Interview with David Ellis

FILM PRODUCER OF
RUDOLFO ANAYA: THE MAGIC OF WORDS

Roberto Cantú

Roberto Cantú: One of the highlights in the Rudolfo Anaya conference was the partial screening of your film *The Magic of Words*. I personally felt very thankful for your courtesy in allowing us to show your film as a work in progress. We opened the conference with its screening, and as anticipated, the audience was thrilled and inspired by your film, asking where it could be purchased. Before going into such details, tell us about your background. What kinds of films have you made?

David Ellis: I started working in television in 1974 in Albuquerque, New Mexico, where I was a cameraman at the local NBC affiliate. After two years, I moved to the local PBS station as a producer and made programs on the arts and public affairs. As an independent producer, I produced and directed the prison film *Doing Time* (1980), made at the state Penitentiary of New Mexico and completed just eight weeks before the facility was destroyed in America's worst prison riot. Since then, I've worked at NBC News and started my own production company, completing several documentary, educational, and corporate video programs for clients in New York, Fort Worth, Los Angeles, and Tokyo. My educational productions include art history films made at the British Museum; Metropolitan Museum of Art, New York; and the Los Angeles County Museum of Art. My documentaries have been broadcast on national PBS, the Discovery Channel, Disney Channel, and on foreign television.

RC: How did you come to make the film *Rudolfo Anaya: The Magic of Words*?

DE: I first met Rudolfo Anaya in 1994, when I interviewed him for a film I was making on New Mexico called *Land of Enchantment*. He was captivating and poetic in his comments. At the time, I thought he would be a good subject for a film. In 2004, when I moved from Los Angeles to Albuquerque, I contacted Rudy to ask if he had been the subject of a film. And when he said no, I knew I'd gotten lucky: I had found the subject for my next production. Rudy's answer when I posed the question of doing the film: "Yes, come on. Let's make a film."

RC: What was involved in making this film?

DE: My first concern was how to raise the money to make the film. When you're an independent filmmaker, as I am—meaning you're not employed by a TV network, or by a production company with a deal at a network or cable outlet—it's a burden to find funding for every project. It's never easy and rarely fast. I knew this was not going to be a commercial documentary—that is, it was unlikely to generate enough money on completion to attract investors at the beginning. And most people don't realize that PBS doesn't fund productions, so that was out. That meant going to the most likely source of support for an educational documentary: foundations. I wrote my first funding proposal for *The Magic of Words* in 2005 and submitted it to the McCune Charitable Trust. And got lucky. McCune was the first money in and gave the project enough for me to film the key interviews with Rudy and supporting footage as well. But raising the rest of the money was much more difficult: it took nine years. That forced me to shoot a little bit when I got small grants, write other proposals, and shoot more when I had my next grant. It's a difficult way to make a film, but in the end, it worked. I received support from other foundations, the State of New Mexico Film Office, and the City of Santa Rosa, New Mexico, where Rudy grew up. But it wasn't until July 2013 that I received a grant that made possible the completion of the film. I shot some key scenes that I'd been waiting literally years to film and then spent months on the editing. The project was finally completed in July 2014.

RC: Since it took more than nine years to plan, shoot, and complete *The Magic of Words*, how did your project grow from an initial idea to its final version as a film? How did you select the vivid landscapes and biographical background that substantially frame the story you tell in the film? How many people did it take to make this documentary?

DE: It can require a lot, which is surprising to many people. Sometimes, the production team may be just three people (cameraman, sound person, and director); sometimes, you need many more if you're working on a complex project, which requires multiple lighting technicians, one or two production assistants, an art director and assistant, and actors for dramatizations. But as a director who is also a cameraman, there were days when I went out alone to film. In the case of this film, a three-person crew was used most of the time.

RC: No doubt you accumulated many hours of film footage over the years. From all the material you shot, what did you leave out?

DE: Every film has "outs," shots and scenes that just don't make the final cut. It may be for reasons of time—not enough of it in the final show—or because the initial idea for the material didn't work out. Or, sometimes, you have an abundance of riches, which happened on *The Magic of Words*. Too much good footage. Each of the interviews I did was filled with rich material, not all of which could be used.

RC: Based on ten years of work with Rudy on your film project, what are some of your lasting impressions? What kind of person is he?

DE: Rudy is a remarkably kind, humble, and sensitive person; it's obvious from the moment you meet him. And he's a real storyteller, drawing people to him. The video crew saw this right away and was excited. And you have to realize that experienced video crews are often world weary. They've traveled widely, worked countless fifteen-hour days, and aren't often surprised or impressed by the subjects they cover. They've been there, done that. But it was different with Rudy Anaya. Rudy was a star! We all felt privileged to have participated in the day's shooting. It was less like work and more like a visit with a favorite grandfather.

RC: What motivated you to keep going when you had so much trouble raising money?

DE: Making a biographical film about a living person is a heavy responsibility. There is a responsibility to fulfill: you've been entrusted with someone's life story. I take that responsibility very seriously. There's no question of stopping or giving up the show. It will be completed, no matter what, whether it's difficult to do or not.

RC: How did you choose the interview subjects? And how did you choose what to include from the interviewees?

DE: Even though it was frustrating that the film took so long to complete, there was an unintended benefit. The longer I knew Rudy, the more I learned about the film's direction, and what questions I should ask his friends and colleagues, who would enrich the film. Each new interview mirrored my experience with Rudy. There was a compounding effect so that the more interviews I did, the more informed I became about Rudy Anaya, the writer and the person. Choosing the interview comments to use is hard because each person is interviewed for hours and says a lot of interesting and helpful things. The first step is to get transcripts of all the interviews, and then in the editing room, you listen and watch and make your decisions.

RC: What are the pitfalls of making a film about a writer?

DE: You don't want to make a film that moves slowly because it has too many interviews. But it's essential to hear comments from others about the subject of the film—and that means interviews. Hopefully, you speak with intelligent and articulate people like those who contributed so importantly in *The Magic Of Words*. And the result—even though they are what is sometimes dismissed as "talking heads"—is a film that provides a context to understand the subject.

RC: Where will the film be shown?

DE: I am offering the film to national PBS for broadcast and also hope for a showing on the Spanish language channel Vme, an affiliate of PBS.

For that network, I will produce a Spanish language version, meaning I will record the narration and all the interviews in Spanish. Apart from television, the film will be marketed to middle schools and high schools around the country, accompanied by a teacher's guide.

RC: Where can the film be purchased?

DE: *Rudolfo Anaya: The Magic of Words* can be purchased online at anayafilm.com

For questions, contact David Ellis at ellisfilm@aol.com.

Contributors

Mario Acevedo is the author of the national best-selling Félix Gómez detective-vampire series from HarperCollins. His debut novel, *The Nymphos of Rocky Flats*, was chosen by Barnes and Noble as one of the best paranormal fantasy novels of the decade. His short fiction is included in the anthologies *You Don't Have A Clue: Latino Mystery Stories for Teens* and *Hit List: The Best of Latino Mystery* from Arte Público Press, as well as in *Modern Drunkard Magazine*. He has ghostwritten numerous novels and is a coauthor of the thriller *Good Money Gone*, winner of Best Novel: Adventure or Drama—English in the 2014 International Latino Book Awards.

Heiner Bus was a professor of American studies at the Universities of Mainz, Trier, and Bamberg until his retirement in 2006. His Ph.D. thesis on Saul Bellow was followed by a book, *Studien zur Reiseprosa Washington Irvings* (1982), based on research at Yale University with the support of an ACLS postgraduate grant (1972–73). Subsequently, he specialized in U.S. ethnic literatures, with a strong focus on Chicano literature. Besides editing a bilingual anthology, *Recent Chicano Poetry/Neueste Chicano-Lyrik* (1994), with Ana Castillo, and a special issue of *Hispanorama* on Chicano literature in 1990, he published numerous essays on Asian American, Jewish American, African American, Native American, and Chicano literature in anthologies and scholarly magazines in Germany, the United States, France, Spain, Turkey, and the Netherlands. He also published on American English in German newspapers, German-Turkish migrant literature, Western writing, Charles Brockden Brown, the New Journalism, North African slavery as culture contact, and American hemispheric identity.

Roberto Cantú, born in Guadalajara, México, is emeritus professor of Chicano studies and emeritus professor of English at California State University, Los Angeles, where he teaches courses on the European novel (seventeenth to nineteenth centuries) and on Latin American, Mexican, Mexican American, and Mesoamerican literatures. Included in his many publications is his translation from English to Spanish of José Antonio Villarreal's novel *Pocho* (1995). Cantú is the editor of *An Insatiable Dialectic: Essays on Critique, Modernity, and Humanism* (2013); *The Willow and the Spiral: Essays on Octavio Paz and the Poetic Imagination* (2004); and *The Reptant Eagle: Essays on Carlos Fuentes and the Art of the Novel* (2015). He is coeditor (with Aaron Sonnenschein) of *Tradition and Innovation in Mesoamerican Cultural History* (2011). In 2010 he was recognized at his campus with the president's Distinguished Professor Award.

Robert Con Davis-Undiano is Neustadt Professor and Presidential Professor of English at the University of Oklahoma. He is executive director of the *World Literature Today* organization, which publishes *World Literature Today* and *Chinese Literature Today,* and he teaches in the areas of Chicano and Mexican-American studies, American studies, critical theory, and cultural studies. His research is primarily in Mexican-American literature and culture, but he has also written *The Paternal Romance* (Illinois 1993), *Culture and Cognition: The Boundaries of Literary and Scientific Inquiry* (with Schleifer and Mergler, Cornell 1992), and *Criticism and Culture: The Role of Critique in Modern Literary Theory* (with Schleifer, Longman 1991). In 1999, he edited with Rudolfo Anaya a *Genre* special issue on "Chicano/a Studies—Writing into the Future," and he has edited ten other books and has published some sixty articles. He is the editor of the book series (Univ. of Oklahoma) "Chicana & Chicano Visions of the Américas," which has published volumes by Rudolfo Anaya, Denise Chávez, Demetria Martínez, Carlos Morton, Rigoberto González, Leroy V.

Quintana, and many others. His most recent book, *Mestizos Come Home! Making and Claiming Mexican American Identity*, will appear in 2017 from the University of Oklahoma Press.

Ramón A. Gutiérrez is currently the Preston and Sterling Morton Distinguished Service Professor of American History and the College at the University of Chicago. Born in New Mexico, raised in Albuquerque, and educated at the University of New Mexico and the University of Wisconsin, he has held posts at Pomona College and the University of California, San Diego. At UCSD he was the founding chair of the Ethnic Studies Department and its Center for the Study of Race and Ethnicity. Over the years, his research has focused on the racial and ethnic legacies of the Spanish conquest of the Américas, studying the religious aspects of cultural change. He is the author or editor of several books, among them *When Jesus Came, the Corn Mothers Went Away: Marriage, Sexuality, and Power in New Mexico, 1500–1846* (1991); *Festivals and Celebrations in American Ethnic Communities* (1995); *Mexican Home Altars* (1997); *Contested Eden: California before the Gold Rush* (1998); and *Mexicans in California: Transformations and Challenges* (2009).

Spencer R. Herrera is an associate professor of Spanish at New Mexico State University, where he teaches Chicana/o literature, culture, and film. He is the coauthor of *Sagrado: A Photopoetics across the Chicano Homeland* (2013), winner of a Border Regional Library Association Southwest Book award, a New Mexico–Arizona Book award, and a Pima County Public Library Southwest Book of the Year award. He is the author and editor of *Before/Beyond Borders: An Anthology of Chicano/a Literature* (2010). He also guest edited a special issue on Chicana/o literature for *Revista Casa de las Américas*, a premier Latin American journal published in La Habana, Cuba. He was born and raised in Houston, Texas. He completed his Ph.D. in Spanish with a minor in film at the University of New Mexico.

María Herrera-Sobek is associate vice chancellor for diversity, equity, and academic policy and a professor in the Chicana and Chicano Studies

Department at the University of California, Santa Barbara. She held the Luis Leal Endowed Chair in Chicana/o Studies from 1997 to 2009. She received her Ph.D. in Hispanic languages and literature from UCLA and has taught at UC Irvine, Harvard University, and Stanford University. Her publications include *The Bracero Experience: Elitelore Versus Folklore* (1979); *The Mexican Corrido: A Feminist Analysis* (1990); *Northward Bound: The Mexican Immigrant Experience in Ballad and Song* (1993); and *Chicano Folklore: A Handbook* (2006). She has edited or coedited several books, including the following: *Chicano Renaissance: Contemporary Cultural Trends* (2000); *Perspectivas transatlánticas en la literature chicana: Ensayos y creatividad* (2004); *Violence and Transgression in World Minority Literatures* (2005); *The Norton Anthology of Latino Literature* (2011); and *Celebrating Latino Folklore: An Encyclopedia of Cultural Traditions*, 3 volumes (2012). She was also the editor or coeditor of several special journal issues: *Journal of American Studies of Turkey* (*JAST*); *ConcentricJournal* (Taiwan); *Nerter* (Canary Islands); and *American Studies Journal of Germany*. In addition, Herrera-Sobek has published more than 140 scholarly articles and book chapters and published poetry extensively in journals and anthologies.

Monika Kaup is a professor of English and comparative literature at the University of Washington, Seattle, where her teaching and research areas include U.S. Latino/a literature, U.S.-México border literature and culture, hemispheric American studies, baroque/New World baroque/neobaroque studies, and twentieth-century U.S. fiction. She has completed two related projects on the New World baroque and the neobaroque. The first, *Baroque New Worlds: Representation, Transculturation, Counterconquest* (coedited with Lois Parkinson Zamora, 2010) is a collection that traces the changing nature of baroque representation in Europe and the Américas across four centuries. *Neobaroque in the Americas: Alternative Modernities in Literature, Visual Art, and Film* (2012) is a comparative, hemispheric study of the neobaroque—the twentieth- and twenty-first-century recovery of the baroque—in modern and postmodern North American, U.S. Latino, and Latin American literature, film, visual arts, and theory. Her other publications include

Rewriting North American Borders in Chicano and Chicana Narrative (2001) and *Mixing Race, Mixing Culture: Inter-American Literary Dialogues* (coedited with Debra Rosenthal, 2002). She is currently at work on a new book project entitled "Post-Poststructuralism: New Realisms in Contemporary Theory and Post-Apocalyptic Narrative," which investigates the rise of new realisms in contemporary theory after poststructuralism and explores its arguments via close readings of contemporary postapocalyptic narrative.

Enrique R. Lamadrid teaches folklore, literature, and cultural history in the University of New Mexico's Department of Spanish and Portuguese. His research interests include ethnopoetics, folklore and music, Chicano literature, contemporary Mexican poetry, and literary translation. His field work centers in New Mexico but ranges as well into México, Spain, the Andes, and the Caribbean. His research on the Indo-Hispano traditions of New Mexico charts the influence of indigenous cultures on the Spanish language and imagination. His literary writings explore the borderlands between cultures and their natural environments, and between popular traditions and literary expression. Lamadrid was awarded the Chicago Folklore Prize for his 2003 ethnography *Hermanitos Comanchitos: Indo-Hispano Rituals of Captivity and Redemption* and the Américo Paredes Prize in 2005 for his cultural activism and museum curatorial projects.

José E. Limón is a professor of English at the University of Notre Dame, where he also holds the Julian Samora Endowed Professorship in Latino Studies and is director of the Institute for Latino Studies. Limón has published in major scholarly journals and has authored four books: *Mexican Ballads and Chicano Poems: History and Influence in Mexican-American Social Poetry* (1992); *Dancing with the Devil: Society and Cultural Poetics in Mexican-American South Texas* (1994); *American Encounters: Greater Mexico, the United States, and the Erotics of Culture* (1998); and *Américo Paredes: Culture and Critique* (2012). A new book, "Neither Friends, Nor Strangers: Mexicans and Anglos in the Literary Making of Texas," is in progress. In his former position as professor of English and anthropology at the University of Texas at Austin, he directed thirty Ph.D.s to completion, with twenty-eight of these currently in tenure-track positions across the country, from Brown University to the University of California, Santa Cruz.

Francisco A. Lomelí is a professor in the Spanish and Portuguese and Chicana/o Studies Departments at the University of California, Santa Barbara. He has been chair of three departments: Chicana/o Studies, Black Studies, and Spanish and Portuguese. He has also served as director of Education Abroad Programs for the University of California system in Costa Rica (1994–1995) and in Chile and Argentina (2011–2013). His publications cover a wide gamut of topics in Chicano studies and Latin American literature. Some of his works include *Dictionary of Literary Biography* (1989, 1993, 1999), *Handbook of Hispanic Cultures of the United States: Literature and Art* (1993), *Chicano Literature: A Reference Guide* (1984), *The Writings of Eusebio Chacón* (2012), *Life and Writings of Miguel de Quintana* (2004), and *Barrio on the Edge* (trans., 1998). He has also delivered numerous papers in many universities in the United States, México, Ireland, Italy, Chile, Spain, Russia, France, and Germany, among others.

John M. D. Pohl is an adjunct professor of Art History at UCLA and teaches in the Departments of Anthropology, Chicano Studies, and Fine Arts at California State University, Los Angeles. He is an authority on American Indian civilizations and has directed numerous archaeological projects in Canada, the United States, México, Central America, and Europe. A specialist in the ancient arts and writing systems of the Américas, Dr. Pohl serves as the Peter Jay Sharp Curator and Lecturer in the Art of the Ancient Americas at Princeton University and has designed, written, and produced exhibitions as well as documentary and feature films on American Indian history for many other institutions around the country as well as in Europe. Most recently, Dr. Pohl curated the exhibitions *The Aztec Pantheon and the Art of Empire,* for the Getty Villa Museum in 2010, and the *Children of the Plumed Serpent: The Legacy of Quetzalcoatl in Ancient Mexico,* for the Los Angeles County Museum of Art and the Dallas Museum of Art in 2012.

Rosaura Sánchez is a leading scholar in the field of literary criticism, linguistics, and theory; the former chair of the Department of Literature (1995–1998); and former coordinator of the Third World Studies Program at UCSD (1980–1982). She is the author of numerous scholarly articles and reviews, especially of lengthy and detailed introductions to the novels and letters of María Amparo Ruiz de Burton. Dr. Sánchez has published seminal books, such as *Chicano Discourse: A Socio-Historic Perspective* (1994) and *Telling Identities: The Californio Testimonios* (1995). She coedited with Beatrice Pita the groundbreaking book *Conflicts of Interests: The Letters of Amparo Ruiz de Burton* (2001). She is also the author of the short story collection *He Walked in and Sat Down/Entró y se sentó* (2000) and, with Beatrice Pita, coauthor of a science fiction novel, *Lunar Braceros 2125–2148* (2009).

Horst Tonn is a professor of American studies at the University of Tuebingen, Germany. Educated at the Free University Berlin and the University of Texas at Austin, he has previously taught at the Universities of Mainz/Germersheim, Erlangen, and Duisburg. As a visiting scholar, he taught at California State University, Fullerton, and at Poone University in India. His major research areas are Chicano literature and U.S.-Mexican border culture, documentary (writing and film), the representation of war in the media, cultural globalization, and participatory culture. His two book publications are on the contemporary Chicano novel (1988) and on the history of documentary writing in the United States (1996). Besides numerous articles, he has coedited books on the role of war correspondents in media society (2007) and on cultural globalization (2007).